The Death of American Antisemitism

The Death of
American Antisemitism

SPENCER BLAKESLEE

Westport, Connecticut
London

Library of Congress Cataloging-in-Publication Data

Blakeslee, Spencer, 1935–
 The death of American antisemitism / Spencer Blakeslee.
  p. cm.
 Includes bibliographical references and index.
 ISBN 0–275–96508–2 (alk. paper)
 1. Antisemitism—United States. 2. Jews—United States—Politics
and government—20th century. 3. United States—Ethnic relations.
I. Title.
DS146.U6B55 2000
305.8′00973—dc21   99–29576

British Library Cataloguing in Publication Data is available.

Library of Congress Catalog Card Number: 99–29576
ISBN: 0–275–96508–2

First published in 2000

Praeger Publishers, 88 Post Road West, Westport, CT 06881
An imprint of Greenwood Publishing Group, Inc.
www.praeger.com

Printed in the United States of America

The paper used in this book complies with the
Permanent Paper Standard issued by the National
Information Standards Organization (Z39.48–1984).

10 9 8 7 6 5 4 3 2 1

For Barbara, the embodiment
of the expression
besherta.
Through her
comes my strength.
With her
comes my joy.

Contents

Preface

It is likely that a great many people reading this book's title will say, "Wait a minute, antisemitism is dead? I remember something antisemitic that happened just a few years ago," or, "One of my best friends is Jewish, and she says antisemitism is always a threat." Just as often they will then go on to relate something awful that happened to someone in their family, a neighbor, or a coworker that was clearly antisemitic. Their tales would be true, regardless of how dated they might be, and I could add several examples from my own experience. Others will ask, "What about Crown Heights [1991], wasn't that antisemitism at its worst?"[1] This book is not about individual incidents of antisemitism, as appalling as they may have been, but about the overall safety of America's Jews at the beginning of the twenty-first century. It examines the emotional significance antisemitism continues to exert on the consciousness of substantial numbers of American Jews and the political necessity antisemitism continues to exert on a small group of Jewish advocacy organizations (JAOs) that purport to represent Jewish interests. All of this emotion and political necessity in spite of the statistical reality that since the end of World War II anti-Jewish beliefs have almost disappeared from the American cultural scene. The vast majority of Americans are simply not antisemitic!

But a caution is also in order at this point. The near disappearance of antisemitism in America over the past sixty years does *not* mean it has disappeared in other parts of the world. A careful examination of the sociocultural fabric of several European countries (not to mention the Arab countries) quickly reveals the tenacity and persistence of antisemitism in these parts of the globe. A few examples will serve to highlight the extent of the problem.

Fifty years after World War II a young woman writes a book (and movie) about the nascent antisemitism in her small Austrian town (*Nasty*

Girl). The duplicity of the Swiss banking institutions and their treatment of confiscated Jewish wealth were brought to light in a series of sweeping legal and moral indictments. There is uneasiness in Germany over the reality of pro-Nazi fringe groups and the reign of terror they brought against recent immigrants. There is persistent fear on the part of Polish peasants that "the Jews will come back," and this in a country with no more than four to five thousand Jews—down from 3.3 million in 1939! Finally, the recent rash of synagogue desecrations in Russia, and the openly antisemitic stance of the Russian National Unity group as reported on December 16, 1998 in the *Boston Globe* by David Fillipow in an article entitled "Public Discontent Fuels Hate in Russia." It is a sorry list, indeed, and no one, Jew or non-Jew, of conscience can ever safely ignore these rumbling undercurrents of Jew-hatred. No, antisemitism is not gone from the world's stage, but it is nearly so from the American scene. It is to this limited but enormously powerful world citizen (the United States) that I have turned an analytical eye in regard to its emotional and political understanding of a disappearing prejudice.

This book is about the continuing necessity for the real or imagined presence of antisemitism and the impact that presence has on the twin issues of Jewish identity and organizational necessity. It is an attempt to urge America's Jews and their organizations to move toward issues of greater importance to them that will assure their continuance in both the twenty-first century and beyond. Does this sociological assessment of Jewish identity and survival mean that the individual Jew and his/her opinion about antisemitism and his/her own identity count for little in a decidedly large discussion? Not at all. Those individual opinions have never been more important than they are today in a period of escalating intermarriage between Jews and non-Jews, and the low birthrates among Jewish families.

The present birthrate for Jewish families (approximately 1.8) is not sufficient to even replace the current population of American Jews. The exception to this arithmetic average is the Orthodox Jews. They are opposed to abortion and many forms of birth control and are consciously seeking a higher birthrate. It currently stands at approximately 3.4 children per family. Added to this biological reality of underreproduction among the larger population of American Jews are the ongoing tensions embedded in the question, "Who is a Jew?" The divisiveness among the major branches of Judaism (Reform, Conservative, Orthodox, and to a much smaller degree, Reconstructionist) is incredibly painful to those religious Jews who want to worship according to their conscience but still remain one with their coreligionists. Added to the religiously observant Jews are the millions of Jews who claim the right to their identity as Jews, but who want nothing whatever to do with the religion of their forefathers and -mothers. Are all of these Jews in fact *Jews*? If they are, how are these differences in interpretation to be reconciled in the face of an inevitable assimilation that results in more and more Jews (of whatever stripe) opting out each year?

A clear implication of these multiple pressures is that every Jew in this country will have to decide what being Jewish means to her/him, or if there is any reason to continue to identify oneself as Jewish. In a very real sense, the decisions today's Jews make about their identity will shape the content and expression of American Jewry for decades to come. Whether or not the numerous Jewish organizations in the United States, and in particular, those held in high reverence for their pioneering work in Jewish defense, will play any role whatever in this identity/continuity challenge turns on a number of complex factors. This book addresses several of those factors and represents an attempt to contribute to our collective understanding of the rapidly changing textures of American Jewish life.

As each succeeding group of "strangers to these shores" (Parrillo, 1997) was assimilated, the memories of prejudice, discrimination, and physical attacks that often marked their journey into America's mainstream did not immediately abate. Long after they had assimilated as Americans, individual members of these social/ethnic groups held on to their memories of those outrages, and frequently the "idea" of those prejudices outlived (by decades) the pain of actual experiences. A residual belief often persisted in those communities that as good as life was, there was always the possibility that they could once again find themselves objects of renewed attack. Nowhere was that sentiment more prevalent than in the Jewish community.

For Jews, this victimization and revictimization had occurred frequently during their long diaspora history. These were a people who had justly earned a near permanent sense of foreboding about their safety and tranquility. But, in contrast to other countries in which Jews settled, America proved to be a very different experience for the Jew. White, Protestant America did not welcome Jews with open arms, but neither did it greet them with pogroms, or government policies specifically written to drive them out. As Jews steadily adapted to this new world, success followed in a number of occupations, and Jews (like every other ethnic group before them) began assimilating into the general population. America proved to be more than a safe place in which to pursue a livelihood. In time it produced the most successful Jewish community history had ever seen! But with that success came a larger question—can Jews accept that success and still call themselves Jews?

It was the plight of Jews in other parts of the world that prompted small groups of prosperous American Jews early in this century to form defense organizations as formal mechanisms to protect and advocate for the interests (and sometimes the lives) of their coreligionists overseas. The influence of prominent leaders in these American Jewish organizations was substantial in terms of the help they were able to extend both to afflicted Jews still in Europe and increasingly to the fast growing population of newly arrived Jews in this country. The issue of Jewish safety in America differed in very significant ways from what Jews had experienced in Europe. The crudeness of American nativists when combined with the imported mentality of a European bred antisemitism was no less disruptive, if not as physically destructive, to the peace and tranquillity of America's Jews. Protection from a variety of direct physical assaults was necessary, as was the advocacy for dealing with the frustrations of being denied a host of basic civil rights. It was the Jewish defense organizations that led the fight for Jewish safety and the legal battles for obtaining those common civil liberties; and antisemitism was at the core of the mission statements of these organizations. In all four of the JAOs examined in this study, antisemitism was their *raison d'être*. The history of these organizations and the importance of antisemitism as their primary mission are discussed in detail in parts one and two of this book.

Chapter one briefly describes the history of the Jewish experience in America, and the antisemitism that often accompanied it. This brief history lesson is followed in chapter two with a detailed description and discussion of sixty years of tracking antisemitic opinions and, in more recent times, the occurrence of antisemitic incidents. Chapters three, four, five, and six focus on the history and organizational characteristics of the American Jewish Committee (AJC), Anti-Defamation League (ADL), American Jewish Congress (AJCg), and Jewish Community Relations Council (JCRC); the four JAOs discussed in this study. Chapter seven pulls together these organizational characteristics into a portrait of the JAOs and the influence the lay leaders hold over their day-to-day operation and their decision-making process. It is here that we learn the extent of the political importance antisemitism carries for these organizations.

Perhaps the best way to observe all of these complex factors is to examine them during the JAOs' involvement in actual antisemitic incidents. Part three does that, giving the reader firsthand exposure to advocacy techniques and results. Chapter eight presents the first of three antisemitic incidents in which these four organizations involved themselves. In the first incident, the American Jewish Committee withdrew, at the last minute, from a long-awaited black/Jewish historical exhibit because the Nation of Islam had inserted several antisemitic panels into the exhibit material.

In the second incident, described in chapter nine, a black professor at one of the "seven sisters" colleges insisted on using a highly volatile book compiled by the Nation of Islam as a textbook in his Black History Course. In the third incident, the focus of chapter ten, the fiery leader of the Nation of Islam, Minister Louis Farrakhan, gave a speech to an overflow crowd at the University of Massachusetts at Amherst. The next day the JAOs held a joint press conference to make sure that several of the antisemitic allegations he had made after the press had left the night before were not omitted from the extensive media coverage the speech received.

All of the data presented to this point suggest that several conclusions can be made, and having made them, they must, in turn, lead the JAOs and America's Jews to consider new directions they can pursue in the future. Further, these conclusions should prompt a serious effort to create a new basis for understanding the threat of antisemitism. Part four addresses those conclusions and their implications.

Chapter eleven discusses the paradox of public opinion of attitudinal antisemitism, which is at an all-time low, and the inexplicably high levels of Jewish foreboding about the supposed threat of American antisemitism. It discusses what we know about antisemitism, what we don't know about antisemitism, and what we don't want to know about antisemitism in the United States. It tackles the elusive problem of defining antisemitism and the pressing need for new and better polling instruments. The black community is examined as a case in point.

It is unreasonable to conclude, chapter eleven argues, that these JAOs, still deeply influenced by an immigrant mentality (and the antisemitism that went with it), are equipped to assume a role in the mounting dilemma of Jewish identity or continuity in America. This last chapter illustrates the inroads that 100 years of assimilation have made on American Jewish identity. Given these inroads, it stands to reason that if, at some point in the future, there are no, or very few, Jews, then there is little reason for any Jewish organizations, let alone the JAOs examined in this study. On the other hand, if American Jews decide to continue identifying themselves as Jews, by whatever formula, can the JAOs survive without making substantial changes in the way they do business?

A NOTE ON SPELLING "ANTISEMITISM"

Richard S. Levy (1991) points out that "Jew-hatred," Jew-baiting," and "Judaeophobia" existed long before the term "antisemitism" came into vogue in late nineteenth-century Germany. Antisemitism is a descriptive expression for Jew-hatred coined by the failed German journalist and full-time antisemite Wilhelm Marr in 1879. Europe's other political agitators, and their presses, quickly adopted this new expression. It didn't contain the word "Jew," and it gave their collective expressions of repugnance for Jews a pseudoscientific cachet. Jews could now be considered as bearers of obvious (if impossible to define) racial attributes, rather than members of a specific religion or as people of undefined national origin. Such a distinction is ludicrous since there is no such thing as a "semitism" that an "anti" could oppose. It is an expression that never refers to any of the other members of the semitic family of languages. It refers only to Jews, and only in negative ways. Throughout this book antisemitism connotes attacks against Jews as individuals and Jews as a community.

NOTE

1. In four days of rioting in the Crown Heights section of Brooklyn, New York, following the accidental death of a seven-year-old black child, a Jewish scholar was murdered and millions of dollars in damages were done to Jewish homes and businesses. The neighborhood is almost equally divided between Hasidic Orthodox Jews and blacks.

Acknowledgments

There are a great many people one encounters while writing a book, and this has been no exception. There are too many of these people who have given me assistance at one point or another to recall with complete accuracy or fairness. However, there is a group of people to whom I am deeply indebted for different forms of assistance, support, and critiques that they provided at different times during the writing of this manuscript. They include Jack Wertheimer, Jerome Chanes, Jonathan Sarna, Earl Rabb, Gary Tobin, Daniel Elazar (deceased), Helen Fein, Ron McAllister, Michael Brown, Gordana Rabrenovic, Debra Kaufman, Sherry Israel, Arnold Dashefsky, Henry Tischler, Barbara Weiss, Arlene and Howard Weintraub, and Calvin Goldscheider. In the early days of this effort there was the spiritual and intellectual companionship of Rabbi Bernard Mehlman, and throughout the writing there has been the support, patience, and encouragement of my colleagues and students at Northeastern University and Framingham State College. They patiently endured what must have seemed like endless conversations about various portions of this book. Four of my students, Christina Cain, Erin Feeley, Beth Grupposo, and James Leach, must be recognized for their willingness and enthusiasm in undertaking the tedious task of checking citations, bibliographic references, and misspelled words. To all and each of these stalwart souls I am deeply grateful for their wisdom, guidance, and patience. There is my deep appreciation to the professional leadership of the four JAOs discussed in this study, Dr. Lawrence Lowenthal (AJC), Mr. Martin Goldman (formerly AJC), Mr. Leonard Zakim (deceased, ADL), Ms. Sheila Decter (AJCg), and Ms. Nancy Kaufman (JCRC). Their honesty and candor about themselves and their organizations could only have come from dedicated leaders who have only the best interests of their constituencies in mind. Not suprisingly, we often saw issues differently, but they never withheld key information or their cooperation throughout the long months of interviews. Their help was valuable beyond words. A special note of appreciation is made to Ms. Cyma Horowitz, principal librarian at the American Jewish Committee's Blaustein Institute for Human Relations in New York City. No matter how short the notice, she always had the requested material (and often more) waiting for me. Thank you for your help, Cyma.

There is one individual who deserves special praise because of the unique mentoring role he extended that was of critical value in helping me think through problems of logic and common sense. He is Dr. John Weiss, a distinguished historian and authority on the ideological roots of European antisemitism that culminated in the Holocaust. He patiently helped me understand that an author need not lose commitment to his subject simply because there was a more direct, jargon-free way of telling the story. Thank you, John!

There are family or kinship systems that provide support and nurture to the first-time author, and I have been particularly blessed with a large network of supportive people. They have included my granddaughter (Isabel Rose) and her mom (Nance) and dad (Steven) in Olympia, Washington, a Hebrew calligrapher of breathtaking talent who is also my brother Lawrence, a dear group of stalwart friends my wife and I have come to think of as "our crowd," and the editorial staff at Greenwood Publishing, Dr. Jim Sabin, my acquisition editor, Ms. Maralee Youngs, copyeditor, and Ms. Elizabeth Meagher, my production editor, who disproved the belief that writers and their editors are natural antagonists; they are natural collaborators, and thank heaven for it. The inevitable errors of judgment that appear here and the conclusions I put forth in this book are solely my responsibility.

I have dedicated this book to my beautiful wife, Barbara, and in doing so have, perhaps, introduced some readers to the wonderful Yiddish word *besherta*. In the infinite reaches of the universe there is the knowledge that some souls must have time together on earth (*besherta*), and G-d allows that to take place. This has been the blessing that came to me late in my life in the person of Barbara. Her patience, prodding, and never-flagging love has made my life a miracle.

Abbreviations

AAUP	American Association of University Professors
ACLU	American Civil Liberties Union
ADL	Anti-Defamation League
AIPAC	American Israel Public Affairs Committee
AJC	American Jewish Committee
AJCg	American Jewish Congress
AJYB	*American Jewish Year Book*
BBURG	The Boston Banks Urban Renewal Group
BG	*Boston Globe*
CCI	Council on Community Inter-Relations
CCNY	City College New York
CJF	Council of Jewish Federations
CJP	Combined Jewish Philanthropies
CLSA	Commission on Law and Social Action
EJ	*Encyclopaedia Judaica*
FEPC	Fair Employment Practices Commission
FHA	Federal Housing Authority
JAO(s)	Jewish Advocacy Organization(s)
JCC	Jewish Community Council (predecessor to the JCRC)
JCRC	Jewish Community Relations Council
JPS	Jewish Publication Society
JTS	Jewish Telegraphic Service
KKK	Ku Klux Klan

NAACP	National Association for the Advancement of Colored People
NJCRAC	National Jewish Community Relations Advisory Council
NJPS	National Jewish Population Survey
NOI	Nation of Islam
NORC	National Opinion Research Center
NOW	National Organization of Women
NPOs	nonprofit organizations
RHSPAC	The Roxbury Heritage State Park Advisory Commitee
SR	*The Secret Relationship between Blacks and Jews*, Vol. 1
UAHC	Union of American Hebrew Congregations
UJA	United Jewish Appeal
WJCg	World Jewish Congress

Part One

Introduction

_____ *Chapter 1* _____

Jews, America, and Antisemitism

INTRODUCTION

On November 25, 1998, the *New York Times* ran an ad sponsored by the Anti-Defamation League (ADL). It proclaimed, "One out of eight Americans has hard-core Anti-Semitic feelings. Does this sound like a problem that doesn't exist?" The day before the *Boston Globe* ran an eight-paragraph article from the Associated Press entitled, "Blacks More Antisemitic than Whites, Survey Finds." There was more that was not said in these two items than that was said. For example, in the instance of the *Boston Globe* article, the reader does not find out how the survey (sponsored by the ADL) of black attitudes toward Jews was conducted, what questions were asked, or what the results were that led the ADL to make the claim it did. Nor did the article reveal what depth this antisemitism had assumed among blacks, or in what areas, or, for that matter, how antisemitism was understood in the black community.

What the article did do was send a not-too-subtle message that blacks are antisemitic, and that is nonsense. America's black community is not monolithic. The variations in the black community are as wide and deep as those in the Jewish community. This kind of reporting suggests that the antisemitism that does afflict certain portions of the black community is actually endemic to the entire community; it is reckless to suggest such a thing. To begin with, there is no such thing as "black antisemitism." Certainly there are blacks that are antisemitic, just as there are Asians, Hispanics, feminists, or labor leaders who are antisemitic. The big difference between those groups and "black antisemitism" is that we never read about "Hispanic antisemitism" or "feminist antisemitism." It is time for the ADL and the other Jewish advocacy organizations (JAOs) to get much more specific about who in the black community it is they think is antisemitic, and more important, what level of threat they believe this poses for Jews. In addition to blacks and other whites another readership (America's Jews) was important to the ADL, and I will say more about the impact these ads and articles have on them in a moment. Second, what is the reader to conclude after reading the ADL's ad?

The ad boldly claims, "One out of eight Americans has hard-core Anti-Semitic beliefs." The ADL goes on to say that these one out of eight persons who are hard-core antagonists toward Jews total approximately 35 million Americans. There are 35 million Jew-haters—I'm more than a little skeptical of such a claim. I don't believe it, and I am not convinced that the ADL does either (based on the comments made to the author during the research for this book). Also, precisely what are those "hard-core beliefs," and at what level of intensity do they differ from moderate- or mild-core beliefs? We never find out. What the reader can safely conclude from both the article and the ad is that the last months of any year are active fund-raising months for organizations that depend on donations and contributions (approximately 40 percent of all charitable giving occurs during the last two months of the year). This includes the ADL and other Jewish organizations, and this is the time to take advantage of the tax deduction a contribution to their efforts to fight antisemitism represents.

Several days after the first article appeared in the *Boston Globe*, a longer article by Julia Goldman entitled "Anti-Semitism in U.S. Drops, but Stays High Among Blacks" appeared between November 27 and December 3, 1998 in Boston's *Jewish Advocate* and hundreds of other Jewish newspapers across the country. The article revealed that the ADL's statistics came, once again, from the same eleven beliefs about Jews it had constructed in 1964! The other important issue in this debate is, "What was the likely impact those statistics had on a certain segment of American Jews?" As these findings did in the past, they once again could be counted on to raise already high levels of apprehension among some Jews to still higher levels. As reported in chapter two, there are significant numbers of American Jews who know they have never been safer from attack or calumny than they are in America, but they continue to feel a powerful sense of "foreboding" about their future based on the past. Antisemitism has raised its ugly head on more than one occasion in this country, and it could again. So, these fears are not entirely groundless, but when placed in the context of an ethnic group that is almost totally accepted as mainstream Americans, it is not unreasonable to conjecture that these continuous reminders of the past only serve to fuel an almost baseless paranoia. It is time for the Jewish advocacy organizations to stop fueling this anxiety and turn their attention (and money) to more productive and positive Jewish venues. Those are the issues this book addresses—the continuing political and emotional necessity of a threat that has virtually vanished from the conscious mind of most Americans. Framed as a question it becomes, "Why does antisemitism continue to serve substantial emotional and political needs for some of America's Jews, and most decidedly for the organizations that purport to serve the best interests of America's 5.5 million Jews?

To answer this question it is necessary first to go back in time and examine the American Jewish experience, and the antisemitism that frequently dogged that experience, and then to come forward to the present time when the threat of antisemitism has largely disappeared, but the emotional and political purposes it serves are still healthy and thriving. That is where the research for this book began.

In 1992, I found myself exceedingly puzzled over the apparent escalation of antisemitism in the black community. Over the next several months my puzzlement escalated to scholarly curiosity, and it rose, yet again, to what became a broader and deeper examination of the reality of antisemitism in America today, and the ways in which it impacts everyone it touches, for example, Jews and non-Jews, formal and informal organizations alike. What was it that had fueled my puzzlement about the status of antisemitism in America to begin with? It started with a full-page essay in the July 22, 1992 *New York Times* (op-ed section) entitled "Black Demagogues and Pseudo-scholars," by Henry Louis Gates, the chair of Harvard University's Afro-American Studies Department.[1]

Gates clearly and convincingly disavowed the antisemitism, demagoguery, and pseudoscholarship of a handful of strident black separatists led by Minister Louis Farrakhan, the fiery leader of the Nation of Islam (NOI). Farrakhan has been aided in his campaign of twisted allegations of supposed Jewish wrongdoing by a small coterie of devoted mouthpieces such as Khallid Muhammad, Professor Leonard Jeffries (City University of New York), Professor Tony Martin (Wellesley College), and Steve Coakley of Chicago.

Their main source of "reliable" information about the Jews comes from an incendiary book compiled by the Historical Research Department of the NOI (and soundly thrashed by Gates in his article) entitled *The Secret Relationship between Blacks and Jews* (1991, hereafter *SR*). Its 334 pages and 1,275 footnotes form a strange compilation of frequently distorted snippets of information taken from different Jewish sources that reminds one of ransom notes constructed from words cut out of magazines and newspapers and then pasted together to form a ransom demand. In this case the people being "held up" are unsuspecting members of the black community. The book has become the bible of black separatist groups and is sold wherever the NOI is speaking, and in some bookstores catering to Afrocentric clientele. As infuriating as its overall antisemitic portrayal of the Jews and the issue of slavery is, its content is so muddled that only a few stalwart individuals have made any attempt to debunk the book allegation by allegation. One refutation was provided by David Brion Davis, the Yale

University black history scholar, in 1992 ("Jews in the Slave Trade"); and a second one in 1994 by Harold Brackman, a Holocaust scholar at the Simon Weisenthal Institute in Los Angeles.[2] On first reading the Gates article, I thought, "Who are these people, and why are they saying such terrible things about my people?" Up to that day I had never thought of the black community as antisemitic, but perhaps I was wrong.

In the same time frame in which the Gates article appeared, four incidents of antisemitism (three of which are reported in detail in this book) occurred in Boston, Massachusetts. The one incident not reported in complete detail in this book was actually the first in this series of antisemitic incidents, and it took place on the campus of Tufts University in Boston, Massachusetts. In the spring of 1992 the Tufts Islamic Society, in conjunction with the Middle Eastern Studies Group and the university's Vice President's Office, invited Kahllid Abdul Muhammad of the NOI to speak on the subject of "Israel's relationship with South Africa." Muhammad claimed that "Israel and South Africa had a biblical mandate to oppress Palestinians and black people; that Jews own the world-wide transit of gold and precious gems, and with names like Goldstein and Silverstein it is understandable why they call it Jewelry"; and finally that "Jews were never slaves in Egypt and that blacks are the real Chosen people." He had used the Tufts forum as an opportunity to rail against Jews, who he said were the principal benefactors in the enslavement and transport of millions of black slaves to America during the despicable middle passage. Much to their credit the Tufts University Islamic Society later rescinded their support when several members expressed discomfort with Muhammad's brand of Islam.

The reaction by Jews in the audience to Muhammad's comments was stunned disbelief and outrage. But it was a reaction that did not reach outside the campus, except to a small group of Jewish scholars and Jewish organizational professionals who were informed of the incident. Muhammad's performance became one in a collection of speeches and talks by strident and noisy spokespersons for black separatism. Over the next three years their inflammatory rhetoric grew more inventive and crude in their allegations of Jewish wrongdoing toward blacks.

The JAOs in Boston took no action in the aftermath of the Tufts incident, but in fairness to them, they had not been invited to the talk. Nobody at the Tufts Hillel, or in the Jewish organizations, felt there was any reason for concern; they all had been caught off-guard. What most impressed me about the entire incident was the level of outrage, fear, and paranoia it triggered in the Tufts Jewish community, and among the Jewish organizational professionals who learned of it.

The Tufts incident became a focal point during a national meeting on antisemitism (The Salzberg Conference on Anti-Semitism, November 6, 1992) in Waltham, Massachusetts. During this meeting loud demands rang out in the room for justice, or at least a lawsuit against the NOI and possibly

Tufts University. Other participants lamented, "After all we [Jews] have done for the blacks, why have they turned on us in this way?" A third group voiced the fear that antisemitism was staging a frightening comeback, and added, "What are we going to do about it?" The other three incidents reported in chapters eight, nine, and ten followed the Tufts incident in quick succession. As I listened to the outrage, fear, and paranoia that Muhammad's remarks had generated, I wondered how extensive antisemitism was in the black community. After several months of analyzing what historical/statistical data was available on antisemitism in the black community, it turned out that the results were confounded by a number of factors, for example, how do blacks understand antisemitism as compared to whites, do the items in the survey mean the same thing to blacks that they do to whites, and, finally, what level of threat to Jewish security do these antisemitic blacks carry for Jews?

As the other three antisemitic incidents began to unfold, my interest moved increasingly away from any real or latent antisemitism among blacks to the more intriguing question of how prominent Jewish advocacy organizations made decisions about antisemitism, regardless of its origin. How did they decide what had to be done, and who made those decisions? What processes did they go through in carrying out those decisions? Did they collaborate in confronting incidents of antisemitism? As a result of their vigorous advocacy, were these JAOs able to construct any mechanisms to prevent the reoccurrence of antisemitism in the future?

Over the next three years, dozens of interviews were conducted with key Jewish professionals in these organizations, as well as others connected with the three antisemitic incidents. Added to these interviews was the historical information found in archival material from the four organizations, as well as letters, memos, documents, and even scraps of note paper, if they seemed relevant to increasing my understanding of how Jewish organizations actually dealt with antisemitism, and why it continued to absorb so much of their time and effort. What emerged from all of this interviewing and reading was the conclusion that antisemitism continues to possess substantial emotional and political weight for large numbers of America's Jews and the organizations that purport to represent their interests. Three key questions reached out for answers:

1. What are the internal politics that persuade these JAOs that antisemitism is a continuing threat to Jewish safety in the United States, when in reality, Jews in America today have never been safer, or less likely to find themselves the object of an antisemitic attack or canard? The fact is that since the end of World War II antisemitism, by whatever measure you choose, has dropped to near-negligible levels! Coupled to these facts is another question that asks, What factors continue to shape the opinion of substantial numbers of American Jews that antisemitism is still a substantial threat to their safety?

2. How are organizational politics distorting the JAOs' moral capacity to serve other more important issues in the Jewish community?

3. How many Jewish organizations does it take to fight antisemitism in America today?

   Not for the first time did I discover that the needs of select individuals in an organization often overrode whatever its public relations material said was its stated mission. This self-service has substantial implications for how problems are defined by these organizations, who decides something is a problem to begin with, and how the problem, incident, or issue is finally acted upon.

   Integral to this discussion are the implications these questions carry for America's Jews, and their quest for an explainable identity in a highly pluralistic society. America's Jews are casting about for new forms of organizational leadership in their struggle for identity and continuity in the face of massive assimilation into late twentieth-century American society; they are not finding it! Does this failure of leadership on the JAOs' part call for new organizations, or a rethinking in some strategic way the mission and goals of the present organizations? Certainly a compelling element in this discussion is the way, or ways, in which these JAOs will continue to represent themselves to the Jewish and non-Jewish communities. This becomes an important question in light of the escalating level of the Jewish intermarriage rate and the impact this is having on the number of Jews that will exist in the next century. If the Jews of America are so nearly assimilated into the general society that they virtually disappear, then what use is there for the JAOs, no matter how successful they were in the past?

   Finally, there is the question always asked of social scientists about any "regional" study: Can the results generated by this study be generalized to organizational behavior on a national basis? Yes, it can. The organizational characteristics and decision-making processes reported here are replicas, in all respects, of the JAOs' structure and behavior at the national level. Furthermore, we can expect to see the same patterns of organizational decision making and leadership in the face of antisemitism regardless of where in the United States it occurs. Three of the four organizations discussed in this book (American Jewish Committee [AJC], ADL, and the American Jewish Congress [AJCg]) are branch offices with national headquarters in New York City. The fourth, the Jewish Community Relations Council (JCRC), has no national office, and is a local entity. The National Jewish Community Relations Advisory Council (NJCRAC), located in New York City, is an umbrella group that provides an advisory and public relations function to the 114 Jewish Community Councils throughout the United States. It has no power or authority to directly influence the decision making of any of these community councils. The Boston JCRC was an important ingredient in this study because it was directly involved in the two of three

antisemitic incidents, and its participation tells us much about Jewish organizational structure, whether or not it has a national office. If, as this book
proposes, antisemitism is an artifact of a recent past in American society,
where did it come from to begin with?

To properly understand the motivations that energized these JAOs in their
confrontations with American antisemitism, it is necessary to understand the
Jewish migration to America and the antisemitism that was part and parcel
of that resettlement process. It is also important to understand the centuries-
long influence that the ideological form of European antisemitism imposed
on the mind of every non-Jewish immigrant who came to America from the
several countries of Europe.

EUROPEAN ROOTS OF AMERICAN ANTISEMITISM

Throughout this book I will make a distinction between "ideological" antisemitism and "attitudinal" antisemitism. The former was a product of centuries of European bigotry and Jew-hatred, and was sanctioned by official
state and church policy. Through these political and ecclesiastical processes
the Jew was marginalized in countless ways, and his death at the hands of
mobs was frequently ignored, or directly ordered by the state. By contrast,
the latter expression, "attitudinal" antisemitism, is a variant of that earlier
European brand of bigotry and discrimination. It formed the background
mentality of what would become American antisemitism. As vituperative,
and infrequently deadly, as this American brand of antisemitism was, it
never became official state or federal policy, and that is a powerful distinction to keep in mind.

No political candidate, however antisemitic, has been successful in placing an openly anti-Jewish plank in an American political platform. Unlike
Europe, no antisemitic political party has successfully captured the attention
of any more than a disturbed fringe element in American society, and none
of these groups has been successful in making it to the election ballot. In
spite of these clear differences, it is essential to understand the pivotal role
this European legacy played in shaping the foundational base of the JAOs'
operations, and the residual memory that antisemitism still carries for large
numbers of American Jews. In combination, they have formed the yin and
yang of a political/emotional nexus that continues to define the identity of
both groups in unique ways.

The Jews who came to America were the Jews who had fled the countries
of Europe to make a better life for themselves and their families and to escape the prejudice and discrimination of those native lands. The Europeans
who populated America (from its earliest days) were the same Europeans
steeped in an ideological antisemitism that had discriminated against the
Jews in their native lands for centuries. The European antisemitic predispositions arrived in this country long before the huge influx of Jews began to

arrive in any numbers in the mid-nineteenth century. However, there was a major difference in the anti-Jewish hatred that had festered in Europe for centuries, and the ways in which those images of centuries-old antisemitism would shape the attitudes of Americans toward Jews.

In Europe, anti-Jewish hatred was an ideology legitimated by church and government policies that restricted the Jews' movements, the Jews' incomes, and the Jews' occupations. In America, however, it was the "idea" of the Jew (not an ideology) that came here with the English, German, and French settlers. It was anti-Jewish sentiment that was embedded in the teachings of the Christian denominations, their sacred documents dating back centuries, and the shared beliefs of clergy and congregant alike about "the Jew." It was an image tightly bound to the New Testament injunctions about Jews as "Christ killers!" It also was an image that manifested itself in unsavory liturgical depictions of Jews that was eventually extended into an unflattering portrayal of Jews in plays, books, and poetry. Shakespeare's *Merchant of Venice* is one example.

It is in Europe we must look to find the source of the most pernicious and destructive myths about the Jews. Myths that acquired increased legitimacy as the Christian world expanded and Jews struggled to maintain a presence. But, anti-Jewish hatred did not start with Christianity. Attacks on Jews predated the Christian variety by hundreds of years. There was the Jew-hatred of Roman emperors intent on expunging the presence and the power of Jews in pre-Christian times. For example, in 167 BCE ("Before the Current Era") Antiochus Epiphenus desecrated the temple in Jerusalem by broiling a pig and pouring its juices over sacred Jewish scrolls, the Torah. He defended his actions by proclaiming that the Torah was inimical to the interests of the empire (Wistrich, 1991; Seltzer, 1980).

In spite of these national desecrations, the Jews often enjoyed a quiescent, if sometimes tenuous, relationship in the states (that would eventually become Europe) in which they resided over many of the next thousand years. The Jewish Diaspora had started long before the destruction of the second Temple in 70 CE ("Current Era"). Jews were an active part of Greek society dating back to the fourth century BCE. They had arrived in the Crimea and France at the very dawn of the Christian era. Jews settled in Italy in the second century BCE, in Germany in the fourth century CE, and Poland in the tenth century CE. But this accommodative coexistence with their Christian neighbors changed dramatically in the thirteenth century.

Early in the thirteenth century, Jewish safety and privacy was permanently disrupted with the founding of the mendicant friars—the Dominicans and the Franciscans (Cohen, 1982). For the next three hundred years, the Catholic Church advanced its anti-Jewish agenda through these mendicant friars.

The principal activities of the mendicants were conversion, teaching, and itinerant preaching. In these various capacities, they also taught intolerance for the Jews to local clergy and laity alike. They overlooked no opportunity to preach anti-Judaic homilies, and in their quest to rid Western Europe of the Jews, they directly contravened the earlier Church dictates of Augustine of Hippo (354–430). Hippo's teaching provided much of the substance for medieval Christian thought, and he instructed that "God had ordained the survival of the Jews, in order that their presence and continued observance of Mosaic Law might aid the Church in its mission to the Gentiles" (Cohen, 1982:14). The Church neither discouraged nor interfered with the friars' attacks on Jews, and eventually the Church entrusted the entire leadership of the inquisition to those same mendicant friars. They were quick to spread any distortion or calumny about the Jews as they traveled across Europe. The collection of medieval falsehoods that grew out of their enmity formed the basis for an ideological Jew-hatred in Europe that lasted for centuries, and remnants of it can still be seen today in various European countries and Russia. A handful of these myths deserve separate comment because they ultimately played a powerful role in the formation of American anti-Jewish beliefs.

"Deicide," literally one who killed God, plus the New Testament belief that Jews were people of the past and Christians were people of the future, provided the foundation for centuries of Christian anti-Jewish bigotry. While a handful of Jewish priests colluded with Roman authorities in the crucifixion of Jesus, it was a Roman decision and a Roman execution that killed Jesus, not "The Jews." Furthermore, that collusion cannot be passed down to their descendants, regardless of the high priest's cavalier attitude toward future generations of Jews. Over the centuries that this myth flourished, culminating with the Holocaust, the last words Jews about to be murdered frequently heard was "Christ killer!" (Poliakov, 1965:25).

"Well poisoning" grew out of the fiction that a Christian child had been drowned in a town well as part of a secret Jewish rite of sacrifice that was a part of a larger plot to kill all Christians. This myth was often heard in the aftermath of large scale deaths from such diseases as typhus. The average citizen's knowledge of the conditions that bred these devastating diseases was negligible, but frequently, Jews paid for that ignorance with their lives. A terrifying variant of the well poisoning myth occurred in the fourteenth century with the appearance in Europe of the Black Plague.

Physicians, kings, and religious leaders were all stymied by the appearance and ferocity of the Black Death; its origins remained a mystery until recent times. It was variously attributed to something in the air or something contracted from being out-of-doors, so people crowded into already cramped and unsanitary quarters, only aggravating the spread of the disease still further. Nothing they did seemed to forestall the agony and disfiguring death that marked the plague. According to Norman Cohn ([1968] 1996), "it was . . . concluded that some group of people must have introduced into the water supply, a poison concocted of spiders, frogs, and lizards—all of them symbols of earth, dirt, and the Devil—or else maybe of basilisk-flesh. As the

plague continued and people grew more and more bewildered and desperate, suspicion swung now here, now there, lighting successively on the lep-
ers, the poor, the rich, the clergy, before it came finally to rest on the Jews,
who thereupon were almost exterminated" (87). Within a short time many
of the people in these towns came to realize that the Jews in their community
were dying at the same rate as everybody else. But a great many Jews had already died at the hands of mobs before this obvious reality penetrated most
people's mind.

The "blood libel" myth customarily depicts a group of Jews bleeding a
Christian child to death. One of the better known reproductions of this
myth can be seen in the woodcut of the murder of Simon of Trent (Wistrich,
1991:70–71). The alleged purpose of this sacrifice was to obtain Christian
blood that was then used for baking the unleavened Jewish bread, *matzah*.
One of the simpler forms of bread, *matzah* is comprised of very few ingredients, and blood is not one of them.

"Host piercing" is the quintessential Christian myth about the Jews. It is
a concoction that alleges Jews collected the small wafers used in the
Christian service of communion, and then pierced them with a needle or a
knife. Thus, metaphorically rekilling Jesus, since the host is the physical representation of the body and blood of Jesus. Jews, however, never accepted
Jesus as the Messiah, nor did they ever partake in any religious ritual involving a small wafer of bread. Thus they had no firsthand knowledge of
why this small wafer should hold any importance whatsoever. It is a myth
that betrays its purely Christian invention.

"Money lending and usury" are frequently raised criticisms of the Jews
("they care more for money than people," "they control international finance," and so on, and so on), and like the other myths already discussed
this one contributed substantially to the ideological brand of European antisemitism. Like the other myths already discussed, this one also had its origins in the Middle Ages. The Lateran Council of 1215 ruled that Jews be
disbarred from all civil and military functions and from owning land. These
disbarments became Canon Law (Cohn, 1970:79).

Few avenues were left open through which Jews could earn a living, or ac-
cumulate wealth. They could lend money, which was outlawed as usury by
the Church, and they could keep their wealth (such as it was) in highly liq-
uid forms, easy to quickly transport. Europe was growing, and the mon-
archs of these states often ordered Jews to lend money to the state so it could
pursue its military escapades. The unsavory image of the Jewish money
lender grows out of medieval portrayals of the Jews not giving the humble
peasants full value for any goods they received. For example, a Christian
wife (it was seldom the husband involved himself in negotiations involving
money) could not borrow money when times were lean from anyone but a
Jew. She was frequently outraged to discover that the quilts made by her
grandmother, and handed down over the generations, were not worth a

great deal of value in terms of lendable funds. Under these circumstances the Jew was often depicted as a "blood sucker" (Wistrich, 1991:27), a depiction that has persisted down through the twentieth century and appears today in the demagoguery of Louis Farrakhan and the NOI.

The frequently heard characterization that "Jews stick together too much," or "Jews are clannish" has both a Jewish and an anti-Jewish history. This insistence that Jews stick to their own kind had its origins in the Hellenistic period. No other nation at that time denied the gods of its neighbors; on the contrary, it recognized them, including them in praise with their own deities. This pan-religiosity was used with considerable success by the Greek ruling authorities in creating a social bond between the various people in its domain. None of these people except the Jews refrained from dining at the same table with their neighbors, or partaking of the sacrifices offered to their gods. None of these people except the Jews refused to send gifts to its neighbors' temples. None of these people except the Jews were unequivocally hostile to intermarriage. As a result of their monotheism and observance of strict dietary and marriage laws, the Jews were viewed by their Greek counterparts as misanthropic, flagrantly denying the Hellenic principle of the unity of mankind. As the dispersion of Jews moved across Europe in the ensuing centuries, they took these strict religious beliefs with them, often living in separate parts of the cities in an effort to retain their singular identity. The institution of the ghetto in the sixteenth century served both purposes: it segregated the Jews as chattel of the state from the rest of the populace, and it provided the Jews with the privacy they sought for their religious observances (Wistrich, 1991:37).

But segregation didn't stop with the ghettos. Jews were further segregated by requiring them to wear certain articles of clothing that clearly identified them as Jews, hats, for example, of a certain shape (*Encyclopaedia Judaica*, v3, 1972:129–134; hereafter *EJ*). Another device were "Jew badges," ring shaped pieces of cloth (variously colored white, yellow, or blue), that Jews had to prominently display on their outer garment (Wistrich, 1991:70–71).

Christian antipathy toward Jews only heightened with the arrival of the Protestant Reformation. The Catholic Church was joined in the sixteenth century by the Protestant denominations that formed in the aftermath of the Reformation. Its most prominent figure, Martin Luther, added his fury to the prevailing Christian hatred toward the Jews. At first, Luther was content to pursue the dictates of St. Paul and try every means possible to convert the Jews as evidence of this new Protestant mission. When his efforts proved as futile as other missionaries' efforts before his, he launched scathing and violent denunciations of the Jews.

Luther drew much of his anti-Jewish rhetoric from the writings of Anton Margarita (b. 1490), an apostate and anti-Jewish writer who was the son of a rabbi in Regensberg. He denounced the Regensberg Jewish community, and converted to Catholicism in 1522, and later became a Protestant. His first anti-Jewish book, *Der Gantz Judisch Glaub*, was published in Augsburg in 1530. It was so poorly written that when his allegations about Jews proved to be unfounded, he was imprisoned and later banished from Augsburg. However, his book was reprinted several times (Frankfort, 1544, 1561, 1689; Leipzig, 1705, 1713) and was widely read. It strongly influenced Martin Luther, who quoted it many times in his *Von den Juden Und Lhren Luegen*.

In 1543 with the publication of *Concerning the Jews and Their Lies*, Martin Luther proposed to his readers some "honest advice." Luther suggested seven steps should be taken to deal with the Jews. They ran the gamut: burning their synagogues; putting them in stables like gypsies; destroying their prayer books and Torah; putting their rabbis under a threat of death for teaching. Finally, Luther intoned, "let the young and strong Jews and Jewesses be given the flail, the ax, the hoe, the spade, the distaff, and spindle, and let them earn their bread by the sweat of their noses as is enjoined upon Adam's children. To sum up, dear Princes and nobles who have Jews in your domains, if this advice of mine does not suit you, then find a better one so that you and we may be free of this insufferable devilish burden—the Jews" (*EJ*, v3, 1972:159). Luther's indictment of the Jews and his demands for severe punishment lodged in the German Christian mentality and helped fuel a resultant German Protestant antisemitism that culminated in the horrors of the Holocaust as the ultimate mechanism to free Europe of "this devilish burden."

By the Enlightenment period, and with it the emancipation of Jews throughout most of Europe, it became increasingly awkward for even the most dedicated Jew-hater (particularly those in government) to sustain their public attacks on Jews based purely on these myths. This was particularly true in Germany and Austria, which had never embraced the democratic ideals of the Enlightenment mentality. Something new was called for to deal with "the Jewish question," and the increasing assimilation of Jews into mainstream European society. That something was the formulation of the expression "anti-Semitism." It was first coined by a full-time antisemite named Wilhelm Marr (1818–1904).

Marr was an unsuccessful journalist and petty agitator who started his political career in the midst of the 1848 social protest movement in his native Hamburg. His 1862 anti-Semitic pamphlet *Der Judenspiegel* (Jews Mirror) was followed by the influential *The Victory of Judaism over Germandom, Considered from a Non-Religious Point of View*. By 1879 it had gone through twelve editions. Marr abandoned the religious identity of Jews, and insisted that Jews be treated as a race, and for the words Jew and Judaism he substituted "Semite" and "Semitism," which, with the prefix anti, went on to gain international currency. Marr introduced the expression "anti-Semite" into the political vocabulary in 1879 by founding the League of Anti-Semites (*Antisemiten-Liga*), which organized lecturers and published a short-lived monthly. The league failed as an organization, but it was historically important because it was one of the first efforts at creating a popular political movement based solely on antisemitism. His later antisemitic pamphlets were poorly received, and he retired in obscurity (*EJ*, v3, 1973:10–15). Marr had created a dubious standard for labeling anti-Jewish beliefs in the modern world, and in so doing, he introduced a huge readership to the destructive myths and distortions about Jews that had abounded in Europe for centuries. The idea of Jews as a race persisted in Europe and the United States until after World War II. Even some Jews gave the concept credence. The aftermath of Marr's agitation led to oblivion for him, but it triggered the imaginations of other individuals who hated Jews. The next international outburst of Jew-hatred found its voice in Russia.

Between 1897 and 1905 a specious collection of articles began circulating that focused on an alleged conspiracy by Jews to control worldwide finance, banking, and the newspapers. They became known as *The Protocols of the Elders of Zion*. Serge Niles, a former officer of the Cheka (the Russian Secret Police under Nicholas II), and a Russian Orthodox "priest" of questionable authenticity, began circulating the first copies of the *Protocols* in 1905. This collection of twenty-four (sometimes twenty-seven) protocols had supposedly been fashioned at secret meetings coincident with the first Zionist Congress in Basel, Switzerland, in 1897. The *Protocols* allege that a powerful and mysterious group of Jews had supposedly worked out an elaborate set of plans (the protocols) that would enable them to disrupt all of Christian civilization, and on the ruins of Christendom erect a world-state ruled over by Jews. The *Protocols* were first printed in abbreviated form in the Russian language in 1903 in the newspaper *Znamia* (Banner), and subsequently in book form in 1905. They were translated into German, French, English, and other languages of the Western world and they soon became *the* sacred book of anti-Semitic writings. It had its greatest impact on Germany in the years after World War I.

The conspiratorial secrecy that pervades the *Protocols* is the same trademark characteristic that pervades the NOI's *The Secret Relationship between Blacks and Jews* or *SR*. Wherever the NOI makes an appearance, copies of the *SR* are always for sale, and frequently the *Protocols* are for sale on the same table. The *Protocols* have enjoyed a huge and diverse distribution from its first public release in 1905 up to the present day. The most thorough discussion of the *Protocols* can be found in Norman Cohn's *Warrant for Genocide* ([1968] 1996).

The expression antisemitism did not mean the same thing in America that it did in Europe. Where the latter was ideological (i.e., often racial), the former was attitudinal (i.e., negative beliefs about Jews). Thus, almost immediately, a definitional problem became apparent—what did the expression antisemitism mean in the American context? To this day that definitional vagueness has not been satisfactorily answered. Whatever it meant, and means, Jews in America, virtually from their first days in this country, encountered anti-Jewish hostility and animosity. American antisemitism was not only attitudinal, it often expressed itself in blatant forms of discrimination in housing, education, and employment, and very infrequently turned deadly, as in the case of the lynching of Leo Frank.

JEWS, AMERICA, AND ANTISEMITISM

The history of Jews in America has been told in a number of excellent studies: Nathan Glazer ([1957] 1989), Arthur Hertzberg ([1990] 1998), Jonathan Sarna (1986b), Howard Sacher (1992), Jacob Marcus (1995), and the American Jewish Historical Society's five-volume edition on the history of the Jews in America (1992). There are several excellent studies of the prejudice and discrimination Jews suffered during their passage into American society. These include Leonard Dinnerstein (1994), Frederic Jaher (1994), and Jerome Chanes (1995). My comments over the next several pages are not designed to compete with these excellent studies or to deny the reader the opportunity to pursue these accounts of the American Jewish experience and antisemitism from a firsthand perspective. Rather, my brief narrative history of the American Jewish experience is to weave from several sources a brief tableau of both the history of the Jews in America and the antisemitism that dogged their heels until approximately sixty years ago. Several of the specific instances of antisemitism that involved the JAOs are covered in greater depth in the chapters devoted to the history of the JAOs. For this reason, the next several pages discuss and describe this interrelationship between history and antisemitism during three broad periods of American history: 1654 to 1800, 1801 to 1900, and 1901 to the present day. Antisemitism in America has been uneven but never totally absent from any of these historical periods. It rose and fell with the circumstances of the day, but was a constant undercurrent from the arrival of the first Jews in 1654. It was inevitable that the European history of ideological antisemitism, fueled by centuries of Christian doctrine, would make its way to this country as the "invisible baggage" (Sarna, 1986b:3) of every European immigrant group who came to America.

The same can be said of negative attitudes toward American Jews today. As negligible as they are, antisemitism persists as a fixed ingredient in the manifestos of fringe groups scattered around the country, whose members count anything different or liberal in the surrounding social fabric as a direct threat to their freedom and liberty.

1654 to 1800

When the Portuguese retook Recife, in the colony of Brazil, from the Dutch in 1654, the Jews were expelled. Twenty-three of those expelled Jews came north and landed on America's shores (Hertzberg, 1990:19). Many more of the Jews who had comprised the small Jewish community in Recife went back to Holland (Glazer, [1957] 1989:13–14). This small group of twenty-three Jews is frequently described as the first Jews to settle in this country. They were, in the sense of establishing themselves permanently in America, but they were not the first Jews to see the new continent, or to roam its shores. To understand the arrival of earlier, unnamed Jews to this continent, it is necessary to understand the expulsion of the Jews from Spain in 1492, and from Portugal five years later. Some Jews under Spanish rule at that time capitulated to the demands of the Roman Catholic Inquisition, and gave up their faith for a forced conversion to Christianity. Others gave up their faith in public and continued to practice their Judaism as crypto Jews, or Marranos. Some of those crypto Jews came to the new world with Christopher Columbus, and others came, but never stayed, on later voyages of discovery.

Many of the Jews expelled from Spain on the order of Queen Isabella and King Ferdinand (on the eve of approving Columbus's voyage in 1492) fled to Portugal only to find themselves expelled from Portugal in 1497. A large percentage of these twice-expelled Jews made their way to Amsterdam; Holland was the only country in Europe where they were allowed to live, legally. As employees of the Dutch West Indies Trading Company, they made their way to Brazil and the Caribbean basin islands with Holland's westward expansion and colonization. It was from this population of Jews that twenty-three of them found themselves in New Amsterdam, the predecessor of New York. Peter Stuyvesant, the governor of New Amsterdam, did not welcome them with open arms; he was openly hostile to their being in his colony, and before letting them disembark, demanded of the Dutch West Indies Company an indemnification to insure that the Jews did not become a financial burden. He received it, but the events of the next few years showed that not only did the Jews take care of themselves, but they were quick to establish several successful business ventures that contributed to the civic welfare of New Amsterdam (Sarna, 1986b:3).

Was Stuyvesant anti-Jewish? Yes, but was he antisemitic? No, the expression "antisemitism" did not exist until two other events had occurred: the emancipation of the Jews at the end of the eighteenth century, and the creation of the expression antisemitism in 1889 by Wilhelm Marr, as discussed above. Stuyvesant was reacting to those first twenty-three Jews in the same way he would react to any pre-emancipation Jew—with distrust and general loathing. But it must be remembered that he was no better inclined toward Quakers or Lutherans, either. He wanted no one in his colony that could conceivably disrupt his rule of social order.

The Puritan experience in New England forever left its social (if not religious) imprint on Boston and other New England cities, although its actual history spanned only a short period, from approximately 1630 to 1684. In 1684 King Charles II of England ordered a halt to the Puritan experiment.

The Puritans considered Boston a new Zion, the "city on the hill" that would bear redemptive power in the New World. They declared themselves, not the Jews, God's chosen people, but in doing so, they also adopted a substantial Hebraic liturgy. At one point prominent Puritans attempted to convince skeptics that their missionary travels to the Indian tribes of Maine were an archeological expedition to prove that America's native citizens were actually the lost tribes of Israel! John Winthrop, the first governor of Massachusetts, was portrayed as the Moses to the New World. But as far as Puritanism's relevance to actual Jews, there was none (Hertzberg, 1990:38–40).

In the late seventeenth century, Cotton Mather, a leading spokesperson for the Puritan movement, took to wearing a Jewish skull-cap (*kippah*) and calling himself a "rabbi." He published a conversion textbook drawing extensively on Hebrew biblical citations as a way to prove to the Jews the inevitability of their conversion to Christianity. The few Jews who resided in the colonies ignored it. With all of this interesting tension between Puritan aspirations and myths and the reality of the colonies' handful of Jews, there were almost no openly anti-Jewish actions. One example occurred early in the eighteenth century in the person of Judah Monis.

In 1720 an Algerian Jew named Judah Monis arrived in Boston from New York. He converted to Christianity after about two years, received a masters degree from Harvard, and then stayed on to teach Hebrew (Sacher, 1992:36). He authored the first Hebrew grammar text in America, but he could not have done any of these things (teach and write) had he not converted to Christianity. Harvard would not have hired him if he had not, and there is no record that Monis particularly missed his Jewish roots after his conversion. He died peacefully in Boston, and to this day a small stipend is distributed annually to the Unitarian-Universalist Society (Boston, Massachusetts) from a trust fund Monis established specifically to benefit the Unitarian Church and its ministers (Hertzberg, 1990:42). Harvard continued to successfully deny Jewish students admission to its colleges and would not hire practicing Jews as faculty members for another two hundred fifty years.

By 1700 there were only 200 to 300 Jews in the colonies, and they were clustered in the major shipping centers of New York, Philadelphia, Baltimore, and Charleston, South Carolina (Sarna, 1986b:296). The colonial period was virtually free of antagonisms toward Jews (Hertzberg, 1990:59). The principal charge in almost any economic conflict between Jew and Gentile was that the Jews had killed Jesus. By and large, this handful of Jews who lived and worked in the colonies were ignored; and if any thought was given to them, it was by the different Christian denominations intent on converting them from Judaism to Christianity. As the new country moved toward the Revolutionary War, and its establishment as a democratic society, the number of Jews continued to slowly increase, but with these growing numbers came increased incidents of antagonism toward some Jews.

The population of Jews had grown from the original twenty-three in 1654 to approximately 1500 by 1750 (Sarna, 1986b:296). As meager as their numbers were, the fact remains that several Jewish names had become prominent by 1780: Haym Solomon (a Philadelphia businessman); Mordecai Sheftall (a leader of the Jewish community in Savannah, Georgia); David Franks (who sold provisions to both the British and the Patriots) and his daughter, Rebecca Franks (who married an English officer and spent the rest of her life on a baronial estate in England); and Aaron Lopez (one of America's leading shipowners, and unfortunately, also one of its leading traffickers in slaves) (Hertzberg, 1990; Sacher, 1992; Marcus, 1995). While none of these Jews made any significant impact on the American Revolution, they were significant "simply because they were there" (Hertzberg, 1990:65). But through their presence and influence, these Jews (and others sympathetic to the Jews) were instrumental in getting various "Christian oaths of office" rescinded in several of the founding states.

In 1777 only New York gave political equity regardless of religion, but in the next several years other states quickly followed New York's example, including Virginia, Georgia, South Carolina, and Pennsylvania. One of the better known efforts to rescind the Christian oath was the struggle that marked the passage of Maryland's "Jew Bill." Its significance lay in the fact that it reflected the general population's willingness to liberalize its treatment of Jews through election to public office. First introduced in 1797, the bill sought to repeal the requirement that anyone dealing with the law declare their belief in the Christian religion (Sarna, 1986b:34). As Sarna relates, it didn't pass, and was reintroduced annually until 1826 when it did pass, and two Jews, Solomon Etting and Jacob I. Cohen, were promptly elected members of the Baltimore City Council.

Yet, in spite of meager numbers and a general desire on the part of the emerging states to liberalize restrictive laws against Jews, there were incidents of abysmal prejudice leveled at some Jews. In 1778 several Jews in Savannah, Georgia, sent their families to Charleston, South Carolina, while they remained behind to fight the invading British forces. On December 1, 1778, an anonymous letter appeared in the *Charleston Gazette* accusing the Jews of disloyalty for supposedly abandoning the fight for liberty to save their own ill-gotten goods. The writer characterized the Jews' behavior as a pointed dismissal of the colony's plight. The next day in the same paper an equally anonymous "American and true-hearted Israelite" heatedly declared that the accusation was patently false and that only their women and children were relocated to remove them from possible harm; the men had stayed behind to do their patriotic duty (Hertzberg, 1990:67).

A similar economic incident occurred in 1784, this time in Philadelphia. Miers Fisher, a former Tory, had returned to Philadelphia to set up a bank, and claimed he would offer lower interest rates, thereby protecting the citizens of Philadelphia from "Jewish usury" (Hertzberg, 1990:67). Haym

Solomon writing anonymously as a Jewish broker lashed out at Fisher demanding to know how he dared accuse the Jews of such calumny when it was a known fact that Jews were among the most patriotic defenders of America. He went on to point out that it was patently unfair of Fisher to paint all Jews with the same brush simply because a few members of the Jewish community had behaved in an unscrupulous manner (Hertzberg, 1990:67).

By the turn of the century (1800), there were approximately 2000 to 2500 Jews in the United States (*Leo Baeck Institute Year Book*, 1967, 10:69), but now families and synagogues, as well as individuals, were being tracked through the census. Jewish families now totaled approximately 600, and they were served by only a handful of synagogues. In addition to this modest growth, there were also expressions of the continuing seeds of distrust and outright loathing for Jews held by some in the surrounding society. In one such instance, in 1790, Jews were described as "clannish," and Dr. David Nassy, a Philadelphia physician, came to their defense, pointing out that several Jews in Philadelphia had married Christian wives and attended synagogue while their wives attended church. They were accepted as part of the better reaches of society, and it was doubtful, according to Nassy, that such integration could support a charge of self-segregation (Hertzberg, 1990:67).

In 1800, Benjamin Nones, a prominent figure in the Philadelphia community was attacked in the *Gazette of the United States* (a Federalist publication) for being a Jew and a Republican (what is today a Democrat). He immediately took up the charge and defended himself on both counts, as a Jew and as a Republican, in an impassioned letter that included praise for the revolutions in America, France, and Holland, because these were the only countries that had given equality to the Jews. He included with himself as a Jew not only Abraham, Isaac, and Moses, but also Jesus and the twelve apostles; he said, "I feel no disgrace in ranking with such society, however it may be subject to the illiberal buffoonery of such men as your correspondents" (Hertzberg, 1990:68). He asked, rhetorically, Given these predispositions to greatness, how could he as a Jew be anything but a Republican?

1801 to 1900

Between 1801 and 1840, over 750,000 immigrants came to the United States from Europe (Marcus, 1995:77), and with a few exceptions they came from lands that considered Jews inferior. On the stage and in popular writings, the Jew was frequently portrayed as unscrupulous and unsavory, although the direct experience Americans had with Jews was laudatory and praiseworthy; and there was substantial respect exhibited for the Jew "in reality," as contrasted with the mythical "idea" of the Jew. Yet, parallel to these sentiments of acceptance, prominent authors such as Washington Irving, James Fenimore Cooper, and Henry Clay wrote disparaging comments about Jews. Added to this was that fact that a great many Americans believed that this was a Christian nation, and as such, Jews (as outsiders) were not entitled to its many amenities and privileges (Marcus, 1995:78).

By the early 1800s there were a number of Jews serving the government of the United States in various capacities. Uriah Phillips Levy was a prominent naval officer: he started out as a deckhand at age ten and rose through the ranks to commodore and earned the title "hero" for his actions during the War of 1812; Mordecai Manual Noah was a writer and politician. But both of these men were attacked by anti-Jewish forces in the government who contended that they were not worthy to hold positions of trust or to represent the U.S. government in delicate relations with foreign countries. Both men had their defenders in the government, including President James Madison, and both went on to perform illustrious service to the United States.

By and large, the Jewish community was free of problems during the early decades of the nineteenth century. The same could not be said of the Christian communities. In its various forms and denominations it suffered serious defamations. A convent school was burned in Boston and fires destroyed several churches in Philadelphia. Dozens of Christians were murdered, and campaigns were mounted that drove the Mormons out of upstate New York and into the deserts of Utah. Freemasons were denigrated, and the abolitionist preacher William Lloyd Garrison was dragged through the streets with a rope around his neck. "Nothing like this happened to Jews in America, and they knew it," noted Jacob Marcus (1995:82).

By 1801, there were only seven synagogue communities in all of North America; by 1840, sixteen new synagogues had opened their doors (Marcus, 1995:90). Beginning slowly in the 1820s and peaking in the 1850s, increasing numbers of Jews left Europe for America. Some of these new immigrants were from Eastern Europe, but the vast majority of these new immigrants were German Jews. Once here, they quickly discovered they had to share living space and opportunity with hundreds of thousands of other newly arrived nationalities: Poles, Germans, Swedes, Italians, Irish, and a steady stream of French and English, all intent on settling in the new world. By the late 1830s, there were approximately 15,000 Jews in America, and in the next twenty years that figure ballooned to between 125,000 and 150,000 (Sarna, 1986b:296). During the same period, this flood of new people brought over 3,000,000 new souls of all varieties to America; yet, the peak years for immigration—Jewish and non-Jewish—were still decades away![3] One group of Jews the new arrivals had to deal with were the settled and successful families of Sephardic Jews who had been coming to this country for literally centuries.

The Sephardic Jews, who preceded the wave of German Jews (sometimes referred to as the "second wave"), came to America between 1830 and 1860 and were already settled and prominent in American life. They were prosperous merchants who had formed themselves into a quiet and unobtrusive community of Jews who were just as quickly assimilating into the general society.

By 1830 the intermarriage rate between the Sephardic Jews and non-Jews was on the order of one in three. They bore famous names: Frank, Lopez, Cardozo, Sachs, Gratz, Touro, and Levy, and the history and legacy of these "Grandees" (a Sephardic Jewish elite in America), as Stephen Birmingham (1971) described them, dated back to the founding of this country and before. The arrival of the first wave of German Jews with their less polished manners and the economic reality of peddling to make a living (rather than some more refined undertaking) did not encourage these more established and private Jews to throw open their arms, homes, or salons to the newcomers. If anything, they drew back still further into the warmth and familiarity of their own social constellations.

In terms of any anti-Jewish sentiment, these first arrivals held themselves aloof from the common calumnies that sometimes arose in the surrounding gentile community. On the other hand, they did not shirk from speaking out against injustices aimed at other Jews. The general quiescence of the times (from the colonial period to the Civil War) largely left them alone; a condition that would begin to sour (for all Jews in America) with the approach of the new century, and the promise of still greater and greater numbers of immigrants, Jewish and non-Jewish alike.

The Jews who came to America from 1830 to 1860 were from Germany, Austria, and Bavaria, and they outnumbered arriving Jews from other parts of Europe by overwhelming proportions. They came in two groups, those who were virtually driven out by restrictive government regulations and near poverty, and the more modernized and economically secure German Jews who would follow a few decades later. The revolution that swept Europe in 1848 would be the deciding factor for many of the later group of German Jews to set sail for America. Collectively the German Jews had become America's *nouveau riche* by the turn of the century, but in the beginning, that first group of German Jews to arrive in America were poor and lacking in definable skills that would assure them jobs in the burgeoning cities in which they settled. What they lacked in occupational preparedness, they made up for with drive, ambition, and daring. They would characterize themselves as adventurers and felt no shame or compunction in strapping a homely pack on their back and setting off as peddlers.

The early histories of famous names like Seligman, Bache, Guggenheim, Lehman, Rosenwald all began with some form of peddling or merchandising before moving into finance, bond marketing, and general banking. As these German Jewish peddlers moved west from the East Coast, they left telltale signs of their journey behind them on the frontier and further west to California: Mogen Davids over doorways, Hebrew letters to identify an earlier Jewish ownership, and synagogues. Barry Supple reports that by 1860 there were new congregations in Alabama, California, Georgia, Illinois, Indiana, Maryland, Wisconsin, and Washington, DC (Sarna, 1986b:73).

The father of J. S. Bache & Co., Semon Bache, worked in a Mississippi store. Marcus Goldman, of Goldman Sachs & Co., peddled for two years before opening a men's clothing store in Philadelphia in 1848. One of the more adventurous entrepreneurs was Meyer Guggenheim. He peddled shoestrings, lace, needles, pins, and polishes (furniture and stove). He perfected a stove polish that he sold wherever he could reach by auto or train. Eventually he opened a wholesale household products company in Philadelphia. The Guggenheim family would not only succeed in peddling and banking, but would make a name for itself in railroad ownership as well (Supple in Sarna, 1986b:75).

Henry Lehman arrived in this country in 1844 and peddled for a living in Alabama for a year before founding a general store with his brothers (Lehman Brothers). Their cotton brokerage business would bring them into one of the best known anti-Jewish incidents of the Civil War period—the issuance of Ulysses S. Grant's Order #11 (Sarna, 1986b:75). Samuel Rosenwald peddled throughout the South and Midwest (sometimes on foot), and after establishing a store in Springfield, Illinois, became the father of Julius Rosenwald, the future president of Sears Roebuck (Sarna, 1986:75).

Lazarus Strauss began peddling in 1852 in the South and established a store in Georgia. After the Civil War he moved north and established a crockery business. The family went on to found R. H. Macy & Co. Two other names are important to this discussion of German Jews because of their eventual involvement with anti-Jewish behavior: the first is Joseph Seligman; the other, Jacob Schiff. Seligman arrived in America in 1837 and began peddling in the area of Mauch Chunk, Pennsylvania (now Jim Thorpe, Pennsylvania). He saved a modest sum of money and with his brothers established dry goods stores first in Pennsylvania, and then expanding to Alabama, Missouri, and New York State. With the discovery of gold in California they went into business in San Francisco. In a single generation the Seligman family had made itself wealthy by moving Jewish enterprise across the entire country, and then moving on to a larger fortune in the world of finance (Sarna, 1986b:75–76).

Schiff was a part of the second generation of German Jews to come to this country. He entered in 1865, founded a small brokerage firm, went back to Germany in 1872, but returned to America to join Kuhn Loeb & Company where he would stay for the remainder of his days. He married the daughter of Solomon Loeb and went on to become the president and driving force in Kuhn Loeb. In company with several other prominent New York German Jews, Schiff would help form the American Jewish Committee in 1906 (see chapter three). Schiff's background was representative of the second wave of German Jews to arrive in America. They came from financially comfortable, educated families. They would be the transformative force in moving many of these earlier family fortunes, which had started with peddling, into security brokerage and investment banking.

They would also bring the predominant form of Judaism to this country as well, that is, the Reform branch. Supple (Sarna, 1986b:82–83) provides the reader with a graphic representation of the "Family Business of German Jewish Origin." It is interesting to note the way in which intermarriage kept many of these families and businesses tightly connected to one another.

Moving toward the years of the Civil War, America's Jews came out as early advocates for the abolition of slavery, but, in the South, a handful of Jewish landowners were slave owners as well. The Civil War produced one horrendous incident of antisemitism, and it was Grant's Order #11 of December 17, 1862. It demanded that all of the Jewish merchants from his military district in Western Tennessee pack up and leave because of their alleged trading with the enemy across Union lines (Dinnerstein, 1994:32). The only merchants identified as smugglers were Jewish, and undoubtedly some of them had engaged in such activity. On the other hand, Hertzberg (1990) contends that the group of staff officers that persuaded Grant to sign the order to begin with were deeply involved in the smuggling being carried out by several gentile firms, and they saw the expulsion of the Jews as a way to reduce competition and, thus, increase their own profits.

The reaction to the order was instantaneous and vociferous, particularly from the Jewish community. Jews inundated the White House and Congress with letters of outrage. The Congress rescinded the order in a matter of days and based its decision on the Constitutional protection against singling out one group for such treatment. Behind this constitutional argument stood President Abraham Lincoln. He demanded, in private correspondence, that Grant rescind his order immediately and publicly admit his error. Grant did, and he refused to ever discuss the incident or the president's stinging rebuke again during his lifetime. But in spite of the national attention this incident generated, the German Jews were virtually free of very much antisemitic sentiment or behavior. This lack of antisemitic attention changed with an incident in 1877.

By 1877 Joseph Seligman's fortune was assured, and in keeping with his hard-earned social position he took himself and his family aboard his private railroad car and set off for a vacation at the posh Saratoga Springs resort in upstate New York. Unfortunately, much to his dismay and embarrassment, the owner of the resort refused to allow any Jews on the premises. The owner knew who Seligman was, but his fortune as a prominent banker and a popular social lion made no difference. "Persons of the Hebrew faith" were not going to be admitted. Seligman gathered up his family and his dignity and went back to New York City where he promptly put together a syndicate that bought out the Saratoga Springs resort. As the new owner, Seligman's first act was to fire the man who had embarrassed his family a few weeks earlier!

But the rejection went deeper than one resort against one man of the Hebrew faith. These exclusionary restrictions against Jews were becoming increasingly prominent in heretofore white, Protestant enclaves. The Hebrew restriction clause was particularly prominent at resorts throughout New England and New York State. It would eventually—and blatantly—spread to employment and education. This creeping antisemitism, which would reach full bloom by the mid-1940s, was building up strength just as the resettlement of Jews from Eastern Europe was reaching a crescendo.

1901 to the Present

The 1972 film *The Russians Are Coming, The Russians Are Coming* could very well have captured the sentiments of those Jews already comfortably settled in America, some for several generations. The exodus of Jews out of Russia, Eastern Europe, and countries adjacent to them, such as Romania, Lithuania, and Poland, began slowly in 1881. Jews from these parts of Europe had been coming to America in small numbers as early as the 1840s, but with the assassination of Czar Nicholas II of Russia in 1881, Jews began leaving for America in increasingly larger and larger numbers. The exceptional numbers by the turn of the century paralleled the general patterns of immigration into this country from all parts of Europe. This was a period of unrestricted immigration, and the industrialization of this country needed cheap labor; the newly arrived immigrants were fodder for a surging industrial economy that had taken hold of the United States.

By 1900 there were approximately one million Jews in America; by 1910 this number had risen to nearly two million. In the years between 1881 and 1914, the year that serious discussions began on restricting all immigration into this country, over two million Jews had come to America, pushing this country's total Jewish population to approximately 3,600,000, or 3.5 percent of the general population (*AJYB*, 25:337). After 1881 the vast majority of these new Jewish arrivals came from Russia, Poland, and the states that bordered them. The actual borders of Poland and Russia had changed several times over the previous three hundred years, but the Russians were intent on isolating their Jews in a single geographic area—the Pale of Settlement in the years prior to the Czar's assassination.

The Pale covered an area of 386,000 square miles, and stretched from the Baltic Sea to the Black Sea. According to the 1897 census, 4,899,300 Jews lived within its borders, making it the most densely packed geographic area in the world. The Pale held 94 percent of the total Jewish population of Russia and 11.6 percent of Russia's general population. It was the largest ghetto ever conceived, and the living conditions ranged from meager to poverty stricken. It was administered by Jewish councils who could provide no protection whatever from the frequent pogroms that swept through the villages and shtetls within the Pale. People had no room and no way to make a living. While the assassination of Czar Nicholas II of Russia in 1881 triggered massive pogroms in the Pale that led to the death of hundreds of Jews, it was the remorseless poverty that finally drove hundreds of thousands to leave for other countries, but principally the United States (*EJ*, v13, 1972:24–26).

What clearly distinguished these "Russian Jews" (an attribution attached to any Jew who came from Eastern Europe) was their poverty. The middle-class Jews of Russia, and the other Eastern European countries, were just as frequently up-ended during times of political and economic upheaval, but because of their wealth, they were able to relocate to other parts of Russia, or other countries within the Eastern European sphere. The middle-class Jews and the devoutly religious Jews, unlike the poor Jews, never seriously entertained leaving Europe for the United States. The poor had no other choice! They left their motherland because of poverty, not pogroms. Only a small number of the Russian Jews who came to America came because of the violence visited upon them by the pogroms.

Another distinction must be made between the Russian Jews and the German Jews who came to America. While the first wave of German Jews came to this country in similar states of poverty and civil deprivation, they quickly adapted to the booming economic realities of America and made the most of them. They typically rose to middle-class status within one to two generations and were already wealthy when the East European Jews began to flood into America. At this point in their economic drive, German Jews were often able to return to their countries of origin, to reestablish themselves in some cases and in other cases to show off their newly ac-quired wealth to the folks back home. It would be a long time before the poverty-stricken East European Jews would have any such opportunity, and in most cases, it was the last thing they would consider doing. They had come to America to stay, not to go back to the horrendous conditions they fled.

There are few immigrant tales so thoroughly told as that of the East European Jews in the years between 1881 and 1920. Fully two million Jews arrived in this country from Russia, Poland, and the border states during that forty-year period. But the fact remains that just as many Jews stayed in Eastern Europe. While the German Jewish settlers of the second wave were redefining themselves as Americans who held to Judaism as a religious pref-erence, the East European Jews would reflect a staunchly traditional orienta-tion toward their Judaism. They would be citizens of the United States, but they would not stop being religious Jews. In many regards, the intellectual and spiritual treasures of Ashkenazic Jewry had their home and their history in Lithuania, Poland, and parts of Russia. But in the villages and shtetls throughout the Pale of Settlement, the rabbinic authority that constituted the Jewish communal council not only educated the villagers but also dictated every aspect of their daily life. Life was harsh, poor, and strictly observant.

For huge numbers of these impoverished Jews, the trip to America was an escape not only from the dictatorial hand of the state, but from the equally dictatorial and repressive hand of rabbinic rule. An unconfirmed source has said, "The Jews of Eastern Europe not only threw their hands up in joy at the sight of the Statue of Liberty, but also to cast into New York harbor the physical accoutrements of their Judaism. For example, *kippahs*, prayer shawls [*tallits*], and tefilin [small leather boxes containing specific prayers]. Over time New York harbor acquired another layer to its bottom composed of the mounds of cast off prayer paraphernalia of the new Jewish arrivals!"

Rabbis in Eastern Europe admonished Jews not to leave, not to go to America. America was a great moral cesspool in which Judaism and common sense were quickly lost in the quest for money. But to the poverty-stricken Jews of Eastern Europe, the lure of full-time work, adequate housing, if only minimal by anyone else's standards, and finally, freedom from government oppression were too much to ignore in the face of these rabbinic pleas. Once in this country, the rabbis' pronouncements proved all too accurate. In the name of food, shelter, and employment, many a new arrival gave up eating only kosher food, observing the Sabbath, and maintaining other ancient customs. It would be a mistake, however, to conclude that they gave up these religious attachments with any joy; it was always a temporary accommodation to the immediate needs of day to day survival. A small minority of these immigrants was deeply (and often publicly) committed to socialism and Zionism, but the vast majority of East European Jews wanted only relief from generations of poverty. In time (less than a generation, in many cases) these Jews renewed their religious observances, rekoshered their homes, and strictly observed the Sabbath.

The work these newcomers took up was dramatically different from the work previous Jewish settlements had undertaken. The first wave of German Jews had started off peddling and then swiftly moved out across the country establishing their presence and making their fortunes in the wide expanse of a growing nation. Of the newcomers after 1890, few ever left the major cities they had first come to. The "Lower East Side" experience was repeated throughout the country and in every city with a Jewish enclave, for example, Philadelphia, Chicago, and Baltimore.

The demands of the industrial revolution had reached a fever pitch in America by the turn of the twentieth century. Some of these newcomers were skilled tailors, sewing machine operators, cloak makers, and cutters. But even those who had no such discernable job qualifications often said they did, and learned what they needed to do on the workbench. For tens of thousands more who had no job skills, and could learn none in the short time necessary for survival, the back pack and peddling became their path to survival. In time they were all put to work, with the exception of the old-world Talmudists for whom any kind of work beyond studying sacred text was abhorrent. But this was an economy that had no way to compensate Talmudists and they, too, soon took up a pack, or manned a homely pushcart. It was a shameful comedown, but there was no way any of them were going back!

Irving Howe admits, in the preface to the second edition of *World of Our Fathers* (1990), that the passage of time had veiled his retelling of the history of the immigrant experience with a discernible nostalgia: in some ways, a Jewish depiction of the "good old days." But they were not good, they were harsh, brutal and all together unforgiving. It was as if Hobbes's famous proclamation about life and its brutishness had in fact become reality for millions of struggling souls. These hard-working Jews expected nothing for themselves, but all of the tedious work and uncertain living conditions was for the children (*ein das kinder*). The next generation would move up and out, particularly out. The tenements, and the grinding poverty that went with them, were only a way station to a better life. That is how it unfolded for millions of East European Jews as they left the Lower East Side to make homes and livings in Harlem, the Bronx, Brooklyn, and similar Jewish enclaves in other major cities. The lives that unfolded for those successive generations of immigrants were ones of achievement and increasing dignity as Jews moved away from peddling cheap trinkets and knickknacks in the squalor of the tenements for more stable occupations in the professions and small business ownership. But for a time, and for virtually everyone who would pass through those portals, the squalor and noise were part and parcel of daily life.

Deborah Dwork (in Sarna, 1986b:102–117) captures all of this grimness and oppression in her fact-based retelling of Jews on the Lower East Side. As a medical historian she quickly demonstrates, based on her examination of early-twentieth-century public documents, not only the physical inadequacies of tenement conditions of the time for the hundreds of people jammed into them, but also the countless ways in which those tenements directly contributed to disease and death. But, as later chapters in this study will relate, the East European Jews were a hardy lot, and boisterous as well. They are the Jewish immigrants most Americans associate with "the Jews." They established the Yiddish press, the music halls of Second Avenue, the motion picture industry, and they provided the backbone (and often the voice) for the American labor movement in the first years of the 1900s.

The stories of life as an immigrant as told by Jewish writers and journalists frequently offer the insight and poignancy that stolid facts alone cannot convey. Mary Antin, in *The Promised Land* (1912), Henry Roth, in *Call It Sleep* (1934), Abraham Cahan, in *The Rise of David Levinsky* (1917), Anzia Yezierska, in *Bread Givers* (1925), and Michael Gold, in *Jews Without Money* (1930) all tell the story of life as an immigrant East European Jew. A collection of Yezierska's short stories was turned into a silent film in the early 1920s and entitled *The Hungry Heart*. It is an astonishing film not only for its portrayal of life on the Lower East Side of New York, but also because it is filmed on location, in the Lower East Side, and the appearance and conditions of the tenements are captured vividly, if unintentionally, by the film. But all of these depictions were of separate groups of Jews: Jews separated by language, class, and customs from their coreligionists.

The idea that Jews were all of one nation never really worked in reality, not in Europe, and certainly not in America. The Sephardic Jews had little, if anything, to do with the German Jews and the same proved true between German Jews and East European Jews. The caste system was virtually impenetrable. The Sephardic held themselves apart as the "Grandees," and the German Jews quickly formed themselves into "Our Crowd." Collectively, the Sephardic and German Jews became the "Uptown Jews," and the mass of East European Jews became the "Downtown Jews," each division as different from the other as Jew is from gentile. But, the fact remained that they were coreligionists, even if they could never agree on what the observance of that religion consisted of. The German Jews, like their predecessors the Sephardic, would help their Russian coreligionists in their time of need. The German Jews were liberal with their money and support when it came to their newly arrived brethren. Part of this response was rooted in a genuine observance of millennia old doctrines of Jewish social service. It also represented a more practical reality, the continuing uneasiness of the German Jews toward the East European Jews. An uneasiness that would not pass even with the eventual and obvious prosperity of the East European Jews; prosperity was not the whole answer.

The German Jews knew they had to do those things that would relieve their coreligionists of suffering, homelessness, and disease, but they also wanted these new Jews (greenhorns), these "kikes"[4] to become Americans of a Jewish persuasion as quickly as possible. They feared the reaction of the larger gentile community to these obvious outsiders, the extent to which their "otherness" would trigger animosity toward all Jews and ultimately give rise to new bouts of antisemitism. Their fears were not entirely unfounded. Antisemitism in word and deed was growing more apparent in America as the country moved toward its first quarter century.

The East European Jews were just as intent on becoming Americans as anyone before or after them, but this didn't include becoming like their coreligionists from Germany. The persistence of those countless differences becomes fully apparent when we examine the founding fathers of the Jewish defense agencies in chapters three, four, and five.

Whatever their differences, the sheer presence of 3.5 million Jews in America was increasing the specter of anti-Jewish hostility throughout the country: the various nativist and populist movements, plus the efforts of several members in the U.S. government who wanted to protect "America for Americans" by demanding stringent restrictions on all immigration. These demands were directly targeting the Jews, but it also included huge numbers of Southern Europeans, particularly Slavs and Italians, whose homelands were caught in economic and agricultural depressions. Two incidents during this time (1908–1917) were laced with overt suspicion of and antagonism toward Jews.

In the first, Theodore Bingham, police commissioner of New York City, published an article in *Harper's* in September 1908 entitled "Foreign Criminals in New York" in which he argued that Italians and Jews were at the center of most criminal activity in the city. Given the population of Jews in the city at that time (approximately one million), Bingham went on to allege, "It is not astonishing that half the criminals should be of that race." The response from the Jewish community, and particularly Jacob Schiff, by then one of the key figures in the new American Jewish Committee, was so strong and unrelenting that Bingham retracted his entire statement in a matter of a few days (Hertzberg, 1990:205). Schiff's response when combined with the residual anxiety of East European Jews about the role of the law and its connection to antisemitic attacks was a powerful ingredient in the overwhelming Jewish response to Bingham's broadside condemnation of Jews as a "criminal race."

The fact of the matter is Jews were involved in a host of criminal activities at the time of the Bingham report, and it included prostitution, bank fraud, arson, and gambling. What distinguished a small handful of professional Jewish criminals (such notorious gangsters as Arnold Rothstein, Meyer Lansky, Bugsy Siegel, Louis "Lepke" Buchalter, Dutch Schultz, and Abe Reles) from the rest of the Jews who tried their hand at crime was the fact that the nonprofessional's involvement in crime lasted less than a half generation. Short-term involvement in crime was part of an economic passage into the main stream, not a full-time occupational choice (Hertzberg, 1990:207).

The second, pivotal, antisemitic incident that had been fulminating since 1896 was the literacy requirement imposed on newly arrived immigrants. First proposed by Senator Henry Cabot Lodge (Massachusetts), it specified that entry into this country could only occur if the immigrant was "literate in English, or the language of his native country" (Hertzberg, 1990:192). East European Jews were not literate in English, and frequently did not speak or write the language of their native country, for example, Poland and Russia. What they were literate in was Yiddish.

As opposed to Yiddish as significant numbers of German Jews were (Rabbi Isaac Meyer Wise found Yiddish abominable), they immediately joined the battle against this thinly veiled attempt to categorize Jews as an inferior race based on literacy. The arguments for and against literacy testing moved through the highest levels of the U.S. government for several years without any satisfactory resolution. In 1911, Congress issued the forty-two-volume Dillingham Report on Immigration. The report's sole purpose was to preserve America for older (original) Americans over the burgeoning influx of newer less capable immigrants. America, at least the white, Anglo-Saxon portion of it, was becoming increasingly apprehensive over the unfettered appearance of millions of "less able" new citizens. White America outnumbered the new arrivals by a large majority, but one of the underlying anxieties among the restrictionist camp was that white America would soon be outnumbered by people of foreign extraction, and their prerogatives and privileges would be lost to that foreign element. The Dilllingham Report was couched in the language of racial and ethnic differentiation.

In 1914, Isaac Hourwich of the American Jewish Committee released his book, *Immigration and Labor*, that attacked the commission's reliance on "zoological species" as a mechanism for contrasting immigrants with older American stock. At the same time, Franz Boas, a Columbia University anthropologist who had been measuring cranial capacity for years, was virtually ignored when he proved that cranial capacity was the same for immigrants as it was for the rest of white America (Hertzberg, 1990:194). In 1917 the Dillingham Report was fully rejected by Congress. Hertztberg's (1990) conclusion to this struggle is worth repeating in full: "The end of the battle over literacy tests came in February 1917, when Congress overrode President Wilson's veto. The bill that was sustained had exempted from the literacy test those aliens who could prove that they were 'seeking admission to the United States to avoid religious persecution—whether such persecution be evidenced by overt acts, or by laws, or governmental regulations.' Illiterate Jews from Czarist Russia thus had precedence over illiterate Italians from Sicily" (193). While the literacy battle was over, the attempts to enact restrictive immigration legislation, as a way to reduce the number of Jews coming into America, went on unabated.

It must be noted that two other phenomena were going on at the same time as the struggle over literacy was taking place during the late teens and early twenties, and they underscore the efforts by nativists to restrict immigration. The first was the pseudoscience of eugenics. It had found a receptive audience, first in England and then America. In a series of genetically based arguments, eugenicists argued that the native stock of a country (like its apples and potatoes) could be improved and enhanced through an intentional tinkering with human genetics. In other words, the favorable, desirable stock of a country (in America's case, white, Anglo-Saxon Protestants) could be preserved and enlarged at the expense of less attractive foreign stock.

The second ingredient influencing the discourse on immigration restriction that was directed at Jews was the "Red Scare." The aftermath of the Russian revolution in 1917 brought a great deal of attention to the small number of extreme socialists and, now, a smattering of communists, who were Jewish and living in the United States. The newly emerging government in Communist Russia was populated with a number of Jews, and to the many admirers in the United States of Marx's and Engels's theories, it appeared that their "struggle" had finally achieved resolution. They may have been small in number in this country, but they were loud and strident in their demands and in their use of other forms of agitation. Women like Emma Goldman and men like Alexander Bergman teamed up as unabashed radicals and terrorists. Their plans included bombing the Carnegie Steel Company in Pittsburgh, Pennsylvania (Sacher, 1992:296–298). The connection between Bolshevism and Jews was quickly made, and the term became Jewish Bolshevism. Over one thousand communists and radicals were arrested, tried, and in the main, deported back to Russia and Europe before the Red Scare died out. But the fuel it lent to the efforts of the nativists and the restrictionists was of immeasurable value in pushing the loyalist necessity for restricting the entry of unsavory aliens to this country.

Immigration restriction legislation was approved by Congress in 1921, and again in 1924. The legislation used a complicated quota system based on the number of persons from each European country living in America at the time of the 1910 census to decide how many immigrants would be allowed into America each year; the original quota was 3 percent from each country. But it soon became apparent by the number of exceptions that were being granted, not only to Jews, but to Italians and Slavs as well, that these percentages had to be refigured. It was, in 1924, downward to 2 percent, and the base year was shifted back to 1890, a year in which a small number of Jews came to this country as contrasted with the next twenty-year increase to 1910. In 1890 approximately 40,000 Jews came to this country as contrasted with approximately 93,000 Jews in 1910 (Sarna, 1986b:296). Under this new quota system virtually everyone from Asian countries was kept out. The Immigration Restriction Act was ratified in 1929 and signed by the president into law with the largest quota allocations favoring immigrants from Great Britain, Ireland, and Germany (Dinnerstein, 1994:98).

With the enactment of the immigration restriction law, the open door to America and its promise of freedom from political tyranny and the promise of economic opportunity had been slammed shut. The flow of Jews and Southern European natives virtually stopped. For example, between 1920 and 1924, 10.3 percent of all immigrants into this country were Jewish. From 1925 to 1929 that dropped to 3.7 percent! The antisemitic forces in the U.S. government had finally found a way to legally shut off the influx of East European Jews into the United States. Nobody inside or outside of the government could have predicted the devastating consequences these quotas would have on Europe's Jews a little more than a decade later.

The 1920s was a period of unparalleled opportunity for millions of people in this country, including Jews. Fortunes were made virtually overnight, but under this euphoria rustled the seeds of civil discontent. The Ku Klux Klan saw its membership and popularity reach its peak during the early years of the 1920s. This increase in membership when combined with other populist/rural sympathies fueled increasing demonstrations of anti-Jewish animus; an animus that would only deepen and worsen during the depression years and the years of World War II. One of the first and most dramatic examples of this unthinking hatred of Jews erupted in Atlanta, Georgia, in 1915 with the lynching of Leo Frank. Frank, a young, Jewish plant manager, had been accused of the rape and murder of a young factory employee by the name of Mary Phagen. The charges were upheld, Frank was found guilty, but his sentence was commuted to life in prison. This commutation so outraged the ordinary citizens of Georgia that they pulled Frank from a jail cell in neighboring Marietta, Georgia, and murdered him in August 1915. Frank's death would be the only lynching of a Jew in all of U.S. history.

The Frank murder was highly significant for another reason. Because of the increasing levels of antisemitism in Europe and at home, three of the four Jewish advocacy organizations discussed in this study came into existence. In fact the Leo Frank case was the galvanizing issue that brought the ADL into the public eye. The other two organizations had, like the ADL, been organized to directly combat antisemitism. Antisemitism was nothing short of a growth industry in the early years of this century. But on another level, each of these organizations saw themselves, and presented themselves, as the "voice" of the Jewish community. The dissension and lack of accommodation that took place among these three defense organizations was legendary and would reappear at key points in their mutual histories over the next several decades.

Nativist sentiments ran high during the 1920s, and none other than Henry Ford involved himself in an antisemitic representation that spanned almost the entire decade. Ford had enthusiastically embraced the *Protocols of the Elders of Zion* and went on to finance their publication in this country. Ford had acquired his own newspaper, the *Dearborn Independent*, as a vehicle for expressing his business and personal philosophy. It became the instrument through which he published the *Protocols* under the title of "The International Jew." Ford's editors would make detailed and extensive comparisons and extensions of each of the Protocols in serial form. Ford was totally indifferent to the fact that the *Protocols* had long ago been proven a forgery. He defended his publication on the basis of his belief, "That's what is happening." The *Dearborn Independent* became much more than the mouthpiece for the republication of the *Protocols*. They became Ford's personal venue for spewing his anti-Jewish sentiments on a number of issues.

The popularity of the series was as impressive as it was disturbing, and the articles were gathered together as a book entitled *The International Jew*. But the outcry against the *Dearborn Independent* and Henry Ford built quickly in both the Jewish and Christian community. Louis Marshall of the AJC demanded a cessation of the publication. But the attacks on Jews that appeared in the *Dearborn Independent* continued. It was not only reprinting the *Protocols*, but it frequently printed specific attacks on "the Jews" for a long list of wrongs allegedly perpetrated against gentiles of humble origin as well as the highly placed and influential (Leo P. Ribuffo in Sarna, 1986b:175–190).

The *Dearborn Independent* was condemned by the Federal Council of Churches, and in January 1921, 119 prominent Christians, including William

Howard Taft, Woodrow Wilson, and Cardinal William O'Connell, signed "The Perils of Racial Prejudice," a statement asking gentiles to stop their propaganda against Jews (Sarna, 1986b:183). The hue and cry did not end with this demand, nor did it end publication of Ford's newspaper. Demands continued to be lodged to stop the publication of the *Dearborn Independent* by both Jewish and non-Jewish groups, but with Henry Ford fronting all of the money for the paper, it was doubtful that it stopped publishing because Jews and some Christians didn't like what it was saying. The pressure on Ford, however, continued with a boycott organized and supported by a variety of Jewish and Christian groups. Both Ford and the paper were sued for millions of dollars claiming defamation and slander by a variety of persons. Finally, in 1927 under enormous pressure from the White House and the American Jewish Committee, Ford signed a formal retraction of his charges of all wrongdoing by Jews.

Louis Marshall of the AJC may have been satisfied with Ford's lame excuse that he did not know what his editors were writing in his name, but very few others believed Ford. Some people raised the possibility that Ford's signature on the retraction had been a forgery. This proved to be true. Ford admitted to a confederate of Huey Long, Gerald L. K. Smith (a conservative Christian evangelist), that he had allowed an employee by the name of Bennett to sign Ford's name to the retraction letter. Ford further encouraged Smith to reissue *The International Jew*, which he did. In 1940 Ford told the *Manchester Guardian* that the Jews had started World War II. Not surprisingly, Ford like Charles Lindbergh was an instant success with Adolf Hitler. Both of these "staunch" Americans received medals from Hitler personally, and that was covered extensively by the international press.

As the depression deepened during the 1930s, the antisemitic rhetoric of politicians and agitators grew louder and more insistent. Jews were not only "international bankers," they were "blood suckers," and Bolsheviks as well. They were taking jobs away from deserving gentiles in areas such as teaching and social work. Increasingly, Jews were excluded from attending the country's top universities and colleges on the pretext that they were over represented in the student body. This policy was public knowledge at Harvard, Columbia, and Princeton Universities. Jewish faculty, in all disciplines, found it nearly impossible to secure tenured positions in prestigious colleges such as Dartmouth and Wellesley. Where Henry Ford's specious mutterings about "the Jews" had reached perhaps a million people all told through the written word, the avid audience of another antisemite during the depression, Father Charles Coughlin, the radio priest, reached several million every week.

Antisemitic rhetoric increased exponentially after the 1933 election of President Franklin Delano Roosevelt in this country, and the appointment of Adolf Hitler as chancellor of Germany in the same year. The antisemites inside and outside of government were quick to seize on Roosevelt's comfortable relationship with prominent Jews. He had appointed Jews to his cabinet, as well as several lower level executive positions. With Hitler's assumption to power in Germany, several German *Bunds* began appearing in American cities across the country, particularly in those cities with substantial German populations. Coughlin's following attracted millions of ordinary citizens, Catholic and non-Catholic alike, but he also attracted a mixed bag of bigots and Nazi sympathizers. Even though several leading Catholic prelates opposed Coughlin, the Vatican would not condemn his teachings (Dinnerstein, 1994:113). It finally took World War II to silence Coughlin and others like him under the Enemy Sedition Act of 1917. For the first time in their memory, ordinary Jews were frightened about their personal safety, and thousands of them stopped any form of religious observance; others simply converted out of Judaism.

In 1935 *Fortune* magazine reported the results of a survey it had conducted on American antisemitism. The survey asked a revealing question: "Do you think Germany is being helped or hurt by the Nazi exclusion of Jews?" Throughout the country, half of all respondents felt that Germany had been harmed by Nazi policies toward Jews. But in the Midwest and far West, when those who were indifferent to the plight of the Jews were combined with those who actually thought the persecution of the Jews was helping Germany, the total opposed to Jews was more than 50 percent of all responses. *Fortune* magazine was not impressed (and said so) about these less than encouraging results from a significant percentage of America's population (Hertzberg, 1990:251).

Newspaper advertisements now began appearing that sought "Christian applicants," or "receptionist wanted for Christian office," and "Christian men to sell our products." Ads with this sort of wording were showing up in every paper in the country, including the prestigious *New York Times*. Housing developments, resorts, and innumerable clubs were closed to "those of the Hebrew faith." In the textile industry in New York, Chicago, and Philadelphia, sewing machine operators, who were largely Jewish, lost virtually all of the wage gains they had achieved during the 1920s. Pay was cut (more than once), and working hours were extended to fifty-five and sixty hours per week. *Fortune* magazine found itself explaining to its readership that there were more poor Jews in America than there were rich, and that Jews did not control the major financial institutions. But for millions of Jews who were subjected to the indignities of antisemitic canards, publications, and demagogues, a genuine sense of foreboding had overtaken them. Things were not as good for the Jews as they had been even ten years before.

The late 1930s ushered in the era of public opinion polling, and for the first time politicians, businessmen, and academics could probe the great American psyche on all manner of things. Opinions about Jews were very much a part of that enterprise. In chapter two I summarize the significant opinion polls on beliefs about Jews from the depression years through World

War II, when antisemitic attitudes were at their highest in this country, and up to the present time. I will defer any further discussion about antisemitic attitudes during the war years to that more in-depth presentation. But suffice it to say antisemitism had never been worse in the United States, nor would it be again. Suspicion, hatred, and animosity toward Jews was evident in a 1938 poll that found 77 percent of respondents said "no" to the question, "Should we allow a larger number of Jewish exiles to come to the United States to live?" (Dinnerstein, 1994:127). This country's unwillingness to admit war refugees, particularly Jews, into the United States during the war years is still a hotly debated subject.

The war years brought a different problem to the major Jewish organizations in the United States, and to Jews in general in America: What to do about the mass slaughter of Jews in Europe being carried out by the Nazi regime? In recent years there has been a number of excellent studies about this failure to do enough to help the Jews of Europe escape certain annihilation in the death camps of Poland. The debate is not yet finished, nor is there a completely satisfactory understanding as to whether the allied powers and the Jewish organizations did enough to effect rescue of the doomed Jews of Europe.

During the unfolding of the events that eventually enveloped Richard Nixon and finally led to his resignation in 1974, observers asked, "What did he know and when did he know it?" That same question has been asked repeatedly of the allied governments and the Jewish organizations about their knowledge of the events surrounding the attempted destruction of the Jews by the Nazi regime. Arthur D. Morse, in *While Six Million Died* (1967), and David Wyman, in *The Abandonment of the Jews* (1984), argue convincingly and poignantly that the Jewish organizations and the allied governments knew all the facts of the slaughter from the very beginning, but did nothing (until near the war's end) to rescue Jews. By contrast, William Rubinstein, in *The Myth of Rescue* (1997), portrays the same events in a much more controversial treatment, arguing that the Jewish organizations were not equipped to take any direct action to get Jews out of Europe once the mass-slaughter began. The allied governments could not do anything more than win the war to insure the protection of all war-torn refugees, including the Jews.

Rubenstein raises two points that will forever haunt the actions of both good men and venial about those years. The first is that we too frequently observe history from the safe remove of time, and ask, "Why didn't they do more?" The reality is that we are all bound up in our histories as they are occurring, and few of us are prescient enough to predict an accurate future under the pressure of horrendous events. The second point is the far deeper complexities that would have accompanied any effort to get Jews out of the extermination camps and into safe refuge. Given that Hitler had agreed to such a proposal, what would the allies have done with millions of starving, diseased, and, frequently, dying men, women, and children if they were turned over to the allied powers? How would they have been moved from the death camps and ghettos, housed, fed, and protected? How would they have been transported during a time of war, and where would they have taken up life in safe territory, in the United States, Britain, Canada, the African countries, where? The infrastructure such a massive relocation would have required is staggering to contemplate.

This is not to dismiss the bureaucratic fumbling and ineptness of America's State Department; it was simply appalling. The U.S. State Department had its antisemites, but worse, it had otherwise good men who were simply indifferent to the plight of the Jews. The Jewish organizations were, true to form, busier arguing with one another, over who represented the Jews, than coming together over the common cause of rescuing Jews to do much more than lodge continuous complaints with the U.S. government. Hertzberg (1990: 298–300) argues, pragmatically, that the Jewish organizations could not take any direct hand in rescuing the Jews of Europe. This was a time of global war, and the likelihood of interfering with the prosecution of such a momentous event in any substantial way was incomprehensible. We must also recall Rubenstein's enjoinder about history (1997), and not overlay the reality of Jewish organizations of today on the reality of those same organizations during the war years. These were not powerful organizations, either financially or politically. While their voices were acknowledged in Washington, they did not have the history of advocacy success that they do today. These were essentially very small organizations, with often painfully small budgets. What they were able to do, in spite of their internecine conflicts, is still remarkable. A reading of the correspondence exchanged between these organizations with State Department officials and other Jewish organizations is some of the saddest reading extant. As the reader pursues page after page of letters, memoranda, and interoffice correspondence, it becomes painfully clear how deep the frustration and near-despair ran among the authors of those letters (see Friedlander and Milton, Archives of the Holocaust [1993]).

The years immediately following World War II did not see an instantaneous drop in America's antipathy toward Jews, but as the revelations about the Holocaust, the war-crime trials, and subsequently, the establishment of the State of Israel became widely known, those negative opinions did begin to drop significantly. They dropped to such an extent that the ADL even considered, briefly, changing its name in the belief that its major work had been completed. It had not, but the public admission of antisemitic beliefs was becoming more and more unacceptable in the face of economic success in post–World War II America; and Jews were participating in that success as well.

Just as other Americans were relocating to the suburbs, so too were the Jews, in huge numbers. They were building new synagogues and temples by the hundreds in those suburbs, and their design mimicked the churches and cathedrals of their Christian neighbors. It was the era of the "Gentlemen's Agreement," and while Jews were increasingly welcome in business, the professions, and the upper levels of the academic world, any gentile friendships often ended at 5:00 P.M.; Jews went to their homes, and gentiles to theirs.

The end of the war brought enormous advances in technology (particularly the technology of death), politics, and the economy. New social support programs were launched that facilitated a quiet revolution, that is, "How and when American Jews became white folks." How and when Jews moved from the status of being a distinct group of "others" to membership and acceptance in America's dominant white society: understanding how this shift in perception took place is important to this study.

In 1995 Noel Ignatiev published *How the Irish Became White*. The thesis of his study was the ways in which outsiders are classified, and held down, when they are labeled as something other than white. The story of the Irish in America, and specifically the famine Irish after 1847, is a classic study of moving from a denigrated class of "others" to membership in white, mainstream America. Over a much longer time frame (3.5 centuries), and no less impressive, is the important transition that America's Jews made from the status of "near white" to mainstream white society. Now comes Karen Brodkin with an equally provocative title *How Jews Became White Folks and What That Says About Race in America* (1998), in which she points to several changing properties in the American socioeconomic complex that moved Jews from being a racially fixed status of "other" to that of white— like other folks! Three of the most pivotal ingredients affecting this change were education, occupations, and housing, all of which occurred in the immediate aftermath of World War II.

The G.I. Bill and federally funded home-loan programs favored Jews just as it did vast numbers of other white males. In fact, Brodkin refers to these programs as "affirmative action programs for white males" (42). They were government-sponsored and -supported programs that pointedly ignored all females and black males. The opening of these educational opportunities through government subsidy made it possible for tens of thousands of Jews to move up and away from the trade occupations of their fathers' generation. With this move came better paying and more prestigious jobs in all sectors of the economy. By the mid-1960s, and into the 1970s, Jews shattered virtually all of the restrictive glass ceilings of earlier generations. Occupational mobility went beyond representation in the professions; it cleared the way for Jews to move into the upper echelons of major corporations and top institutions of financial management.

If education underwritten by the G.I. Bill triggered one of the biggest college-building booms in U.S. history, then government-subsidized home-loan programs fueled a mammoth home-building boom that transformed housing starts into a primary economic indicator. Jews by the thousands from all across the country left the inner cities to move into cramped, small, quickly built houses on minimal footage, and away from the noise and danger of the city. The country was moving to the suburbs and the U.S. government was making it all possible, at least for white citizens. Where Jews had lived in distinctly Jewish enclaves for three generations, they now shared space with Catholic, Protestant, and nonreligious whites. Now the Petersons, Smiths, and Washingtons were the Jews' neighbors; they were no longer the "gentiles" or the "goy." These three sociocultural benchmarks, that is, education, employment, and suburbanization, were at the very heart of transforming Jews from "not quite white" to white like other folks.

As important as *how* Jews became white folks, is *when* it all happened. By and large, it all happened in the ten years following the end of World War II. At the war's end, a great many people in the United States still harbored ill will toward Jews, but with the rapid changes mentioned above, and the horrendous revelations emerging about the Holocaust, average citizens in America were increasingly keeping their anti-Jewish beliefs to themselves; they had to. Jews were in the same classrooms as their children, Jews were sitting next to them at work, and living next door to them in the recently developed suburbs.

But as auspicious as this "whitening of American Jewry" was, it also carried the seeds of a problem more serious than antisemitism, that is, intermarriage between Jews and non-Jews. Assimilation theorists (Gordon, 1964; Alba, 1985, 1995) have proposed that the last fateful step in an ethnic group's absorption into the dominant society is marriage across ethnic and, particularly, religious lines. This has happened to America's Jewish community, and in a relatively short time frame. In 1965 the intermarriage rate between Jews and non-Jews was on the order of 9 percent. Of those Jews who married between 1965 and 1974, 25 percent married non-Jews. In the next ten years the intermarriage rate rose to 44 percent, and in the years between 1985 and 1990 marriages between Jews and non-Jews rose to 52 percent (Linzer, Schnall, and Chanes, 1998:30). In some areas of the country, San Francisco most notably, the intermarriage rate is thought to be on the magnitude of 70 percent. Philosemitism (i.e., a distinct liking of Jews, and finding Jews interesting and attractive) may prove to be more injurious to the future continuity and vitality of American Jewry than antisemitism ever was.

CONCLUSION

In this first chapter I have attempted to briefly recount the historical experience of Jews in America from their arrival in 1654 to the present time. I have not attempted in this brief sketch to present all of the significant events or, for that matter, even most of the events, that Jews participated in during this three-hundred-fifty-year odyssey. Rather, I have attempted to portray the relationship of Jews in America in tandem with the animosity, discrimination, and antisemitism they encountered during three consecutive time periods: 1654 to 1800, 1801 to 1900, and 1901 to the present. As horrendous as this passage has sometimes been, the native animosity toward Jews has been dropping sharply and steadily, particularly over the past fifty years. Both negative attitudes toward Jews and intentional incidents of provocation have nearly vanished—not disappeared, not by any means, but dropped to a point that makes their significance questionable.

In chapter two, an in-depth portrait is drawn to acquaint the reader with precisely how antisemitism has been measured since the introduction of opinion polls in the 1930s. It discusses the serious problems that undergird the integrity of these polls, and the questionable usefulness of these surveys in understanding the extent of anti-Jewish sentiments within the larger American social structure.

NOTES

1. My interest in antisemitism predated my becoming a Jew by two full decades. In fact, my interest in things Jewish could be traced back even further to my youth and to several confusing and distorted messages I had heard about "the Jews" from people I loved and respected. Years later, and considering myself reasonably well educated, I was still at a loss to understand why antisemitism has enjoyed the history it has. Now, even still better educated, and securely Jewish in my private life, I can say (with modest confidence) that as unacceptable as antisemitism is to me, I think I am beginning to understand its history and the terrible impact it has had on the Jewish people.

2. In an unpublished paper entitled "Unicorns and Zebras: Postmodernism and the Embedded Problematics in Black Antisemitism" (1993), I consumed six pages refuting three of the NOI's allegations that had appeared in one paragraph of the *SR*!

3. I have used Sarna's statistics (1986b) to support my comments on population changes in the American Jewish community. I have done so because those statistics are quite likely the most accurate. Sarna constructed his population statistics from collective retrospectives on population changes during the nineteenth century. For the twentieth century, Sarna drew upon Jack J. Diamond, "A Reader in Demography," *American Jewish Yearbook*, 77 (1977), pp. 251–319; and Abraham J. Karp, *Haven and Home* (New York, 1985), p. 374. An exhaustive source for Jewish demographic data can be found in Jacob Rader Marcus's, *To Count a People: American Jewish Population Data 1585–1990* (1990). The problem with Marcus's data is that it includes virtually every citation concerning Jewish population, and those citations frequently disagree with one another.

4. "Kike" is a term of uncertain origin but attributed to the German Jews and their observation that many of the newcomers' last names ended in "kie" (e.g., Warshowskie, Bronowskie, Ciminski), a combination that quickly fused into kike.

Chapter 2

Measuring Antisemitism: Fifty Years of Decline

When studying antisemitism in America it must be understood from two perspectives, its prejudicial form and its discriminatory form. Gordon Allport ([1954] 1979:6) offers a definition for a prejudicial attitude. It is a feeling that is "favorable or unfavorable, toward a person . . . [but is] not based on actual experience." This is considerably different from action fueled by those beliefs, discrimination, and, in some violent or socially unacceptable way, depriving those persons of their civil liberties or jeopardizing their physical safety. Accounts of antisemitism in America from 1653 to the early 1930s focused on incidents rather than attitudes (Sarna, 1986a; Dinnerstein, 1994; Jaher, 1994). In the mid-1930s, when public opinion polls began growing in popularity, we saw for the first time the results of nationwide surveys that included negative beliefs about Jews. This concentrated focus on negative beliefs about Jews overshadowed accounting for antisemitic incidents (including exclusionary measures in multiple contexts), which at this point assumed a secondary place in the minds of most Americans. Antisemitic incidents and attitudes began to run together for most people.

The JAOs, however, continued to investigate the incidents, while the large polling firms like Gallup, Roper, and National Opinion Research Center (NORC) told America what their attitudes were about Jews. It was not until the 1960s that Jewish organizations began funding formal research on the extent of antisemitic beliefs, and in the process, created a substantial body of social-science research on antisemitic attitudes. The results of this research, however, were problematic. One problem was the lack of any clear definition of antisemitism. References to antisemitism were couched in a way that led the reader to believe that everyone simply understood what the expression meant. That assumption is still true today, even though a number of scholars continue to struggle with accurately defining antisemitism. Another problem with the data is that there were few attempts to understand the inter-item dynamics of the questions asked. In other words, some respondents would respond to a question in a negative way because of their answers to other similar questions or their beliefs about Jews and business.

A major criticism of this data is that it failed to acknowledge that the significance of one item would outweigh the combined significance of several other items. What makes this body of research useful to us today is that it was the first serious, scientific attempt to examine a long-standing issue in intergroup relations. It produced several useful insights as well as complications for later investigators. Perhaps the most significant contradiction is that these negative beliefs, which supposedly measure American antisemitism, are still assumed to be accurate indicators of antisemitism today.

This is not to suggest that the Jewish organizations were doing no research on antisemitism and its allied manifestations of group prejudice and discrimination; they were. Prominent among these early researchers was the AJC and its groundbreaking study by Adorno et al. (1950) on the nature of the authoritarian personality. These are people who prefer or believe in a system in which some persons control while others are controlled (dominance and submission). It was not until the early 1980s that separate statistics began appearing once again on the occurrence and location of antisemitic incidents (e.g., swastika daubing, desecration of buildings, hate speech, and physical violence against Jews). The ADL was the principal reporter of these incidents, but in later years, their reports were enhanced by statistics provided by federal and state law enforcement agencies. Two key studies during the 1960s provided the basic data on which future studies of American antisemitism were based, and they need to be clearly understood because of the impact they have had on how Jews and their organizations continue to understand American antisemitism today.

The first study was carried out by Charles Stember (1966), and the second was a collection of research studies funded by the ADL beginning in the mid-1960s and ending in the early 1980s. They were collectively grouped under the title, "Patterns of American Prejudice Series."

STEMBER'S ORIGINAL FINDINGS

Stember's primary goal was to trace the path of antisemitism in America as seen through the results of dozens of public opinion polls conducted from 1938 to 1962. He did not set out to create a "single number" index of antisemitism, or to ascertain who was more or less antisemitic in some hierarchical way. That task, and the indices it would produce, would flow from the research of other social scientists. Stember wanted to determine first and foremost the content of antisemitic attitudes and the way those attitudes had changed over a two-decade period. On the other hand, as a social scientist, he did want to know if there actually was an attitude called antisemitism, or if the negative beliefs Americans held toward Jews (at any given time) were simply transient, situationally fixed, and possessed no structural framework. Stember posited the legitimacy of an antisemitic attitude by applying John Harding, Bernard Kutner, Harold Proshanky, and Isidore Cohen's three components of attitudes (1954) toward ethnic groups: (1) The cognitive, consisting of perceptions, beliefs and expectations regarding a group; (2) The affective, comprising friendliness, hostility, and other feelings which the group inspires; (3) The conative, which contains prevailing opinions on how members of the group should be treated in specific social contexts (Stember, 1966:40). For example, the cognitive component addressed such issues as the perception of Jews as a race and questions about qualities the respondent found objectionable in Jews (e.g., unscrupulous, selfish, clannish). The affective component (the most difficult to isolate and measure since it deals with feelings) addressed such issues as beliefs about the size of the Jewish population in the United States and how much or how little antisemitism there was at a particular time. The conative component addressed issues of associating with Jews, such as working next to a Jew, or having Jews as neighbors, or the extent to which Jews should be admitted to colleges. These components proved to be valuable in codifying the data that the dozens of opinion polls provided. Harding's components will be revisited in the last chapter, in conjunction with the discussion about the necessity for new definitions of antisemitism and its continuing reality in the minds of the American public.

Over 250 questions were represented in the collection of data that Stember examined, and many of them were repeated dozens of times. Given Harding's components and Stember's massive collection of data, Stember concluded that he had tapped a genuine set of antisemitic attitudes about Jews in America.

The polls Stember examined included 40 Gallup polls from 1937 to 1961; 37 NORC polls from 1942 to 1957; 3 polls from the Psychological Corporation (1944, 1948, and 1953); 17 polls from Opinion Research Corporation from 1938 to 1946; 4 polls from the Office of Opinion Research (long defunct) from 1941 to 1945; and 19 polls from Elmo Roper from 1935–1952 (231–234). The total came to 83 opinion polls and thousands of questions. From this collection of polls, and the questions asked about Jews in America, Stember compiled 131 tables of differentiated data about how Americans felt about their Jewish fellow citizens (209). He grouped his concluding analysis about antisemitic beliefs into five broad categories: (1) changes in imagery, (2) association with Jews, (3) attitude components and their interrelations, (4) active hostility toward Jews, and (5) the effects of the war (including the Holocaust), and included also a separate analysis of distinctive trends in population subgroups. (This clustering of data in broad categories became particularly important in the ADL studies that followed in later years.) From this mass of data, Stember isolated twelve negative beliefs about Jews that had shown the greatest long-term decrease from 1938 to 1962 (table 1). Next to each item in the table I have indicated the original Stember table in which they were first reported.

Stember posited that, by 1962, four of the twelve items listed in table 1 had ceased to significantly function as manifestations of American antisemitism: Number 4—Jews are too clannish; Number 7—Jewish neighbors are objectionable; Number 8—Colleges should limit numbers of Jews; and Number 12—Jews have too much power in finance.[1] The decline in virtually all items prompted Stember to remark, "One fact consistently emerges from

Table 1
Stember's 12 Characteristics of Antisemitism

		1938* (%)	1962 (%)
1.	Jews are a race (table 2)	(1946) 42	23
2.	Jews have objectionable traits (table 12)	(1940) 63	22
3.	Jews are unscrupulous (table 12)	(1940) 51	27
4.	Jews are too clannish (table 12)	(1940) 17	18
5.	Jewish businessmen are less honest (table 16)	47	18
6.	It would make a difference (to employer) if person were Jewish (tables 28, 30)	(1940) 43	6
7.	Jewish neighbors are objectionable (table 32)	25**	3
8.	Colleges should limit the number of Jews (table 38)	26	4
9.	Would not marry a Jew (table 40)	57	37
10.	Jews have too much power (table 50)	41***	17
11.	Jews have too much power in business (table 53)	47	47
12.	Jews have too much power in finance (table 53)	42	18

* Tracking these twelve characteristics did not start uniformly in 1938. Where there is difference in the date the question was first asked, it is noted.
** This index rose to 42 percent by 1942.
*** This index rose to 55 percent by 1946.

our analysis: *Antisemitism in all its forms massively declined in the United States between prewar or war years and the early 1960s*" (209, italics added). Stember (217) expressed optimism that the downward trend in American antisemitism would continue in the future.

Stember analyzed trends among different population subgroups as well (e.g., age, sex, income, religion, urban/rural, region, and voter/nonvoter). Stember retained six of the original twelve items: (1) Jews are a race; (2) Jews generally have objectionable qualities; (3) Jewish businessmen are less honest than others; (4) would object to having a Jewish employee; (5) would object to having a Jewish neighbor; (6) think Jews have too much power in the United States. To these he added three additional items: (7) Jews tend to be more radical than others; (8) would vote for an antisemitic Congressional candidate; (9) think Jews are a threat to the United States. From his results it can be concluded that men who are low wage earners, have less than a high school education, and do not live in the city are more likely than other Americans to be more antisemitic.

In spite of Stember's excessive optimism, his analysis of dozens of polls, and hundreds of questions about Jews, provided future researchers with a quantitative baseline from which to launch further research on American antisemitism. He identified scores of negative beliefs about Jews that had enjoyed public favor at one time or another, and over a substantial period of time. His study encouraged future researchers to adopt more robust research on the inherent strength of the principal areas of negative beliefs about Jews. Did he produce an "overall measure" of antisemitic belief? Yes and no, depending on how you understand the word overall; yes, insofar as the attitudes reported represent the collective (or overall) opinions of the general population about a discrete attitude called antisemitism; no, insofar as his research provided the reader with a "single number" indicator of the strength of an antisemitic belief.

The single number referent would emerge from the work of the second set of studies, which were conducted by a group of social scientists under the umbrella title, "Patterns of American Prejudice Series."[2] Two studies from that collection directly relate to the present study: Selznick and Steinberg (1969) and Marx (1967), the first because it became the basis for all future reports of the level of American antisemitism using the same collection of beliefs about Jews, and the second because one chapter in it discussed antisemitism among blacks.

SELZNICK AND STEINBERG

At about the same time as Stember's work was going to press the ADL commissioned the "Patterns of Prejudice in America Series." Five of the seven volumes in the series addressed antisemitism and based their results on an analysis of a national opinion survey conducted in 1964 by NORC, three weeks before the presidential election. The 105 questions included 27 about Jews. They asked about everything from electing a Jew as president to the frequency of contact with Jews under various circumstances (e.g., work and neighborhood). One question listed eighteen negative beliefs about Jews.[3] Based on the level of "yes, no, don't know" responses to the list of eighteen beliefs about Jews, they concluded that "a good guess would put American antisemitism between 26 and 42 percent, or at about a third of the population" (Selznick and Steinberg, 1969:19).

From these eighteen items, the authors selected eleven antisemitic beliefs (table 2). Next to their eleven items, I have shown an item from Stember's earlier study that matches it, or is the same in intent.

Gertrude Selznick and Stephen Steinberg (1969, hereafter S&S) then separated their eleven items into six categories of beliefs about Jews. The following descriptions are paraphrased from S&S:

1. Jews as monied (6). A long-standing ingredient in negative characterizations of Jews has been their relationship to money. While Jews (as a group) have high incomes (they are parallel to income levels among Episcopalians), the amount is usually exaggerated in some people's minds. This belief grows out of the long history of ideological beliefs about Jews; it tends to surface more quickly during times of economic crisis. But it also marks the fact that the American cultural scene saw Jews as a salient social category. (Note: This recognition was abetted by studies that focused on the melting pot theory, such as Will Herberg's *Protestant, Catholic, Jew: An Essay in American Religious Sociology* [1955].) Committed antisemites link the amount of money Jews have with their high, even exaggerated, levels of ambition, and from this, embrace a negative conclusion, when, in fact, it is an intentional distortion of otherwise acceptable accomplishments.

2. The Jew as clannish (9). For centuries, in Europe, Jews were segregated by civil law, but Jews also isolated themselves from their gentile neighbors because of their desire to observe their religious practices in private. The ghetto served both purposes, but more often than not under crowded and unsanitary conditions. When the emancipation of the Jews began, in the mid-eighteenth century, they continued to isolate themselves in observance of Mosaic law. But, it gave the appearance of clannishness in a time that called out for greater openness. In later day America, clannishness was found in response to statements about Jews sticking together too much and going out of their way to hire other Jews. After 1948, this clannish criticism included a perception of Jews being more loyal to Israel than to America.

3. The Jew as prideful and conceited (10). This is the concept of the Jews as God's Chosen people. Neither a majority of Jews nor the unprejudiced hold to this idea, but those who are highly antisemitic include it in their litany of complaints about Jews, whether or not it is true.

4. The Jew as dishonest and unethical (10). The ideological hatred of Jews by Europeans owes much to the image of the Jew as money lender and international trader. As a cultural preconception, it came to America along with the waves of

Table 2
Selznick and Steinberg's (1969) "Index of Antisemitic Beliefs"

Item Description	Percent Agree
1. Jews have too much power in the United States (Stember number 10—same)	11
2. Jews care only about their own kind (Stember number 4—Jews are too clannish)	26
3. Jews are not as honest as other businessmen (Stember number 5—same)	28
4. Jews have too much power in the business world (Stember number 11—same)	29
5. Jews are more loyal to Israel than to America*	30
6. Jews control international business (Stember number 12—Jews have too much power in finance)	30
7. Jews are tricky and shrewd in business (Stember number 3—Jews are unscrupulous)	35
8. Jews have a lot of irritating faults (Stember number 2—same)	40
9. Jews use shady practices to get ahead (Stember number 3—Jews are unscrupulous)	42
10. Jews stick together too much*	52
11. Jews always like to head things*	54
Mean percentage of agreement	34.3

* Stember included these items in a cluster he called "distinctive qualities of Jews." See his table 10 (1966:63).

Source: Gertrude J. Selznick and Stephen Steinberg, *The Tenacity of Prejudice: Anti-Semitism in Contemporary America* (New York: Harper & Row, 1969), 6.

immigrants from virtually every country in Europe. In America it manifested itself in agreement to comments such as, "Jewish businessmen are so shrewd and tricky that other people don't have a competitive chance," "Jews are more willing to use shady practices," and "Jews are [not] as honest as other businessmen."

5. The Jew as power hungry (12). Three widely accepted beliefs shaped this category: Jews always like to head things (54 percent); movie and television is controlled by Jews (47 percent); and Jews control international finance (30 percent). This in spite of the fact that a 1936 *Fortune* magazine article convincingly dismissed all three of these allegations as baseless. Jews were dominant in

two areas: (1) textiles, clothing, retailing and scrap metals; and (2) the professions and literary field (13).

6. The Jew as pushy and intrusive (15). This is one of the contradictions of antisemitism, that some people can see Jews as secretive (clannish) and intrusive (domineering) at the same time. This dual characterization has been a central ingredient of antisemitism in different places and at different times. *The Protocols of the Elders of Zion* posited a contrived fantasy that Jews had formed a secret conspiracy to rule the world, and at the same time saw Jews as pariahs and as a people who could only function on the margins of society. Adolf Hitler and his henchmen were very adept at doing the same thing during his reign of terror and destruction. The population of Jews in every community and at every time in history has been small, and yet this idea of the Jew as all-powerful, while remaining insignificant, has always been a central ingredient in the diatribes of dedicated antisemites.

Following this step, S&S cross-validated the eleven items against six other negative beliefs about Jews taken from the original list of eighteen: (1) Jews are always stirring up trouble with their ideas; (2) Jews have stirred up a lot of trouble between Jews and Negroes; (3) Jews today are trying to push in where they are not wanted; (4) you can usually tell whether or not a person is Jewish just by the way he looks; (5) the movie and TV industries are pretty much run by the Jews; and (6) Jewish employers go out of their way to hire other Jews. The authors concluded from their cross-validation that if a person scored high on this collection of eleven items, they were likely to score high as well on other negative beliefs about Jews. Conversely, if they scored low on this collection of items, the same logic would obtain in the opposite direction.

Seven of the eleven items in S&S were chosen from "traditional tenets of antisemitism" (18). To determine who was antisemitic, or more correctly, who was more antisemitic than someone else, S&S constructed an eleven item "index of antisemitism." The intensity of antisemitic belief was determined by how many of these eleven negative items the respondent agreed with. The fewer the items agreed with, the lower the level of antisemitism, and conversely, the greater the number of items agreed with, the higher the level of antisemitism. For example, 15 percent did not agree with any of the eleven items; 15 percent agreed with one; 8 percent agreed with five; and 2 percent agreed with all eleven. The authors divided the sample into thirds based on the number of the eleven items the respondents agreed with: 0–1 item, least antisemitic (31 percent); 2–4 items, middle antisemitic (32 percent); and 5 or more items, most antisemitic (37 percent).

Who is more or less antisemitic was a somewhat arbitrary matter. The average response of 3.75 items would mean 47 percent of the sample population was most antisemitic! The authors raised the bar to 5 items. On this basis approximately a third of the sample (37 percent) was now designated "most antisemitic." By basing the intensity of antisemitism on the number of items a respondent picked, the relative importance of one item compared to another was ignored. For example, "Jews have too much power in the United States," which generated only 11 percent agreement, and "Jews stick together too much," which generated 52 percent agreement, carry exactly the same weight in determining overall intensity of antisemitism. There are other unsettling properties to this index as well.

S&S reached different conclusions from Stember about their respective data. Where Stember believed four items should be dropped because agreement with these negative beliefs about Jews had dropped so low they were no longer reflective of public opinion, S&S argued for the continued use of two of these "dropped" items ("Jews care only about their own kind" and "Jews control international business") based on the argument that they reflected "traditional anti-Jewish beliefs" and the way in which they contributed to a conventional antisemitism as contrasted with a political antisemitism. Where Stember had shown antisemitic beliefs had plummeted in the years following World War II, S&S, writing during the same period using several of the same items, concluded that "a large number of traditional tenets of anti-Semitic ideology are accepted by sizable proportions [of Americans]" (18). Based on their eleven-item index of negative beliefs about Jews, S&S concluded that fully a third of the population held highly antisemitic beliefs.

What is disconcerting in this explanation is the assertion that Stember was somehow wrong in considering the results of multigroup comparisons, and that they (S&S) were more accurate in their findings by asking questions that directly confronted these beliefs (18). Thus, they say, "[T]he conclusion seems justified that conventional antisemitism not only continues at fairly high levels, but has hardly declined since 1952" (18). Where 1952 came into the picture is not explained. The fact remains that we live in a pluralistic society (and did in the 1960s), surrounded by many different groups of people, and narrowing a respondent's answers to one group (Jews) does not give us an accurate reflection of the impact of that pluralism on the perception of an object group's desirability. Pluralism was on everybody's mind and lips during the 1960s, and that preoccupation, plus the overarching influence of the civil rights movement on how pluralism was understood cannot be minimized. The importance of using multigroup comparison questions is discussed more fully in chapter eleven.

In conclusion, the antisemitic index devised by S&S produced an easy to read, shorthand way of numerically fixing the supposed level of American antisemitism, and it is the measure of American antisemitism the JAOs have kept before the public's eye ever since. One must speculate if S&S's criticisms of Stember (1964), and their assertion of an apparent resurgence of antisemitism from 1962 to 1964, was not fueled, in part, by the fact that their study was financed by the ADL, and it is to the benefit of the ADL to demonstrate a problem, rather than a solution.

Ten years after the S&S study, Quinley and Glock (1979, hereafter Q&G) produced a wrap-up volume entitled, *Anti-Semitism in America*. Their examination of antisemitism did not reflect the results of a new poll, but was a summarization of what the "Prejudice in America Series" contributors believed they had learned over the years about American antisemitism. Q&G's comments were based on the original survey data produced in 1964 and to a lesser degree on some data from a 1975 Louis Harris poll. The Harris poll asked five questions that match several of the same items in the S&S study (table 3).

Q&G revisited S&S's six headings of traditional images of Jews (i.e., Jews as monied, Jews as clannish, Jews as prideful, Jews as dishonest, Jews as power hungry, and Jews as pushy and intrusive) and found that the descriptors that composed each of these headings had dropped from 1964 to 1975. The one exception was "perceived loyalty to Israel" (30 percent in 1964, 33 percent in 1975). This is not much of an increase when you consider the massive financial support U.S. Jews rendered to Israel in the aftermath of the 1967 Six-Day War and the 1973 Yom Kippur War. The mean level of antisemitism on the five items from the Harris poll that match the S&S items fell 14-percentage points (37 percent) from 1964 to 1975. But this substantial downward shift in negative perceptions of Jews was not factored into the antisemitic index. Q&G conclude their comments on American antisemitism by saying, "[T]he most reasonable conclusion that can be drawn from the information that does exist is that there was almost an across the board decline in acceptance of traditional antisemitic shibboleths from the late 1930s to the mid-1960s. *Since then there appears to have been no increase in antisemitism*" (xx, italic added). Even though the Harris poll did not replicate all of the items in the index of antisemitism, it is obvious that Q&G

Table 3
Louis Harris 1975 Poll Results

Item Description	1964 (%)	1975 (%)
The movie industry is controlled by Jews	47	18
Jews are not as honest as other businessmen	28	18
Jews are shrewd and tricky	35	21
Jews are clannish	26	27
Jews are more loyal to Israel than to the United States	30	33
Mean percentage of belief	37.3	23.4

have conveniently overlooked the fact that antisemitism dropped substantially in the eleven years between 1964 and 1975, but they offer no explanation whatever to account for this decline.

In 1982 Gregory Martire and Ruth Clark (*Anti-Semitism in the United States: A Study in Prejudice in the 1980s*) reanalyzed the eleven-item index of antisemitism and concurred with S&S's earlier conclusion that they were all interrelated in terms of describing a property called antisemitism. (The statistics they used came from a 1981 poll conducted by Yankelovich, Skelly, and White.) The overall mean percentage of those agreeing with the eleven negative beliefs about Jews had stayed virtually the same at 35.2. If not exhibiting a downward trend between 1964 and 1982, antisemitic attitudes had not risen.

The year 1993 marks the last year the "index of antisemitic beliefs" was used to report negative beliefs about Jews. In 1993 the ADL published the results of a poll conducted for them by Martilla and Kiley entilted *A Survey of Antisemitic Attitudes*. The overall mean response had dropped yet again, this time to 27.4 percent. The ADL conceded that the "most antisemitic" group had to have the bar raised again to properly reflect the changes that had occurred over the previous thirty years. In fact, in an interview the regional director of the ADL in Boston admitted "that the average American is not antisemitic." It is necessary to go one step further in understanding this last effort to paint American antisemitism as a serious problem, and that is to entirely reconstruct the index:

0–1 item	39 %	not antisemitic
2–4 items	36 %	somewhat antisemitic
5–8 items	21 %	moderately antisemitic
9–11 items	4 %	most antisemitic

There is a 73 percent likelihood that the items most frequently agreed with (stick together too much, 51 percent; at head of things, 39 percent; loyalty to Israel, 35 percent; and have too much power, 31 percent) are among the items selected by those considered most antisemitic.

Even if we trusted the validity of the items in the index, and that's risky at this point, it would be foolish to ignore, or minimize the significance of this vitriolic 4 percent. The U.S. population currently stands at approximately 260 million. Excluding children twelve and under and those in prisons we are left with 220 million people, and 4 percent of 220 million is 8.8 million! As one former executive from the AJC told me, "These are not good odds" (Martin Goldman, interview by author, August 29, 1995). They are not, indeed. This population represents more than one openly dedicated antisemite for every Jew in the United States, regardless of the method used to define who is a Jew (see Lazerwitz, Winter, Dashefsky, and Tabory, 1998)! A second aspect of this measurement story is the number of antisemitic incidents occurring in the United States in a given year.

What is the extent of the attacks against Jews at the present time? Given the media attention the Crown Heights riots attracted in 1991, it would be easy to conclude that large numbers of Jews are under threat of attack in the United States. Not so; the incident in Crown Heights (Brooklyn, New York) in the summer of 1991 was an anomaly. Nothing of this scale had happened between blacks and Jews since the Harlem and Detroit riots in 1943. The repercussions of the Crown Heights riot, based on the official indifference to the plight of the Jews, contributed directly to the defeat of the incumbent mayor of New York (David Dinkins), a multimillion-dollar settlement for the violation of the civil rights of Jewish residents, and the imprisonment of two of the rioters for their part in the murder of a young Hasidic scholar. The riot also triggered substantial efforts on the part of residents of Crown Heights, both black and Jewish, to avoid a repeat of the tragic incidents that occurred during the four days of rioting that went unattended by the New York City Police Department.

The incidents of antisemitism reported yearly by the ADL (their annual *Audit of Anti-Semitic Incidents*) are considerably tamer by comparison. They have included graffiti (swastikas and Stars of David daubed on everything from automobiles to locker doors in college dorms), advertisements placed in newspapers denying the Holocaust, hate mail to individuals, and, in rare cases, a rock thrown through a synagogue window.

The ADL has compiled a record of all available data on antisemitic incidents going back to 1980. The number of these incidents climbed slowly during the 1980s and early 1990s, in part because national law enforcement agencies were joined by local police forces in reporting all sorts of hate crimes. But the reporting has been inconsistent and constrained by tight budgets, plus the demands of local citizens to address crimes of personal violence before worrying about hateful speech or graffiti against Jews. In the mid-1990s the occurrence of these offenses against Jews began to drop (table 4).

Certainly antisemitism has not disappeared from the American cultural scene, and law enforcement officials cannot ignore fringe groups like the skin heads, the White Aryan Nation, or Louis Farrakhan's parrots, and their violently antisemitic rhetoric. Nor can we ignore the social and cultural insults that occur from time to time. But, the fact remains that any Jew in the United States today has only a remote probability of being the object of an antisemitic slur or attack. Given this context, it is useful to examine the implications the ADL annual report has for the Jewish community in terms of incurring such an attack.

The 1997 statistics divide out to thirty-five incidents per week, or less than one antisemitic incident per state, per week. The one question that is never raised by the JAOs about these statistics is "Why are they dropping?" It is just as important to understand why a long-standing animosity is de-

Table 4
ADL's Annual Report of Antisemitic Incidents

Year	Number of Incidents	Up or Down (%)
1992	1,730	
1993	1,867	+7.3
1994	2,066	+9.5
1995	1,843	-10.8
1996	1,722	-6.5
1997	1,571	-8.8

clining, as it is to understand the causative factors behind any increase. The way it stands now, the probability of any of America's nearly six million Jews being directly involved in an antisemitc incident approaches the infinitesimal. Jews have never been safer in America than they are today.

At the same time, care must be taken to remember that Jews are not equally represented in all of these United States! They are more heavily concentrated in the large cities, particularly on the two coasts. So, it stands to reason that if you are Jewish and live in these more heavily populated areas of the country, you stand an increased probability of being directly affected by an antisemitic incident. You also stand an increased probability of being involved in any number of other forms of assault and insult, as well. It is one of the risks that go with large-city living.

There is yet another side to this "risk to Jewish safety" question, and that is the fact that many people in the Jewish community believe that a far greater threat to Jewish safety today lies in philosemitism. These are persons who are not Jewish, but who intentionally pursue social, intellectual, and affectional attachments to Jews. This admiration and affection for Jews has been a curious characteristic of American society since its earliest days. One of the more interesting paeans of praise to Jews was written in 1908 by Madison Peters and entitled *Justice to the Jew*. Written by a Protestant clergyman, it is partly a story about how Peters overcame his lifelong antipathy toward Jews, and then set off to discover and recount all of the wonderful things Jews have done for civilization over the past 3,500 years. In a phrase, a great many non-Jews like us—they really like us—and they are marrying our sons and daughters in increasing numbers with every passing year.

This combination of Jewish out-marriage plus cultural assimilation is a much larger problem for the average Jewish family today than is antisemitism.

If this deadly duo (assimilation and intermarriage) accurately reflects the current state of American Jewry, then why do the Jewish advocacy organizations still spend so much of their time and budgets (approximately $100 million per year) combating antisemitism, which is rapidly dwindling from the American cultural scene? Conversely, could their time, talent, and money be better invested in other activities that would contribute to an enhanced Jewish identity? It appears to be a straightforward question, but what adds confusion to an otherwise simple question is the fact that there are significant numbers of American Jews who are convinced that antisemitism is still a serious problem in the United States, and a not insignificant percentage of those Jews are also convinced that antisemitism is going to worsen in the future! Consider the following: Most Jews would tell you they feel no direct sense of threat, nor do they believe that the ghosts of the past (in terms of denial of housing, jobs, or employment) are ever likely to rear their ugly heads again. On the other hand, considerable numbers of these same Jews express the ongoing anxiety that "it could happen again." How do these misgivings translate into hard statistics?

ANTISEMITISM'S IMPORTANCE TO THE JEWISH COMMUNITY

Jewish concern about antisemitism is a confusing and contradictory collection of insights. Four studies completed over the past ten years provide some insight into this confusion, and they hold particular significance for this study. Each of these studies has been conducted with varying degrees of polling rigor:

- Gary Tobin and Sharon Sassler (1988) reported that 77 percent of America's Jews believed antisemitism could become a significant problem in the near future.
- Earl Rabb (1995) surveyed San Francisco Bay area Jews and found that seven out of ten respondents said antisemitism is a serious problem in the United States today.
- Gary Tobin (1996) adds a provocative insight to Rabb's statistics from his (Tobin's) recently completed study of "generation Xers" (interview by author, September 1996). Over 90 percent of these young Jewish women and men (ages 19 to 24) are convinced that antisemitism is a problem in the United States, or that it could become one in the near future.
- Lastly, there is the recent AJC *Survey of American Jewish Opinion* (1998). The AJC found 33 percent of their respondents believed antisemitism is a very serious problem and 62 percent believe it is a moderate problem. Of the AJC sample, 40 percent believe antisemitism will increase (9 percent greatly, 31 percent somewhat) over the next few years.

We cannot, however, leave this discussion of antisemitism without holding the surveys of Jewish opinion to the same critical examination used with the earlier studies of antisemitic attitudes and incidents. If the validity of the items so frequently quoted in attitudinal surveys of anti-Jewish opinion is flawed, then one suspects that the same could be true here, as well. One of the first considerations in any survey is who is the population being surveyed and are certain biases embedded in this sample that would skew their responses, even if the respondents were not consciously aware of them?

Tobin and Sassler (1988) examined opinions about antisemitism among Jews from three collections of data: (1) samples of Jewish populations in seven cities/counties (Kansas City, Missouri; Atlantic City, New Jersey; Baltimore, Maryland; Worcester, Massachusetts; Rochester, New York; and the Essex and Morris Counties, New Jersey); (2) Jewish advocacy organizations and Jewish community federations; (3) a group of 114 Jewish newspapers and magazines. In the first group, the questionnaire was constructed from interviews with ten randomly picked Jews and fifteen leaders in the Jewish community (i.e., rabbis and volunteers in Jewish communal organizations).

From the collection of JAOs surveyed, there were 73 responses from the 215 questionnaires mailed, or 34 percent, and in group three there were 40 responses from the 112 questionnaires mailed, or 33 percent. In group one, 42 percent (on average) believed there was a moderate level of antisemitism in their community, and 11 percent (on average) who said there was a great deal of antisemitism in their community. In the same year (1984), 77 percent of the population surveyed by the AJC (*National Survey of American Jews: Politcal and Social Outcomes*) agreed that antisemitism may become a serious problem for American Jews.

It is possible to compare the responses of groups two and three when they are placed side by side. Their responses to the question, "How important are programs to combat antisemitism" to the Jewish people? are as follows:

JAOs	Jewish Media
72% very important	68% very important

But, when asked, "What is the most important issue facing the Jewish people?" the reponses were:

JAOs	Jewish Media
34% Jewish education of children	53% Jewish education of children

Programs to combat antisemitism slumped to third or fourth place.

Tobin and Sassler's analysis (1988) produces three conclusions about Jewish perceptions of antisemitism: (1) The organizationally affiliated populations (e.g., the JAOs and the Jewish Press) held substantially stronger beliefs about the significance of antisemitism to the Jewish people than those persons sampled in the seven Jewish communities; (2) There were significant differences among the JAOs as well. The responses from the ADL were always higher on the significance of antisemitism than any or all of the other JAOs combined. The respondents in the JAOs were more likely to have personally experienced antisemitism than those from either the community populations or the Jewish media. Again, the ADL's number of personal experiences with antisemitism was always greater than that of the other JAOs, due, no doubt, to the public exposure they receive (and seek) as the dominant organization combating antisemitism in the United States; (3) All of the JAOs and the Jewish media have a stake in antisemitism! Combating it and writing about it means jobs, hierarchies of power, budgets, revenues, and organizational survival.

As comprehensive as Tobin and Sassler's study is, we learn more about what the organizationally affiliated Jew believes is important, or troubling to the Jewish people, than we learn about the larger numbers of grassroots Jews (*amcha*) themselves. This distinction between organizationally affiliated Jews—their opinions, decisions, and predispositions as to what is best for "the Jews"—becomes increasingly important in understanding the political importance antisemitism possesses for those same organizations; a great deal more will be said about this relationship in later chapters.

Rabb's data (1995) presents dilemmas similar to Tobin and Sassler's study. His population of survey respondents was 908 people in the Jewish community who had contributed one dollar or more to the Jewish Community Federation's annual fund-raiser (1). The 108-item questionnaire probed a host of areas from the State of Israel to specific social issues (e.g., crime and poverty).

On the topic of antisemitism Rabb tells us, "[F]ew respondents report they have been victims of antisemitism" (5). However, 68 percent agreed that antisemitism is a serious problem in the United States today, and 35 percent believe that antisemitism is increasing! What is noteworthy about the 68 percent who believe antisemitism is a serious problem is that this population "has been quite consistent for many years" (5). So, in spite of dropping percentages in almost every other general public poll, Jews in the San Francisco Bay area cling to the belief that they are the object of considerable antipathy from their surrounding communities: this from an area where intermarriage among Jews and non-Jews is among the highest in the country. In addition, 38 percent of respondents profess to having heard antisemitic remarks in the past year. Unfortunately, the report doesn't tell us what the remarks were or what made them antisemitic.

The 38 percent who had heard antisemitic remarks, heard them in the previous twelve-month period, but the time period for those who had actually experienced some form of antisemitic discrimination was not stated. So, we don't know if it was the previous twelve months, or possibly, over the person's entire life. With or without a stated time frame, any direct experience with antisemitism was significant for its infrequency. Rabb reports that 2.8

percent experienced employment discrimination; 1.4 percent experienced physical harassment; 1.5 percent experienced government discrimination; and, 0.9 percent experienced housing discrimination. The report does not tell us when these experiences took place or over what time period, and it also does not tell us what form the discrimination took or, more important, what made it clearly identifiable as antisemitic. What had happened to those respondents that led them to believe the discrimination in question was leveled at him/her because he/she was Jewish? Or, alternatively, did these perceived offenses happen for some reason other than the fact that the person was Jewish? We don't find out from the study, but it is important, in the final analysis, to know those answers. The Jews surveyed in Rabb's study were more likely, by virtue of their contributions to the Jewish Community Federation, to be organizationally affiliated Jews, rather than any representative cross-section of the larger grassroots Jewish population of San Francisco.

Tobin's (1996) comments about "generation Xers" has to be taken with some reservation. His analysis of this group has not yet been published, and that renders the authenticity of these claims somewhat problematic.

The AJC *Survey of American Jewish Opinion* (1998) is the most rigorous study in this collection of surveys of Jewish opinions, and it is focused on grassroots Jews as contrasted with those Jews who are organizationally affiliated. The AJC polled 1,001 self-identified Jewish respondents selected from a national consumer mail panel. The sample was demographically representative of the U.S. Jewish population (1).

The results of the AJC's survey are particularly interesting when compared to the same survey done only a year earlier (AJC, 1997). The results are virtually identical. The totals stayed the same, but the numbers shifted between categories: 33 percent of the respondents said antisemitism was a serious problem, compared to 40 percent in 1997, while 62 percent said it was somewhat of a problem (15), compared to 55 percent in 1997. Forty percent believe antisemitism will increase over the next several years, compared to 39 percent a year earlier, and those expressing this belief were (on average) older in both years. On the other hand, these results are substantially the same as Tobin's "generation Xers," who are considerably younger than the AJC population, but who expressed a heightened apprehension about antisemitism. What are we to make of all this pessimism? What is its source?

Earl Rabb, director emeritus of the San Francisco JCRC, and a longtime observer of the American Jewish community, explains these statistics by first pointing out that the preoccupation with antisemitism among America's Jews is their continuing sense of "foreboding" (Earl Rabb, interview by author, September 1996). Jews have long memories; they do not quickly forget the embarrassments and insults of only a few decades ago. Second, antisemitism has enjoyed multiple rebirths over the centuries, and it could happen again. Witness the excesses of history, and it is not hard to imagine Jews could once again become the target for the hate merchants. Recent hate messages by militant right-wing groups, and the inflammatory rhetoric of leading black separatists, is vivid testimony to the persistent popularity of several slanders about Jews, some of them centuries old, but trotted out in new clothing.

A more disturbing (and also, more sociological) alternative explanation is possible. First, it says that antisemitism is the historically proven device for characterizing a whole group—Jews. Thus, antisemitism provides American Jews with a tangible referent for their identity, an identity that Jews have given up finding in their religious history, traditions, or observances. Second, being born ethnically Jewish does not carry the weight it did for past generations of Jews who did not consider themselves religious. Given the impact assimilation has had on the American Jewish community, and the ethnic vanishing act this has produced, it is less difficult to understand the strange logic that supports the idea that occasional outbursts of antisemitism actually provide Jews with a tangible anchor (a negative one, to be sure) to which they can attach a continuing ethnic, if not religious, Jewish identity in a polyglot society.

One source in this study reflected, "[A]ntisemitism . . . fires the blood, it gives identity to the victim, . . . it becomes the way in which members of this group stand out from the general population. . . . [T]ake away antisemitism, and there goes what's left of my identity!" But, as palpable as antisemitism is to those Jews who continue to see it as a problem, or necessity, it is a problem/necessity that continues to elude any precise definition.

When asked what this antisemitism is that Jews are so concerned about, the response given typically parallels Justice Potter Stewart's lament when asked to define obscenity: "I can't define it, but I know it when I see it." Many Jews apply the same logic to antisemitism. They know antisemitism when they see it, but most of them find it virtually impossible to define it with any consistency. Yet, at some point, that is precisely the task the Jewish community and the social scientists must undertake if we are ever to put antisemitism in proper perspective to the rest of Jewish life in America.

CONCLUSION

The questions or statements discussed in this chapter that were used over the years to probe negative beliefs about Jews have been shown to possess two qualities: the measurement methods have been inconsistent, and the questions or statements were rarely defined with any precision. As a consequence, the collective results of all of these studies are misleading in what they supposedly tell us about American antisemitism in the closing days of the twentieth century. What we must conclude from this mass of tangled data is that any problem we had with American antisemitism in the past has long since dwindled to one of minor interest to the American public. At the same time, antisemitism continues to carry a significant emotional impact for substantial numbers of America's Jews and continues to be politically essential to the leadership of the JAOs. For both of these groups antisemitism remains a central ingredient in their lives.

Given antisemitism's near disappearance from the U.S. cultural scene, the obvious question becomes, "Why do the JAOs continue to identify antisemitism as an ongoing threat, and expend millions of dollars promoting that viewpoint?" Just as importantly, why do substantial numbers of Jews continue to believe that antisemitism is a serious problem in America, and one that many of them believe is increasing in severity? The answer to these questions is found (in part) in the histories of these JAOs, the reasons why they were created to begin with, and how over the decades, there has emerged a striking similarity in their organizational structures and behaviors.

In the next four chapters, the history of the JAOs is briefly recounted, and in each case the specifics of their organizational structure is included. Following this, chapter seven pulls together all of the organizational characteristics that the JAOs share and groups them into a summary discussion of the unmistakable similarities that exist among them, and the impact this may have on their very survival.

NOTES

1. Stember's optimism in dropping two of these four items ("Jews are too clannish" and "Jews have too much power in finance") was premature. Both items were subitems of larger categories, unlike the items on Jews as neighbors and Jews being limited in college admission, which were not part of larger categories and did decline sharply enough to warrant Stember's optimism. "Clannishness" was one of ten subitems in a category titled "Qualities Found Objectionable in Jews (1940–62)." "Finance" was one of eight subitems in a category titled "Beliefs Concerning the Nature of Jews' Supposed Power (1938–62)." Stember's optimism was based on the downward slide of negative opinion between 1938 (63 percent) and 1962 (22 percent). He applied the original subitem percentages, for example, 18 percent for "clannishness" and 18 percent for finance to produce his figure of approximately 4 percent. Researchers since Stember have criticized this manipulation as overly optimistic and misleading. Selznick and Steinberg (1969) reinserted both items in their Index of Anti-Semitic Beliefs.

2. The seven volumes in the "Patterns of Prejudice in America Series" are: Gertrude J. Selznick and Stephen Steinberg, *The Tenacity of Prejudice: Anti-Semitism in Contemporary America* (New York: Harper & Row, 1969); Gary T. Marx, *Protest and Prejudice: A Study in the Black Community* (New York: Harper & Row, 1967); Seymour Martin Lipset and Earl Rabb, *The Politics of Unreason: Right Wing Extremism in America 1790–1970* (New York: Harper & Row, 1970); Charles Y. Glock and Rodney Stark, *Christian Beliefs and Anti-Semitism* (New York: Harper & Row, 1966); Rodney Stack, Bruce Foster, and Charles Y. Glock, *Wayward Shepherds: Prejudice and the Protestant Clergy* (New York: Harper & Row, 1971); Charles Y. Glock, Robert Wuthnow, James Piliavin, and Michael Spencer, *Adolescent*

Prejudice (New York: Harper & Row, 1975); Charles Glock, Gertrude Selznick, and Joe L. Spaeth, *The Apathetic Majority: A Study Based on Public Responses to the Eichmann Trial* (New York: Harper & Row, 1966). There is an infrequently mentioned eighth volume in this series that served as a summary statement of the five works specifically devoted to antisemitism. It is: Harold Quinley and Charles Y. Glock, *Anti-Semitism in America* (New York: Harper & Row, 1979).

3. The eighteen items about Jews were: Jews are more willing than others to use shady practices to get what they want; Jews are more loyal to Israel than to America; Jews are just as honest as other businessmen; Jews have a lot of irritating faults; International banking is pretty much controlled by Jews; Jews are becoming more and more like other Americans; Jews don't care what happens to anyone but their own kind; Jews always like to be at the head of things; Jews stick together too much; Jews are always stirring up trouble with their ideas; Jews are warm and friendly people; Jews should stop complaining about what happened to them in Nazi Germany; You can usually tell whether or not a person is Jewish just by the way he looks; The movie and television industries are pretty much run by Jews; Jews have stirred up a lot of the trouble between whites and Negroes; The trouble with Jewish businessmen is that they are so shrewd and tricky that other people don't have a fair chance in competition; Jews still think of themselves as God's Chosen People; Jewish employers go out of their way to hire other Jews (S&S, 1969:Appendix A, p. 10).

Part Two

The History and Structure of the Jewish Advocacy Organizations

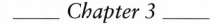

Chapter 3

The American Jewish Committee

INTRODUCTION

Any discussion of the organizational history of the major Jewish defense organizations has to start with the American Jewish Committee. Founded in 1906, it was the first of the big three Jewish defense organizations ostensibly created to speak for the Jewish community. It was followed by the Anti-Defamation League in 1913. The third member of this troika was the American Jewish Congress. It came into existence twice, first, in 1918 as a temporary organization, and then in 1922 as a permanent organization. The fourth JAO examined in this study, the Jewish Community Relations Council, was formed at the end of World War II; however, it was created to combat the same initial issue as the big three—antisemitism.

The American Jewish Committee (AJC) has provided a Jewish voice on national and international affairs since its inception, and its organizational history parallels much of America's pluralistic history, as well as that of the American Jewish experience. The goals of the AJC have evolved during three historical phases over its ninety-year history in America. Its formative period, from 1906 to 1945, was marked by a deep concern for the plight of East European Jews in the aftermath of Czar Nicholas II's assassination in 1881, and the devastating pogroms it triggered all across Russia. The one that gained the greatest public attention was the Kishiniv pogrom of 1903. There followed, in rapid succession, countless other attacks on Jews during 1904 and 1905 (Telushkin, 1991:258–59). The AJC's second historical period, from 1945 to 1967, describes the years following World War II and culminating with the Six-Day War in Israel in 1967.

The AJC's third historical period began in approximately 1967, and continues to the present (Cohen, 1972; Zelin, 1992; Svonkin, 1995). This third period has included the growing fragmentation in the civil rights movement, particularly between blacks and Jews, that was marked by the ascendancy of the black separatist movements in 1966; the Six-Day War in Israel in 1967, and how this war galvanized the American Jewish community to refocus its attention on a more Jewish agenda (as contrasted with intergroup activity); and the publication of the first Jewish family population survey in 1973, which provided important demographic proof that showed (for the first time) the rising intermarriage rate between Jews and non-Jews (Massarik and Chenkin, 1973).

THE AJC'S FORMATIVE YEARS: 1906 TO 1945

In 1906 a handful of wealthy and prominent German Jews founded the AJC in New York City. Prior to formalizing their organization these men had been meeting informally for several years in restaurants and clubs around New York City under a loose confederation they called "the wanderers" (Cohen, 1972:8–9). Their new organization was intentionally oligarchic in design and consisted of sixty people. This "closed" membership did not expand until 1931 when it enlarged its membership to 350, but was still directed by a small executive committee (Cohen, 1972:9). At no time over the next forty years did the AJC's decision making involve more than fifty men, almost all of whom lived and worked in New York City. This committee was self-supporting and all the funds that the AJC needed for its operations were donated by this handful of members.

The original founders of the AJC included Jacob Schiff, banker and head of Kuhn, Loeb Company; Oscar S. Strauss, the secretary of commerce and labor in Theodore Roosevelt's administration; Judge Mayer Sulzberger; Cyrus L. Sulzberger, a successful merchant and a cousin of Judge Mayer Sulzberger; Dr. Cyrus Adler, a scholar and communal leader; and the prominent attorney, Louis Marshall (Cohen, 1972:7; Svonkin, 1995:25–29).

The AJC declared itself the official voice of the American Jewish community from its first days. This presumptive rationale was based on the founders' belief that their sponsorship of several other Jewish institutions entitled them to lay claim to this distinction. Those organizations included the Jewish Theological Seminary, established in 1886 (for the education of Conservative rabbis); the Jewish Publication Society, established in 1888; and the American Jewish Historical Society, created in 1892. While the founders were genuine in their desire to aid the victims of the pogroms in Eastern Europe, they also were intent on establishing themselves as the premier voice of American Jewry.

The AJC's first action (even before it was a formal organization) was to raise funds to aid Jews who had survived the hundreds of pogroms that took place in Russia from 1903 onward. The rallying point for their fundraising was the infamous Kishiniv pogrom. Over the Easter weekend of

April 6–7, 1903, forty-nine Jews were murdered in Kishiniv, Russia. While the numbers were small in comparison to other Jewish disasters (both before and after Kishiniv), this incident touched off international outrage. The founders of the forthcoming AJC raised $1.25 million among themselves in a matter of days. They funneled those funds to local Jewish organizations in Russia that, in turn, used the money to buy food and clothing and, especially, to replace some of the housing that had been destroyed by the Russian marauders. Following their success in mounting this financial form of international relief, these men quickly agreed on the need to establish a more permanent, formal organization to facilitate their mission "to prevent the infraction of the civil and religious rights of Jews, in any part of the World" (Cohen, 1972).

In its next significant undertaking, this new Jewish committee exerted political pressure on the American government to abrogate the 1832 trade agreement with Russia. Two of the committee's members, Jacob Schiff and Louis Marshall, were particularly angered by the pogroms in Russia, and found in the trade treaty with Russia an opportunity to apply pressure directly against the government of Russia. They had been angry for years with the Russian government's flagrant abuse of American Jews traveling in Russia, and the arbitrary laws the Russian government had created that were designed solely to harass Jews. Schiff and Marshall used their personal power and prominence as members of the Jewish community to directly intercede with, first, President Theodore Roosevelt and, then, President William Howard Taft and members of Congress to undertake abrogation proceedings against the trade treaty. To press their discontent with the uneven policies of the Russian government still further, and to gain public recognition and support for the AJC, they launched a series of publicity campaigns and mass rallies, all of which proved effective. By 1911 most of the Jews immigrating to America were former victims of Russian laws and official harassment. They eagerly added their voices to the AJC's protests. The Congress of the United States did abrogate the 1832 Russian trade treaty on January 1, 1913. The committee had been successful in demonstrating that it could exert substantial influence in the realm of international politics (Cohen, 1972:54–80).

In the United States, the AJC's leaders found themselves reluctantly compelled to attend to the well-being of huge numbers of East European Jews who had been pouring into the United States in mounting numbers since 1881. The East European Jews (*"Ostjuden"*) who made their way to America between 1881 and 1920 differed significantly in their understanding of religious, cultural and economic issues as compared to the German and Sephardic Jews who had preceded them to America in the eighteenth and nineteenth centuries. Nevertheless, these new immigrants were still the coreligionists of these earlier Jewish settlers, and they could not be allowed to go without housing, schooling, and employment.

While the more established Sephardic and German Jews kept their social distance from these new arrivals, they contributed their funds unstintingly in an effort to ameliorate the desperate living conditions that prevailed in the swollen tenements of the Lower East Side of New York City. Deborah Dwork (in Sarna, 1986b:108), a medical historian, vividly illustrated the extent and depth of this poverty in the Jewish dominated tenements. She conducted a thorough and painstaking search of public building and utility records from the turn of the century, and produced the following characterization: "In 1900, the Tenement House Committee of Charity Organization Society illustrated this problem by exhibiting a cardboard model of an entire block. The chosen block, bounded by Chrystie, Forsyth, Canal, and Bayard Streets, was in the tenth ward. The 80,000 square foot area boasted thirty-nine tenement houses (nearly all six stories high) with 605 apartments. These buildings housed 2,781 people. . . . There were 264 water closets; only forty apartments had hot water. The one bathtub on the block, wedged in an air-shaft, was obviously unusable. Of the total 1,588 rooms, 441 or 27.7% were completely dark, with no access to outer air; 635 rooms or 40% were ventilated only by dark, narrow air shafts."

The Jews who were forced to live in these squalid circumstances did so willingly, knowing that their children and grandchildren would not. They would sacrifice their dreams, dignity, and not infrequently, their lives, so those who followed them would live the American dream. Life in New York's Lower East Side during those times has been compellingly captured in the writings of Moses Rischin, *The Promised City* (1962); Irving Howe, *The World of Our Fathers* (1989); Abraham Cahan, *The Rise of David Levinsky* (1917); Mary Antin, *The Promised Land* (1912); Anzia Yezierska, *Bread Givers* (1925); and Michael Gold, *Jews Without Money* (1930). Henry Roth's *Call It Sleep* (1934) is perhaps one of the more disturbing treatments of this period of Jewish survival in the *Goldina Medina* (the Golden Land).

These new Jews went on to found the Yiddish theaters, several of the Jewish newspapers that flourished in the United States well into the 1930s, and countless other businesses. They formed trade unions, sponsored socialist political candidates in city elections, and in the process, often shunned any religious connection to Judaism. Given the oppression of the state combined with the inbred life of the Jewish shtetl, it is not difficult to speculate that upon arrival in this country, thousands of these Jewish immigrants tossed any connection to their past religion into New York harbor along with *tallits, teffilins*, and other ritual objects associated with the old world. Those to whom religion was important were deeply observant in the old-world sense of the word—Traditional. The overcrowding, the scarcity of work, and the terrible living conditions brought to the entire Lower East Side an unceasing cacophony. From the street vendors who jammed Hester and Mott streets, to the peddlers who seemed to be everywhere at once, the noise and confusion were overwhelming. While much has been said and written about the New York Jewish experience, it is only because it was the largest Jewish settlement in America. Variations on this poverty, crowding, and oppression happened in every major city in which Jews settled—Philadelphia, Baltimore, Chicago, and somewhat later, Boston.

The Russian Jews met in public parks for huge labor and protest rallies. The union organizing oratory of Samuel Gompers rang out cheek to jowl beside the radical protests of Emma Goldman and Clara Lemlich. It may have been a life overburdened with poverty and hard work, but it was not a life without its savory distractions.

The theaters that lined Second Avenue were boisterous, crude, and hilarious; just what the exhausted garment workers needed after a fourteen-hour day of meeting the demands of an exploding marketplace. The Eddy Cantors, Al Jolsons, and Molly Picones were near-instant successes. Not because their humor was so original, or even that good, but they were "like us." They slipped into Yiddish with the same ease they slipped into costume. The plays that lit up Second Avenue were morality plays plain and simple, particularly when they were reenactments of old-world Jewish favorites.

Unfortunately, one of the unmistakable side effects of all of this noise, humor, poverty, and street corner opportunity was that it certainly didn't meet anyone's definition of the word "refinement." In several instances, the derision and insults that rained down on these awkward but sincere newcomers (greenhorns) was a product of their own self-effacement. They mimicked themselves on-stage and off. If blacks had been quick to learn that "shufflin and shuckin" in minstrel shows was a way to earn a few pennies, then, the East European Jews could be seen as equally alert to the economic possibilities in publicly imitating the Jew's worst caricatures, caricatures that had come to America through expressions of centuries-long, European antisemitism. Needless to say, this "public behavior" did not sit well with the longer established German and Sephardic Jews.

The German Jews of the AJC found this near-total disregard for decorum among the Russian Jews embarrassing and in sharp contrast to their own more conservative and circumspect behavior. Not drawing attention to oneself was seen as a paramount commandment in coexisting with the gentile community, of which they were all a part. Men like Schiff, Marshall, Sulzberger, Adler, and hundreds of other prominent German Jews had labored long and hard (in some cases for decades) at their resolve to be seen as Americans first and Jews by religion, just like their Protestant neighbors. Their sincere desire was for all Jews in America to become Americans as quickly as possible, and not to replicate the customs and beliefs of the shtetl or the ghetto. Part of the reasoning for Jews to become identified as Americans first, and Jews by religion second, was the ancient fear of upsetting the Christian power structure, and possibly triggering antisemitism. But this separation was immediately apparent in the unmistakable differences in how each group conducted themselves during religious observances.

For the German Jews who had brought Reform Judaism to this country, one of the central features of their religious observance was decorum. People dressed for the occasion, rabbis gave sermons, and in time the Reform temples and synagogues installed organs for the playing of sacred music. The Reform services were typically shorter in length, and as much of the service was conducted in German (and subsequently English) as it was in Hebrew. As their commercial success grew, the German Jews began building large, expansive, sometimes ornate synagogues and temples that mimicked in design the churches and cathedrals of the Protestant, Christian establishment. This emphasis on decorum, plus other changes that accompanied it, was in sharp contrast to the more boisterous behavior that took place in the traditional (and entirely Hebrew) services of the East European Jews. Where the Reform Jews had given up wearing the distinctive *tallit* (prayer shawl) and the *kippah* (the traditional male head cover), these and other objects (*teffilin*) were still steadfastly retained in the more traditional services of the East European Jews. Over the passage of several years, the German Jews in New York City came to be known as the "Uptown Jews," and the East European immigrants were the "Downtown Jews" (Sanders, 1969).

Because its members were successful businessmen, financiers, and professionals, the AJC had a distinctly elite air about it. It resembled the *shtadlanims,* that is, Jewish agents to the court rulers of eighteenth-century European monarchies. The Jewish governing councils (*Kehillas*) had disappeared with the emancipation of the Jews, but their descendants brought the spirit of the "court Jew" and the *Kehilla* with them to America (Elazar, [1976] 1995:258). Men like Jacob Schiff and his colleagues in the AJC attempted to reestablish this European form of Jewish governance through an American version of the *Kehilla*. The concept never took hold, in part because the East European Jews would not recognize the *Kehilla* as having any authority over their lives. This was America not Europe, and the very democracy that was so appealing to the long-oppressed immigrant, was precisely the reason that a throw back form of governance from eighteenth-century European Jewish life would not sail.

The AJC's leadership continued to hew to its elite selectivity, and for decades it excluded Jews of East European origins from serving on the board of directors, or in major lay leadership positions. The AJC saw itself providing financial and other assistance to those impoverished Jews in need of help during their transition into American life, but that help did not extend to admitting them to their largely closed society. This antipathy toward East European Jews was also based on long-standing cultural and language differences. The *Ostjuden* generally were not educated in the Central European sense of the word (i.e. enlightenment). They often did not speak their own national language (e.g., Polish or Russian), and certainly not German.

The Hebrew they spoke was reserved for sacred texts. Hebrew was for speaking to God, not other Jews. They spoke Yiddish, a language that was centuries old, and used a combination of Hebrew characters and a derivative form of Low German. To the educated German ear, Yiddish was a harsh tongue, an inferior dialect of German that automatically placed the speaker one rung (at least) down on the social hierarchy of Jewry. These newly arrived Jews (and the "new" distinction often persisted for decades) were the "country bumpkins," and while the more refined German Jews in the AJC found them worthy of their help, they did not extend them membership in the AJC.

With the onset of World War I, the AJC and American Jewry found itself in a rapidly changing America. The huge immigration flow from different parts of Europe was reaching its peak years. Over two million Jews had come to America since 1881 in search of relief from poverty and oppression, and seeking the opportunity to better their lives. The AJC, in company with the other JAOs, had successfully fought various immigration restrictions, particularly the racist requirement of literacy tests as a determinant of fitness to stay in this country (Cohen, 1972:49).

In the aftermath of their participation in the post–World War I negotiations in Paris, the AJC was painfully aware of the growing "America first" sentiment that was gaining strength in the United States. The original immigration restriction forces had gained significant momentum in Congress, and in conjunction with the growing appeal of groups like the Ku Klux Klan (KKK), and the antisemitic writings of Henry Ford, large numbers of Americans were demanding a curtailment of open immigration. Even some in the American Jewish community supported restricting the immigration of more Jews from East Europe, fearing the increased possibility of a gentile backlash against all Jews. The anti-immigration forces prevailed, and in 1921 a bill was introduced to curtail immigration to certain specific quotas per country. The Immigration Restriction Act became law in 1924 and would prove to be the harbinger of great suffering for Jews stranded in Europe during World War II. It was this bill that would prohibit a more generous attitude on the part of America toward Jews seeking to escape the murderous onslaught of the Nazi death machines. With the menace of Nazism growing in Europe, antisemitism in this country had begun to heat up. There was a growing resentment toward the increasingly powerful concentration of political power in key urban areas from rural populations in the United States. A natural target for this growing frustration was the Jew.

Antisemitic rhetoric in the United States became increasingly prevalent and public in the late 1920s when Henry Ford published *The Protocols of the Elders of Zion* in his own newspaper, the *Dearborn Independent*. In the 1930s, radio priest Father Charles Coughlin included antisemitic diatribes as part of his Sunday radio program, and his broadcasts reached a huge American audience in comparison to Ford's paper. By 1945, public opinion polls on antisemitic attitudes had reached their highest levels in the country's history (see chapter two). In the aftermath of revelations about the Holocaust, brought to the general public's attention for the first time during the Nuremberg War Crime Trials, antisemitic attitudes in America began dropping significantly. As a result of these shifts in public opinion, the AJC began a serious study of prejudice and antisemitism by commissioning Theodor Adorno et al. to conduct one of the earliest studies on prejudice and discrimination, *The Authoritarian Personality* (1950). It was only one of a number of publications the AJC had sponsored or authored since the 1930s. More would follow in the decades after World War II. In the early 1950s, the AJC began compiling what became the most thorough database on black/Jewish relations from the Jewish perspective.

THE AJC'S SECOND PERIOD: 1945 TO 1967

Following World War II, and with it the near-successful destruction of European Jewry, and the formation of the new State of Israel in 1948, the AJC's mission to the Jewish community changed in a number of significant ways; their interests now shifted to a greater emphasis on domestic U.S. affairs. The emerging State of Israel became increasingly identified with the international interests of Jews, thus diminishing the international influence of the AJC. While they were not publicly opposed to the formation of the State of Israel, in private, most of the AJC's members were anti-Zionist (Zelin, 1992:133–34). Jacob Schiff, for example, was outspoken in his belief that Jews could not benefit from the establishment of an Israeli state. In his opinion it was the responsibility of America's Jews to be Americans first and Jews by religious choice, and not risk appearing to hold divided loyalties between the United States and Israel. It was not until 1962 that the AJC opened its first office in Jerusalem (Zelin, 1992:135). Beginning in the early 1950s and forward to the mid-1960s, the AJC in company with the other two JAOs (the ADL and the AJCg) shifted their focus from an international emphasis to more of a intergroup emphasis (Svonkin, 1995).

One of the first steps the AJC undertook was to begin actively recruiting a larger membership. They did so for two reasons: (1) To help defray the costs of an increasingly expensive operation. It was no longer possible for the handful of prominent Jewish men who ran the AJC to carry the entire financial burden of the organization. Nor did they think it was advisable. (2) Enlarging the membership base increased the legitimacy of the organization in several more Jewish communities in America than New York City.

In 1945, as a part of a strategy for recruiting this larger membership, the AJC opened chapter offices across the United States to provide the organizational structure that was needed to facilitate communications with new members and new locations. The chapter office not only became the vehicle for assuring closer communication with members, but it also put the home office of the AJC closer to any local issues that had national implications for the quality of Jewish life in America. These branch offices were feedback and information gathering offices for the AJC. Between 1945 and 1949 the AJC attracted 18,000 new dues-paying members; by 1960 membership had grown to 23,000 (Zelin, 1992:129).

The Roosevelt Administration in Washington, DC had instituted sweeping new social service policies during the 1930s, thereby eliminating the need for many of the social service agencies connected to immigrant relief organizations. The AJC, along with hundreds of similar organizations, had moved away from providing direct social services to Jews. Their goal now became one of advocating for Jewish protection (against antisemitism), and more actively pressing for the enlargement of Jewish civil rights, such as open access to education and employment, principally in the United States.

The AJC has long had an informal reputation as the think tank of the Jewish communal world, a reputation expanded when they established the Blaustein Center for Human Relations and a specialized library of American Jewish history in 1959. By the early 1960s, over 100 professional researchers staffed the center, conducting research on intergroup and community relations. With the end of World War II, and with antisemitic attitudes falling in the United States, the AJC turned its attention increasingly to intercommunity and intergroup activities (Zelin, 1992).

This shift in the committee's domestic role after World War II represented a major change in its goals from those at its inception four decades earlier. The committee now emphasized improving intergroup and intercommunity relations between Jews and other groups. While the AJC continued to keep a watchful eye on antisemitism, it also recognized that Jews were living in a pluralistic society with many different groups who were all struggling to assimilate into mainstream American society (Svonkin, 1995:57).

During the 1950s and early 1960s, at the height of the civil rights movement in the United States, the American Jewish Committee, in company with large numbers of other liberal Jews, actively supported black America's quest for improved housing, and expanded employment and educational opportunities. These were all issues Jews could identify with based on their personal experience; however, Jewish enthusiasm for black civil rights cooled rapidly with the emergence of black militancy (often anti-Jewish) in the mid-1960s. In 1967, as a result of the Six-Day War, Israel become a greater concern for the AJC than black civil rights.

THE AJC'S THIRD PERIOD: 1967 TO THE PRESENT

Although the committee had begun to make active, if restrained, overtures to Israel in the late 1950s, it was not until the Six-Day War that the committee decided that support for Israel had to become a more significant part of its basic mission statement. It did not ignore antisemitism in America, but the committee did devote a considerable portion of its resources to the continued existence and prosperity of Israel and sought to expand its staff and revenues to maintain this increased level of activity. To a great many Jewish communal leaders it was apparent that the Holocaust was not the last attempt to eliminate Jews; the Six-Day War between Israel and its Arab neighbors was seen by many Jewish communal leaders as a second attempt at annihilation in this century.

In the early 1970s the AJC prepared a new set of goals in a formal mission statement that is still operative today. Their new statement included nine goals: protecting the security of Jews everywhere by advancing human rights; combating antisemitism; supporting Israel's peace goals and strengthening Israel's relations with the United States; safeguarding American democracy by fighting bigotry and discrimination; nurturing pluralism and cooperation among diverse groups; supporting public policy issues that benefit Jews and Americans as a whole; enriching American Jewish life by strengthening the Jewish family; fostering an understanding of Jewish history; and enhancing the relationship between American Jews and Israelis (AJC announcement, September 1984). This mission statement, the third major revision in the committee's history since its formation in 1906, focused on three key issues: antisemitism, Israel, and Jewish identity. They remain central to the AJC's mission twenty-five years later.

Because of its persistent threat to the safety of the Jewish people, antisemitism has been the primary target of the AJC's activities. Israel became important to Jews everywhere but not to the AJC until the aftermath of the Six-Day War in 1967. Jewish continuity is a relatively new concern on the committee's priority list. After the 1971 National Jewish Population Survey (NJPS) documented the increase in intermarriage by American Jews, the JAOs, including the AJC, took no action on the findings. Jewish intermarriage and the continuity of Jewish identity was a problem for some other Jewish organizations, most commonly thought to be the synagogues. Today the issue of Jewish continuity is on every Jewish organization's agenda, even if they do not know what they are supposed to do about it.

The evolving mission statements of the AJC demonstrate how the organization has changed since its founding in 1906. In the first period it directed most of its attention and influence to international events; in the second period, to domestic issues; and in the third, the present period, to both international and domestic issues.

This third period is the focus of the present research. In particular, how nonprofit organizations such as the JAOs will reshape their fundamental goals in ways that will permit them to balance the goals of organizational mission with the need for organizational survival. These dual goals must be seen in the context of six Jewish concerns today:

1. The influence antisemitism will exert in an era when attitudinal antisemitism continues to drop in intensity

2. The continuing ambivalence in the black/Jewish relationship

3. The relationship between American Jewry and Israel

4. The changing contours of civil liberties in America

5. The continuing erosion of the American Jewish population due to intermarriage

6. The implications that all these concerns possess for the organizational survival of the JAOs.

LEADERSHIP CHARACTERISTICS OF THE AJC

The AJC has a dual emphasis on international and national issues, and a dual constituency. The mission statement of the AJC says its advocacy is directed at "Jews everywhere," and "Jews of America" (AJC mission statements, 1994, 1995, 1996). Worldwide there are approximately 13 million Jews, of which approximately 6 million are in the United States (AJC, 1996:171). The AJC's primary constituency is the Jews of America, but in practical terms this translates to the AJC's lay leaders, key contributors and financial supporters, and, on occasion, influential Jews in the at-large community, whether or not they are AJC members.

Oligarchy has been the major form of organizational power in Jewish organizations. JAOs are an example of classic oligarchies (Michels, 1958). This is not unusual in advocacy organizations in general, because as leaders select like-minded peers with whom to consult when making important decisions, the circle of advisors tends to narrow to a small handful (Mansbridge, 1980). It is perhaps ironic that in America, where the nonprofit sector is considered characteristic of a pluralist society, some of the organizations that comprise this sector are frequently not particularly democratic in their leadership and decision making. Power and control in Jewish organizations is held by a small number of influential lay leaders (Elazar, [1976] 1995:426). These are the elected presidents, vice presidents, chairs of the board, and chairs of the significant committees and commissions that pass on resolutions for programs and resource allocations.

In the AJC's organizational hierarchy, only a few large, influential contributors are at the apex of the lay leadership. Directly beneath them in influence and power are a narrow band of substantial contributors who eschew any public attention or direct involvement in the day-to-day decision making of the AJC. Beneath them is a still wider band of contributing members and the professional staff. At the bottom is the widest band representing the at-large Jewish community who rarely contribute any money to the AJC. For the majority, their knowledge of AJC affairs ranges from ignorance of its existence to recognition of the name, but little, if any, knowledge of its work.

The influential contributors at the top of the elected leadership comprise the president, board of directors, and key personnel who sit on the principal national and local committees and commissions and who make all of the planning decisions on future programs and budget allocations (Howard Weintraub, interview by author, March 1995). In spite of their substantial financial influence, only a few members of the AJC's executive board and executive committees make the major decisions that determine the direction of the organization. This is an indication of the persistence of oligarchy in JAOs. The small numbers that comprise the oligarchies in the JAOs does not, perforce, exclude the opinions and concerns of Jews not in leadership positions, but any recommendations they offer up will be adopted only if influential members of the executive board and appropriate committees are sympathetic. These formal committees and commissions define the direction of Jewish advocacy and make its decisions (Woocher, 1991:172–73).

Beyond planning, program adoption, and resource allocation, actual decision making flows from two lines of authority: a small, relatively closed, predominantly male group of elected lay leaders; and the professional staff who are hired and paid as employees of the advocacy organizations. These professionals provide essential research and background on key issues before significant policies or programs are considered for adoption. This restriction of decision making to a limited few blurs any absolute distinction between the locus of control (elected lay leaders) and the locus of implementation (the professional staff).

The large contributors who become the leaders (president, chairman of the board, directors of significant committees and commissions) in the AJC are recommended by a nominating committee and chosen by the board of directors. Virtually all of the candidates are long-standing members of the AJC, or another Jewish communal organization, and are prominent in their chosen professions and in their local communities (Weintraub, interview).

Positions on the boards of directors, governors, and key committees for lay leadership are persistently difficult to fill because there are few volunteers, and because some volunteers are poor leaders. Daniel Elazar ([1976] 1995:430) summarizes the leadership quandary in the following way: "Since community leadership by and large consists of filling vacuums, it is often more difficult to recruit leaders and to determine whether they are representative or not. It is not as if many people were clamoring for a few places—indeed, it is just the other way around."

The AJC requires those on their board already be successful in their professional lives and able to set their own schedules to accommodate committee needs. So, the board is represented by successful business executives and owners, bankers, financiers, doctors, lawyers, and judges who are likely to possess the autonomy in their positions, which is needed to carry out committee business. The demographics of the AJC's lay leaders reflect these preferences.

In 1990 the national lay leaders of the AJC were predominantly male (71 percent) and married (81 percent). Their average age was fifty-four; 62 percent had annual incomes over $100,000, and 85 percent claimed a synagogue affiliation. The elected leaders of the AJC were predominantly liberal (only 16 percent Republicans) and Reform in their religious affiliation (67 percent) (Zelin, 1992:174). The AJC's lay leaders today differ only slightly from those who sat on its board in the mid-1980s. On average they are slightly younger, and some acquired their leadership skills through their social activism in the civil rights and antiwar movements of the 1960s.

To be considered for a position on the committee's national board of directors a candidate must be dedicated to the AJC; be able to serve on committees and commissions; raise funds from associates and others in the community; and donate $5,000 to the national AJC ($750 to the chapter AJC). While the professional staff is vital to the day-to-day operation of the organization, there are many more qualified people who can serve as professional staff than there are qualified candidates for elected lay leadership positions.

The professional staff differs in several respects from the elected leadership. To begin with, the members of the professional staff usually come out of a social science/social welfare background and have often attended professional school for their training. This in contrast to the elected lay leaders whose education has frequently been in business or law. Some of these professionals are among the committee's chapter directors. For example, the director of the Philadelphia AJC chapter is Dr. Murray Friedman, a leading authority on antisemitism and the black/Jewish relationship. In addition to his AJC duties, he teaches at Temple University. Other staff personnel include professional fund-raisers, public relations experts, legal analysts, and social scientists who are investigating changing patterns in antisemitism, race relations, and the growing threat from militia groups. For example, there is Kenneth S. Stern, author of *A Force Upon the Plain: The American Militia Movement and the Politics of Hate* (1996). Stern is the AJC's expert on hate crimes and hate groups. His analysis of these groups accurately predicted the bombing of the Alfred P. Murrah Building in Oklahoma City in April 1995.

The professional staff members have substantial influence on the programs that will be adopted by the lay leaders. Within certain national guidelines they can confer with almost any other group in the chapter's community, that is, the different civil rights groups (e.g., black, Hispanic, and Asian; Gay Rights; and women's movements), economic round tables, and public sector social service agencies. Fundamental decisions about organizational direction are made by the elected lay leaders, but it is the staff professionals in consultation with their local and national lay leaders who make the daily decisions in their respective communities. This has proven to be an excellent working relationship between the two lines of authority (Elazar, [1976] 1995:366). This relationship between professional staff and the elected lay leaders is found throughout the nonprofit sector.

This combination of elected and professional leaders working together in representative oligarchies form the power base of today's JAOs. Day in and day out they select strategies that will satisfy the dual goals of the formal mission and that of the organization's continuing survival.

THE AJC TODAY

The overall membership of the AJC today is approximately 45,000; total employment is approximately 335. The AJC's annual budget is approximately $19.8 million, and its ideology is described by committee insiders as "centrist," as contrasted with liberal or conservative. Over its ninety-year history, it has moved from an elitist organization representing the financial power of a handful of men to a cosmopolitan organization with international and domestic interests. From its inception, it has attempted to carry out its advocacy in a diplomatic fashion, campaigning and intervening on key issues largely from behind the scenes. The leaders of the AJC steadfastly prefer this approach; but of late, the AJC has taken out full-page advertisements on a range of issues, including antisemitism, the State of Israel, and Jewish identity.

Since the 1930s, the AJC has published over 1,000 studies, pamphlets, and books in addition to its regular monthly and annual reports and magazines. The majority of these studies have been released since 1945. The AJC's best-known external publication is *Commentary* magazine, published monthly since 1945. The AJC sponsors *Commentary*, but the magazine maintains a separate corporate and editorial identity. It is widely read in the secular community for its discussion of international and national political issues, and a handful of specifically Jewish topics. Since the early 1970s *Commentary* magazine has become a decidedly conservative voice in the Jewish community. For the past ninety-five years the AJC has published an annual almanac of world Jewish affairs called the *American Jewish Year Book*. Finally, the AJC publishes the *AJC Journal*, a newsletter focusing on current events within the committee, and distributed monthly to all AJC members.

Although the committee's formal mission statement says that its constituency is the at-large Jewish community, the AJC has no direct mandate from that community. The objectives in its mission statement are so broad, altruistic, and long term they are virtually impossible to dispute. There are no mechanisms, formal or informal, through which members of the American Jewish community can express their opinions of the activities or decisions of the AJC. Jews can write a letter to the editor of their local newspaper, or they can call the AJC offices to register their opinion. The absence of any feedback mechanisms from the American Jewish population to the AJC continues to reinforce the oligarchic nature of the AJC's decision making.

There is a steady exchange of information and opinions between the thirty-four local chapters and the AJC's national office in New York City.

The chapter office first and foremost fulfills the national agenda of the committee in a particular region. A major responsibility of the chapter office is to keep the national office apprised of what is going on in the chapter's region, particularly about those events that are consistent with the AJC's advocacy positions. While reliance on the telephone is evident from even the briefest visit to an AJC office, e-mail is equally important, and the chapter office transmits a substantial amount of correspondence every day between the national office and the chapter office. E-mail has proven particularly useful in determining the content of letters and press releases that must be coordinated before they are released.

The Boston chapter of the AJC celebrated its fiftieth anniversary in 1996, and was one of the first chapter offices the AJC established after World War II. Boston, like all chapter offices, has the same organizational structure and leadership characteristics as the national office of the AJC.

Unlike the ADL, the AJCg, and the JCRC, which were all well established in Boston by 1946, the AJC had no office in Boston during the turbulent years of the 1930s when antisemitism was climbing in Boston as it was in other U.S. cities. By the 1950s it was involved, along with the other JAOs, in fighting the restrictive quota systems in local colleges that limited admission of Jews as students or hired as faculty. The fight over these restrictive codes is covered more extensively in the next two chapters on the ADL and the AJCg.

During the late 1960s the AJC was involved, along with other Boston Jewish organizations, in efforts to resolve the religious and racial conflicts that arose as the Boston neighborhoods of Roxbury, Dorchester, and Mattapan were transformed from Jewish to black neighborhoods. Over the past several decades, the Boston chapter of the AJC has operated quietly but persistently in fostering intergroup religious affairs and intercommunity programs fostering black/Jewish relations.

The Boston chapter currently has three employees: a director, a professional associate, and a support person. From time to time several unpaid volunteers also work in the office and on special projects. The Boston chapter has an eighty-five-member member board of directors, and twelve-member executive committee. Members belong to the AJC, not the chapter, although a member's entire experience may be with the chapter. The current budget of the Boston chapter of the committee is $250,000. The annual budget is distributed from the New York office to the chapters based, in part, on the previous year's achievements and, in part, from the amount of contributions generated by the chapter. The chapter budget is augmented with specific fund-raising events featuring prominent speakers from the Jewish and secular community. The chapter's professional employees and its lay leaders come from two different groups. There is no career crossover from the professional ranks to elected leadership. In fact, there is no clear-cut career path for professional staff at the AJC. If they leave one chapter, they may go to another at a different location, or they may leave Jewish advocacy altogether and go into entirely different fields such as teaching or politics.

CONCLUSION

This chapter has presented the history and organizational characteristics of the American Jewish Committee since its inception in 1906. It provides a basic framework for understanding not only the AJC, but the history and the similar organizational profiles adopted by the other three JAOs. Those histories and organizational profiles appear in the next three chapters.

_____ *Chapter 4* _____

The Anti-Defamation League

INTRODUCTION

The Anti-Defamation League (ADL) came into existence seven years after the American Jewish Commitee formed in 1906 and shared a number of the same characteristics as the AJC beyond their German-American founders. Most notably, the ADL shared the same historical periods in the evolution of its goals. But, unlike the AJC's clearly stated intention to carry out its mission to the Jewish people in a circumspect and diplomatic fashion, the ADL would be very public and, if necessary, undiplomatic in its condemnations of antisemitism. The ADL would quickly establish its reputation as the best-known Jewish agency in the United States to publicly combat antisemitism and, eventually, other hate crimes.

During the ADL's formative period, from 1913 to 1945, America's Jews and their lay leaders were becoming painfully aware of the mounting presence of domestic antisemitism, as well as the long-standing international variety. While it was the Kishiniv pogroms of 1903 that brought the AJC into formal existence, it was the arrest and conviction of a young Jewish plant manager, Leo Frank, in Atlanta, Georgia, that was the catalyst for the ADL's formal origin. The second period from 1945 to 1967 reflects those years immediately after World War II that saw the formation of the new State of Israel, revelations of the horrors of the Holocaust, and the first substantial indications of a sharp drop-off of antisemitism in America. The ADL's third historical period began about 1967 and continues to the present. Unlike the AJC's clearly stated intent to function "in the background," the ADL was very public and forthright from its very first days in its condemnations of antisemitism.

THE ADL'S FORMATIVE PERIOD: 1913 TO 1945

The ADL started life in Chicago, Illinois, as a separate operation of the Independent Order of B'nai B'rith (Moore, 1981:102–64; Wertheimer, n.d.). Following its formation in 1913, and particularly after the lynching of Leo Frank in 1915, the ADL quickly established itself as an identity separate from its parent organization, the B'nai B'rith. In spite of this separate identity, the ADL received much of its funding from B'nai B'rith for several years after its founding.

B'nai B'rith was founded in 1843 as a Jewish fraternal organization similar to other American fraternal organizations such as the Odd Fellows Lodge. B'nai B'rith directed its considerable energies (and finances) to helping tens of thousands of newly arrived immigrant Jews with their immediate social needs (e.g., housing, clothing, and medical care), and with other practical necessities such as the formation and operation of a Jewish Burial Society. From approximately 1890 onward, B'nai B'rith was reporting national and international incidents of antisemitism in its journal, *The Menorah* (Moore, 1981:103).

Like the founders of the AJC, the leadership of B'nai B'rith in 1913 was largely drawn from prosperous, middle-class, German American Jews in the Midwest and South. These men were becoming increasingly apprehensive about the threat to their prosperous Jewish image posed by the rising tide of Jewish immigrants from Eastern Europe. These immigrants were sometimes blamed for a growing domestic antisemitic backlash, and some of the Jews in B'nai B'rith even fantasized about a pre–Civil War "golden age," when Southern Jews and non-Jews enjoyed mutual harmony. But increasing numbers of non-Jewish Americans were beginning to invoke traditional Christian stereotypes of the nefarious Jew, blaming crime, radicalism, urban immorality, and other disturbing forces on these immigrants. The racist ideologies with which many prominent Americans reacted to the great waves of immigration was a perpetual threat to the Jewish community and the ADL. In 1907, Congress had established the Dillingham Commission on immigration, and the ADL had unsuccessfully tried to block publication of the commission's forty-two-volume report in 1911. The report described positive and negative categories of immigrants and urged tests and other obstacles to curb "undesirable" immigration. The ADL was eventually successful in getting the much feared literacy test portion of the commission's requirements dropped from general immigration requirements (Moore, 1981:106).

Equally disturbing to America's newly prosperous German Jews, with their concern for propriety, was the flourishing world of Jewish show business: the actors, actresses, comedians, vaudevillians, and singers. The success of these Jewish performers often entailed pleasing gentile audiences by fostering and mimicking Jewish stereotypes, and they persisted in these portrayals despite the anger it raised among the more refined German Jews in both the AJC and the ADL (Moore, 1981:105, 114).

Domestic antisemitism peaked dramatically in the 1913 murder trial of Leo Frank, a manager of a family-owned pencil factory in Atlanta, Georgia. It ultimately resulted in his conviction and lynching in 1915 by an out-of-control mob. Frank was arrested in April 1913 for the alleged murder of one of his female factory employees, Mary Phagen. The ADL became an immediate and staunch defender of Frank's innocence, but its advocacy did not prevail at the time of the incident. The ADL stood by its claim of Frank's innocence in the long decades after his lynching and in 1986 saw him exonerated of all charges in the aftermath of a 1982 death-bed confession by another employee, Alonzo Mann. He admitted seeing a third employee, Jim Conley (the state's main witness against Frank), carrying the dead girl's body. Conley threatened Mann with death if he ever revealed what he had seen. Mann held his terrible secret for 67 years! Leo Frank's murder by an unruly mob on August 16, 1915, stands to this day as the only American Jew ever lynched (Dinnerstein, 1994).

In September 1913 Adolph Kraus, president of B'nai B'rith, reacted to the Frank case by inviting fifteen prominent Chicago members to form the Anti-Defamation League. In approximately one year (1914–1915), 150 prominent Jews from across the country were appointed to the league's executive committee. These men (like their counterparts in the AJC) were drawn from the ranks of successful Jews of German origins. They held the same nativist American predispositions toward citizenship and religion as the founders of the AJC: You were an American first, and a Jew by religious choice.

But the organized Jewish community was divided in its reaction to the Leo Frank case, with some leaders urging Jews to distance themselves from the trial, treating it as a purely legal matter for the courts to settle, not as a political question in which they should intervene. For example, the AJC "did not want to be considered as championing the cause of Jews who were convicted of crimes" (Dinnerstein, [1968] 1987:76). It was feared that raising questions about the American legal system (there were serious doubts about Frank's guilt from the very outset) might provoke a gentile backlash, one that would surely arise from Jewish organizations championing a "Jewish" criminal (see Louis Marshall letter to Simon Wolf in Moore, 1981, n. 12).

The AJC had always maintained that it was in the American Jews' best interest to maintain a low profile, but Sigmund Livingston didn't agree. Livingston, a founding member of the ADL and its president for decades, made it clear from the outset that the ADL would fight antisemitism openly, in print, and through the intervention of prominent regional and national personages (Moore, 1981:109). The quiet diplomacy of the AJC would not be the ADL's forte. The ADL's more confrontational approach appealed to a growing Jewish middle class, which believed it was being treated like a scapegoat amid charges of being the cause of change, civil disturbance, and an end to traditional life as white, Protestant America had come to know it.

From its beginning, the ADL concentrated on domestic issues of concern to the Jewish community. This is not to say that the ADL felt any lack of concern for the plight of Jews in Europe, but rather, that their sympathies (and their financial contributions) for their coreligionists in other parts of the world were funneled through B'nai B'rith. The focus of the ADL from its inception was on the safety and fair treatment of America's Jews.

In striking back at the stereotypes that had played so fearsome a role in the Leo Frank case, the ADL lobbied against those stereotypes and their dissemination by newspaper advertising that used expressions and phrases to discriminate against Jews in housing, resort accommodations, and employment. For example, ads included such expressions as, "clerical jobs for young Christian women," "We do not rent to persons of the Hebrew faith," and "delightful house available in Christian neighborhood." The Hebrew exclusion clause was commonplace in ads for resorts in the New England area and the mountain regions of New York State (Cohen and Wexler, 1989: 2, 9). One of the narrators in this third volume was David Rose, who started his legal career in 1932 as a representative of the ADL in Boston, and concluded it in New York City as chairman of the ADL's national executive committee. The ADL was successful in persuading several major American newspapers—including the Jewish-owned *New York Times*—to change their advertising policies. Nevertheless, Jewish communities in several Southern towns felt a visceral fear after the Frank case that persisted for decades, and it mandated silence on their part about controversial issues, especially race. Having felt the sting of lynching, however, the ADL joined black civil rights organizations in successfully battling and passing antilynching laws (Moore, 1981:111; Belth, 1979:43–44).

The success of the ADL in their direct interventions into biased advertising and restrictive rental policies played a prominent part in transforming the country's attitude toward matters of fairness and discrimination, but it also triggered serious ambivalence among other Jews. Adolph Kraus, president of B'nai B'rith, and Sigmund Livingston took the lead in the struggle over newspaper advertising. But both men were elitists, of German Jewish background, who found much to dislike in the new *Ostjuden*, and sometimes even publicly criticized them for their uncouth and obnoxious behavior that, allegedly, triggered antisemitic responses by the gentile community (Moore, 1981:113–14). In effect, some Jews were proclaiming their shame about other Jews, setting the stage for the much-analyzed self-hatred that preoccupied later Jewish leaders and intellectuals.

The ADL greatly enhanced its reputation for public confrontation by reacting vigorously in the 1920s to auto maker Henry Ford and the explicit antisemitism in his publication, the *Dearborn Independent*, which drew heavily on *The Protocols of the Elders of Zion*, a forgery constructed by Russian antisemites in the 1890s. One of the first admitted authors of the *Protocols* was Gottfried Zur Beek (Ludwig Mueller). His work was entitled *Die Geheimnisse der Weisn Von Zion*, 4th ed. (*The Protocols of the Elders of Zion*). Its message was supposedly an alleged secret Jewish conspiracy to conquer the world, in communion with communism and giant capitalism, thereby, ruthlessly subverting traditional Christian verities in a vengeful Jewish drive for power.

The Ford piece is a skillful send-up on the legitimacy of the *Protocols* and represents one of the first large-scale printings of the document in the United States. Norman Cohn, in *Warrant for Genocide* ([1968] 1996) provides one of the most thorough comparisons between certain sections of the *Protocols* and the possible source of much of its inflated dialogue, a work by Maurice Joly, written in 1864, and entitled *Dialogue aux enfers entre Montesquieu et Machivelli*. The Joly monograph is a thinly veiled attack on Napoleon III in the form of twenty-five dialogues, and many of its passages resemble the language found in *The Protocols of the Elders of Zion*. Ford's immense prestige as an American folk hero gave this scurrilous writing some credibility, particularly in the disturbing aftermath of World War I and the Russian Revolution of 1918.

The ADL mobilized prominent Jews and non-Jews to publicly oppose Ford's message. They formed a coalition of Jewish groups for the same purpose, and raised constant objections in the Detroit press. Before leaving his presidency early in 1921, Woodrow Wilson joined other leading Americans in a statement that rebuked Ford and others for their antisemitic campaign. A boycott against Ford products by Jews and liberal Christians also had an impact, and Ford shut down the paper in 1927, recanting his views in a public letter to Sigmund Livingston, ADL (Cohen and Wexler, 1989, n. 1). Ford came under severe pressure from government and business leaders, but contended he had no direct hand in the writing of "The International Jew." In spite of this attempt to distance himself from the material, the tract had grown to a four-volume collection before its distribution was halted in 1942.

While publicly confronting Henry Ford and the powerful Ku Klux Klan (KKK) during the 1920s and 1930s, the ADL was also restructuring itself in an effort to eliminate the remnants of its quasi-fraternal origins, and was dealing with the new leadership of Alfred M. Cohen, new president of the B'nai B'rith. Cohen, formerly president of the board of governors of the Union of American Hebrew Congregations (UAHC) represented the traditional German Jewish views (Moore, 1981:118–19). The ADL had grown increasingly independent of B'nai B'rith, which nevertheless continued to provide them with financing. By the late 1930s, the ADL and the AJC had joined forces in the battle against Nazi antisemitism and its American sympathizers, whom the ADL studied in careful detail (Cohen and Wexler,

1989:18). When World War II ended, the goals and mission of the ADL had to be reexamined in the light of a changed world and a quickly changing American scene.

THE ADL'S SECOND PERIOD: 1945 TO 1967

The end of World War II brought a series of changes to the ADL. The Holocaust had nearly eliminated Jewry in Central and Eastern Europe, its ancient heartland. But the Zionist ideal had triumphed as thousands upon thousands of Jewish refugees made their way to Palestine to begin the serious business of founding the new State of Israel. The question now became what initiatives Israel would embrace, what physical and political boundaries it would draw, and how Jews in other parts of the world, particularly the United States, would relate to it. Would Israel compromise American Jews with the old charge of dual loyalties—United States and Israel?

The ADL attempted to finesse the issue by applauding the new state, not only for its contribution to world Jewry, but for the place it was assuming among democratic governments. Just as the nations of Central and Eastern Europe had enriched the world by acquiring statehood since the mid-nineteenth-century, so, it could be argued, Israel had finally fulfilled its millennia-old destiny in 1948 (Moore, 1981:128). Just as Poland, Ireland, and Italy enjoyed the interest and support of their brethren in the United States, so it was natural for American Jews to show similar inclinations toward the new citizens of Israel, many of whom were directly related to American Jews.

In America, Jews had benefited from the wartime boom and from the continuing decline in the social antisemitism, which many American Christians had supported or at least tolerated. Overt expressions of antisemitism were now equated with Nazism and were avoided as a social embarrassment. The ADL even considered for a brief time dropping the word "defamation" from its title (Moore, 1981:123).

This increasing acceptance of Jews by U.S. society, when added to government support through the financial vehicles like the G.I. Bill, enabled many Jews to begin entering top-ranked colleges and universities, and thus preparing themselves to enter better paying professions. They were quickly gaining the occupational and economic security needed to move to the suburbs along with millions of other post–World War II families.

Increasingly, the Holocaust was seen as a major American Jewish issue, the horrifying, yet logical culmination of centuries of anti-Jewish discrimination and oppression. The major American Jewish organizations competed for preeminence in analyzing and discussing the underlying forces of prejudice and discrimination, but in the absence of any unifying structure or centralized leadership, their efforts were fragmented. This sense of individuality in the face of a common struggle was partially remedied in March 1944 with the formation of the National Jewish Community Relations Advisory Council (NJCRAC), which the ADL joined. The NJCRAC functioned as an advisory and coordinating umbrella organization fostered and financed by the Council of Jewish Federations, whose growing power in major U.S. cities stemmed from its hold on Jewish charitable purse strings. (A more extensive treatment of the NJCRAC appears in chapter six.) In 1951 the NJCRAC pressed for the creation of an all-inclusive coordinating agency, to include the AJC, the AJCg, the ADL, and the UAHC, the organizational arm of Reform Judaism in the United States. The Jewish War Veterans also were to be represented, as were fourteen of the newly formed Jewish community councils (JCCs), including the Boston, Massachusetts, JCC.

In an attempt to both unify and clarify Jewish communal activity, the NJCRAC recommended assigning accountability to the Jewish organizations based on a specific expertise, and in the process, eliminate wastage and overlapping responsibilities. The NJCRAC retained Columbia University sociologist Robert MacIver to do an organizational analysis of the Jewish organizations. MacIver's 1951 report triggered considerable debate, and some outrage, among the organizations that were part of the study. (A larger discussion of the MacIver report appears in chapter six.) Several of the Jewish agencies that were a part of the study found much in MacIver's study to praise and support, but the ADL and the AJC were deeply distressed by what they regarded as the report's clear intent to undermine their prerogatives. In 1952 they quit the NJCRAC, protesting the MacIver recommendations, and did not return to NJCRAC membership until 1964.

Nathan Belth (1979) argued the ADL's position. He feared a gradual overcentralization, "the eventual creation of a single agency," that would quietly erase the reasonable, defensible, ideological differences among the various Jewish advocacy groups, not least, those of the ADL and the AJC, who might be led where they did not wish to go, thereby risking betrayal of much of their membership in the process. Belth's complete response can be found in MacIver's Report on the Jewish Community Relations Agencies (1951:205–28).

The ADL substantially shared the concerns held by the established German Jewish community toward the new Jewish generation rising to prominence after 1945. The ADL also feared that the local chapters which it had faithfully represented, and its relationship with B'nai B'rith, would be pushed aside in a new drive by the NJCRAC to seize centralized control of the principal Jewish agencies, thereby creating something akin to a Jewish "papacy."

Deciding which policies to pursue in the late 1940s and early 1950s regarding issues of social welfare and discrimination heightened tensions between the liberal and conservative voices within the ADL. Unlike the AJC or the AJCg, the ADL was not a membership organization. The liberal influence was strongest at the ADL's local and national headquarters, and among its paid staff and volunteers who flocked in as the ADL became visibly more dynamic and activist. Both the professional staff and the volunteers were talented, dedicated, and cohesive: they enjoyed a substantial level of cooperation (Cohen and Wexler, 1989:17–18). Both the professionals and the volunteers argued that the ADL should be focused on racism and discrimination in general, for example, the deepening civil rights struggle in the black community, and not just with Jewish issues.

By contrast, the conservative influence (populated by prominent lay leaders in New York and Chicago) argued that the ADL's focus should be narrower, its energies and resources concentrated on specifically Jewish problems. Even though these lay leaders' influence was overrepresented, much of ADL policy tended to reflect the outlook of the professional staffers, that is, the full-time workers who were making the small, daily decisions by which policies were both shaped and implemented (Cohen and Wexler, 1989:25–26). The number of professionals increased in the early 1960s, particularly in the ADL's Civil Rights Commission, the cutting edge of the ADL efforts in the area of civil rights and discrimination.

The professional staffers were, however, primarily responsible for one significant misreading of history. They were deeply concerned about antisemitic hate groups and their leaders, such as Gerald L. K. Smith and his Silver Shirts, who continued to spew their distorted invective even after 1945. In reality, the influence of these fringe groups had plummeted sharply in the years after World War II and the mounting revelations about the Holocaust. But the ADL feared that these highly marginal groups might follow the historical trajectory of the former Nazi party and rebloom with new strength and visibility. So, the ADL infiltrated these groups, tracked their planning, and exposed them to a broad American public, which knew little about their existence (Cohen and Wexler, 1989:18). David Rose later admitted ruefully "that many of our concerns were magnified in our own minds, based upon hysteria" (18). However, this infiltration of fringe groups and the systematic collection of personal data would, several years later, bring both praise and condemnation to the ADL. The increasing popularity of these fringe groups in late-twentieth-century America has vindicated the extensive research and tracking activities the ADL undertook after World War II. It may have been overzealous at the time, but the ADL did compile a large collection of data that is proving useful today in understanding the historical structure and function of these groups.

The political climate had changed since the 1930s. No longer were Jews isolated in American life; they had acquired allies. The post–World War II economic boom had lifted many Jews into the ranks of the middle class, while the Holocaust, the birth of Israel, and the liberal Truman Administration provided the political force to consolidate economic change. Meanwhile, Jews were concerned about the separation of church and state, about prayer and the teaching of religion in public schools, and about possible tax benefits for religious schools (Cohen and Wexler, 1989:21).

After 1945, it became possible to pursue legislative remedies, not merely representation, in discussions and appeals to the Christian conscience. In 1948 the AJCg, with its Commission on Law and Social Action (CLSA), led other Jewish organizations in pressing for the Fair Employment Practices Commission (FEPC). Judge A. K. Cohen of the Boston ADL was appointed to the three-member FEPC board. The American labor movement joined the vigorous lobbying for the FEPC, arguing successfully that discrimination because of age or sex must be banned. Eventually, discrimination in accommodations and employment were also included as a part of the charter of the FEPC ban (Cohen and Wexler, 1989:15–16).

A turning point for the ADL was its decision in the mid-1950s to join other human relations agencies in filing an *amicus curiae* suit in the *Brown vs. Board of Education* case, in which the U.S. Supreme Court decided during its 1954 session to finally outlaw segregation in schools. By throwing the influence and resources of the liberal Jewish community behind the black struggle to enter the American mainstream, the ADL was reaffirming its own traditions and beliefs, while declaring its support for the broad, liberal segment of American society that opposed discrimination.

But the ADL's newly liberal position upset many of its Southern supporters, isolated as they were among whites in whom antisemitism and racism were more pronounced than elsewhere in the country; no one had forgotten the Leo Frank lynching. The ADL's legal support of *Brown vs. Board of Education* had fostered controversy in its own ranks. In spite of this internal dissension, the ADL became increasingly involved in the black civil rights struggle from the 1950s forward as its Civil Rights Commission attacked segregation in education, housing, and employment.

THE ADL'S THIRD PERIOD: 1967 TO THE PRESENT

The ADL, like the AJC, reached a point where it shifted its attention from principally intercommunity concerns to those issues that directly related to Jewish welfare. This shift in emphasis was triggered for the ADL in the same way it had happened for other American Jews—the Six-Day War in Israel in 1967. The outbreak of war in the Middle East provided the ADL with a quintessential Jewish issue to deal with, and one that every Jew could identify with—another attempt at the destruction of the Jews in the twentieth century!

The Six-Day War in Israel galvanized every American Jewish organization into statements and actions that lent direct and unqualified support for the safety and future of the new Jewish State; the ADL became one of Israel's staunchest supporters. The ADL, like the other organizations in the field of intercommunity relations, had, by 1966, come face to face with the often volatile black separatist side of the civil rights movement. Like its sister organizations, the ADL found itself excluded from these newer organizations that had formed under the banner of a more militant, and often strident, appeal to black pride as well as black civil rights. The ADL did not abandon its coalitions in the black community, but it did shift its public emphasis to hate crimes with an emphasis on antisemitism and racism.

Over the past three decades, the ADL has broadened its original mission of fighting antisemitism to include a wide-reaching attack on all forms of prejudice and discrimination. For example, a program begun in Boston entitled "A World of Difference" has grown from occasional spots on television to a complex array of teaching devices used nationwide. A search on the Internet brought up three pages of citations on the ADL's activities in a number of areas including issues of national concern (e.g., church and state issues, the Supreme Court's decision on the KKK, and an *amicus curiae* brief upholding the conviction of Myron De La Beckwith [the murderer of civil rights leader, Medgar Evars, on June 12, 1963]), and international issues (e.g., British Heritage Magazine apologizes for antisemitic ad at ADL urging, U.S. response to Saddam Hussein, and support for a war crimes disclosure act in the case of Bosnia).

A brief history of the ADL's legal efforts can be found in the ADL *Litigation Docket*. This study highlights the activities of the ADL's legal affairs department and includes descriptions of *amicus curiae* briefs, filed before the Supreme Court (and lower courts) involving discrimination in housing and employment, sexual orientation, religious accommodation, religious displays on public property, and hate crimes. The ADL regularly publishes *ADL on the Frontline*, a monthly newsletter (formerly known as the *ADL Bulletin*, which started in 1940) that highlights current activities by the ADL around the globe on matters of terrorism, hate crimes, antisemitism, and civic and educational activities; *Law Enforcement Bulletin*, a specialty newsletter sent to law enforcement agencies throughout the United States (began publication in 1989 and is released semiannually); and *Dimensions: A Journal of Holocaust Studies*, a publication of the ADL's Braun Center for Holocaust studies.

In recent years, the ADL has written extensively about the antisemitism emanating from some black leaders, most notably the Nation of Islam and its leader Louis Farrakhan. ADL special reports include *Louis Farrakhan: In His Own Words* (1985), *Louis Farrakhan: The Campaign to Manipulate Public Opinion, A Study in the Packaging of Bigotry* (1990), *The Anti-Semitism of Black Demagogues and Extremists* (1992), *Farrakhan Unchanged: The Continuing Message of Hate, the Ongoing Record of Racism and Anti-Semitism by Louis Farrakhan and the Nation of Islam* (February/March 1994).

The ADL's mission statement has shifted gradually over the past three decades as a result of the Jewish community's expanding acceptance in American society. These changes parallel the changes seen in the AJC in chapter three. An earlier concern with actual defamation, and outright insults and warnings of exclusion of Jews, has given way to a focus on broader issues. Today's mission statement of the ADL includes confronting anti-semitism, advocating for Israel, and representing Jews around the world. Recent ADL research has included monographs on militia groups, pro-Nazi enclaves, the religious right, and Holocaust denial. ADL titles include: on militia groups, *Paranoia as Patriotism: Far-Right Influences on the Militia Movement* (1995); on skinheads, *Young Nazi Killers: The Rising Skinhead Danger* (1993); on church-state discrimination, *The Religious Right: The Assault on Tolerance and Pluralism in America* (1994); on the Nation of Islam, *Jew Hatred as History: An Analysis of the Nation of Islam's Secret Relationship between Blacks and Jews* (1993); on Holocaust denial, *Hitler's Apologists: The Anti-Semitic Propaganda of Holocaust "Revisionism"* (1993); on international issues, *Extremism in the Name of Religion: The Violent Record of the Kahane Movement and Its Offshoots* (1995); on ex-tremists, *The Freeman Network: An Assault on the Rule of Law* (1996). The ADL thus maintains a scholarly commitment to the study of prejudice, an-tisemitism, and the Holocaust, as well as tracking antisemitism and hate crimes in this country.

While David Rose may have lamented that much of the ADL's research during the 1940s on fringe groups had been a hysterical overreaction, the passage of time has demonstrated the ADL's foresight in this area. The recent surge in activity among far-right-wing groups and radical militia groups came as no surprise to the ADL. They had hung onto those historical files, and they proved useful in understanding the motivation and psychology of these latest hate groups.

At this century's end the ADL, like the AJC, is principally concerned with three issues: antisemitism, Israel, and the status of Jews around the world. It is the least explicit of all the advocacy organizations in its statements about Jewish continuity, but the "representation of Jews around the globe" is understood to subsume many of the issues surrounding Jewish identity.

THE ADL'S ORGANIZATIONAL CHARACTERISTICS

The ADL's organizational characteristics and the role they play in decision making parallel the AJC's (see chapter three). For example, first, the ADL's founders were prosperous German Jews who, like the founders of the AJC, resisted membership by, or election of lay leaders from, the East European Jews. The B'nai B'rith (ADL's parent) didn't deny membership to East Euro-pean Jews to the fraternal organization, but B'nai B'rith did deny them lead-ership roles in that organization. They reasoned that the first task of the East European Jews was to become an "American," and if possible, a prosperous American; a great many of them did!

Second, the ADL pursues advocacy goals to and for the Jewish commu-nity as well as those goals that will ensure its own organizational survival. It serves multiple constituencies involving worldwide Jewry as well as American Jewry. Like the AJC, the impact of key contributors and elected leaders carries more weight in ADL decision making than the opinions of the at-large Jewish community.

Third, the power exercised by the representative oligarchies is the same in the ADL as it is at the AJC; its organizational hierarchy is based on the same logic as the AJC. The election of officers and the selection of lay leaders for the various commissions and committees is directly comparable. The qualities of the ADL's elected lay leaders possess the same dimensions as the AJC's, namely, prominence in their respective business or professional community, a dedication to the goals and ideology of the ADL, and a willingness to participate in ADL business that may require meetings outside the person's homebase.

Fourth, the qualifications of ADL's professional leaders include education in the social sciences, social welfare, or law. The role the professionals play in decision making on formal programs and projects parallels the AJC.

Just as there are similarities, there are differences between the ADL and the AJC, and these include the following four. First, the ADL has no direct members in the same sense as the AJC or the AJCg, but it is a part of B'nai B'rith, and considers that membership its membership as well. All ADL activities are reported to B'nai B'rith members, and fund-raising by the ADL is also directed at the B'nai B'rith membership list.

Second, an unspecified donation is required to qualify for election to lay leadership. Additionally, the ADL has a voluntary contribution program involving an annual donation of $1,000. Of the ADL's funds, 35 percent comes from non-Jewish sources that include individuals, corporations, and grants.

Third, beyond a financial contribution, the ADL employs a selection criteria for electing lay leadership called the "3Ws": wealth, wisdom, and work. The first, wealth, is self-evident. The second, wisdom, may describe a prominent scholar (lay or religious) whose work on behalf of the ADL's goals would qualify him/her for an elected position. The third, work, is the dedication of the individual who is willing to advance the overall mission of the ADL through in-kind labor or extensive volunteer work. Any of these three attributes could qualify an individual for election to a lay leadership position. The ADL board of directors, and its major committees, are predominantly businessmen, bankers, and lawyers, but there is also a scattering of academics, social workers, authors, rabbis, and union officials (Leonard Zakim, ADL, interview by author, July 22, 1994).

Fourth, while the AJC describes its ideology as "centrist" in political terms, and prefers backstage diplomacy in its advocacy, the ADL's ideology has always been more confrontational, particularly when it comes to anti-semitism. The ADL leans more to the right of the political spectrum and will exert direct pressure on local and federal policy makers, and it will go directly to the press and other media in decrying incidents of antisemitism.

The ADL's consistent use of newspapers and the involvement of prominent citizens began early in its history and remains one of its primary protest techniques (Moore, 1981:108–109).

FEEDBACK MECHANISM BETWEEN THE ADL AND THE JEWISH COMMUNITY

Like the AJC, the ADL has no mandate from the Jewish community to represent it, nor does it possess any formal feedback mechanisms to determine if its actions on behalf of that community are seen as effective or even necessary. For example, attitudinal antisemitism (as reported in chapter two) has been dropping over the past three decades, yet studies of the Jewish community show a continuing sense of foreboding among some Jews about the presence (or possible presence) of antisemitism in the general community. These contradictory results leave the reader in a quandary as to what the exact status of antisemitism is in the United States, and which set of statistics the ADL focuses on.

In a recent incident, the ADL's probity about collecting data on extremist groups was called into embarrassing scrutiny. In 1993 the ADL's San Francisco office was raided by the city police looking for evidence of illegal spying on American citizens. All of the Jewish advocacy organizations and the San Francisco District Attorney came to the ADL's defense and the charges were dropped in November of 1993. But the feedback to the larger Jewish community was only through the public media (Wertheimer, 1995:72). There has been no formal attempt to evaluate the effectiveness or the direct impact of the ADL's activities in its fight against antisemitism.

In spite of the fact that the ADL has no grassroots participation in its program planning or decision making, it has tens of thousands of devoted and enthusiastic supporters. Its present employment is approximately 400, and it has an annual budget of $34.5 million. Its ideology is more conservative, or "right of center" than the AJC, but it is not possible to label it as conservative in the political sense of the word. Its ideology propels it to seek fair treatment for all persons, coupled with the belief that antisemitism is a recurring phenomenon (Zakim, ADL, interview).

Over the past eighty-three years, the ADL has matured as an organization from an explicitly elitist oligarchy to a more cosmopolitan (although, no less oligarchic) organization with worldwide interest in the prevention of terrorism, hate crimes, and prejudice (Wertheimer, 1995).

Substantial interorganizational communications take place on a daily basis between the ADL's national office and its regional offices. ADL has offices in New York City (the national office), Washington, DC, an overseas office in Jerusalem, and thirty-five regional offices throughout the United States. Communication with these offices goes on around the clock. The likelihood of an incident of hate, prejudice, or antisemitism occurring and the national office not knowing about it is not possible. However, this has a competitive side to it as well. The ADL is the most frequently thought of organization when it comes to antisemitism, and often the first to be contacted when an incident does occur. The ability of the other advocacy organizations to be heard on an incident of antisemitism is frequently overwhelmed by the ADL. Two of the three incidents reported in this study provide evidence for the strong presence and influence of the ADL.

THE BOSTON CHAPTER OF ADL

Unlike the AJC, the ADL has never commissioned a full historical treatment of itself. Deborah Moore's study (1981), although brief, is one of the best accountings to date. An equally useful corroboration for virtually everything that transpired in the ADL's history from its inception to the late 1970s can be found in Nathan Belth (1979). Belth was the ADL's respondent to Robert MacIver's report in the early 1950s and was the ADL's secretary at the time. While his book is about antisemitism in America, because of his long association with the ADL, it is considered a parallel history of the ADL as well. A great deal can be learned about the ADL, particularly at the regional level, from a seven-volume oral history project started several years ago. It reports thirty years of reminiscences by its past directors.

The Boston regional office opened in 1934, with Benjamin Epstein as its director (Moore, 1981:4). Above him was Judge A. K. Cohen, the creator and first chairman of a board of directors that would broaden ADL activities in New England; David Rose served as vice chairman.

The Boston ADL had its work cut out for it; the Great Depression, mass unemployment, a crisis atmosphere, and the rise of Nazism all combined to heighten an entrenched antisemitism during the 1930s. If Boston's Yankee variant was social, educational, and occupational exclusion, its Irish manifestation was frequently violence, with schoolboy gangs assaulting young Jews, while the police often turned a blind eye, or arrived "too late." A focal point for violence was the doorstep of Dorchester's Hecht House, a large settlement house where Jewish children were sometimes attacked. The authorities passed off these assaults as "boys will be boys," mere pranks, unworthy of serious attention (Moore, 1981:3). Two other studies are particularly useful in understanding the nature and expression of antisemitism in Boston during those years. The first is John Michalczyk (1995), and the second is Jonathan Sarna and Ellen Smith (1995:8–14). Sarna and Smith provide an extended discussion of antisemitism in Boston.

New England was populated with antisemitic resorts, most notably in the ski areas of western Massachusetts and New Hampshire, whose advertising warned Jews off with coded phrases such as "churches nearby." Nor was the notice "Gentiles Only" unknown.

Boston's antisemitism in the 1930s was fed by the popularity of Father Charles Coughlin, the radio priest, whose eagerness to blame the world's ills on Jewish bankers and big capitalists grew after 1938 (Sarna and Smith, 1995:11–12). After World War II, Boston was to acquire a homegrown version of Coughlin in the form of Father Leonard Feeney, a charismatic but openly antisemitic Jesuit priest whose highly vocal insistence that Catholicism was the only path to salvation gained him a youthful following, but also roused intense anger among Jews and Protestants (Sarna and Smith, 1995:13; Cohen and Wexler, 1989:12–15). Feeney's Sunday speeches on the Boston Common required a police presence to avert violence. His fiery rhetoric also divided a great many Catholics, who feared his oratory would stir a backlash that would block their entrance into the American mainstream. Although Feeney was excommunicated in the 1950s for violating Catholic doctrine, it came too slowly to satisfy many Jews who held strong memories of the Holocaust.

Meanwhile, organizational problems, and the turf struggles they signified, continued to plague the world of Jewish activism. Benjamin Epstein of the Boston ADL was promoted to the New York office. In a separate action, the American Jewish Conference was formed, adding another name to the long list of Jewish organizations, and adding to the divisiveness among them regarding their institutional claims. Competition was intense over funding, jurisdiction, membership, program activities, responsibilities, and credit. Some resolution was achieved in 1947, two years after the Jewish Community Council of Boston was formed; the ADL's David Rose was elected its vice president.

Rose recalled that the competing groups eventually united in the battle against anti-Jewish discrimination in admissions to higher education. The ADL in Boston was particularly concerned about discriminatory quotas in medical schools, but encountered flank attacks from Jewish groups, particularly the Jewish Community Council, which tolerated, even defended, the status quo, thus offering sustenance to the school authorities who had created these admission limitations. Rose testified to his disappointment that his alma mater, Boston University, was among those schools tilting its admission preference against Jews. Its president, Daniel Marsh, strongly opposed the FEPC, and Rose was part of a group that confronted Marsh on his opposition to the law (Cohen and Wexler, 1989:12–15).

All this was part of the sustained postwar attack by Jews on their tacit position as Boston's second-class citizens. Assaults on their children by gangs, which the police ignored, stirred a sense of terror and of ghettoization, of limiting Jews to certain neighborhoods. This was true in the more attractive suburbs as well where informal real estate restrictions were common. Jews were excluded as a matter of course from leading Boston social clubs (for example, the Union Club), where Boston's leaders met to shape the city's future. It was the same situation in top executive positions, especially in banking, finance, insurance, and the public utilities. The occasional token Jew in such companies was there largely to accommodate Jewish customers (Cohen and Wexler, 1989:10–12). Jews also were largely absent from Boston's great cultural, educational, medical, and charitable institutions, as they were from crucial political posts, those that drew votes from outside the narrowly defined Jewish constituencies of Wards 12 and 14 (Cohen and Wexler, 1989). Jews did receive a few appointive political posts, but none of great significance.

The Boston office of the ADL has an organizational structure that parallels its national office. It has twenty-four employees: ten professionals, nine support personnel, and the balance a work force augmented by numerous volunteers. New England ADL has a ninety-four-member board of directors and a thirty-member executive committee. The entire executive committee sits on the board of directors. There is no specific dollar amount for election to a board position, but the usual donation is $1,000. Additionally, the ADL voluntary contribution program in the Boston chapter called "The New England Thousand" currently has over 600 donors of $1,000 or more annually.

The Boston ADL budget is approximately $1,000,000 (contrasted with $34.5 million nationally). Boston was one of the first regional offices of the ADL and is one of its largest. Like other regional offices, New England holds special fund-raising events honoring prominent persons inside and outside the Jewish community. All funds raised ($5 million in 1997) are sent to the national office of the ADL, and the region's budget request is returned to Boston.

The similarities in the relationship between the national and chapter offices of the ADL and the AJC are so striking that many in the Jewish community see these two organizations as two sides of the same coin. For several years the AJC and the ADL conducted joint fund-raising campaigns. While the AJC is described as centrist, the ADL is more conservative.

The interorganizational communications between the ADL's national office and the chapter office is as rigorous as it is with the AJC, but the ADL in Boston appears to have greater autonomy at the chapter level, particularly on issues of antisemitism. Like the AJC, the ADL is directly responsible to its national policies on issues of antisemitism, Israel, and, increasingly, Jewish identity and solidarity.

If the history and the organizational characteristics of the AJC and the ADL follow almost parallel paths, the same cannot be said of the American Jewish Congress and the Jewish Community Relations Council. There are significant differences between the historical and organizational characteristics of the AJCg and the other two national organizations, and there are several similarities between the AJCg and the JCRC.

_____ *Chapter 5* _____

The American Jewish Congress

INTRODUCTION: 1916 TO 1922

The years between 1916 and 1920 were the American Jewish Congress's (AJCg) temporary period prior to becoming a permanent organization in 1922. By 1916 approximately two million East European Jews had taken up permanent residence in the United States, joining the one and a half million who were already here. The Jewish organizations that would help these new arrivals make their adjustment from old-world ways to American ways were undeniably generous with their help and money. Yet, for all the success these *Ostjuden* enjoyed in their new country, the established Jewish organizations did not see them as capable of holding elected lay leadership positions in their organizations.

These newly arrived Jews from Eastern Europe were determined that their voices (often radical in tone) would be heard in some formal organizational way. Europe was in the third year of World War I, and the United States was just months away from formally entering it. Once again the Jews of Europe, particularly in Russia, were suffering disproportionately from the anguish of war. America's *Ostjuden* were prepared to help their European cousins just as the German Jews of an earlier generation had come to the aid of the victims created by the 1903 Kishiniv pogroms. This time, however, there was a major difference. The German Jews had helped the afflicted Jews of Russia sincerely and quickly, but it was from the safety of distance that the expression "coreligionists" was created. This generation of East European–bred American Jews frequently were directly related to the Jews being persecuted in Europe; these victims of tyranny were family.

In the United States, Sanders's "downtown Jews" (1969) were moving from peddling and working the sweatshops of the garment district to mercantile ownership and prosperity in other fields as well. They chafed under the disdain they encountered from the more elite, settled German Jews who had preceded them to America. Democracy was the watchword of these most recent arrivals, and they embraced the accompanying "Americanizing" it entailed with boisterous enthusiasm.

Organizers of this new Jewish congress in 1916 included the charismatic Rabbi Stephen S. Wise (who had issued several calls for such a congress), Bernard G. Richards, Rabbi Judah Magnes, a social activist and radical organizer, and Louis D. Brandeis, who would serve as the first head of the new organizing committee (Frommer, 1978:51–112). Their desire to form a broadly representative Jewish congress to provide more than financial support to the beleaguered Jews of Eastern Europe was in sharp contrast to the more elite character of the ADL and the AJC. These early founders believed that Jews everywhere had the fundamental right to live their lives unfettered by tyranny, to practice their professions, and to participate in the daily life of their communities free of harm or prejudice. Lastly, the founders of the AJCg pointedly rejected the organizational structure adopted by the AJC, a closed committee, or the ADL, a closed membership of only a few prominent members drawn from the B'nai B'rith. They consciously chose an organizational structure that hewed closely to a democratic form of governance.

The AJCg original organizational strategy focused on four objectives: first, taking the initiative, not laying low; second, relying on the force of massive Jewish activism, not the influence of a handful of prominent individuals; third, appealing to a conscious Jewish identity, not appeals to gentile sensitivities and misgivings; and fourth, emphasizing those issues that would yield far reaching political change, not simply maintaining the conservative status quo (Frommer, 1978:63).

This activist strategy disturbed the leaders of the AJC and B'nai B'rith: first for fear of an antisemitic backlash in response to such aggressive public stances, and then by the inherent threat it presented to the German Jewish prevailing domination of American Jewish politics. Another Jewish organization could mean disunity and dispersion of Jewish representation that could split or even dissipate the power base of such established German Jews as Louis Marshall, Jacob Schiff, and Cyrus Adler. Marshall refused to join any organization that involved a new "Jewish Congress," whose goals, and radicalism, he sharply rejected. Marshall sent Richards a tightly packed thirteen-paragraph letter on March 16, 1916. He told Richards that he would not join an organizing effort that would result in an American Jewish Congress. Marshall's letter emphasized two major themes: first, that such a congress constituted a breach of faith with the AJC on the part of the new congress's organizers for even raising the idea of another organization that would represent Jews; and second, the fear that quiet diplomacy and reasoned debate would be converted into mass meeting disruptions whose end result would be immeasurable harm to the American Jewish community and to the efforts of all right-thinking men to help assuage the misery of Jews in Europe. In addition to his refusal to support this new congress, Marshall included a carefully worded defense of his own American Jewish Committee (AJCg Archives. Marshall to Richards letter, March 16, 1916. Box 1).

In spite of this conservative resistance, the American Jewish Congress continued to build membership strength. It acquired all 50,000 members of the fledgling (and financially struggling) American Zionist Movement. The AJCg's growing membership frequently included a variety of radicals, socialists and labor unionists (Frommer, 1978:64–65). The Zionist presence and influence was substantial from the AJCg's first days. It was only after a reorganization in 1928 that other voices began to be heard (Chanes, 1994:8).

The United States entered World War I in April 1917, and President Wilson made the unprecedented request of the organizers of the AJCg that they postpone its formal opening until the war ended. The AJCg executive committee accepted Wilson's plea, and the American Jewish Congress formally opened in mid-December 1918 as a temporary organization. The newly formed AJCg selected nine delegates to participate in the Paris Peace Conference of 1919. In Paris the AJCg's delegates argued, with some success, for minority treaties that would help safeguard the Jews in Czechoslovakia, Poland, Rumania, and the new "successor states" of Central and Eastern Europe. The founders of the American Jewish Congress rightly assumed that the bitter ethnic and religious rivalries (that had existed, in some cases, for centuries) in these regions virtually ensured discrimination against minorities by their new governments, unless legal restraints were enacted (Frommer, 1978:110).

Their official presence at the Paris Peace Treaty talks gave the newly formed American Jewish Congress an opportunity to make several demands in a recognized international assembly. The delegates from the AJCg made five demands: (1) the right of refugees to return and become citizens of the new states; (2) legal equality for all citizens, no matter their race, religion, or nationality; (3) minority representation in the various parliaments; (4) the right of minorities to use their own languages and manage their own communal organizations; and (5) no religious discrimination. There was, however, little optimism among Jewish activists here or abroad regarding the potential effectiveness of these measures, since they lacked any enforcement powers. The delegates returned to the United States and, in true democratic fashion, adjourned *sine die* (Tenofsky, 1979:63).

Less than three years later, in 1922, the organizers of the AJCg decided it had to continue the defense of Jewish interests overseas by establishing itself as a permanent institution. But being a temporary organization that had represented the U.S. government at well-financed postwar peace talks was a very different thing from attempting to carry on those same demands from a considerably less secure financial base. From its first days as a permanent organization, the AJCg was plagued by a persistent shortage of funds with which to carry out its mission to the Jewish people.

The AJCg goals evolved over the same three historical periods as those of the AJC and the ADL. The first period, from 1922 to 1945, emphasized the plight of international Jewry; specifically, the Jews of Eastern Europe. The second period, between the end of World War II (1945) and the Six-Day War in Israel (1967), marked the formation of the AJCg's highly respected Commission on Law and Social Action (CLSA). The third period, 1967 to the present, parallels the initiatives pursued by the AJC and ADL, that is, emphasis on intergroup and intercommunity activities.

THE AJCg'S FORMATIVE PERIOD: 1922 TO 1945

The AJCg began with a strongly Zionist and Eastern European orientation, and only in the late 1920s did it shift its primary attention from the Jews of Russia, Poland, and Rumania to Jews in the United States. The AJCg's plans to re-form itself as a permanent organization met with the same divisiveness and antipathy from the other Jewish organizations it had encountered in its earlier, temporary years. But, in the United States, federal and state legislation, courts of law, and public opinion could be used to confront antisemitism in politics, housing, higher education, and employment.

The AJCg rightly concluded that antisemitism in America had a relatively shallow growth-history and one that lacked the political/ideological backing antisemitism had enjoyed in Europe. The AJCg reasoned that antisemitism would be gradually erased through education, the force of reason, and the enlistment of people of goodwill in search of real solutions to discrimination. These proved to be naive assumptions. This strategy of education, goodwill, and reason was first enunciated in 1917 by H. Pereira Mendes, a leading Sephardic rabbi (Frommer, 1978:497–98), but it proved inadequate in the face of the notorious "blood libel" incident in Massena, New York, in 1928. In that case, local Jews were accused of kidnapping a gentile child and using his blood for religious purposes. The accusation attracted national attention, but when the child reappeared (unharmed) several days later, city officials issued only a mild apology to the Massena Jewish community. (See also Dinnerstein, 1994:101.)

From its first days as a permanent organization, the AJCg was hampered by a persistent lack of funds with which to organize extensive educational and legal campaigns. But their activities were hampered also by the constant disagreements between the religious and secular segments of the Jewish community as to just what was in the best interests of America's Jews. For example, resolutions for a program of uniform Jewish education were rejected because of internal bickering, as was the concept of "uplifting Jewish ethics and values in modern society." Even the issue of the Ku Klux Klan (KKK) couldn't bring harmony to the AJCg in their attempts to combat domestic antisemitism.

During the 1922 presidential election, the AJCg wanted both the Republicans and the Democrats to make a public rebuttal of the antisemitic diatribes of the KKK. The disagreement over the wording and even the necessity of asking for such a declaration created so much upheaval in the AJCg that one of its leaders, Samuel Untermeyer, threatened to resign. It wasn't a question of rebutting the KKK, but it was, in Untermeyer's opinion, undignified and uncouth to stoop to such tactics. In his estimation, "the American Jew can well afford to treat their [KKK] assaults with the silent contempt they deserve and to allow such sporadic outcroppings of bigotry and intolerance to exhaust themselves and to die the death they deserve" (Frommer, 1978:501–3).

In spite of this persistent lack of funds and the divisiveness in the Jewish community, the AJCg decided in 1929 to undertake vigorous countermeasures to combat economic and educational discrimination against Jews in the United States. But their commissions on economic discrimination and on discrimination in education met with only lukewarm reception in the larger Jewish community. A great many Jews were reluctant to support these measures ideologically or financially. By the early 1930s, a crisis atmosphere had begun to build everywhere as the world headed into a global economic depression and the rise of Nazism in Germany.

In 1933 the AJCg mission statement emphasized five initiatives: Zionism, that is, helping build a Jewish national home in Palestine; encouraging Jewish consciousness; fostering cooperation among Jewish organizations; providing relief for impoverished or destitute Jews; and protecting Jewish interests everywhere in the world by fighting discrimination and gaining equal opportunity. In effect, the congress was leaving behind its narrow focus on Eastern European Jewry and developing a global, and especially American, orientation in its advocacy efforts (AJCg Archives. Constitution and bylaws, 1933–1968. Box 1). The outbreak of World War II refocused all of the JAOs' attention on the horror unfolding in the death camps in Poland.

By 1943 the revelations that had begun as rumors that Jews were being gassed and incinerated in Poland (and elsewhere) were being confirmed by authoritative, firsthand accounts. Those reports and telegrams sparked the AJCg into action, just as it had the other American Jewish organizations. As Jews and as organizations, they individually and collectively appealed to Capitol Hill, to the White House, and to the State Department, but their efforts at saving any of Europe's Jews proved ineffective. Two excellent sources detail the efforts and failures of America's Jewish organizations to do more to save Europe's Jews during World War II. The first is a twenty-two volume collection entitled *Archives of the Holocaust*, edited by Henry Friedlander and Sybil Milton (1993). It is a massive collection of correspondence from and between the Jewish advocacy organizations dating from the early 1930s to the end of World War II, and beyond. The second is *American Jewry during the Holocaust*, edited by Seymour Maxwell Finger (1984). Both of these collections are painful but necessary reading if one is to fully appreciate the conflict embedded in the various attempts at action by the Jewish community during this time.

Both collections relate in minute detail the realization, frustration, and inability of American Jewish leaders to do anything to stem the disaster occurring daily in the death camps of Eastern Europe. This is not to excuse the timidity and unwillingness of several of the leaders of prominent American Jewish organizations to believe what was placed before them in the way of evidence; it was tragic by any measure. One of the more tragic incidents that took place during this time was the Reigner telegram (by way of the British Jewish community) to World Jewish Congress president, Stephen S. Wise, detailing the extent of the killing then going on in Poland. Its revelations were so horrific that most authorities (on both sides of the Atlantic) doubted its authenticity. Gerhart Reigner recalls that disaster of inaction in poignant detail in his essay in Seymour Finger's collection (1984:1–16, app. 5). It is not surprising to find two sides to this story of rescue, given the complexity of the times. In the well-known study by David S. Wyman, *The Abandonment of the Jews* (1985), Wyman castigates the American and British governments, as well as the Jewish organizations for their callous disregard of the Jews. A recent publication takes a different stand altogether, William D. Rubinstein's *The Myth of Rescue: Why the Democracies Could Not Have Saved More Jews from the Nazis* (1997).

All three of America's Jewish defense organizations essentially accepted President Roosevelt's wartime strategy of disregarding the interests of minorities, be they Jewish, African American, or Japanese American, while striving for an all-inclusive coalition of allied forces throughout the world. Roosevelt and his advisers argued that victory in Europe would solve all problems, and that any special consideration granted to Jews, even those being annihilated in the Holocaust, could stir up antisemitism here and abroad (Wyman, 1985).

During the 1930s and 1940s, the AJCg undertook to fight antisemitism through its own committee on defamation. It established the committee's mission as one of combating anti-Jewish sentiment and anti-Jewish organizations using formal legal action. This was done in an effort to foster an improved understanding of different aspects of Jewish life in America. The AJCg mounted a highly visible campaign to refute the antisemitic preaching of the radio priest, Father Charles Coughlin. While both the AJC and the ADL were equally troubled by Father Coughlin's pronouncements, they would not publicly join the AJCg or support the AJCg's efforts for ideological reasons (Frommer, 1978:516–17). The AJC and the ADL felt that the AJCg had overstepped its boundaries by moving into the area of antidefamation, for which each of these other organizations was already well known.

In 1942, however, the Council on Jewish Federations (the fund-raising arm of Jewish welfare) attempted to form a single operating body to fight antisemitism in America. It would comprise four Jewish organizations: the AJC, the ADL, the AJCg, and the Jewish Joint Distribution Committee. It did not really establish itself as a collective force against antisemitism, because the AJC and ADL were adamantly opposed to such a collective effort. In the end, the AJCg went its own way and established a commission on antisemitism. Once again, divisiveness had dictated the direction of Jewish advocacy.

The American Jewish Congress also sponsored formal, legal action against the stringent quotas on Jewish admissions imposed by a host of America's prestigious universities (Boston and Harvard Universities and Wellesley College). The ultimate effect of these restrictive student admission quotas and faculty hiring restrictions was to drastically retard the placement of Jewish faculty and students, thereby curtailing Jewish entry into the upper classes of American life. Jews were also being systematically excluded from employment in higher paying prestige jobs, and thus, prevented from progressing too far up the American social ladder. During this time the AJCg was also addressing the parallel problem of employment advertising that was aimed at Christian applicants and often specifically excluded Jews from consideration.

After World War II, the AJCg formed the Council on Community Inter-Relations (CCI). It was headed by the social scientist Kurt Lewin, who had fled Nazi oppression in Germany and resettled in America. He resumed his earlier studies of aggressive behavior in social groups while in the employ of the AJCg (Frommer, 1978:521–22). Many of Lewin's basic observations about aggression and intergroup relations can be found in Lewin, Lippitt, and White (1939:230–60).

The CCI program focused on the "group life" aspect of Jewish/non-Jewish relations as distinguished from the individual or the national/political aspects of antisemitism; it involved a very different methodology than previously used in researching intergroup relations. The CCI undertook short-range projects on Jewish defense and anti-Jewish friction; medium-range projects, devoted to determining the underlying causes of particular anti-Jewish incidents and then creating programs to alleviate the accompanying tension; and long-range projects that Lewin hoped would provide greater insights into the larger forces underlying group friction. Lewin's group would then develop therapeutic action to deal with the issues. The way in which the CCI functioned under Lewin's direction provides valuable insights into how decisions were made by the AJCg in those days, and the role social science research would ultimately play in the success of another effort of the AJCg, the Commission on Law and Social Action (CLSA).

THE AJCg'S SECOND PERIOD: 1945 TO 1967

By mid-1945 the war in Europe was drawing to a close and the AJCg was preparing to move into its second period and to the formation of its best-known commission, the Commission on Law and Social Action. In 1945, the year of final victory over Germany, the brilliant jurist and legal writer

Alexander Pekelis was leading the AJCg. Under his guidance, the AJCg established the Commission on Law and Social Action (CLSA), a major innovation that soon became the AJCg's vanguard mechanism for attacking discrimination and prejudice. It quickly became well known for its legal advocacy in attacking antisemitism and for its support of civil rights cases that encompassed a variety of complaints by other minority interests, not just those of America's Jews (Frommer, 1978:522).

Pekelis believed the other Jewish organizations were fighting antisemitism backwards. Rather than throwing a lot of resources at each and every offense, it made more sense to secure a comprehensive approach to the situation. The end result of Pekelis's policy was to carefully pick situations that could be won and, at the same time, possessed larger, more general characteristics of discrimination. The win would blunt the societal impact of discrimination in its most broadly understood meaning, again, not just for the Jews. Pekelis held "[t]he conviction that legal skills, social science training and the capacity for social action must be joined if specific tasks are to be defined intelligently and pursued successfully" (Konvitz, 1950:226).

Led by an executive committee and bolstered by a professional staff, the CLSA was careful to avoid wasteful commitments on legal cases that seemed likely to be irrelevant to broader questions of discrimination. Instead, the CLSA picked its targets carefully in its efforts to promote equality and civil liberties. It emphasized reaching beyond antisemitism, defamation, and discrimination directed only against Jews, to combat racism in general (Tenofsky, 1979:68). The AJCg realized that these issues were interconnected; that the avowed racist was very often the avowed antisemite, and vice versa. The CLSA subsequently forged important alliances with other civil rights organizations such as the National Association for the Advancement of Colored People (NAACP) and the American Civil Liberties Union (ACLU).

The AJCg frequently launched "test cases," not so much in hopes of winning (particularly in the South where judges were notoriously conservative), but rather in the course of establishing a process for making claims, setting legal parameters, and laying the foundation for later cases. Its other legal mechanism was frequently the *amicus curiae*, or "friend of the court," which were supportive legal briefs filed to serve similar functions. The AJCg's success in the use of *amicus curiae* briefs was exceptional (Svonkin, 1995:242–45; Tenofsky, 1979:76).

Frank Sorauf examined *amicus curiae* cases from 1920 to 1966 and found that the CLSA (formed only in 1945) had filed twenty-four *amicus* briefs, while the NAACP had only filed fifteen *amicus* briefs since its founding in 1909. During this same time period, the ACLU won 51.9 percent of its cases (Tenofsky, 1979:215).

By comparison, the AJCg won 65 percent of the cases it brought, and in the process, was often hobbled by inadequate financing. The AJCg attributed this exceptional *win* record on the part of the CLSA to five factors: (1) a continuous flexibility in adjusting to changing social circumstances; (2) the adoption of a systematic, step-by-step approach to every case it considered; (3) its wealth of experienced staffers and legal researchers; (4) a carefully enunciated set of rules about selecting only promising cases; and (5) a cohesive and highly centralized organizational structure. Sorauf (Tenofsky, 1979:216–220) suggested that the overall success of the AJCg can be attributed to five things: (1) a well developed staff with expertise and long experience in questions of separation of church and state; (2) the one-step-at-a-time philosophy that reflected the CLSA's thinking on educating as well as winning; (3) its adherence to its own rule that it would only litigate the most promising cases, not every case with which it came in contact; (4) the importance of controlling information (This factor allows the AJCg to build a case slowly, but with absolutely accurate information. In twenty of the twenty-two cases the AJCg participated in, it was involved from the very earliest days of the case.); (5) group cohesion. No local branch would take a position contrary to the national offices on an issue. None of the AJCg's local chapters would consider litigating without support of the national office.

The CLSA made extensive use of the social-science data gathered by Kurt Lewin and his research on group behavior. Lewin's findings provided a solid alternative to the traditional mythology that typically surrounded matters of race and religion. It was Lewin's research that successfully raised issues linking prejudice and economic inequity. Lewin's researchers worked closely with the CLSA lawyers, and with the AJCg's social activists at the local, grassroots level, where complaints with potentially large-scale implications usually started. These collaborations between CLSA and Kurt Lewin produced litigation that generally extended beyond Jewish interests alone. The CLSA contended that Jews were best protected as individuals when they were safeguarded as a group. This reasoning made it essential to enter the struggle of other minorities who were being treated unjustly as well. Such was (and continues to be) the nature of pluralist societies, and it led the CLSA to legally confront groups such as the Ku Klux Klan, as well as to pursue civil rights violations in alliance with the federal government.

One of the AJCg's best known legal victories came about as a result of the efforts of the CLSA. It was a series of test cases the CLSA mounted from 1945 onward against the explicit exclusion of blacks from the 23,000-unit Stuyvesant Town housing development on Manhattan's Lower East Side (Tenofsky, 1979:78–86). Already a huge real estate developer in the 1930s, the Metropolitan Life Insurance Company had used federal and private money to replace rotting tenements with mass housing development like the Stuyvesant project.

The Stuveysant Town case spawned dozens of ancillary suits charging discrimination in various forms, including taxpayers' suits and the abridgment of Fourteenth Amendment rights. A great many of these cases were success-ful, and each of them added a little more ammunition to the original test case. These suits were as much educational advocacy as they were legal bat-tles. This was an advocacy measure that the AJCg and the CLSA would use repeatedly in the 1950s and 1960s.

Either on its own initiative or in company with other advocacy groups such as the ACLU and the NAACP, the CLSA sponsored several legal suits to break the ban on renting to black tenants. Racial discrimination in hous-ing was unlawful, it argued, particularly when federal money was involved. No matter, contended the insurance company. The decisive factor was that Stuyvesant Town would be managed as a private enterprise, and constitu-tionally no one could dictate the company's rights to choose its own tenants (Tenofsky, 1979:81).

This traditional view prevailed for years, despite legal suits attacking it in whole or part. One appeal even reached the U.S. Supreme Court, but failed. Nevertheless, public opinion was being affected, though private property was virtually noncontrollable until the late 1960s, when the laws changed regarding fair housing and private ownership. The courts reversed them-selves on Stuyvesant Town in 1968, declaring that private housing could not legally impose racially based restrictions on prospective tenants.

This case demonstrated the legitimacy and influence that the AJCg's legal advocacy had gained over the previous half century. In some cases, entire sec-tions of an AJCg brief were restated in Supreme Court decisions. This often happened in cases regarding the issue of separation of church and state, where contemporary sociological and psychological data were brought forward in cases involving religion in public schools, just as the CLSA had done in those cases involving racial and religious discrimination (Tenofsky, 1979:216).

Several other examples highlight the extent of the CLSA's legitimacy in le-gal circles. Justice Felix Frankfurter had only a CLSA brief as virtually his sole source of argument in a case regarding religious expression in the Illi-nois public schools. Similarly, Chief Justice Earl Warren cited a brief from the CLSA in opposing an argument for school prayer. A CLSA brief was prominent in a case of church and state relations, concerning the applicabil-ity of unemployment compensation for Seventh Day Adventists who were dismissed for refusing to work on Saturdays. As a final example, the CLSA brought suit to end the free distribution of Gideon Bibles to New Jersey school children; this practice of distributing free Bibles in public schools was later ended throughout the country (Sorauf, 1963).

The emergence of black separatism in the civil rights movement in 1966 when coupled with the Six-Day War in Israel in 1967 affected the AJCg no less strongly than it had its sister organizations, the AJC and the ADL. But unlike those two organizations, the AJCg had always been a supporter of Zionism dating back to its founding in 1922. A substantial number of its members had come from Zionist organizations, and the formation of the

State of Israel after World War II was the realization of a long-nurtured Zionist dream. However, the domestic future of the AJCg was more uncertain at this point in time than it was for either the AJC or ADL.

THE AJCg'S THIRD PERIOD: 1967 TO THE PRESENT

The AJCg once again begun shifting its goals in the mid-1960s. Its bylaws began placing heavy emphasis on activism in many forms. These included the monitoring of church-state relations, of far-right-wing political groups, of Moscow's pressures on Soviet Jews, and of the Arab Boycott of Israel. The AJCg also monitored political events in West Germany, in the United Nations, and in the realm of human rights. Liberal humanitarianism was the theme, plus the central thesis that antisemitism in America stemmed from larger social problems, which once removed or reduced would benefit Jews by making the country a safer more equal place to live for everyone.

Along with this shift in goals, outside observers noted that perhaps the AJCg's halcyon days had been reached by the late 1960s, in part, because of the final vindication of the CLSA's struggle with the Metropolitan Life Insurance Company and their exclusionary policies in their sprawling housing developments in New York City. Both Jack Wertheimer (1995) and Stuart Svonkin (1995) commenting on the "golden age of intergroup activity" in the Jewish advocacy field, that is, 1945–1967, suggest that the major issues that the AJCg was established to address had largely been achieved by the late 1960s.

The AJCg has been a prominent voice in the decades-long struggle over the separation of church and state. In 1984 it founded the Institute for Jewish-Christian Relations. The institute seeks to promote dialogue on theological issues between Jewish and Christian scholars. It focuses on theological and scholarly activities such as interpreting the scriptures and Mosaic law in Judaism and Christianity. It meets periodically, and when it does it produces meeting proceedings.

An ironic legal success was the AJCg's response to affirmative action. While affirmative action was an important step toward a more equal society, the AJCg voiced another interpretation to the new act's efforts to balance racial and gender inequality in American education and employment. For America's Jews, affirmative action was a variant of the old quota system of the late 1940s and the 1950s that had denied Jews entry into colleges (both as students and as faculty) and jobs because of restrictive limitations put on the number of Jews that would be admitted or hired. Because of this history, the AJCg found itself in the forefront of the legal battle surrounding the admission of Allan Bakke to the University of California medical school at Davis (1973).

The AJCg argued correctly that the University of California at Davis had no previous record of discrimination to overcome since it was a brand new school at the time Bakke sought admission. Also, Bakke could not be denied one of the unfilled minority slots in favor of a less qualified black applicant due to the school's affirmative action policy. The AJCg's position (in league with six other Jewish organizations) prevailed, and the U.S. Supreme Court ruled 5–4 in favor of Bakke; he was admitted. More recently, the AJCg's resistance to affirmative action can be seen in its support of the decision by the U.S. Supreme Court to not hear an appeals-court ruling that had barred the law school at the University of Texas from considering race in admissions (see Douglas Lederman and Stephen Burd, "High Court Refuses to Hear Appeal of Ruling That Barred Considering Race in Admissions," *Chronicle of Higher Education*, July 12, 1996; Arch Pudington, "What to Do about Affirmative Action," *Commentary*, June 1995). Conservative observers increasingly foresaw a substantial erosion, even elimination, of affirmative action in education and employment over the next several years. As of this writing, affirmative action quotas based on race and gender in education, employment, and federally funded building contracts have been struck down in California and Washington State.

The AJCg faced a dual problem going into the 1980s. Not only had it participated in America's maturing into a country that was less restrictive and more accepting of differences (in no small part because of the efforts of the CLSA), but its survival as a formal organization serving anyone's needs was again in jeopardy because of its chronic lack of funds. The AJCg has only a handful of substantial givers (approximately fifty). Overall, its membership base, while large (approximately 37,000), is not as prosperous as the donors to the AJC and the ADL. Of the three national Jewish advocacy organizations in this study, the AJCg is the smallest with forty employees on its national staff, and an annual budget of approximately $7 million. What delineates a "member" in the JAOs is always something of a mystery rendering total counts suspicious.

From its inception in 1922 (as a permanent organization), the AJCg has persistently found itself short of funds. It comes in last in fund-raising among the prominent Jewish organizations in America. On two separate occasions in 1985 and 1992, the AJCg attempted to alleviate its chronic funding problems by merging with the AJC. The negotiations ended in failure on both occasions because of substantial, and apparently unresolvable, ideological differences. The AJC was the more conservative of the two organizations, and the merger talks triggered deeply held misgivings about the idea of joining forces with the more liberal, and some suggested "radical," AJCg (Sheila Decter, AJCg, interview by author, June 24, 1994).

The AJCg does not support a research or publications effort on the scope or depth of either the AJC or the ADL. The AJCg, because of its primary emphasis on litigation, invests itself heavily in extensive legal research, little of which is seen by the general public. But the proceedings and the legal briefs of the CLSA are maintained in extensive collections. A two-volume history of the CLSA's complete proceedings is housed in AJCg headquarters in New

York City. The AJCg produces four principal publications. The first is *Judaism: A Quarterly Journal of Jewish Life and Thought*. Published since 1951, it presents scholarly articles on religious, moral, historical, and cultural concepts of Judaism. The second publication is the *AJCg—National Report*, published three times per year and devoted to a wide range of AJCg activities. The third is the *Fundamentalist Newsletter* and reports on developments and trends growing out of the fundamentalist Muslim resurgence in Arab countries, and the potential impact this carries for Jews worldwide. The fourth publication (established in 1933) is a monthly house organ that goes to the entire AJCg membership and is entitled the *Congress Monthly*. It covers general Jewish issues in short essays and articles, and includes book and film previews. The AJCg maintains an in-house library at its New York headquarters.

By 1993 the mission statement of the AJCg was broadened to emphasize the protection of democratic institutions in the United States and Israel, while strongly backing the separation of church and state in the United States, and the continued pursuit of the peace process in Israel with its Arab neighbors. The growing cultural skirmishing in the United States led the AJCg to support programs of social and economic justice for minorities, women's social and economic equality, and the acceptance of cultural diversity, while remaining vigilant in its opposition to antisemitism, racism, and bigotry in general. The AJCg also remains solidly behind specifically Jewish concerns, for example, the institutional, cultural, religious, and communal aspects of being Jewish in America, and the need to find creative ways to express Jewish identity, ethics, and values.

The American Jewish Congress is struggling to have its voice heard in the world of Jewish advocacy. Like the AJC and the ADL, it has embraced three fundamental issues in the closing days of the twentieth century: antisemitism, Israel, and Jewish continuity. It is ideologically predisposed to address these issues from a legal stance. In this regard it differs from the AJC and the ADL. Both of those organizations will join with the AJCg in legal confrontations as circumstances dictate, but the AJCg is the Jewish advocacy organization that most frequently initiates the legal battles that will secure a point of justice.

ORGANIZATIONAL CHARACTERISTICS OF THE AJCg

The AJCg is the third member of the "big three" national Jewish advocacy organizations that were formed as Jewish defense organizations, that is, the protection of Jews from the ravages of war and political bigotry. But the leadership of the AJCg (and the subsequent impact this had on goal formation) came from a decidedly different sector of the American Jewish community. In spite of its leadership's differences from the German-Jewish personalities in the AJC and the ADL, the AJCg, as an organization, shares a number of organizational characteristics with its sister organizations. They pursue the same goals of advocacy for the Jewish community, as well as their own organizational survival. First, they serve multiple Jewish constituencies, and as with the AJC and the ADL, the impact of key contributors and elected lay leaders within the AJCg carries more weight in its decision making than do the opinions of the at-large Jewish community. Second, the AJCg is a membership organization and has been since its earliest days. One of its founding principles was to be as representative of the general Jewish population as the word "congress" usually implies (Wise, 1916:4).

Early in its life, the AJCg's initial membership was greatly enlarged when it absorbed the entire membership (50,000) of the American Zionist Movement. Membership today is a highly fluid figure ranging from approximately 35,000 to approximately 50,000 (Rufner and Fisk, 1996:2410–11).

Accurate estimates of membership in both the AJCg and the AJC are difficult to pin down. While Rufner and Fisk's *Encyclopedia of Associations* (1996) and AJCg literature claim it has a membership of 50,000, *The American Jewish Year Book* (AJC, 1995:73) maintains it is closer to 35,000. The question is what is a member? Is it a fixed annual donation?; subscription to the AJCg *Congress Monthly* (or any of the other AJCg publications)?; a donation to a fund-raiser?; and so forth? Anyone who appears on a mailing list for contributions (or some other AJCg-related reason) seems potentially to count as a "member." It is unlikely that anyone in the AJCg can answer the membership questions with complete accuracy. Annual fees from members are augmented by contributions received from approximately fifty substantial donors, plus contributions that are made as a result of special fund-raising events such as recognition dinners and special topic meetings. In recent years the AJCg has augmented its operating budget with funds arising from a handful of estates and endowments bequeathed to it over the past several decades.

Third, the presence of representative oligarchies, and the exercise of power and control this facilitates, parallels the oligarchies found in both the AJC and the ADL. The AJCg's organizational hierarchy is distributed in the same patterns as the AJC and the ADL (AJCg Archives. Bylaws, parts 1, 2. Book 1). (See also chapter seven herein for a comprehensive comparison of these characteristics.) The election of officers and the selection of lay leaders for the AJCg's various commissions and committees follow the parameters of the AJC and the ADL. The qualities expected of the AJCg's elected lay leaders includes prominence in the local community and dedication to the AJCg's ideology and its overall mission.

Fourth, the qualities of its professional leaders include an education frequently based in the social sciences with an emphasis on political science and law. The importance of the professional's role in shaping programs and projects parallels that of the professionals in the AJC and the ADL.

The AJCg and the ADL and AJC differ in two significant ways. First, the AJC and the ADL lay leaders will raise funds beyond their personal contributions; this is neither expected nor encouraged on the part of the board members of the AJCg. The annual contribution necessary to qualify for consideration as an elected lay leader on the AJCg board of directors is $1,000; it rises to $1,500 for consideration as a member of the executive committee. Of this contribution, $100 represents the person's annual membership fee. The AJCg's governing council and board of directors have approximately 200 elected lay leaders, and its executive committee has approximately 50 elected lay leaders. Its formal committees are overrepresented by lawyers and constitutional law experts. Considering the AJCg's emphasis on legal redress to correct social inequities, this legal overrepresentation is not surprising. There are some business, finance, and social service professionals elected to the board as well.

Second, the ideology of the AJCg is decidedly different from the other two national organizations. It is liberal, socially active in a number of spheres, and intentionally litigious. The AJCg has enjoyed its greatest success in the courts and before federal and state lawmakers. It is just as concerned with antisemitism as its two sister organizations, but not as a thing unto itself. Rather, the AJCg views antisemitism as a manifestation of other deep-seated societal aliments. It believes that the alleviation of these systemic ailments will relieve Jews of the burden of antisemitism while it eases poverty, unemployment, and substandard housing in the larger society.

As with the AJC and the ADL, the AJCg has no direct mandate from the Jewish community to speak in its name, nor does it possess any formal feedback mechanisms to determine if its programs and activities on behalf of that community are seen as desirable or effective. Ideologically, the AJCg considers itself more *grassroots* than the other two organizations, yet persons familiar with the organization express the belief that if American Jews want to know more about what the AJCg is doing, "They should join up" (Decter, AJCg, interview).

THE AJCg TODAY

At this writing, the AJCg is directing its energies and resources at eight specific program areas: (1) a *Hasbara* (Hebrew for "public relations") program with mid-level Israeli officials that brings them to the United States to facilitate a better understanding of American Jewry; (2) a mayor's conference that takes up to fifty U.S. mayors (per year) to Israel to study, firsthand, problems that are shared by American and Israeli municipalities; (3) the conduct of an extensive litigation program on the issue of church-state relations; (4) monitoring the Nation of Islam (NOI) and its attempts to secure additional government funding for its projects; (5) the analysis of voting patterns by black and Jewish members of the U.S. Congress on issues before federal law makers, for example, affirmative action, congressional redistricting, and the minimum wage bill; (6) outreach programs to the black media, including black college newspapers, to determine what is being said about the Jewish community, and submitting material for inclusion in these media outlets that describes the Jewish community and its activities; (7) social welfare—outreach and legislative advocacy that affect both the black and the Jewish communities, for example, the minimum wage bill and the efforts by the Jewish community to improve black/Jewish relations; and (8) extending outreach and physical support to black churches destroyed in the recent burnings in the South (Phillip Baum, interview by the author, AJCg headquarters, New York, NY, July 22, 1996).

Turning to the AJCg's chapter offices, the fundamental purpose of the chapter offices is to represent the ideology and programs of the national office at the local level, and Boston does that for the AJCg. As early as 1917, James Michael Curley, then mayor of Boston, invited the nascent American Jewish Congress to Boston to discuss a variety of issues on the subject of Zionism (Sarna and Smith, 1995:95–96). During the 1930s a loosely organized "lawyer's committee" represented the AJCg's name in Boston, but little else was known about the AJCg in Boston until its formal incorporation papers were filed in 1944. A year earlier, one member of this lawyer's committee, Lawrence Shubow (ultimately, Judge Shubow of the Brookline District Court), organized a large and successful public protest against the atrocities being waged against the Jews of Europe under Hitler. The rally/protest was held at the Boston Garden auditorium, and attracted thousands of Jews from the entire New England area (Lawrence Shubow, interview by author, August 3, 1994).

In the mid-1940s Shubow cochaired the Commission on Law and Social Action (CLSA) in Boston and became the regional director of the AJCg in Boston in 1947. The Boston chapter of the AJCg has supported or directly involved itself in a host of issues including the changing racial/ethnic composition of the Roxbury/Mattapan neighborhood; the peace process in Vietnam at both the national and chapter level; the organization and implementation of a meals-to-home program for AIDS sufferers; and the sponsoring and organization of a minority student mentoring program in the Boston public schools. By contrast, during the 1980s, the AJCg took a position opposite from the other national Jewish organizations on the question of the Jewish settlements in the West Bank and Gaza. The AJCg did not believe these settlements would successfully serve Israel's peace process over the long term. The Jewish right in the United States strongly criticized the AJCg for taking what they saw as a "dovish" position on Israel's security. As events between Israel and Palestine have unfolded, these Jewish settlements and the redistribution of land have repeatedly stalled the peace process.

The Boston office of the AJCg has two professional staffers, one full-time director and one part-time professional; one part-time support person; and up to six volunteers at any given time. The elected lay leadership of the Boston chapter is a fifty-four-member board of directors and a six-member executive committee. The contribution to qualify for consideration to a board or executive committee lay leadership position is $425 annually, a portion of which is the annual membership fee. All of the AJCg chapter offices have their own CLSA group. In Boston this group numbers approximately 200 and is composed almost entirely of lawyers. The CLSA in Boston meets monthly and consistently attracts approximately 20 to 25 of the CLSA's members.

The current budget of the Boston AJCg is $125,000 (in contrast to the national budget of $7.1 million). The Boston office's budget is distributed from the New York headquarters based, in part, on the previous year's program achievements, and, in part, on the amount of contributions generated by the chapter. The chapter budget is augmented by specific fund-raising events. The struggle for money, and the impact this has on the things the AJCg can afford to do, can be seen in the example of their 1996 budget. The 1996 budget of the Boston AJCg was $125,000, down from $150,000 in 1995; a 20 percent cut in one year. This placed constraints on some of the programs sponsored by the Boston office.

The communications between the national office of the AJCg and its chapters is as frequent and varied as it is in the other two organizations. The Boston chapter has substantial autonomy on the issues and incidents it will pursue in the greater Boston community. This heightened autonomy became particularly apparent in the incident at Wellesley College (chapter nine) involving the use of the NOI's *The Secret Relationship between Jews and Blacks* (1991).

In summary, as renowned as the AJCg and its CLSA division are in the legal pursuit of civil rights, the American Jewish Congress (nationally and at the chapter level) is financially struggling to keep its head above water. While it is unlikely the AJCg will go out of business, knowledgeable sources in the Jewish organizational community do suggest that the AJCg will ultimately have to merge with one of the other Jewish organizations if it expects to continue its mission to the Jewish community. This option (merger or consolidation) is discussed in greater detail in chapter eleven.

Chapter 6

The Jewish Community
Relations Council

INTRODUCTION

The Jewish Community Relations Council (JCRC) is the least "defense" oriented of the JAOs in this study. While it was founded on the specific mission of combating local incidents of antisemitism, its mission quickly expanded to encompass larger, intercommunity social problems. This is not to suggest that it does not or would not join any protest against an egregious attack on the Jewish community; it does, and two of the three incidents reported in this study provide ample evidence of its due diligence in combating antisemitism.

The history and organizational characteristics of the JCRC (known as the Boston Jewish Community Council [JCC] until 1985) must be viewed differently from the other three JAOs in this study. First, the Boston JCRC is a local organization with an emphasis on local Jewish community issues, as contrasted with the national emphasis of the other three organizations. Boston was not only home to the nation's first Jewish Federation (in 1895), it was a city that was predisposed to the idea of a locally controlled JCC. The American Jewish Congress had some early roots in Boston when Mayor James Curley invited the AJCg to hold a meeting in Boston in 1917 prior to its formal beginning in 1922. The Boston JCC, during the 1930s, had begun shaping an organizational identity for itself separate from the Boston Jewish Federation. This was several years before the majority of Jewish Community Councils were formed in other cities in the United States in the mid-1940s.

Second, the Boston JCC expanded into an umbrella function for several other Jewish organizations, and this move was consistent with the decision in 1945 to form the National Jewish Community Relations Advisory Council (NJCRAC). Prior to this decision, each community council had operated independently as a Jewish community service organization. The local Jewish

Community Councils could thus provide a coordinating role for and in company with the several national Jewish organizations that were establishing branch or chapter offices in major U.S. cities after World War II. The Boston JCRC became an organizational model for several other Jewish councils that came into being in other U.S. cities in the late 1940s and 1950s.

Third, the JCRC must be viewed differently because its national affiliate, NJCRAC, came into existence at the behest of the Council of Jewish Federations with the general agreement of the existing Jewish Community Councils, in 1945. In the other three JAOs, the national organization came first and the branch or chapter office followed several years later. This turnabout in the order of origin had significant implications for interorganizational communications and decision making and will be addressed in greater detail later in this chapter.

In spite of the unfolding disaster in Europe, antisemitic attitudes among Americans were reaching an all-time high by 1945 (see chapter two), and the Jewish Federations around the country were doing their best to cope with antisemitism on a local level. After World War II, antisemitic attitudes and incidents dropped off in Boston just as they had everywhere else in the United States. But decades of abuse were not quickly set aside. Antisemitism remained a central issue in the mission statement of the Boston Jewish Community Council for several more years.

THE BOSTON JEWISH COMMUNITY
RELATIONS COUNCIL

During the 1930s the forerunner of what would come to be known as the JCRC in Boston was the Associated Jewish Philanthropies, a pioneering group that struggled with antisemitism in Boston, and was led by Casper Grosberg (Segal, 1985:2). The Boston Associated Jewish Philanthropies changed its name to the Jewish Community Council in April 1944, and it continued to oppose antisemitic violence that focused primarily on Boston's 70,000 Jews who were concentrated in Dorchester, Hyde Park, Mattapan, and Roxbury. The JCC pursued a strategy of fighting antisemitism that emphasized intercommunity relationships that focused on local, neighborhood issues, as well as issues that affected the entire city. The JCC would dispatch speakers, form seminars, cultivate the media, and distribute agency literature in an attempt to advance an educational attack on antisemitism. The basic assumption was that community problems could be solved if coalitions of like-minded citizens of goodwill, Jews and non-Jews alike, could be created (Segal, 1985:5–6).

These campaigns were followed in the late 1940s into the early 1950s with a challenge to the "release time" program, by which Boston public schools released Christian and Jewish students—some 85 percent of all students were eligible—from regular school classes to receive religious instruction in nearby churches and synagogues. By voting against that practice on the basis of separation of church and state, the JCRC effected a paradoxical result as the after-school enrollment in the Jewish Education Bureau's programs rose significantly (Segal, 1985:8). In the 1950s, the JCC joined a broad religious and ethnic coalition led by Father Robert Drinan, later a liberal congressman, to reform the McCarran-Walters immigration law.

In the early 1950s the AJC had initiated a campaign to eliminate the ethnic distinctions called for by the new immigration act. A lot of Americans were still uneasy about immigration and "foreigners" after the war ended. Drinan and the JAOs successfully persuaded Congress to drop the ethnic/racial codes, but (like the Jewish education issue) this, too, had a paradoxical effect. Of the 365,000 refugees brought to America, only 16 percent (65,000) were Jewish (Goldberg, 1996:129). A large number of low-level Nazis and Nazi sympathizers were brought into the United States because of the changes inserted into the final version of the law. An authoritative account of this period can be found in Leonard Dinnerstein's *America and the Survivors of the Holocaust* (1982).

By the 1960s prosperous Jews were following the classic post–World War II American migration from the inner city to the suburbs, in this case to Brookline, Chestnut Hill, Newton, and Sharon, Massachusetts. This suburbanization and resettlement of Boston's Jews began immediately after World War II and picked up speed by the late 1950s and early 1960s. The migration to the suburbs was facilitated by low-interest government mortgage loans for veterans, and by the newly formed Federal Housing Authority (FHA). But the side effects of this flood of relatively cheap money often left the elderly and poor stranded in a deteriorating core city. Boston was no exception to this pattern, and those left behind in the ethnic/racial resettlement of Roxbury, Mattapan, and parts of Dorchester were aging and poor Jews. They were frequently the parents of younger Jews who had moved to the suburbs. The war years had brought thousands of blacks north, and that included to Boston, because of its shipyards and heavy concentration of naval repair depots. Blacks had been moving into some neighborhoods of Boston in small numbers dating back to the 1940s, but a combination of rising housing costs, institutional racism in commercial banking, and the virtual unavailability of loan money resulted in very few black homeowners in the city of Boston. With the introduction of federally backed FHA loans this began to change dramatically in the late 1960s. A thorough retelling of this period in Boston Jewish history can be found in Levine and Harmon's *The Death of an American Jewish Community* (1992).

The practice of *block busting* was endemic, as unscrupulous real estate dealers resorted to blatant fear tactics to stampede Jewish homeowners into selling quickly and moving to the suburbs. Rumors abounded that the arrival of blacks would only bring increased crime, a decline in the quality of schools, and an overall deterioration in the quality of life; much of this misinformation had been started by the same real estate dealers and salesmen.

These block busting tactics were sharply focused at the remaining, often older and poorer, Jews who remained behind after the great exodus to the suburbs years earlier.

Hillel Levine and Lawrence Harmon (1992:6) show that Boston's key banks and Mayor Kevin White's city government had sought to appease aspiring black middle-class home buyers by creating a financial group called The Boston Banks Urban Renewal Group (BBURG). The banks set up a real estate zone in which blacks could buy houses with guaranteed FHA money, but they could not use this money to buy homes in other parts of Boston. In effect BBURG intended (with the blessing of the city) to create a black ghetto in the Jewish neighborhoods of Roxbury, Mattapan, and portions of Dorchester. Political leaders in South Boston, East Boston, and Boston's North End refused to allow any discussion of blacks moving into their neighborhoods, and consequently, the city and the bankers concluded that only the Jews would allow such a concentration of blacks in their neighborhoods. Some Jews could not leave, and some didn't want to in spite of the scare tactics used by real estate salesmen. Tensions between blacks and Jews rapidly escalated.

BBURG was an overly optimistic plan to provide cheap mortgage money that could be used only in a carefully delineated geographic area. The loans were federally guaranteed by the FHA, which protected the banks against any loss. But the plan conveniently ignored the reality of paying monthly utility bills. Then, there was maintenance and upkeep on an aging housing stock. These recurring expenses of home ownership when added to the cost of new roofs and furnaces frequently overtaxed the limited incomes of these first-time home buyers. Not surprisingly, expenses went unpaid, repairs were not made, and, as a consequence, the homes and the neighborhoods quickly began to deteriorate. Encouraging a black property-owning class in Boston would presumably stabilize a city whose civic leaders wanted desperately to avoid racial violence (Levine and Harmon, 1992). The presumption was badly flawed, and violence became a daily reality in these neighborhoods, much to the embarrassment of the mayor and a host of community groups.

For example, the Grove Hall area in Roxbury had been predominantly Jewish for years. In 1967, in the aftermath of successful militant black organizing efforts, the popular slogan "black power" was heard across much of the land. Racial tensions in Boston reached a peak at 5:00 P.M., Friday, June 3, 1967, in the Grove Hall area. A riot was triggered when welfare protesters refused to leave a claims office. By 9:30 P.M. thirty people had been seriously injured and over $500,000 in property damage had been done (Levine and Harmon, 1992:99–103).

The departure from Roxbury to the suburbs of an anchor synagogue, Temple Mishkan Tefila, signaled the departure of major Jewish institutions, and raised a cry of desertion among those not-so-wealthy Jews who were forced to remain behind (Levine and Harmon, 1992:58–65). The Mishkan Tefila building went through a succession of occupants and was eventually transferred for $1.00 to Elma Lewis who used the former synagogue as a fine arts school for black youths. This exchange of funds, as told by Levine and Harmon (1992), was a confrontation filled with tension and bitterness. In reality, it was more of a joke than an affront. Counsel for Ms. Lewis, Lawrence Shubow, gave Lewis the $1.00 to seal the deal, and said on reflection, "it was no big deal" (Lawrence Shubow, interview by author, August 3, 1994).

Both the JCRC and the Combined Jewish Philanthropies (CJP, the new name for the Boston Jewish Federation) were active in attempting an orderly ethnic/racial transition in the Roxbury/Mattapan neighborhood, but the sense of fear and panic was not easily overcome. The JCRC's strategy was one it had frequently used in other situations, an intercommunity coalition with an emphasis on issues that affected both the black and the Jewish communities, and the city as a whole. The basic assumption remained the same: that community problems could be solved if coalitions of like-minded citizens of goodwill, Jews and non-Jews alike, could be created. A coalition was formed with backing from church, synagogue, business, and school leaders. In company with the CJP, the JCC opened a multiservice center on Blue Hill Avenue.

The center would provide care and basic human services for elderly, often poor Jews who had been left behind and who would eventually be moved into public housing in the Brighton neighborhood and elsewhere in the greater Boston area. In a matter of two and a half years the Roxbury/Mattapan area was transformed from a bustling Jewish community to a predominately black community, accounting for the majority of Boston's 120,000 black citizens. Levine and Harmon (1992:66–91) provide an excellent discussion of how the demographics in Roxbury/Mattapan changed from 1955 to 1975.

The question of what happened, why, and whether or not the Jewish community of Roxbury/Mattapan could have been "saved" became an active and bitter debate with the publication of Levine and Harmon's book in 1992. The authors strongly suggest it was the block busting by real estate salesmen that drove Jews out of these neighborhoods and that certainly contributed to the "white flight" that occurred in the aftermath of the BBURG fiasco. On the other hand, the authors completely ignore the fact that Jews had been moving out of these neighborhoods for the suburban towns of Brookline, Newton, and Sharon, Massachusetts, since the 1930s. Of greater importance to this story is that the authors present compelling evidence that the rank-and-file Jews were let down by prominent Jewish leaders who were less concerned about Jewish welfare and safety than they were about maintaining good relations with black activists and white liberals. One attempt to soften this criticism appears in Jonathan Sarna and Ellen Smith's, *The Jews of Boston* (1995:129–62). Gerald Gam's essay, "In Search of Suburbs: Boston's Jewish District, 1843–1994," was an attempt to blunt the criticism of the Jewish communal organizations pictured in the Levine and Harmon book. It didn't accomplish that goal, but was instead an interesting and nostalgic retelling of being Jewish in Boston; in the process, however, it still avoided the sensitive issues touched on by Levine and Harmon.

Changing issues in the 1980s brought a vigorous response from the Jewish Community Council. In 1980 it established the Women's Issues Committee to deal with the question of abortion, equal pay and economic issues in general, and antisemitism in the women's movement (JCRC, 1994).

A second JCC committee undertook an examination of a host of discriminatory issues, including antisemitism, bigotry, unemployment, tax reform, health care, real estate issues, and crime and violence in Boston (JCRC 1994). Community alliances were formed around such diverse issues as care for the elderly, the immigration of Ethiopian Jewry to Israel, separation of church and state, and interfaith panels in school districts (JCRC, 1994). In 1985 the Boston JCC added "advisory" to its title to become the Jewish Community Advisory Council, to reflect its changing charter and increasing involvement with a number of other community coalitions in Boston.

The JCRC has involved itself with a number of key historical issues as well as local/community issues, for example, Sephard '92, a worldwide commemoration of the expulsion of the Jews from Spain in 1492; organized commemorations of the fiftieth anniversary of the Warsaw Ghetto uprising (April 1944); and participation in the establishment of the New England Holocaust Memorial (1996). The JCRC has also been instrumental over the past fifteen years in strengthening connections, among both Jews and non-Jews, with the State of Israel. The JCRC has sponsored and escorted tours of Israel with Boston business leaders, labor officials, and politicians. This has been an effort to learn from the Israelis more about their successful efforts with resolving urban problems similar to those that plague Boston. It has been also an opportunity to forge new economic/business relationships (Nancy Kaufman, JCRC, interview by author, July 7, 1994).

All these activities, commissions, and committees conformed to a mission statement, which has changed little since the JCRC's formalization in 1944, when its purpose was defined as strengthening "the dignity, security and integrity of Jewish life" in Boston and its environs (Segal, 1985:4–5). This entailed representing the Jewish community in intergroup relations, encouraging cooperation and harmony between Jews and non-Jews, working with Jews abroad, and strengthening civil rights. Future emphasis is likely to focus on issues of Jewish continuity, and Israel/U.S. relations (Kaufman, JCRC, interview).

ORGANIZATIONAL CHARACTERISTICS

The JCRC possesses organizational characteristics that are similar to the other three organizations. First, the JCRC pursues the same primary mission as the three national organizations, namely, an advocacy mission to the Jewish community, while assuring its own organizational survival. Its Jewish outreach is confined to the greater Boston area (Kaufman, JCRC, interview); however, because of its regular interface with the State of Israel, its collaborative efforts with that country are as highly regarded as similar collaborations on the part of the other three JAOs. Like the other three JAOs, the JCRC's key contributors and elected lay leaders have the principal impact on organizational decision making, as contrasted with any input from the at-large Boston Jewish community.

Second, the election of officers and the selection of lay leaders for the JCRC's various committees follow the same steps already seen in the other three JAOs in this study as found in the archives of the Jewish Community Relations Council of Greater Boston bylaws (adopted: March 13, 1985). The same can be said about the qualities expected in a lay leader in the JCRC, that is, professional accomplishment, community prominence, and a solid understanding of and commitment to the JCRC ideology. The qualities of the JCRC's professional staff, including educational background and the role they play in organizational decision making and program design, parallel the pattern already seen in the other three JAOs. In a similar fashion the organizational hierarchy of the JCRC exhibits the same characteristics found in the other JAOs, that is, a handful of powerful contributors occupy the very top positions in the organization.

Third, the JCRC and the ADL are alike in that they have never formally analyzed the demographics of their lay leaders. But where the ADL accedes to the similarity between its demographics and those of the AJC and the AJCg, the JCRC is not able to speculate on any similarities or differences between itself and the other organizations in this study. It has never had a reason to formally examine this dimension (Kaufman, JCRC, interview by author, July 1996).

While age and gender can be estimated by attending several meetings, it is not possible to look at a group of people in a meeting (only a portion of which is the lay leadership) and say anything accurate about marital status, occupation, income, religious branch of Judaism, or synagogue/temple affiliation. Beyond the obvious observation that most people in the meeting are probably Jewish, with the exception of outside visitors, little else is available on the demographics of the JCRC. On the other hand, those persons most likely to be considered for an elected lay leadership position in the JCRC come out of the same Jewish population that provides elected lay leaders to the other three JAOs in this study. Consequently, simple logic leads to the conclusion that the lay leadership of the JCRC would at least approximate several of the same demographic characteristics as the lay leaders in these other organizations.

There is a second level of lay leadership to consider in the JCRC's case, however, that is not present in the other three organizations, and that is the seventy-eight representatives from other Jewish organizations that form the backbone of the JCRC's board of trustees. The representatives from those

Jewish service organizations are more often the professional leaders rather than the lay leaders of any of those forty-two Jewish organizations. For example, the executive directors of the other three JAOs sit on JCRC's board of trustees. From another perspective, the similarities between the JCRC and the other three JAOs are offset by their differences.

First, the JCRC, unlike the AJC and the AJCg, is not a membership organization. It views the forty-two Jewish organizations that form the core of its board of trustees as significantly reflective of the entire Boston Jewish community. Each of these organizations has one or more representatives on the JCRC board of trustees as proscribed in the bylaws of the Board of Trustees (Article IV, sections 1, 2, 3). The Combined Jewish Philanthropies holds the largest number of seats (six) because of its direct financial support of the JCRC. These seventy-eight representatives are directly involved in the JCRC's planning process on current and future activities and future programs.

Approximately every ten years, the JCRC reaches out to the greater Boston Jewish community through an opinion survey. The survey was conducted to determine the demographic profile of the Boston Jewish community in 1975, 1985, and again in 1995 (Israel, 1985, 1995). The differences between the 1985 and 1995 studies are worth noting. Both are basically designed to reveal the financial health and capacity for giving on the part of the respondent, but beyond that maze of figures is a genuine effort to determine social service need and whether or not the respondent wanted that need filled by a Jewish outlet. The 1985 study actually provided information on such things as the sampling technique and the actual questionnaire that were used. By comparison, the 1995 report is little more than a snapshot of dozens of demographic indicators. Nothing in the 1985 or 1995 study is useful in terms of determining whether or not the general Jewish population surveyed was satisfied with the performance of the JCRC or thought it should be doing something else with its money, but at a minimum the JCRC is making an effort to stay in touch with the Boston Jewish population, if only once every decade. This survey of Jewish beliefs and demographic characteristics is exceptional, as compared to the other three JAOs, simply because it was done at all.

Second, where the expectation exists at the ADL and the AJC that lay leaders will raise additional funds beyond their own contributions, this does not happen at the JCRC. The JCRC requires no annual contribution or separate contribution to be considered for an elected lay leadership position on the board of trustees or the executive committee. This does not mean that the lay leadership of the JCRC does not make financial contributions in support of the Jewish community. The members of the executive committee (as well as designated representatives from the forty-two organizations) are all prominent members of the Boston Jewish community who usually make their financial contributions through the annual fund drive of the Combined Jewish Philanthropies. Another second characteristic worth noting is that some of the JCRC's elected leaders have served as elected lay leaders on the boards of other Jewish organizations (such as the ADL, AJC, AJCg), thereby establishing a history of Jewish philanthropy and service before being considered for lay leadership at the JCRC.

The JCRC's board of trustees has approximately 160 members including the 78 representatives from the other Jewish organizations; 16 former presidents of the executive committee, and upwards of 60 other members from social service, governmental, and religious organizations in the Boston community who sit on the board of trustees at any given time. The JCRC has eight officers (a president, three vice presidents, secretary, assistant secretary, treasurer, and assistant treasurer), and an executive committee of twenty-one elected lay leaders. The JCRC's ideology is, and always has been, an intercommunity-oriented organization. This is in contrast to the defense and intergroup emphasis of the other three JAOs in this study. The JCRC's emphasis on the redress of basic social inequalities in the larger community through coalitions and collaboration with other advocacy groups make it more like the AJCg than the AJC or the ADL.

The Boston JCRC has four professional employees, two support people, and several unpaid volunteers as circumstances require. The current budget of the JCRC is approximately $600,000, of which approximately $450,000 is a direct grant from the Boston Jewish Combined Philanthropies. JCRC also receives funding from the United Way, reflecting their status as one of the United Way's significant agencies. Very little additional fund-raising is sponsored by the JCRC, but when it is done it is usually in the spirit of raising partial, offsetting funds for a particular project. The Boston/Israel trips are one example.

Antisemitism was the formative basis for the first Boston Community Council in the 1930s, just as it was for the other three JAOs, but as the end of World War II approached, the present council formally came into existence (Segal, 1985:5). The incorporation documents carried an implicit and explicit new emphasis—communities did have a number of problems, and if communities could find ways to work together in coalitions, many of these problems could be eased, if not solved. Antisemitism became one of a collection of community-based problems along with racism, inadequate housing, and a host of other civil issues the JCRC addressed. Antisemitism continues to be a priority for the JCRC, but it is not a first priority. In the future, more emphasis will be placed on Jewish continuity, relations with the State of Israel, and the quality of Jewish community life in Boston.

THE JCRC, NJCRAC, AND DECISION MAKING

The Boston JCRC is responsible for balancing the needs of several Jewish organizational interests, while still carrying out its mission to the local Jewish community. The first of these is the major Jewish agencies in Boston that sit on its board of trustees. Second is the Boston chapters of the other JAOs to whom the JCRC provides a coordinating function. The third is the JCRC's interface with the New York offices of the National Jewish Community Relations Advisory Council (NJCRAC).

The difficulty with attempting to balance a coordinating role and a collegial role simultaneously with the other three national advocacy organizations in this study becomes clearer when actual decision-making incidents concerning antisemitism are examined. The JCRC has no direct authority over these other organizations, or for that matter, over any of the other thirty-nine Jewish organizations with representatives on its board of trustees. They can only advise and recommend those actions the JCRC believes will best meet the needs of everyone concerned. On the other hand, the JCRC recognizes that its visibility on certain issues is essential, such as antisemitic incidents possessing national as well as local significance. This visibility is essential, if the JCRC expects to be seen by its constituency as diligently fulfilling its mission. Because of this sensitivity, the JCRC, on occasion, finds itself competing for visibility with the other three JAOs as well as attempting to function in a collaborative fashion. The tensions this creates can be better understood in the context of two of the antisemitic incidents discussed in chapters nine and ten, the Wellesley College affair and the speech by Louis Farrakhan, respectively.

The NJCRAC is the third major organizational entity with which the Boston JCRC interacts regularly. The NJCRAC is not a "national office" in the same sense of the word as it is customarily used by the national offices of the other three organizations. NJCRAC is virtually a parallel organization to the local Jewish Community Relations Councils and functions in a national coordinating and policy advice role to them. It cannot get directly involved in any functional way with local council decision making.

Historically, the AJC, ADL, and AJCg had been involved, to a limited degree, in combating local incidents of antisemitism in the 1930s, often in connection with the local Jewish Federation, from whom they received small amounts of funding. But, with the increasing menace of Hitler's Germany during the 1930s and culminating in the outbreak of World War II in 1939, many of the community relations councils (Boston among them) were spurred to seek more direct mechanisms for combating local incidents of antisemitism than the national organizations could provide. The community relations councils wanted to respond to antisemitism much as their local fire departments responded to a fire or civil emergency, quickly and with local talent.

The Council of Jewish Federations in 1944 brought together the four national organizations (the AJC, the ADL, the AJCg, and the UAHC) following a failed attempt earlier (1938) to coordinate the activities of the different Jewish organizations in the United States; they suggested a different approach. In company with fourteen community councils from around the country (including Boston) they created the National Jewish Community Relations Advisory Council. It became the first issues-oriented, nationwide Jewish organization whose mission was to deal specifically with issues of local concern. Today, NJCRAC is composed of 13 national Jewish organizations and 117 local community relations agencies (Chanes, 1994).

From its inception, the NJCRAC has taken its message of nondiscrimination, civil liberties, socioeconomic justice, and separation of church and state to the highest levels of government, Congress, the federal courts through *amicus curiae* briefs, and the White House. However, the NJCRAC remains relatively inconspicuous as a planning, coordinating, and consensus-building body (its annual budget is $1.8 million, and it has seventeen employees) whose charter specifically prohibits any direct involvement in local community decision-making activity (Jerome A. Chanes, interview by author, May 10, 1996). As a formal organization, it often stands (uneasily) in the region framed by two questions: Who represents the Jewish community? Who can best present the American Jewish position to the U.S. government? The local councils, who financially sustain the NJCRAC, identify critical issues, help to formulate NJCRAC's relevant policies, and then assist in shaping the strategies required to implement these policies. NJCRAC assembles all of this input and communicates it nationwide to all of the affiliated JCRC councils.

The NJCRAC, nevertheless, faces certain inherent difficulties. The JAOs have an expectation that NJCRAC will support their interests and their respective missions to the Jewish community. The local community relations councils are often critical of the NJCRAC's policy of maintaining a low profile. The Jewish Federations feel that the NJCRAC should be more responsive to them, since a significant percentage of the council's funding comes from the federations. Some of this uneasiness with NJCRAC on the part of its key constituents occurred early in its history when it sponsored the MacIver study.

NJCRAC had been in operation for seven years when it commissioned Robert M. MacIver, a distinguished Columbia University professor of sociology, to conduct an in-depth analysis of Jewish communal organizations in the United States. One of NJCRAC's goals was to see if there were ways to eliminate the expensive duplication of effort and the frequently overlapping programs that plagued these agencies. In his *Report on the Jewish Community Relations Agencies*, Robert MacIver's (1951) study not only pointed out where many of those duplications existed, but he also remarked on the widespread dissension and rancor that seemed to pervade Jewish communal work. MacIver and his colleagues had uncovered the extensive competition among the Jewish organizations. Much of it centered on which of them was best equipped to address certain issues. He pointed out the economies of size that could be realized by emphasizing expertise and strength in specific areas of service delivery and then ceding responsibility for action to the organization that best possessed it. He saw no sense in every Jewish organization making its voice heard on every issue or involving itself in every form of service delivery. He discussed the secular nature of the Jewish organizations' lay leaders and the dominant influence that oligarchy played in their decision making. Toward the conclusion of his extensive report, MacIver recommended shifting a certain amount of power to NJCRAC to effect a more centralized coordination of Jewish communal work in America. If MacIver had made anything approaching a mistake, it was in his advocacy for NJCRAC's (his employer) possible role in future Jewish communal work.

A careful examination of MacIver's report is revealing. Its 261 pages actually contain two reports. The first portion is his analysis and recommendations (135 pages); the second is the reactions of the various Jewish organizations. In the first portion of the report he provides a carefully reasoned community-based study (by an acknowledged leader in the field) of the pressures and problems impacting the principal Jewish organizations in America following World War II. The responses by the Jewish organizations to MacIver's recommendations were swift and decidedly mixed. The majority of the national Jewish organizations who read the study judged its findings believable and its recommendations sensible. But, the AJC and ADL flatly rejected the study and accused the NJCRAC of attempting to create a single organization (under NJCRAC's executive guidance) that would become the "voice" of the American Jewish community. They argued that the dissension MacIver had found in the Jewish communal world was simply the long-standing preference by the American Jewish community (a gross presumption by itself) to remain independent of any single voice. It seemed that the longer the response to MacIver's findings was, the more negative the assessment. For example, the Jewish Labor Committee's response was three pages; the AJC's was twenty-four. In 1952, after lodging their strongly worded rejection of MacIver's study, the AJC and ADL resigned from NJCRAC and did not return until 1964.

Like the JCRC on a local basis, the NJCRAC can only provide advice and recommendations, in this case to the local community councils. It cannot tell them what to do in any specific situation. For example, the Boston JCRC is not bound to any regular communications with NJCRAC, except only insofar as it will strengthen the basic concepts of coordination and collaboration in a community relations context.

On May 10, 1996, in an article entitled "NJCRAC to Open Washington Office," published in *Forward*, the NJCRAC announced plans to go *national*. Any expansion into a national posture would provide NJCRAC with a more direct context within which to exercise its mission of Jewish communal relations at the national political level. In an era of falling Jewish philanthropy, NJCRAC's lay leaders seemed convinced there was enough additional money available to support this move to go national on their part. It remains to be seen if NJCRAC can establish itself as another national organization in Jewish communal affairs and not risk splintering an already loose confederation of national Jewish organizations. Given the independent operation of the 117 community councils there is no assurance that these local councils will be particularly enthusiastic about submitting to any more direction from NJCRAC (as a national organization) than they presently do without it.

In conclusion, chapters three, four, five, and six have provided a historical overview of the four JAOs in this study of the formal organizational response to antisemitism. Organizational characteristics, including leadership (on the part of the elected lay leaders and their professional cadre), goal setting, primary constituencies, membership, budget, and communication mechanisms were examined; similarities and differences were noted. These characteristics are brought together and further analyzed, discussed, and compared in greater depth in chapter seven.

_____ *Chapter 7* _____

A Collective Portrait of the Jewish Advocacy Organizations

INTRODUCTION

This chapter brings together and discusses the several characteristics of the Jewish Advocacy Organizations' (JAOs) organizational structures. This assortment of structural characteristics is examined from several perspectives: the JAOs' fundamental missions; what constituencies they serve; leaderships (lay and professional); and the ingredients that guide decision-making processes.

Jewish organizations began to appear almost from the first day Jews set foot on American soil. As an "outsider" group, Jews knew that any organizational needs they might have would have to spring from their own efforts. A brief review of the history of Jewish organizations in America forms a necessary backdrop to any discussion of the JAOs' organizational characteristics.

JEWISH ORGANIZATIONS IN AMERICA

Jews in Europe, particularly Eastern Europe, typically lived out their entire lives in communities with only one synagogue. That one synagogue (and its rabbi) provided religious instruction and guidance, and just as often it formed the center of the Jewish community's civic activities as well. Life inside the ghettos and restricted quarters was governed by the Chief Rabbi and a governing council. The Jewish portion of the city's taxes was collected by these councils and forwarded to the city fathers as a lump-sum payment from the "community." Civil law was interpreted by Jewish experts for the benefit of Jews living in the quarter, and Jewish life was translated and explained to the world outside the ghettos by this same power structure. Thus, the Chief Rabbi and the Jewish council held a lynch-pin role in the entire process of communication.

In contrast to Europe's restricted quarters, magisterial rabbis, and powerful governing councils, Jews in America established their communities with several synagogues or temples; competition had come to American synagogue life. Jews had, in Leon Jick's words (1976), made America a "community of synagogues." In a similar fashion, the establishment of American Jewish protective and beneficial organizations followed the same pattern of a "community" of organizations, often competing with one another for precedence in their particular undertakings. Where the religious, civic, and judicial affairs of Jews in Europe had been controlled by a single organization called the *kehilla*, American Jews would not wait on a governing council to make their decisions for them; life in America moved too fast for that level of contemplation. But, as seen in chapter three (the history of the AJC), the legacy of that form of oligarchic rule was still appealing to the German Jewish immigrants. They may not have been successful in resurrecting the *kehilla* in America (Arthur Goren in Sarna, 1986b:149–55), but the strength of that mentality—a few powerful persons making decisions of substantial consequence for the entire community—proved to be too enticing to be left behind in the old country.

Jews began forming diverse organizations shortly after their arrival during the colonial period. These earliest organizations, often religious in nature, provided a limited number of social services for newly arrived groups of Jews. Some of these organizations were societies that provided burial services in the Jewish tradition, and others were more fraternal in nature, providing warmth and comfort to Jews who had come from the same geographical area in Europe.

During the peak years of Jewish immigration into America (1881–1920), dozens of Jewish organizations were established that continue to operate to this day. Four of the oldest Jewish organizations are B'nai B'rith (1843), United Order of True Sisters (1846), Free Sons of Israel (1849), and Brith Abraham (1859). Other prominent Jewish organizations that formed during this period included Union of American Hebrew Congregations (1873), Hebrew Union College (1875), Hebrew Immigrant Aid Society (1880), Jewish Theological Seminary (1886), Yeshiva University (1886), Jewish Publication Society (1888), Central Conference of American Rabbis (1889), American Jewish Historical Society (1892), Jewish Chatauqua Society (1893), The Boston Jewish Federation (1895, the first federation in the United States), National Council of Jewish Women (1893), Gratz College (1895), Jewish War Veterans (1896), Jewish Labor Bund (1897), Jewish Communal Service Association (1899), National Jewish Hospital (1899), The Rabbinical Assembly (1900), and The Jewish Museum (1904) (*AJYB*, 1996:467–524).

Scores of Jewish social welfare and mutual aid organizations were quickly formed during this period of open immigration, but they were often short lived. They provided their services to small groups of Jews, then disbanded, and left virtually no records of themselves for future historians.

Three of the four JAOs in this study were formed during this period of mass immigration. They followed a long list of other religious and ethnic assistance organizations in America that had been formed to ease the transition to America from the old country on the part of the newly arrived immigrant (e.g., German, Irish, and Italian). But a shared Judaic heritage often proved insufficient in uniting groups of such disparate and heterogeneous backgrounds. There were deep differences of opinion, and often outright divisiveness, among religious and secular Jewish factions. Anti-Zionist socialists tangled with pro-Zionist social democrats and free-enterprise conservatives. Assimilationists who fully embraced the American way of life found themselves in constant disagreement with the religious zealots who rejected it. There was a persistent tension between Jews from a German background and those of East European origins. Conservative, liberal, secular, religious, Jews in America differed on just about every social, political, and economic issue affecting Jewish life. "[U]nified communal action was virtually out of the question. Jewish pluralism, rivalry, and conflict made that an impossibility" (Diner, 1994:287). This divisiveness remains a characteristic of the American Jewish community and its organizations to this day (Wertheimer, 1993b, 1995). In spite of the disagreements and divisiveness, it is important to understand both the JAOs' organizational characteristics and what it is they do as advocacy organizations.

JAOs AS FORMAL ORGANIZATIONS

As formal organizations, the JAOs are a subset of a large and diverse collection of organizations called advocacy groups, for example, National Association for the Advancement of Colored People (NAACP); National Organization of Women (NOW); National Congress of Puerto Rican Rights; and Asian American Voter's Coalition. This collection, in turn, is a subset of a still larger economic classification called nonprofit organizations (NPOs). This "third sector," as contrasted with the private and the public sectors, shares a number of similarities, whether the organization in question is the Lilly Foundation, the Nathan Cummins Foundation, or a two-person organization advocating for the preservation of a threatened species. The principal characteristics they all share include tax exempt status under provision 501(c) 3 of the Internal Revenue Code; a heavy reliance on volunteer labor; and capitalization not based on stocks and bonds but on land, buildings, and invested assets. The NPOs are further enjoined from distributing any surplus funds, either internally or externally, and they are not subject to oversight or accountability. These characteristics, plus several others that advocacy groups (specifically) share, provide a necessary background to understanding the organizational structure and behavior of the JAOs in this study.

The fundamental purpose of advocacy groups is to obtain for a particular group (e.g., women, blacks, Jews, and gays) protection from discrimination and a broader participation in the civil liberties of the larger society. They utilize coalitional bargaining, political lobbying, and exert pressure for changes in the law. Advocacy organizations infrequently employ civil disobedience to secure their goals but will often mount substantial publicity campaigns as a way to draw the public's attention to an issue or to the organization or to both. A fuller explanation of the mechanics and processes of advocacy organization is necessary to fully appreciate how the JAOs get their work done, and that discussion appears under the heading "Defining Jewish Advocacy."

Today, there are approximately 300 Jewish organizations of national scope and less than a dozen of them would fit the definition of an advocacy organization. They include the four JAOs in this study, the American Israel Public Affairs Committee (AIPAC), the Jewish Labor Committee, the Conference of Presidents of Major Jewish Organizations, the Commission on Social Action of Reform Judaism, and the Jewish War Veterans. Beyond this national collection of 300 Jewish organizations, there are literally hundreds of other Jewish organizations nationwide that provide some form of social service. Added to these hundreds are the thousands of Jewish organizations at the local level. Some of these are branch offices, or regional affiliates of the national organizations, but however many of them there are at any given point in time, they represent a veritable alphabet soup of initials. The handful of organizations that consider themselves advocacy organizations are powerful and well known, yet considering how much of American Jewry's business is conducted by them, remarkably little is known about precisely how they are organized, how they function, and who benefits from all of this application of power. The simple answer to the last part of the question is the Jewish community, but examining the question more deeply the answer becomes another question: "Which Jewish community?" The literature on this aspect of Jewish organizational life is decidedly thin.

THE JAOs' ORGANIZATIONAL CHARACTERISTICS

An examination of the demographics and leadership structure of the JAOs in this study reveals several interesting similarities. A questionnaire was completed on each of the JAOs and included questions on gender, age, personal income, religious affiliation, and political affiliation of key lay leaders. Questions were also asked about budgets, fund-raising, and the primary mission of the JAO. What emerged from the answers to these questions is a picture of two populations running the JAOs: the elected lay leaders and their professional staff. There are a handful of clerical and support personnel, as well as occasional volunteers, but the real work of the JAOs is done by these two groups of leaders. As a consequence, decision making is confined to a small handful of organizational insiders.

The JAOs' chapter/local offices are organized as replicas of their national offices. The AJC and the AJCg are membership organizations while the ADL and the JCRC are not. Each chapter is headed by an executive director who is supported by a small staff. The chapters' boards and committees, like their national offices, are populated by elected lay leaders.

The AJC has approximately 335 employees, nationally, and an annual budget of $19.8 million. The ADL has approximately 400 employees and the largest operating budget of the big three—$34.0 million. The AJCg, the smallest of the JAOs, has approximately 54 employees and a budget of $6.5 million. The fourth JAO, the JCRC, has 37 employees in Boston making it one of the most powerful councils in the United States. The other 113 JCRCs have as few as 3 and as many as 50 (or more) employees. The Boston JCRC receives almost one-half of its annual funding ($750,000) from the Boston Combined Jewish Philanthropies.

The compositions of the boards of directors and executive committees are the same at the local and national levels. The people who sit on these policy-making boards, and they number in the dozens (in Boston, e.g., AJC, 85; ADL, 94; and AJCg, 54), come from established professions and occupations including law, medicine, finance, the courts, social work, a few rabbis, but almost no academics.

Membership dues are often construed as flexibly as the numbers that constitute total membership itself in the AJC and AJCg. However, in all cases but one, a donation is required to occupy one of the coveted board positions. This donation ranges from $5000 (annually) for a seat on the AJC's national board ($750 on the Boston board), to $475 for a board seat on the AJCg, nationally or locally. The Boston ADL, not being a membership organization, picks its board members from an audience of approximately 600 contributors collectively referred to as "The New England Thousand." Each of these persons contributes at least $1000 annually to the ADL and from this group several dozen persons are elected to board and committee positions. The exception to this pattern of donor gifts is the JCRC. It is not a membership organization, and its advisory board is comprised of representatives from forty-two other Jewish organizations in the Boston area. Each of those organizations, however, may have its own requirements concerning financial contributions and election to a board seat. The Boston JCRC also has a thirty-seven-member executive committee, and sixteen of those thirty-seven are past presidents of the JCRC.

The professional staff has the highest visibility in the organizations' decision making; the lay leaders, the most influence. The executive committees make recommendations on formal programs and projects with assistance and advice from their professional staff. Key executive and board members are involved in all decisions involving antisemitism. The JAOs' lay leaders do not automatically exclude the opinions and concerns of Jews outside this small group, but any outside opinion will be directed to the appropriate internal committees and councils (Elazar, 1991:167–190). Complex organizations in both the public and private sectors often have interlocking boards of directors, but this is almost never seen among the JAOs, even though there is only a limited number of qualified leaders for those board positions. On the other hand, when a board member's tenure is up in one organization, it is not unusual to see them move to a similar position on the board of an ideologically compatible JAO (Jack Wertheimer, interview by author, April 11, 1996; Lawrence Shubow, interview by author, August 3, 1994). Former board members are still substantial contributors and they continue to influence decision making in the JAOs because of their financial power. This "voice" is seldom ignored, even long after their formal term has expired.

DEMOGRAPHIC CHARACTERISTICS
OF THE JAOs' LEADERS

The demographics of the leaders of the JAOs were difficult to dig out and equally difficult to update. These demographics are the properties that put a human face on the leadership of the JAOs, and the organizations are not particularly enthusiastic about providing this data. The AJC's demographics were used as a baseline for collecting similar information from the other JAOs. A reasonably complete set of demographics was found for the AJC in a study by Richard Zelin (1992) and then updated through the present study's more recent questionnaire. Zelin's demographies and those in the present study showed almost no change. The demographics for each of the JAOs in the present study were collected through the questionnaire already described and then were followed up with corroborating interviews with each organization. Given the remarkable similarity these organizations share in other areas it naturally follows that great similarity will be displayed in this data as well.

The lay leader in the AJC is male (71 percent); married (81 percent); average age, fifty-four. Of lay leaders, 62 percent earn over $100,000 a year; 53 percent consider themselves political liberals and 16 percent conservative. If they are denominationally affiliated, 67 percent are Reform, 22 percent are Conservative, and only 1 percent are Orthodox.

The ADL confirmed in interviews (Sally Greenberg, interview by author, July 18, 1996) that their demographics are virtually the same as the AJC, but a larger percentage of their lay leaders are male, and politically they consider themselves more conservative than the AJC.

The AJCg is 59 percent male, 77 percent married,with an average age of fifty-three. They are politically liberal (80 percent versus 5 percent conservative), and 60 percent earn over $100,000 yearly. Their denominational choice is 31 percent Reform, 38 percent Conservative, and 2 percent Orthodox.

The JCRC does not keep any demographic records on its leadership, but it does not vary much from the other three organizations. Attendance at board meetings presents a similar picture in terms of age, occupation, and gender to the other three JAOs. Given the criteria for selection to any lay leadership role in Jewish communal life, it is unlikely these basic demographics will vary much from one Jewish organization to the next.

Certainly, there are some differences from one organization to the next. For example, the AJCg's lay leaders tend to affiliate with Conservative Judaism, whereas the largest percentage of ADL and AJC lay leaders affiliate with Reform Judaism. Age, income, and gender are virtually identical in all four organizations. Two-thirds of the AJCg's elected leaders hold graduate or law degrees, not surprising given its Commission on Law and Social Action (CLSA). The professional group least often seen among the JAOs' lay leaders is academics, who are not seen as sufficiently pragmatic to deal with the day-in, day-out problems of Jewish advocacy. Taken collectively, these demographics produce a composite picture of the JAOs' lay leadership ranks.

JAOs AND THEIR FEEDBACK MECHANISMS

The at-large Jewish community has negligible input to the JAOs' decision-making process. None of the JAOs systematically gather opinions from the at-large Jewish community about new programs or work already completed on the community's behalf. At annual and biennial national meetings, lay leaders assess new programs (Howard Weintraub, interview by author, March 2, 1995). The lay leaders evaluate the professional staff, but no one evaluates the lay leaders. From inception, each of these JAOs has positioned itself as the self-appointed spokesperson for the Jewish community, but in reality none possess an explicit mandate from the at-large Jewish community to speak for them or to carry out any actions in the community's name.

A COMPOSITE PICTURE OF THE JAOs

This collection of organizational and demographic data makes it possible to construct a composite picture of the JAOs as organizations and to put a face on their lay leaders and professional staffs. The JAOs are organized and staffed in identical ways. Their financial conditions vary according to their fund-raising ability, but the way in which lay leaders are elected, contributions sought, and formal programs approved and implemented show only narrow differences among the four organizations, and those are frequently differences in process rather than content. Of particular significance is the fact that the Jews they represent total no more than 20 percent of the identified Jewish community in the United States, and possibly less; a population of Jews that is usually identified as the "giving" community.

Given this data, the lay leaders of the JAOs can be collectively described as: male; middle aged; well educated; affluent; politically liberal; and where religiously affiliated, predominantly Reform or Conservative. There is little evidence that the Orthodox community participates to any great degree in the affairs of the JAOs, or for that matter, that the decisions of the JAOs are seen as particularly benefiting the closely woven Orthodox community. This is the profile Aviva Cantor (1995) attacks in *Jewish Women/Jewish Men: The Legacy of Patriarchy in Jewish Life*. In her discussion of Jewish organizations, she describes the lay leadership as a *macherocracy*, an extension of the Yiddish term *macher*, or men who run the show (255).

Whether or not the reader agrees with Cantor's strident criticisms of these *machers*, she has captured the essence of Jewish communal structure and power at the national level. She says, "The structure and process [is] undemocratic, hierarchical, and sexist. . . . [It is] geared toward providing these relatively few men with a monopoly on validation in the form of high status and with an ersatz definition of masculinity, i.e., 'Jewish leader' " (255).

Cantor describes the structure of these Jewish organization as consisting of a few men at the top of the hierarchy who give a large sum of money ($100,000 a year is not uncommon), and for their largesse expect to be accorded recognition and positions of power and visibility. At the next level in this hierarchy there is a thin layer of prominent givers who only want to write a check and eschew any further involvement. Below them is a substantial strata of contributors who donate smaller amounts of money, and whose participation in day-to-day activities is limited. Finally, there is the broad base made up of everybody else in the Jewish community who may or may not contribute to Jewish causes, or who even care much what the Jewish organizations do, but out of some idea of loyalty, contribute a few dollars from time to time (1995:256).

The demographics and organizational characteristics developed for this present study parallel Cantor's observations. For example, the JAOs have no mandate from the at-large Jewish community to conduct affairs in their name. The symbiosis between contributing and leading in the advocacy organizations has been male dominated since their inception. On the other hand, Cantor's categorizations cannot be applied unilaterally, particularly at the local level. Examining the membership of the four JAOs' boards of directors revealed that the AJC's board is 44 percent women, the ADL's board is 35 percent women, the AJCg's board is 32 percent women, and the JCRC's board is 26 percent women. This puts Boston's female representation on the JAOs' boards of directors well ahead of the national experience. Additionally, the past twenty years have seen increasing numbers of women assuming key professional staff jobs in the JAOs, but the point at which women will assume key lay leadership roles in the same organizations, and in significant percentages, is still a question mark.

J. Allan Whitt et al. characterize Cantor's *machers* as "big linkers" (1993:30). They go on to suggest, "[B]oards are likely to continue to select people who are like themselves, especially for those powerful multi-position slots at the top of the organizational hierarchy." These small groups of men (and some women) who dominate the power structure of these JAOs have done exactly what Whitt et al. are suggesting: They have reproduced and re-placed themselves with like-minded people for at least four generations. To some degree the extent to which problem selection and decision making by the JAOs are controlled, first by oligarchy and secondly by ideology, can be seen to follow certain patterns of behavior in attempting to accomplish their goals.

DEFINING JEWISH ADVOCACY

JAOs share certain behaviors with other types of advocacy organizations. In his discussion of interest group activity, David Truman (1971) has sug-gested three consistent behaviors in advocacy groups: First, they *share a col-lection of attitudes*. For the JAOs, one of these is that antisemitism will be challenged whenever or wherever it occurs. Any individual or group in American society, organized or not, who engages in antisemitic behavior can expect a reaction from the JAOs. Second, advocacy groups *make certain claims* on other groups. For example, JAOs seek out collaboration with Christians, blacks, feminists, labor unions, among others, in opposing anti-semitism. Third, JAOs *encourage the establishment, maintenance, or en-hancement of behaviors* that will insure the continued safety and protection of Jews. These initiatives typically include demands for apologies for offen-sive language or behavior, restitution for damage to property, lawsuits to compensate individuals and organizations for slander or defamation, and specific legislation or ordinances to prevent a repeat of the offensive behav-ior in the future.

Like other advocacy groups, JAOs use oppositional advertising, op-ed pieces in the media, public confrontation of offenders, targeted publications, and funding for research to insure their message is disseminated as widely as possible.

Beyond the fixed issue of antisemitism, JAOs advocate for the welfare of Jews in two other venues: legal and legislative action for the wider partici-pation of Jews in the dominant society; and sponsorship of focused research and education programs to expand racial and ethnic tolerance and accep-tance. These tactics make the JAOs similar to scores of other advocacy groups in the United States.

The JAOs' mission statements claim they are the "voice" of the Jewish community, but this is not a monolithic community, and it is certainly not a community of one mind about its own identity; America's Jews do not hold a single, unified definition of themselves. The community, particularly in the United States, is composed of several communities, that is, religious, secular, and ethnic, all calling themselves authentic Jews, and all holding strong opinions about what issues reflect their interests.

The JAOs take seriously the welfare and protection of Jews, however this fractured community chooses to identify itself. Yet, on closer examination, these same organizations often respond more immediately to the needs of their boards of directors, contributing members, and significant financial supporters than to some abstract entity formulaically known as the "at-large population of America's Jews" (Howard Weintraub, interview).

The JAOs do not engage in social protest, nor do they directly provide any social services. More often they distinguish themselves through the use of quiet diplomacy on international issues (see particularly the history of the AJC, chapter three) and legal redress on domestic issues (see the histories of the ADL and the AJCg, chapters four and five, respectively). All of the JAOs have professionally trained staffs on their payroll. Increasingly, they are graduates of advanced Jewish communal programs found in major universities, and their education has included modern management skills and advanced technology applications. But for all of these fairly general descriptors, just what is it advocacy organizations do, and, specifically, what is Jewish advocacy?

According to Earl Rabb, Jewish advocacy is based on a two-millennia history of Jews defending Jewish interests in the public arena through community relations. Changing political circumstances often gave rise to trying different advocacy techniques, some radical but always consistent with a concept of Jews caring for their own best interests (1991:1–2).

In one of the few treatments of Jewish advocacy found in the literature, Rabb (1991) presents Jewish advocacy as a collection of seventy-five propositions: sixteen of them designed to deepen an understanding of the types of antisemitism advocates are likely to encounter; others focused on Israel, church-state separation, and defending/assisting Jews abroad. In a skills section, Rabb discusses methods for influencing public policy, the media's role in Jewish advocacy, the creation of educational programs in schools and in the larger Jewish community, and advocacy leadership. In arguing that advocacy is the most appropriate means for dealing with antisemitism, his advocacy propositions parallel Truman's (1971) observations on the establishment, maintenance, or enhancement of behaviors implied by shared attitudes. In Rabb's opinion (1991:2), Jewish advocacy's principal goal is what they perceive to be the security needs of the Jewish community.

Consistent with Rabb's sixteen propositions are Leonard Zakim's nine rules (1993) for establishing advocacy relationships, and then working with these relationships as coalitions. His rules include realizing that your partners know little or nothing about the Jewish community; never neglecting your partners; establishing bilateral relationships in your partners' organization; turning up where you are least expected, and then helping; and seeking opportunities for pointed conversations with your partners that help resolve problems or develop projects but do not allow them to dissolve into discussions about long-standing differences with no intention of developing plans or resolving differences. Again, highly pragmatic advice, reflecting the influence of the author's legal training. Before moving on to how the JAOs make decisions, it is important to discuss a key property embedded in all of these organizations, that is, their internal system of power.

It is ironic that in the most developed of all democratic countries, much of the JAOs' work is carried out by small, carefully cultivated groups of people that are, in Robert Michels's language, "oligarchies" (1958)—small groups of people at the very apex of the organization's hierarchy, where decisions are often made by a few for the benefit of a few. Michels paints a gloomy, but realistic, portrait of democracies that we can use as a metaphor for complex organizations, particularly the JAOs. Most nonprofit organizations, and the JAOs figure prominently in this group, stoutly defend the democratic process of seeking their constituency's input and opinion, even if they cannot recall the last time they did it. They admit under some probing, however, that they seldom even think of "the constituency" when they make top-level decisions. The rationale here is that their decisions are always designed with the interest of America's Jews in mind, therefore all Jews benefit, whether or not they know it.

Historically, the leaderships of virtually all of America's first corporations (e.g., Harvard University, the Massachusetts Bank, all orphanages, common schools, hospitals, and medical societies) were in the hands of society's most highly placed citizens: landowners, ministers, and professionals (Peter Hall in Powell, 1987:3–7). Later, foundations and trusts were often formed to extend familial dynasties with little or no loss of direct organizational control and virtually no oversight (Hall in Powell, 1987:7). The NPOs that grew out of these earlier corporations were as securely locked into bureaucratic behavior and hierarchical structure as any organizations in the for-profit or public sectors. Decision-making power in these organizations was (and still is) the privy of a small group of individuals who hold clearly vested interests in the organization.

NPOs do not mimic the democratic ideals of the society they serve. Their leadership structure typically drifts into a self-preserving, conservative system of power that Michels (1958) called the "Iron Law of Oligarchy." It was, according to Michels, so corrosive that he considered it a "disease" (1958:365), an affliction that would eventually overtake all organizations, regardless of the pluralistic, inclusive ideals they professed at the time of their founding. Ultimately, the original goals of the organization are displaced by narrower instrumental goals, often focusing on the personal sinecure of the leadership as a form of organizational survival. Michels (1958) identified three factors that are central to the eventual drift by all organizations into oligarchy:

1. *Technical factors* (41–44). The organization's leadership advances the central belief that strong, directive action will assure their and the organization's future. In

assuming this posture, they take control of the organization's agenda (mission), its communications, and the management of any internal dissension. The discussion following on the JAO as an oligarchy demonstrates how long this has been true of these organizations.

2. *Characteristics of leaders* (83–84). These characteristics of leaders include charisma, strength of personality, and specific talents. The success these leaders enjoy leads them to relish the psychic rewards of leadership (e.g., association with other high ranking officials in other organizations, trappings of office, and the gratitude and flattery of the represented), and this leads them to cling to power at all costs (85). The qualities of charisma, personality, and proven records of accomplishment are all attributes the JAOs actively seek out in recruiting new leadership talent. These qualities are frequently taken for granted because of the individual's success in his personal life. It is precisely these characteristics that lie at the base of Cantor's criticism (1995) of patriarchy in the Jewish organizations. A sample reading of Jewish newspapers from across the United States always reveals several pages devoted to the pictures of smiling dignitaries receiving praise and media attention for their contribution (usually financial) to myriad Jewish organizations.

3. *Characteristics of the organization's constituency.* Michels (86) emphasizes two persistent characteristics of the organization's constituency: a general incompetence on the part of the rank and file to care for their own best interests; and the general indifference (50) and apathy of the constituency to the affairs of the organization. This combination of human failing and general disinterest provided the organization's leadership with a practical moral justification for its actions. "After all," they will say, "if we don't do it, who will?" This inability to manage one's existence in a complex state has always been the motivation for the formation of governments, legislatures, laws, and regulations. In turn, it spawns the organizations necessary to insure the domestic tranquility of its citizens. But, in exchange, those same citizens give up to that government bits and pieces of their self-determination over how their lives will be lived. The JAOs function through a similar logic. Jews need protection from adversaries (antisemites), and someone to argue their case for equal rights before an indifferent government; it is the basis for all advocacy in any society. The indifference or apathy of the membership is always a given.

Oligarchies, seen as the concentration of power in the hands of a select few (almost always men, making decisions for those few), did not start with Michels's gloomy predictions, they have been central to the Jewish community for centuries.

JAOs AS OLIGARCHIES

Over several centuries (at least since the crystallization of the idea of the Jewish polity as an aristocratic republic during the Second Commonwealth [Elazar, 1995:426]), oligarchy has been the major form of Jewish organizational power, that is, power and control are held by a small number of influential persons (424).

In mid-sixteenth-century Europe, the oligarchies represented the Jewish community's elite leaders. At their best they exercised a "trusteeship," at their worst they made decisions that benefited only them. This aristocratic oligarchy made most of the decisions in European Jewish communities up to and through most of the eighteenth century. It was this same "oligarchic" group who was responsible for the creation of Reform Judaism as a new Jewish denomination in nineteenth-century Germany, and it became America's first Jewish denomination during the German Jewish immigration in the nineteenth century. It is, therefore, not surprising that the spirit and influence of "oligarchy" continues to exert a substantial influence on today's JAOs and their decision making.

Since emancipation in the eighteenth century, the Jewish community in Diaspora has most successfully advanced its goals and protected its safety by settling in pluralistic societies. Jews do not seek this pluralism for its own sake but rather to enable the community to achieve its goals. Like the society surrounding it in the United States, the Jewish community is enthusiastically democratic, but paradoxically, its formal organizations remain elitist and oligarchic. While the JAOs exhibit ideological differences, their decision making exhibits a number of similarities, not the least of which is this propensity toward centering power in the hands of small groups of lay leaders.

Today's JAOs have taken a major leaf from the American democratic experience, and its call for greater inclusivity, and have blended the earlier aristocratic forms of oligarchy with polyarchy, in which no single individual or group is able to totally monopolize power (Elazar, 1995:425). This form of political power is closer in composition to modern coalitions. These multiple (and often highly competitive) coalitions are increasingly common in Jewish organizational life. But, even as coalitions, they seldom, if ever, include the everyday Jew. All of these forces work together to affect how the JAOs formulate and carry out decision strategies.

DECISION MAKING BY JAOs

At the conclusion of a study of the AJCg's Commission on Law and Social Action (CLSA), Elliot Tenofsky observed, "strategic and tactical patterns by the group . . . simply do not exist. Again and again . . . [Tenofsky asked] CLSA officials . . . about recurrent patterns of decision-making, only to receive as [an] answer . . . that whatever . . . tactics [were] involved [they were] largely on an ad hoc basis" (1979:4).

Yet, JAOs, like any other organization, make decisions every day about myriad issues; and their organizational behavior must be more than an ad hoc response to daily events because, minimally, they have figured out how to survive, and that is definitely more than a collection of ad hoc responses. When key personnel in the four JAOs were asked to describe their roles in the three antisemitic incidents examined herein, their responses were lengthy and reasonably clear, although they were not necessarily conscious of any

formal processes that may have shaped their response to a particular incident. Whether or not the professionals in these four JAOs were knowledgeable or conversant about what may have influenced their decision making,
past research clearly shows that a small collection of factors do consistently
influence the JAOs' decision making. In his 1995 study of the American
Jewish community and polity, Daniel Elazar discusses various observable
factors that consistently shape Jewish organizational decision making
(1995). A brief examination of these influence factors reveals how closely
they parallel the basic ingredients of the oligarchy described earlier.

KEY FACTORS INFLUENCING JEWISH DECISION MAKING

Government by Committee

Decision making by committee is the backbone of Jewish organizational life,
"committees are natural arenas for negotiations, and the wide-spread use of
them encourages decision making through . . . consensus" (Elazar, 1995:416).
However, the quest for consensus in these committees often has no effect on the
outcome, because the oligarchic power structure controls the process, and major
decisions are frequently foregone conclusions (416). On the other hand, not all
input from outside of the organizational structure is automatically excluded. An
incident from 1969 points out the reality of this "government by committee."

At that year's General Assembly of the Council of Jewish Federations, a
group of students calling themselves "Concerned Jewish Students" confronted the council over its spending priorities. Hillel Levine (a conservative
rabbi and a sociologist now at Boston University), the group's leader, complained, "Jewish education was the step-child of the federation whose priorities favored a greater mobilization of resources to combat one crack-pot
anti-Semite than to deal with the Jewish education of millions of Jews"
(Silberman, 1985:207). The assembly was startled by the challenge but incorporated many of the group's demands. A number of initiatives were
launched to create outreach to Jewish students. Some failed, and others were
slowly incorporated into existing federation committees.

This organizational power structure also acts as a veto power that influences input from other organizational members and the professional staff.
The JAOs' elected lay leaders have multiple relationships that extend into
their professional and business lives. If a key member of this power structure
vetoes a decision, the other lay leaders are likely to follow suit. Whatever
personal conflicts might pull at these lay leaders, they remain unanimous on
matters of public policy (Zelin, 1992).

Conflict Avoidance

"The avoidance of conflict is a major factor in the American Jewish community" (Elazar, 1995:416). Conflict is avoided, but consensus is not
sought, because that might entail relinquishing power. Conflict avoidance

is the classic mechanism used by a minority in power to avoid weakening any sense of unity among members (418). One reason that avoiding conflict is important for these leaders is that the Holocaust, the ultimate attack on Jewish safety in the twentieth century, has had an enduring impact on American Jewish identity and is a major motivation for conflict avoidance. The enormous impact of the Shoah may not be fully appreciated by persons outside the Jewish community, and it is sometimes taken for granted by those in it. Since the attempted destruction of Europe's Jews, "no issue is allowed to emerge as a matter of public controversy in the American Jewish community if it is felt that this might threaten the unity of the community" (417).

Two other areas have attracted considerable attention from the JAOs in recent years, and they have both demonstrated their capacity for raising the specter of conflict for these organizations: The first is the State of Israel; and the second is Jewish continuity in the United States. In the first, Israel, the JAOs have uniformly, if not always enthusiastically, supported Israel, particularly since the Six-Day War in 1967. Because the AJC was late in openly supporting the new State of Israel, it has often been described as non-Zionist, or anti-Zionist. Since Israel's founding in 1948, the AJC chose not to criticize Israel's political positions, even when it would have been to the AJC's and Israel's benefit to do so. This position largely grew out of the realization that any criticism of Israel could be interpreted as too harsh, or as anti-Israel in its intent. The AJCg, by contrast, took up the cause of Zionism and Israel from the very beginning of its organizational life. In the early 1920s, the AJCg expanded its own membership by taking on the faltering membership of the American Zionist Movement. In recent years the AJCg has criticized Israel over the issue of the West Bank settlements and the occupation of the Golan Heights before other national Jewish organizations said anything.

Today, all of the JAOs regularly sponsor trips to Israel to demonstrate to American politicians and businessmen, who may have doubts about Israel's political policies, that it is feasible and desirable to do business with the only democratic government in the Middle East. The JCRC in Boston has added another ingredient to its sponsored trips to Israel. It uses these occasions as an opportunity to demonstrate to city leaders the ways in which Israel is solving (or at least coping with) serious problems in the inner city that have their parallels in major American cities.

The second issue, Jewish continuity, is a relatively recent addition to the JAOs' agenda as a major topic of concern. The intermarriage rate between Jews and non-Jews was reported at approximately 32 percent in the 1971 National Jewish Population Survey (NJPS). This was up from approximately 7 percent after World War II. In the 1990 NJPS, the intermarriage rate had risen to approximately 52 percent in certain parts of the country, particularly since 1986. The JAOs had not thought of intermarriage, or Jewish identity, or Jewish continuity as their problem. This was something the religious side of Jewry attended to. However, by the mid-1990s they knew it was their problem as well, but had no clear idea what role they would play in reversing this inexorable decline in the Jewish population in the United States.

Local Chapters versus the National Office

Differences of opinions that grow out of the need for greater autonomy on the part of the branch offices to do their jobs effectively and the always present reality of the headquarters' authorities to intervene in every decision have not happened with the JAOs with the same frequency that is found in the private sector. This classic decision-making dichotomy usually does not impede decision-making by the JAOs and their chapters for the simple reason that the national offices automatically involve themselves in every major decision, but not in those of an exclusively local nature. Consequently, the JAOs do not necessarily review each and every decision made at the chapter level. Another factor in this loosening of the headquarters control was the suburbanization of America.

As the Jewish community moved to the suburbs (along with everybody else after World War II), the JAOs' New York headquarters gradually accepted that their absolute authority was going to diminish. During the same time, professionally trained local chapter staff disagreed more often with headquarters and acted independently. Yet, the national office of these JAOs has not relinquished its authority over local issues, particularly those that may possess national implications. On those occasions, the national office will impose itself as the final authority on local decision making (see chapter eight).

Interorganizational Competition (i.e., Duplication)

During the late 1940s and culminating in the early 1980s, Jewish synagogues and temples throughout the United States found themselves providing extensive social, immigrant, and communal activities to their congregants, including such things as day care, elder care, food supplement programs, teen recreational programs, and new immigrant language lessons; the types of services that had traditionally been the purview of Jewish communal organizations (Elazar, 1995:256–59). For years there was an obvious overlap and competition in organizational programs offered by the synagogues and the communal agencies.

The suburban synagogues (many of them the product of a huge synagogue building boom after World War II) were simply responding to the population shift from the core city to the suburbs that took place from the late 1940s and throughout the 1950s. The decades-old Jewish communal agencies were often stranded in the center city, financially unable to make the physical move to the suburbs and their traditional customers. The Jews who had constituted their traditional client base were not willing to commute, sometimes miles, back to the center city to avail themselves of those services. So, increased pressure was placed on the synagogues, and they responded accordingly.

Similarly, the JAOs were faced with the same task of changing their organizational direction and they began to increasingly move away from the international complexities of defending Jews prior to and during World War II, to refocusing themselves on a collection of broader national issues involving relationships with several other groups in American society (Svonkin, 1995). This intergroup-relations period began shortly after World War II and substantially ended about 1967 with the eruption of the Six-Day War in Israel, plus the expulsion of most white and Jewish supporters of the changed civil rights struggle.

The expanding autonomy of the JAOs' chapters, coupled with the acquisition of increased managerial skills among the professional staffs, resulted in the JAOs frequently dealing with the same issues, and they have justified any ensuing organizational overlap on ideological differences and the differing interests of their constituencies. Although duplication may seem unnecessary, "society frequently creates redundant systems to provide alternative means to approach the same goal" (Elazar, 1995:420), and this type of issue redundancy has been a characteristic feature of Jewish decision making for decades. For example, the AJC and the ADL have both conducted extensive research on the social and political implications of Louis Farrakhan, the NOI, Leonard Jeffries, and the impact of radical Afro-centric texts. Both organizations have published monographs and occasional papers on these subjects and distributed them to college campuses across the country. Even though they are researching and publishing the same information on the same subjects, the AJC and ADL do not believe they are duplicating each other's work, because each organization's research studies are directed to a different constituency, and their responses to these issues are based on different political paradigms. Although, what those differences are is often difficult to discern.

Competing ideas may produce clearer thinking and improved understanding of complex issues; on the other hand, the different JAOs may be driven more by the competition for their members' allegiances than by any need for improved decision making. Another aspect of this organizational competition is the stated expertise of each of the JAOs.

Each of the national JAOs has developed areas of distinct expertise, and not surprisingly, each wants this expertise reserved to itself. The AJC sees itself as the principal authority on black/Jewish relations in the United States. The ADL presents itself as the foremost organization on hate crimes, and the AJCg holds itself up as the most experienced and talented Jewish organization at legal and legislative advocacy. For example, when the AJC launched a highly visible campaign against antisemitism in the American farm belt in the mid-1980s, it encountered substantial resistance to its research program from the ADL. The ADL very pointedly said that it did not welcome another Jewish organization conducting research on antisemitism. The AJC retreated from its project in the face of the ADL's criticism.

Innovation and Program Initiation

Innovation in the JAOs is a subject for a separate study. However, it seems likely that "innovation and program initiation are usually dominated by the professionals, if only because they are involved on a day-to-day basis and [they] are recognized as having the programmatic expertise" (Elazar, 1995:422). The choices made by these professionals are supposedly grounded in the needs and desires of the entire Jewish community, but the feasibility of these initiatives and programs are actually determined by elected program committees that meet annually and biannually to determine the eventual use of budgets and personnel. Jewish organizations have adopted increasingly sophisticated and contemporary management techniques, but they may have done so at the cost of distancing themselves even further from the at-large Jewish community they purportedly represent.

Personalities

The personalities of key organizational members exert a powerful influence on group decision making. Lay and professional leaders derive some of their power from their personality and charm, which are bound to sway any organization's decision making. Equally important, however, are the differences in executive style. Executive styles have been shaped by education and experience. Personality conflicts cannot be underestimated, but they occur more frequently in the top ranks of the national organizations than at the local chapters (Elazar, 1995:423). Even though these conflicts take place at the top of the JAOs, their effects often ripple down through the organization, and outward, to coalition partners in other organizations.

Fund-Raising

A seventh influence factor must be added to Elazar's original six, and that is the ever-present necessity for, and pressure of, fund-raising and its influence on the JAOs' decision making. Fund-raising influences the JAOs' decision making in two significant ways: first, almost any gathering brought together in the name of the Jewish community, or of the JAO itself, is a reason for soliciting funds. If the JAO supports a particular cause, political issue, or objects to an incident of prejudice, that support will be made use of for a fund-raising opportunity. Second, whether the JAOs have been successful or not in quelling an incident of antisemitism or prejudice, it will eventually be used to raise funds. This does not mean that decisions would be withheld or markedly altered by the JAOs because of a decision's fund-raising potential. Rather, it signifies that fund-raising is an ongoing, perpetual function of the JAOs, and on occasion the distinction between advocacy for the Jewish community and advocacy for the sole purpose of fund-raising becomes blurred.

The status of Jewish philanthropy and charitable giving has undergone significant changes during the past ten years. Charitable giving to Jewish causes began declining in 1990 and by 1994 donations to the Combined Jewish Philanthropies/Federations fell from $1.2 billion (annually) in 1990 to $752 million as reported by Karen W. Arenson in a *New York Times* article entitled "Donations to Jewish Philanthropy Ebb," December 27, 1995. Equally dramatic was the drop in the federations' contribution to the United Jewish Appeal, from slightly over 50 percent of funds contributed in 1985 to just over 40 percent by 1994. This drop in donations is not from any lack of fund-raising effort on the part of the agencies; rather, it reflects the changing nature of Jewish giving itself. Increasingly, American Jews are sending their charitable contributions in other directions than to established Jewish philanthropies. Jewish money is flowing to art museums, symphony orchestras, and other civic organizations, and in increasing amounts, because these same Jewish supporters are being named to the boards of these previously inaccessible non-Jewish organizations. These are the same organizations that only a few years ago would accept Jewish money, but not the election of Jewish donors to their boards. It is one more indication of the extent to which Jews have been accepted and sought after in the American mainstream. A second reason for this drop in donations is that many of the services provided by the Jewish social service agencies in the past are now readily available from public agencies associated with the United Way and other similar umbrella organizations, and it doesn't make sense to duplicate these services. Finally, some of the decline in giving can be explained by declines in income among some prominent donors brought on by structural changes in the economy and the way wealth is now distributed. Perhaps the best known example of this can be found in the health care industry. The shift to managed care has often negatively affected the incomes of physicians, and that in turn, has affected their ability to sustain previous charitable giving.

A serious question embedded in all fund-raising is whether or not it affects decision making on vital issues. On occasion the JAOs may postpone or even discard their own committee recommendations if key contributors threaten to take their money elsewhere (Goldberg, 1996). Philanthropy is a highly personal matter and donors will withhold (or threaten to withhold) their money for a variety of reasons, and one of the key reasons is the donor's perception that the organization is not making satisfactory decisions, or it is advocating for positions that are totally unacceptable to the donor's values.

Influence over key decisions by major donors is endemic in all voluntary organizations, but seems particularly acute in Jewish organizations. J. J. Goldberg (1996:363) recounts the efforts of Diana Aviva, of the Combined Jewish Federation (CJF), Washington, DC, to convince the federations throughout the country to mobilize against the GOP's "contract with America" proposal for a balanced budget amendment. She argued that if passed, it could lead to a curtailing of federal funds, which in turn would reduce federal support for human services, and that would ultimately strike a major blow to the center of federation activities.

But certain key contributors to the federations, who also composed a small but powerful group of Republicans, bluntly threatened to withdraw their donations if the federations pursued this protest. Top executives in two of the federations backed down under the pressure of losing millions of dollars. The Aviva initiative collapsed when several other cities followed suit. This example not only demonstrates the power of fund-raising to influence decision making, but it also reaffirms the influence of an earlier factor previously made note of in this study, that is, government by committee. Recall that this factor says, "The JAOs' elected lay leaders have multiple relationships that extend into their professional and business lives. If a key member of this power structure vetoes a decision, the other(s) . . . are likely to follow suit."

Another, and perhaps even more dramatic example of this threat to withdraw funds surfaced at the February 1994 annual meeting of the United Jewish Appeal in Denver, Colorado. In his keynote address, Edgar Bronfman of the Seagram Company, a prominent industrialist and well-known Jewish philanthropist, threatened to withhold his money from the Jewish organizations if they didn't shift their priorities from one of defending Jews to one of educating Jews (Jewish Telegraphic Service, February 18, 1994). He strongly recommended a merger among the defense agencies as a way to put their collective budgets to better use for the benefit of the Jewish community. He went so far as to warn the assembled crowd that he and other wealthy Jewish donors would set up their own trust funds to provide money for their education agenda. This, in contrast to what he termed the "defense agencies' [i.e., the JAOs'] obsession with counting swastikas on bathroom walls," as reported in an article in *Forward* entitled "Restructure World Jewry WJC Insists" by Douglas Feiden, Febuary 25, 1994. Bronfman's comments caught the delegates off-guard. They had come to this meeting (as they had in years past) to share their successes, be congratulated, receive awards, but certainly not to hear themselves chastised.

The *Forward* article also quoted the reactions of ADL and AJCg representatives. Abraham Foxman, national director of the ADL, in responding to Bronfman's criticism, said, "Who are we to tell the donors what their priorities should be? The people who swear by us, it's as if they go to our *shul* and they won't be caught dead in any other *shul*." Phil Baum, executive director of the AJCg, dismissed Bronfman's merger suggestion saying, "we serve different constituencies, our manners are different and we look at life in different ways." Since that 1994 meeting, Bronfman and other prominent Jewish philanthropists (e.g., Charles Bronfman, Edgar's brother and also of the Seagram Company, and Leslie Wexner, of the retailing firm The Limited, Inc.) have gone ahead with their plans to set up multimillion dollar foundations to endow Jewish education.

In the present study, this threat to withhold funds occurred on a smaller scale and with no publicity. Some of the alumni of Wellesley College threatened to withhold their annual pledges in the aftermath of the Tony Martin affair (see chapter nine).

SUMMARY

Several themes have been pulled together in this chapter, and they collectively present a reasonably global image of the JAOs as complex organizations. Jewish organizations began to take shape almost immediately after Jews began arriving in America, and by the early twentieth century several of these were advocacy organizations dedicated to the protection of Jewish safety from antisemitism. These advocacy organizations, however, function the same as scores of other such organizations, and consequently they share a number of similarities.

Board membership is more often determined by the size of the person's contribution than by any special talent they may bring to the job. Demographically, the lay leadership of the JAOs is male, married, middle aged, earning over $100,000 a year, and if religiously affiliated, usually of the Reform denomination of Judaism. However, it is important to remember that all of the JAOs are secular, not favoring one branch of Judaism over another. In chapter eleven, a longer, more detailed discussion appears about the "civil Judaism" to which this secularist orientation has given rise.

The composite picture of the JAOs that emerges from these shared characteristics is one of a male-dominated collection of organizations that are largely insulated from the grassroots Jews (*amcha*) they supposedly represent. Each organization claims to be the "voice of the Jewish people," and none of them has any visible mandate from those Jews to speak in their name. They are tightly controlled oligarchies that echo the aristocratic characteristics of a European past that renders most of their decision making undemocratic and of relevance to only a small handful of membership Jews.

Finally, the JAOs' decision-making process is influenced by seven factors that make most decisions foregone conclusions. This adherence by the JAOs to a patterned form of decision making has led to dissension among the several Jewish organizations and to the outright rejection by the JAOs to any suggestion that they alter their spending priorities. This expenditure of millions of dollars to fight a disappearing threat (antisemitism) has been described as a marginal activity, at best, and, at its worst, a squandering of valuable funds that could be used more appropriately for Jewish education.

Given the substance and several dimensions of these descriptive character-istics, it should be possible to view them, firsthand, in some typical organiza-tional context. That examination of the JAOs' organizational characteristics and decision making is described in part three. Chapters eight through ten present the involvement of the JAOs in three antisemitic incidents and the de-cision making it triggered within those four JAOs. The extent to which the JAOs did or did not collaborate on each of these incidents is explored. First insights are provided on how those decisions were framed by the four orga-nizations. As important as these "living case histories" are to advancing our understanding of the JAOs' decision-making processes, they are equally im-portant for what they say about the politically powerful role antisemitism plays in the life course of these organizations.

Part Three

Three
Antisemitic
Incidents

Chapter 8

Incident Number One: A Black/Jewish Historical Exhibit

INTRODUCTION

A common ingredient appears in all three of the antisemitic incidents that comprise this chapter and the two that follow: all of them involved the Nation of Islam (NOI). In the first incident, the Black/Jewish Historical Exhibit, there was a direct confrontation between the AJC and the NOI over a panel of material (deemed antisemitic by the AJC) that was inserted into the exhibit at the last minute by the NOI. In the second incident, a book published by the NOI was used as a basic text in a Black History course at Wellesley College. In the third incident, a speech at the University of Massachusetts at Amherst (UMASS-Amherst) by Minister Louis Farrakhan, the leader of the NOI, turned into a glaring example of the anti-Jewish demagoguery and pseudoscholarship that Henry Louis Gates had decried in his *New York Times* article.

REMOVING "JEWISH" FROM A BLACK/JEWISH HISTORICAL EXHIBIT

A national touring exhibit sponsored by the headquarters office of the American Jewish Committee and focusing on 300 years of black/Jewish relations in America, was slated to open on Sunday, April 20, 1993, at the Dillaway-Thomas House, a newly opened community museum in Roxbury, Massachusetts. The Boston Mosque of the NOI placed three additional display panels into the exhibit that contained several anti-Jewish allegations by Louis Farrakhan (leader of the Nation of Islam) and several quotes about Jewish domination of the African slave trade. These additional panels were placed in the exhibit the night before the show opened to the public. The exhibit's sponsor, the American Jewish Committee, was not advised of this last minute change to the exhibit's original material. Lawrence Lowenthal, the regional director of the AJC (in Boston), was ordered by his national office to remove the AJC display material. Lowenthal was accused in the local press by several black leaders of not behaving maturely. Byron Rushing, a principal organizer of the Boston exhibit and a prominent black state representative for Massachusetts, said he didn't see anything antisemitic in the NOI panels.

The opening of the Black/Jewish Historical Exhibit in Boston on April 20, 1993, chronicling three hundred thirty years of shared history, should have been the penultimate example of black/Jewish intercommunity collaboration at its best. But, by the exhibit's opening day, it was anything but collaborative. It was aborted several minutes before the formal opening ceremonies.

The aftermath of the AJC's refusal to participate in the exhibit left both communities—Jews and blacks—angry, suspicious, and further apart than they had been at any time since the tumultuous days of the early 1970s. It was during those years that the predominantly Jewish communities of Roxbury and Mattapan were being resettled by blacks.

Boston, like every other major city in the United States, was shifting significant numbers of its central city populations to the suburbs. Cheap mortgage money, subsidized by the G.I. Bill, and the FHA made it possible for millions of Americans to know home ownership for the first time in their lives. The Jews of Boston were no less eager to follow their gentile neighbors to the suburbs. Jews quickly began settling into new communities west and south of Boston. But, the time had also come when Boston's civic leaders agreed that the living conditions of blacks in Boston had been substandard for far too long. An ingenious plan was hatched by financial and political figures to provide FHA mortgage money to blacks to buy homes in Boston. Hillel Levine and Lawrence Harmon (1992) refer to the calamitous results that followed as a "tragedy of good intentions." Nobody in Boston's white community fully appreciated all of the forces at play in this saga. They were driven by an unfortunate combination of greed and civic pride that culminated in one of this country's worst examples of equal opportunity housing.

The exodus of Jewish families had begun years before the ill-fated "BBURG" concept was unveiled by the city and the banks. The Jews who had already left Roxbury and Mattapan were well-to-do, middle-class families, who had been in the center city for decades. Among the institutions that had relocated to the western suburbs was the prestigious Temple Mishkan Tefila in 1951. As each family left, those left behind were lower on the economic ladder, and by and large, didn't have the money that such an expensive relocation required; they were content to stay behind.

The banks, civic leaders, and authorities at the FHA were convinced from the very beginning that the only intact communities in the city of Boston where a massive resettlement of blacks was possible were the heavily Jewish communities of Roxbury and Mattapan. Their reasoning was simple: the Jews living in those two communities would offer the least resistance to such a plan. They also knew that neither the Irish nor Italian communities would ever allow such a plan to move ahead in their parts of the city. City officials, bankers, and realtors drew a line around the Roxbury/Mattapan area and declared that the low-interest loans from the FHA would be available only inside those perimeters. Many of the Jewish families sold at depressed prices due to the "block busting" tactics of unscrupulous real estate salesmen, but much to the dismay of many of the black families, they found they had bought into a decaying housing stock. Their newly purchased homes frequently required new roofs, new furnaces, and extensive electrical and plumbing repairs. Black families had qualified for the low down-payment requirements of the FHA, but that left little to no money for these expensive repairs, and the houses and neighborhoods deteriorated further. By the spring of 1992 the Jews had been out of Roxbury and Mattapan for two decades, but the memories of block busting and deteriorated housing had left indelible marks on both blacks and Jews. The Black/Jewish Historical Exhibit would take place in one of the black communities' recently completed community restoration areas in Roxbury, the Dillaway-Thomas House.

The Dillaway-Thomas House, located in Heritage State Park, Roxbury, Massachusetts, is an imposing colonial era home built in 1750 that has been lovingly restored and converted to a museum featuring the history of Roxbury. As one of Boston's oldest neighborhoods, Roxbury is a community rich in history and reflective of Boston's immigrant past. Successive waves of immigrants, starting with the English, then the Irish, then the Jews, and now the blacks have called Roxbury their home.[1]

Today, Roxbury and Mattapan are largely black (approximately 120,000). The black settlement of Roxbury/Mattapan coincided with the resettlement of almost 90,000 Jews who for decades had made this area one of the most heavily settled Jewish communities in New England. The inaugural edition of the *Roxbury Heritage News,* fall 1992, contains a timeline for each of the three centuries from 1600 forward. Its entries are factual, but provide little information about the actual citizens who successively settled the area. It jumps from the British in the seventeenth century to the blacks in the twentieth. The centuries in between are occupied with store and plant openings and significant events in American history, but not much about the people who did all of this settling. The Jews of Roxbury are remarked on, in a single sentence for the years 1950 to 1960, along with blacks as the principal immigrants in the area during that time period![2]

The geneses for the Roxbury community museum and for the Black/Jewish Historical Exhibit had several parallels in terms of time, money, and dedication. The restoration of the Dillaway-Thomas House involved the combined efforts of the Roxbury State Park Advisory Committee, the Massachusetts Department of Environmental Management, and scores of private citizens. Several of these citizens would play significant roles in the historical exhibit.

By early 1992 over $2 million in state and city funds had been invested in the restoration of the Dillaway-Thomas House, and it occupied a prominent place in Roxbury's Eliot Square. It opened to the public on September 27, 1992. Its central mission was educational, but it also strove to provide a point of reference for other social and community initiatives. The museum contains thousands of photos, documents, oral histories, and audio/visual presentations on the history and people of Roxbury. Although the museum highlights over three hundred years of Boston history, heavy emphasis is placed on the presence and history of blacks in Roxbury.

The Roxbury Heritage State Park Advisory Committee (RHSPAC) was made up of prominent black citizens from the Boston area. In addition to educators and other professionals, one of the committee's most dedicated figures was State Representative Byron Rushing (Ninth Suffolk District). The Dillaway-Thomas House project was the basis for a great deal of pride throughout the black communities of Boston, and Rushing was determined that it would come to fruition. It did. In a similar vein he contributed his time and influence to the Black/Jewish Historical Exhibit.

The Black/Jewish Historical Exhibit project in Boston was initiated by Lawrence Lowenthal, executive director of the New England office of the AJC. The American Jewish Archives (on the campus of the Hebrew Union in Cincinnati, Ohio) had notified all of the AJC's U.S. directors in 1990 that their exhibit "Blacks and Jews: The American Experience" was available as a touring exhibit to any Jewish community in America that wanted it, and the AJC would do the fund-raising to meet the financial expenses involved in mounting the exhibit.

The exhibit, designed and assembled by Abraham J. Peck (administrative director and principal archivist), consisted of eleven panels of documents, photos, letters, and other memorabilia depicting the relationship between blacks and Jews from 1654 to 1987. The entire exhibit originated with, and was assembled and distributed by, the Jewish community. The original exhibit ran in Cincinnati, Ohio, from December 1987 to September 1988. The first exhibit had no black partner, although the exhibit organizers had always recommended such a coalition was advisable. One panel in the exhibit was particularly provocative because it spelled out in detail the extent of Jewish involvement in the African slave trade. While the number of Jews was small (less than 2 percent), it was, nevertheless, a factual portrayal of Jewish involvement in this despicable commerce.

Lowenthal's initial reaction to the concept of the exhibit was very positive, and he sought out AJC board member Andrea Gargiulo, a former commissioner of licensing for the city of Boston. Gargiulo was an outspoken defender of black civil rights, and she was held in high esteem in Boston's black community. Lowenthal met with Gargiulo and expressed his enthusiasm for the project, pointing out that it hit every major issue that the black and Jewish community in Boston was struggling with. Gargiulo agreed and added her willingness to participate in planning the exhibit. In 1990 Gargiulo became chair of the first committee to bring the exhibit to Boston. The project ran into problems from the very start.

Lowenthal was initially unable to find a black group to partner with the AJC in mounting the exhibit, and he was convinced that the exhibit could not succeed without one. In fact, the whole idea of the exhibit didn't make a lot of sense without a black partner. The exhibit had already appeared in several cities, including New York City; Newark, New Jersey; Miami, Florida; and Chicago, Illinois. In each of these cities the exhibit had been a joint black/Jewish exercise. Lowenthal was perplexed by his inability to find a partner in the black community. He encountered only lukewarm interest from the NAACP and the Urban League.

Given this lack of enthusiasm from Boston's black community, Lowenthal let the project lie fallow for several months, but continued to discuss it with various people around the city. After substantial persistence, and the passage of several months, a skeleton working committee did come together. By early 1992 it consisted of Lowenthal and Gargiulo from the AJC, Juanita Wade, the director of Freedom House, and John Simms of Freedom House.

In February 1992, Byron Rushing, a member of the Roxbury Heritage Park Advisory Committee, notified Lowenthal that the RHPAC was pleased to join the exhibit effort.[3] Rushing, John Bynoe, RHPAC's chairman, and E. Barry Gaither, curator of the Museum of the National Center of Afro-American Artists, would act as representatives to the exhibit committee's planning sessions; the exhibit committee was now represented by the AJC, the Freedom House, and the RHPAC.

It was originally thought that the exhibit could be showcased in a prominent public building in downtown Boston such as the Federal Reserve Building or the South Station Transportation Center. But because of Rushing's connection with RHPAC it was agreed that the exhibit would open at the newly renovated Dillaway-Thomas House in Roxbury Heritage State Park. Rushing had been largely responsible for securing over $2 million in state and city funding for that project. The location issue was also a question of "white" sincerity. If the AJC was serious about reaching the largest number of people, then it made sense to hold it in Roxbury rather than downtown Boston. Roxbury had, after all, been the scene of much of Boston's black and Jewish history, not Boston's financial district.

Over the next several weeks this newly formed committee (the initial committee had lapsed in the face of the difficulties with obtaining a black partner for the planning committee) attracted other prominent and committed figures from the black and Jewish communities to serve as members. Among them were George Russell, a black executive with State Street Bank, and Sydney Topol, an Atlanta industrialist and president of a Fortune 500 company. Topol had been born in Roxbury, was coming back to Boston, and was interested in black/Jewish relations. Russell and Topol became the exhibit committee's cochairs.

With the committee and financing for the exhibit firmly in place, Rushing raised a new, and in Lowenthal's opinion, excellent idea. Expand the exhibit to make it larger, but also to make it more representative of the community in which it would appear, Roxbury. The AJC material consisted of eleven panels, and as interesting as it was, it was not very substantial. Increasing the number of artifacts made sense in light of the larger display areas available in a commodious Dillaway-Thomas House. The idea of expanding the exhibit to reflect black/Jewish relations in Boston over the past three hundred thirty years seemed an excellent opportunity for extending the exhibit's influence to an even wider perspective than originally conceived.

At this point Bernard Wax, former director of the American Jewish Historical Society (located on the campus of Brandeis University), brought in an exhibit designer named Gill Fishman. In company with Rushing, Wax and Fishman scoured Boston archives and pulled up eighty-seven photographs of the former Roxbury and Mattapan communities. While this searching through archives, basements, and attics was underway, the newly formed exhibit committee raised an additional $30,000 to mount any newly discovered photos on display panels and create a truly large scale display; they did, and the number of panels came to fifty.

The assembling of a large-scale exhibit was now firmly underway, and Rushing introduced a suggestion that would, on later analysis, prove to be the pivotal issue on which the exhibit would eventually come undone. It also led to large-scale animosity and distrust among the organizers and members of the black and Jewish communities of Boston.

In addition to the AJC's eleven panels and the additional photo panels from local collections, Rushing recommended that the exhibit become an "open-ended" exhibit. That is, the exhibit, as newly constructed, involved people from both communities, the Jews of Dorchester, Roxbury, and Mattapan who no longer lived there, and the blacks who moved in when the Jews left. Rushing's concept of an open-ended exhibit would allow people from both communities to bring in from their own homes whatever documents, photographs, or letters they felt would add to the grassroots quality of the exhibit. The danger in this, Lowenthal reflected, was that it opened up the whole community to participate in the exhibit. The planning was now moving steadily and enthusiastically toward a gala opening in spring of 1993.

In early February 1993, George Russell (one of the two cochairs of the exhibit committee) proposed a large breakfast meeting to be held at State Street Bank. The purpose of this breakfast meeting was to tell the power structure of greater Boston what had transpired, what was going to transpire, and to give them the opportunity to meet several of the key players in this multicommunity effort. Over forty people attended Russell's breakfast meeting. Rushing, Topol, and several others would speak. Russell shared the list of invitees with Lowenthal, since they had agreed that Russell would set up the invitation list and Lowenthal would mail out the invitations. Among the guests was Minister Don Muhammad of the Boston Mosque of the Nation of Islam. Lowenthal's response was telling in light of later events: "I saw his name on the list and I made a fatal error! I did not pick up the phone and call George Russell and tell him, 'George, I don't think it's wise to invite Don Mohammed to this breakfast meeting. The AJC cannot deal in any way with the Nation of Islam. It's dangerous.' They could be disruptive, but I didn't do it; I let it go" (Lawrence Lowenthal, interview by author, June 9, 1994). It must be noted at this point that the AJC has a national policy of not appearing in public (under any circumstance) with representatives from the NOI. This policy is based on the reasoning that any such appearance on the part of the AJC would lend credibility to the NOI's antisemitic dema- goguery (archives of AJC board of governor's meeting, June 28, 1993).

The breakfast meeting was held, but Don Muhammad could not attend. However, one of his aides, Alan Thompson (aka Alan X), substituted for him. The upcoming Black/Jewish Exhibit was described in careful detail, and with enthusiasm, by all of the key committee members. During this meeting Lowenthal was approached by Alan X and was asked about an article that Lowenthal had written for the *Jewish Advocate* attacking the book *The Secret Relationship between Blacks and Jews*. In his article entitled "Understanding Farrakhan and His Organization," January 8, 1993, Lowenthal also attacked the NOI's leader, Louis Farrakhan. The NOI reads everything in the Jewish press, and they were angered by Lowenthal's comments. Lowenthal had also "blasted" *The Secret Relationship* on a popular Boston radio talk show (David Brudnoy, WBZ, February 1993). Lowenthal had not actually read *The Secret Relationship*, but he had read a two-page critique of it by Harold Brackman of the Simon Weisenthal Holocaust Research Center in Los Angeles, California, entitled *The Historical Record: Responding with Fact to Charges in The Secret Relationship between Blacks and Jews* [1993?].

When Thompson questioned Lowenthal about his article, Lowenthal ad- mitted that he had not read *The Secret Relationship*; not surprisingly, Thompson's reaction was one of amazement. How could Lowenthal criticize the book if he hadn't even read it? Lowenthal's admission would haunt him for the next several months, and the fallout culminated in a pointed criticism of the Jewish community in the Nation of Islam's publication the *Final Call* and in Tony Martin's book *The Jewish Onslaught* (1993). In the aftermath of the exhibit's failure, Lowenthal received a scolding letter from a key AJC staff member in New York City pointedly reminding him of the AJC's policy concerning nonappearance with the NOI (Stern to Lowenthal, "Interview Regarding Nation of Islam," May 14, 1993).

Unknown to Lowenthal during this breakfast exchange with the repre- sentative from the NOI was the fact that on a separate occasion, before

Russell's breakfast meeting, the Nation of Islam had been invited in to preview the AJC's eleven panels. In fact, the entire exhibit had been made available for a pre-opening viewing by members of the community. One of the AJC panels carried comments that were highly critical of Louis Farrakhan's role with, and his speeches for, Jesse Jackson's 1984 presidential campaign. A number of these speeches contained strongly worded antisemitic allegations or warnings. In addition, the panel made direct comparisons between Farrakhan and the Nazis. The Nation of Islam saw these comments and was outraged. The exhibit was slated to open at the Dillaway-Thomas House on Sunday, April 20, 1993.

In addition to Russell's breakfast meeting, a number of events occurred beginning in February 1993 that virtually assured that the exhibit would not occur as originally conceived. At a small meeting in late January or early February, Byron Rushing, in an enthusiastic declaration, said that the Black/Jewish Historical Exhibit would be opened up to everybody in the community thereby allowing for maximum citizen input. Something went off in Lowenthal's consciousness. After his encounter with Alan X at Russell's breakfast meeting, he had become painfully aware of the impact of the book *The Secret Relationship between Blacks and Jews*, and what effect the NOI's criticism of the Jewish response to it was having in both the white and black neighborhoods of Boston. Now came Rushing's proposal to open the exhibit out still further into the community.

This idea, Lowenthal reasoned, presented a real potential for serious trouble. Lowenthal pointed out to Rushing that participation by "anybody" in the black community could not include the NOI because of the AJC's policy of nonappearance in any public forum with the NOI. Rushing responded indignantly, "Who are you to tell us who we can include, or not include?" Lowenthal responded, "I am speaking on behalf of the American Jewish Committee which began this whole thing [the exhibit], and is financing it. We cannot deal with the Nation of Islam!" Lowenthal couldn't have been clearer in reaffirming the AJC's national policy of nonappearance. The cochair, George Russell, was not in the room when this exchange took place, and was unable to verify what Lowenthal and Rushing had said to one another (Lowenthal, interview).

On April 17, 1993, four days before the exhibit was slated to open, the planning committee met for the last time. It was a final preparation, a last details sort of meeting. It was again held in the State Street Bank's conference room, and a significant exchange took place in the waning minutes of this final meeting. According to Lowenthal, Rushing made two statements. In his first statement, Rushing said that Professor Tony Martin from Wellesley College (one of the central characters in the Wellesley College book incident; see chapter nine) was going to speak at the Dillaway-Thomas House on Saturday, April 19, 1993. This was the day before the Black/Jewish Historical Exhibit would open to the public. Rushing's announcement created an immediate uproar. Lowenthal remembers: "Everybody leaped on that: What? How could you allow such a thing?—Tony Martin?—This is outrageous!" Rushing quickly pointed out that the Dillaway-Thomas House was public property, and Martin had every right to speak there.

In the clamor that followed his first declaration, nobody but Lowenthal, it seems, heard Rushing make a second, and even more alarming, declaration. Lowenthal clearly remembers Rushing saying in a matter-of-fact way (not a whisper, not a bold statement) that "the Nation of Islam is planning to add their input into this exhibit." Lowenthal is unclear about what he did next, but he does remember that he said nothing in response to Rushing's startling announcement—and he is absolutely clear that he heard Rushing make the statement. His failure to make any comment on something this significant would only complicate later events and decisions.

On Saturday, April 19, 1993, Lowenthal and Fishman were installing the finishing touches to the exhibit. In a word it looked "terrific." Then, shortly after 2:00 P.M., Alan X, the aide to Minister Don Muhammad of the Boston Mosque of the NOI, and Lowenthal's earlier antagonist, arrived at the exhibit site accompanied by nine guards of the Fruit of Islam, the security branch of the NOI. This security force accompanies the leaders of the NOI on every public appearance, and they present a formidable image. Immaculately dressed in suits, white shirts, ties, and black sunglasses, they are intimidating by their very presence, even if they never say or do a thing. Their presence was not lost on Lowenthal or Fishman. The exchange that ensued was heated and worth recounting.

Lowenthal: What is this?

Alan X: We have our panels that we're going to add to the exhibit.

Lowenthal: You can't just come in here and add panels to the exhibit.

Alan X: Well, that's what you invited the community to do, and that's what we are going to do.

Fishman (enraged): You can't do that! I'm the creator of this exhibit. You can't just barge in here and add things.

Lowenthal recalled that his indignation had risen to the boiling point. He remembered saying something else to Alan X, but could not recall what it was, and that the NOI security "goons" were doing a lot of heavy-duty glaring. The tension in the room had reached a precipitous level, and at that instant an older, unidentified man with the NOI contingent came into the room. He never identified himself in the overheated atmosphere of the confrontation, but quietly and calmly declared, "We are going to do what we're going to do!"

The older gentleman, Alan X, and the others in the NOI contingent would not allow Lowenthal to see the content of the NOI's panels. They removed the panels from their transport boxes and began putting them up on any open space they could fit them into. The NOI's panels were being interspersed among the other panels, as if they were a regular part of the exhibit. Lowenthal immediately attempted to stop their actions, pointing out that they could not interfere with the layout or content of the present exhibit. What they were attempting to do by just "showing up" and forcing their display material into the exhibit was illegal. Lowenthal pointed out that all of the contents of the present exhibit were copyrighted objects and text. The Nation of Islam contingent insisted they were leaving their panels regardless of the AJC's protestations.

At this point Lowenthal left the exhibit hall, got on a phone, and attempted to reach several key people connected with the exhibit. He was unable to reach either Byron Rushing or Barry Gaither (curator of the Museum of the National Center of Afro-American Artists). After several other frustrating attempts, he did reach his associate director at the AJC, Martin Goldman, and explained to him the disaster that was in the making, as he saw it, unfolding at the Dillaway-Thomas House. But, unable to reach anyone on the exhibit committee, Lowenthal, frustrated but resigned to this failure, helped Fishman with the final details of setting up the exhibit. The AJC panels were mounted on the walls, and the local exhibit of eighty-seven photographs had been mounted and spaciously set up on stands using the available floor space. It was an impressive assemblage, and wound through several rooms. What happened next is a mystery to everyone connected with this incident. The Boston Police arrived and in strength!

Lowenthal did not know the police had arrived because, at that precise moment, he was on a different floor listening to comments being made by Professor Tony Martin (Wellesley College). Supposedly, someone in the mayor's office had called the police as a precautionary measure. Lowenthal speculated that this was done because of the notoriety attending Tony Martin and his recent clash with the AJC (and the other Jewish advocacy organizations in Boston) over the Wellesley incident (see chapter nine). Lowenthal is convinced to this day that Byron Rushing and Juanita Wade (the director of the Freedom House) believe that Lowenthal himself called the police. It turned out it was Lowenthal's associate director, Martin Goldman, who had called a friend of his in the mayor's office, and that person had called the civil disorder unit, who came over to see what was going on. Whatever the intentions were in calling in the police, their appearance left a bad taste in everybody's mouth. The next day, Sunday (the day the exhibit opened), the police arrived once again, but this time they stood out on the street, content to simply watch the proceedings.

But on Saturday evening Lowenthal was still trying urgently to reach someone connected to the committee to discuss the NOI's actions. At 11:00 P.M. Lowenthal was finally able to reach Rushing, and a brittle exchange took place:

Lowenthal: They [NOI] told me, "We have permission from Byron Rushing to put up these panels." Byron, what have you done? How could you possibly do this? You are going to cause a terrible upheaval; a huge scandal that's going to tear apart our committee.

Rushing: What are you so excited about? Why are you making so much of this? It's ridiculous; this is hilarious. I never heard of anything so foolish and ridiculous in my life! You're making a mountain out of a mole hill.

Lowenthal: Byron, take it from me, this is serious.

Rushing: All right, I will go down there [Dillaway-Thomas House] early tomorrow [Sunday] morning. You bring some of your people, and we'll work this out.

Prominent among Lowenthal's "people" was Gary Rubin, the AJC's director of national affairs. Within the national office of the AJC, Rubin had responsibility for overseeing anything that had to do with antisemitism and bigotry. He was slated to speak the next day along with Rushing and a host of local dignitaries. Lowenthal had called Rubin in New York Saturday night, after his conversation with Rushing, and had started off his conversation by saying, "I think we've got a crisis on our hands!" Lowenthal explained the entire situation to Rubin, and they agreed to meet at the Boston airport for a brief conference early Sunday morning. Rubin was flying in from New York City and would arrive at 10:00 A.M. An 11:00 A.M. meeting with Byron Rushing had been arranged by Lowenthal and several other key people from the AJC, including its president.

At 11:30 A.M. Rubin and Lowenthal met with Rushing and other committee members at the Dillaway-Thomas House. The exhibit would open at 1:00 P.M., and over 300 guests had been invited to a series of carefully orchestrated events. The atmosphere in the room was heavy with uneasiness, and the general demeanor was extremely serious. Rubin said, "Let me see the [NOI] panels." The NOI's panel material repeated much of the content found in *The Secret Relationship*. The panels contained excerpts and fragments of information that depicted Jews as heavily involved in the African slave trade. In addition to the slave issue, the panels also portrayed Jews as controlling Hollywood, and, in so doing, exploiting negative images of blacks. The NOI's panels highlighted Israeli (therefore, Jewish) exploitation of black South Africa. The NOI portrayed Jews as "sucking blood" out of inner-city blacks. The Jews were portrayed in these panels as controlling the media in the United States. The NOI's distorted and demagogic portrayal of Jews filled three panels, similar in shape, size, and physical appearance to the American Jewish Archive's original eleven panels. The NOI had emulated the original panels in every way, except the content.

Rubin cast a shocked eye across the NOI's three panels, and said, "We're out of here!" The next few minutes of interchange gives some indication of the swiftness and finality with which the decision was reached to completely withdraw from the exhibit and the months of work that had gone into bringing it to fruition. Lowenthal recalled Rubin stating, "You will not be associated in any way, whatsoever, with this kind of crap. We're [AJC] out of this exhibit!" Lowenthal commented, "Gary, there are 300 people waiting outside, and this thing starts in less than an hour." Rubin responded, "I don't care!"

The dilemma in this declaration by Rubin was painfully real. The director of national affairs for AJC's New York headquarters politely, but unmistakably, was confronting the local leadership of the AJC. The local AJC officials had a lot invested in this program, and they wanted to find a way to work out the differences and still go on with the show. The AJC's national office, in the person of Gary Rubin, was adamant: Under no circumstances would AJC participation continue with the offending NOI panels as part of the exhibit. It would not have mattered if the panels had been moved to their own room. The Boston AJC, and Lawrence Lowenthal, were up against national AJC policy, and that jurisdiction prevailed. All arguments to the contrary, there would be no compromise with national policy, regardless of the embarrassment it caused at the local level. Rubin left the Dillaway-Thomas House in Roxbury, got back on a plane, and returned to New York City. That was the end of AJC participation in an exhibit that was to open in a matter of minutes, and Lowenthal was left with the ensuing mess. Two questions remain to be answered: Did the Boston exhibit open, or was it canceled; and what happened to Lowenthal and the Black/Jewish Historical Exhibit after Sunday, April 20, 1993?

The exhibit did open, and right on time. Nothing short of a fire or some other catastrophe was going to stop the exhibit from opening as scheduled, or the speeches from being given, or the food from being consumed, or the bands from playing, or from scores of people—black and white, Christian and Jewish—from touring the exhibit and viewing the displays, offending panels and all; and that is precisely what happened. Key dignitaries (Byron Rushing, Sydney Topol, and the mayor of Boston) and several political luminaries all spoke. With the speeches over, hundreds of people streamed through the exhibit. Great quantities of food were consumed; bands played. All told it turned out to be a fine afternoon, except for the American Jewish Committee and its regional director, Lawrence Lowenthal.

What of the original eleven panels from the American Jewish Archives' original exhibit; were they taken out? That didn't happen immediately. They remained in place, at least temporarily; nothing was touched. The AJC released a quickly composed press statement that expressed their outrage at the blatant antisemitic content of the NOI's three exhibit panels, and under no circumstances would the AJC be seen as supporting or associating itself in any way with this current version of the Black/Jewish Historical Exhibit.

On Monday, April 21, 1993, the whole affair exploded in the press and other media, and the uproar lasted that entire week. In the days that followed Rubin's decision to pull the AJC out of the exhibit, Lowenthal found himself alone, fighting the aftershock of Rubin's decision and all of the implications Rubin's decision carried for him in the Boston community. Lowenthal appeared on local, national and public television, and radio. He attempted to defend the decision to withdraw the AJC's eleven panels from the exhibit. Lowenthal recalls, "I didn't know what to do, quite frankly. I just didn't know what to do. I guess what I should have done was to have literally removed the panels the very next day, but I just couldn't do it until our local committee reassembled. I just couldn't do it, although I was ordered to. They told me to get rid of those—take those panels out of that building the very next morning, but I didn't do it. The exhibit committee agreed to meet as soon as possible, which wasn't until Thursday of that week. I sort of fudged it. Officially we're out; that's all there is to it." This was the only example Lowenthal could recall of when there had been such a clear difference of opinion between himself, at the local level, and the AJC's national office.

The meetings that took place among the different groups in the city in the days immediately following the AJC's withdrawal from the exhibit were laced with bitterness and anger. Everybody, it seemed, was angry with the AJC. A large number of schools in the area were disappointed, because they had been invited to tour an entire exhibit, not a partial exhibit. Discussion panels on black/Jewish relations had been planned, and they were structured around open debate and discussion. The exhibit would have been neutral ground, providing people with an opportunity to air their sensitivities concerning black/Jewish relations in the city, and to do so in a mutually supportive environment; now that would not happen.

In the immediate aftermath of the exhibit's failure, Lowenthal and the rest of the exhibit planning committee quietly arranged to meet in George Russell's conference room and attempt to make some sort of a deal with the NOI. At one point, Don Mohammed, the leader of the NOI's Boston Mosque, had actually called the AJC's Boston office. His demeanor was conciliatory, and he expressed the opinion that if he had realized how far out of hand the entire incident would go, he would have withdrawn the NOI from the exhibit. In spite of Rubin's direct order, by Thursday, April 29, Lowenthal had not yet removed the AJC's eleven panels. He was still trying to work out some sort of a compromise. The next day, on April 30, 1993, the *Boston Globe* reported those attempts at compromise as "In Shift, Jewish Group to Allow Exhibit to Remain in Roxbury." Nothing could have been further from the facts in the matter.

Negotiations around the composition of the ongoing exhibit continued between the exhibit committee and the NOI. Don Mohammad had agreed to remove their panels along with the removal of the AJC's panels, and leave in place the 87 pieces of memorabilia and photographs that represented local contributions. Only there was one condition—he (Don Mohammad) would be allowed to come and speak to the exhibit committee about the NOI's role. Lowenthal, of course, had to refuse to participate, because of the

AJC's standing prohibition forbidding any public appearance with the NOI. George Russell was perplexed, but Lowenthal explained, "We can't do it, because as soon as Don Mohammed comes to address the committee, which is 90 percent the AJC, it's then on the record that we met with him, and he's very clever. The next thing you know there it will be in the media, 'Jews and the Nation of Islam.' The American Jewish Committee and the Nation of Islam in a conciliatory meeting—and I'm dead! I can't do it George" (Lowenthal, interview).

Russell's initial reaction to the AJC's nonappearance requirement was frustration and anger with the AJC and with Lowenthal. It took a long time before Russell began interacting again with the AJC and with Lowenthal (George Russell, interview by author, March 4, 1996). All of the blacks on the exhibit committee were furious, as were several of the Jewish committee members. Andrea Gargiulo (a part of the first organizing committee for the exhibit) resigned from her board position with the AJC. She could not understand the AJC's refusal to sit down and talk with the Boston leader of the NOI. She had seen Don Muhammad straighten out hoodlums and tough kids and get other kids off drugs, and she felt he should be given a lot of credit. The AJC and Lawrence Lowenthal did not deny the credit due him for the good he had done. But, neither would the AJC ignore the fact that Don Muhammad represented an organization that spewed hate messages against various groups in the white community, including very distorted, and oft-repeated, antisemitic diatribes. On rethinking the whole affair Lowenthal concluded that he had made the all too common mistake of trying to be nice to everybody; it had not worked. Lowenthal mused, "In this business, you cannot compromise with any perceived antisemitism. Once you do, you're held in contempt by the Jews; *you've failed in your charge*"(emphasis added).

The days and months that followed found Lowenthal embroiled in other repercussions from his New York office's decision to withdraw from the Black/Jewish Historical Exhibit in Boston. Most of the fallout was negative, and much of it was personally painful. Events had moved from conception, to planning, to expansion, to implementation, to head-to-head confrontation, and then suddenly, to the collapse of a wonderfully conceived intercommunity collaborative effort. Certainly, the demise of the exhibit, or at least the AJC's portion of it, was sudden; but, in the final analysis, just how collaborative was it? Those questions are addressed more fully in chapter eleven. To understand how extensive the repercussions were and how far afield the discontent spread, we must set aside the discontent and return to the spring of 1993.

Lowenthal and the Boston AJC found themselves ensnared in a classic catch-22 predicament. Nothing Lowenthal had done or would do could reduce the anger felt by the black community or on the part of the members of the exhibit committee. On the other side, the AJC's New York headquarters was angry, and local Jews were angry. In the weeks immediately following the removal of the AJC panels, Lowenthal engaged in a series of conversations with several people from the black community. The animosity over this incident ran so deep in Boston's black community that Lowenthal was never able to communicate, only converse. He felt, on hindsight, that the breach was so profound as to make it "insurmountable" (Lowenthal, interview).

One of these conversations was with a black female, a retired urban planner. For her, the incident was reminiscent of a childhood memory of Jewish arrogance, the Bronx slave market. During the depression of the 1930s, Jewish matrons would drive to a particular intersection in the Bronx, where hundreds of black housekeepers and maids would wait to be picked out to work for the day in the Jewish matron's home. The experience was humiliating and degrading. While the exploitation of blacks was very much a part of the Bronx slave market, some of the veterans of this era admitted that two part-time jobs paid better than one full-time job (Palmer, 1989:72). The possibility of extra wage days was often to be found in the slave market. But, the economic necessities of the depression left deep scars, and this woman remembered it only as one of humiliation and degradation that she ascribed to the Jews.

This daily, and frequently brittle, interface between Jews and blacks in major cities like New York, Chicago, and Philadelphia was only one of countless, if somewhat less degrading, examples of the substantial social and economic differences between Jews and blacks that took place in the course of daily life. Blacks frequently had Jewish landlords; their children's teachers were frequently Jewish, as were their grocer, their clothier, their neighborhood social worker, and on occasion, their probation officer. It was those kinds of childhood memories (memories that overrode any antisemitism on the part of the NOI and their exhibit panels) that this black woman responded to when she reflected on the actions of the AJC on that fateful day in April 1993.

ORGANIZATIONAL IMPLICATIONS

The eleven AJC panels were finally removed a week and a day after Rubin had ordered an end to the AJC's participation in the Black/Jewish Historical Exhibit. Animosity persists to this day. Russell would not turn away from either Lowenthal or the AJC, in part because he is vice president of public relations for one of the city's largest banks; it would not be good business. But at this writing, Byron Rushing will not speak to Lowenthal or to the American Jewish Committee in Boston. Unfortunately, Lowenthal believes Rushing engineered the entire crisis and the eventual necessity for the withdrawal of the AJC's panels with the help of the Nation of Islam.

The misfortunes do not end with just the leftover bad feelings among the players. After the AJC removed their panels, the exhibit, originally slated to run for two months, continued at the Dillaway-Thomas House for another eight months, with the Nation of Islam's panels, and their anti-Jewish sentiments, firmly in place. The one thing the AJC would not do, appear publicly with the NOI (regardless of the forum), had backfired. The AJC's policy of nonappearance with the NOI had, through a series of miscalculations and bungled communications, only entrenched the NOI more visibly in the public's mind, and had done so for a longer time period than the NOI could have arranged under its own initiative, particularly in the city of Boston.

Boston holds a unique position in the activities of the publicity-conscious Nation of Islam. It was Louis Farrakhan's first home, and it is presently the publishing locus for NOI's book *The Secret Relationship between Blacks and Jews*. Boston is the only site in the United States where an incident of the dimensions here described occurred. The American Jewish Archives exhibit had already appeared in Newark, New Jersey; New York City; Chicago; the greater Miami area; and ten other cities before coming to Boston. In each of those cities the exhibit was a joint black/Jewish effort. Only in Boston did the exhibit take on the crisis proportions here reported, and only in Boston was the AJC's portion withdrawn for any reason. The exhibit would be seen in several other Jewish communities in the United States following this incident (Abraham Peck, interview by author, June 11, 1995).

THE ROLE OF THE OTHER JAOs IN THIS INCIDENT

Of the three antisemitic incidents analyzed in this study, the Black/Jewish Historical Exhibit generated the least involvement from the other three JAOs. Where a great deal of dialogue, strategizing, and planning took place with both the Wellesley College incident and the Louis Farrakhan college speech, this incident did not directly involve the other three JAOs in this study. This is principally because of the exhibit's sponsorship. The AJC had initiated this exhibit, and the events that followed were a result of their initiative. There was no need for the other JAOs to be a part of an activity that was under the sponsorship of the AJC. There was no way of knowing, almost to the very end of the incident, how badly it would end. Certainly, the other JAOs would have provided any help or advice had it been requested.

Interviews with the other three JAOs revealed a collection of organizational responses that ranged from pained disappointment that the exhibit had failed to criticism of Lowenthal for "blowing it." There was no reason to step in and provide a solid front in the face of anger from the black community or the eventual eight-month display of the NOI panels. The other JAOs' remarks included: "I wish Larry had paid closer attention to what was going on behind his back." "It wasn't our place to interfere in how Larry carried out his management of AJC affairs." "I felt very sorry for the corner Larry found himself in, but there really wasn't much I could have done that would have made the situation better for the AJC or for the Jewish community." "Unfortunately, we have reaped some of the harvest of anger and suspicion that this incident triggered. I see it in the meetings I go to with black leaders in the community. They weren't even a part of the decision making, but they know all about it, and they don't like how it ended." (Comments provided on the assurance of anonymity [transcripts on file].)

In spite of the sadness and the hardness of these observations, the other three JAOs felt it was unlikely that the public reputation of the AJC was badly tarnished by its withdrawal from the exhibit. In fact, a great many people in the Jewish community saw Lowenthal as a hero of no small proportions—he had stood up to the Nation of Islam.

NOTES

1. The restoration of Roxbury has included a number of efforts to capture its past in a variety of representations. One of these is a collection of impressive stone tablets adjacent to the Ruggles Street transit station. Each of the four stone tablets re-creates a single "letter home" from an English, Irish, Jewish, and black immigrant to the neighborhood.

2. The *Roxbury Heritage News* was published in conjunction with the Black Studies Department, Northeastern University, Boston, Massachusetts.

3. Letter from Rushing to Lowenthal, Febuary 4, 1992.

Chapter 9

Incident Number Two: Antisemitic Book Is Used to Teach Black History

During the 1993 spring semester, Tony Martin, a black professor at Wellesley College, used a book in his African American survey history course (number 206, offered by the Africana Studies Department) entitled *The Secret Relationship between Blacks and Jews, Volume 1* (1991), published by the Nation of Islam. This compilation of assorted facts and exaggerations contends that Jews were overwhelmingly involved in, and responsible for, the African slave trade. Martin was censured by other Wellesley faculty for using the book in his classroom, and for several other anti-Jewish comments he made on campus. His job was protected under Wellesley's tenure policy. When challenged by the Boston media for their reaction to this collection of antisemitic allegations, the JAOs responded as a single voice and published a strongly worded statement of protest and complaint about the book and Professor Martin's use of it in a classroom situation.

JEWISH ADVOCACY'S ROLE IN THE WELLESLEY INCIDENT

On April 5, 1993, the four JAOs in Boston published a joint press release condemning *The Secret Relationship between Blacks and Jews, Volume 1* (hereafter, *SR*), and the teacher who used it in a course at Wellesley College. The book had been at the center of a controversy for months on the campus of Wellesley College, Wellesley, Massachusetts. Professor Tony Martin had adopted the book for classroom use and had praised it as an authentic historical treatment of Jewish involvement in the African slave trade. Professor Martin was under close scrutiny within Wellesley College for his use of the book in his African American history course and for his flamboyant and controversial teaching style. At this juncture, the Jewish community in the greater Boston area, through its advocacy organizations, had decided to speak as one voice and condemn the use of an antisemitic book, and similar anti-Jewish pronouncements by Professor Martin.

Of the three antisemitic incidents reported in this book that triggered the direct intervention of one or more of the JAOs, the Wellesley College incident is perhaps the most complex: it involved all of the JAOs in a collaborative action, something that rarely happens in Jewish advocacy; before the incident's conclusion, this collaborative decision drew in the advice and involvement of several other national and local advisors to the JAOs; and it is the most complex antisemitic incident because the disputed book (*SR*), the instructor (Tony Martin), and the course on African American history continue to be a presence on the Wellesley campus. The immediate dispute has been resolved, but the incident's causative ingredients remain in place as a reminder of what took place and what could boil up again.

The issues in this incident can be divided into three parts: first, the way in which the decision strategy emerged to write and release a joint press release; second, the decision by the JAOs that focused on how they would deal with a slim monograph, self-published by Martin, that described his impressions of a "Jewish conspiracy" he claimed was mounted to discredit him; and third, the status of Wellesley College at this writing. This includes Tony Martin's future, his course on African American history, and his clearly stated intention to continue using *SR* as his text of choice for that course.

THE JOINT PRESS RELEASE

As the spring semester of 1993 opened at Wellesley College, the administration, the Wellesley College Hillel group (the Jewish students' campus organization), and a host of faculty members were beginning to learn more about Professor Martin's Africana Studies course number 206, and his adoption of *SR* as one of his primary texts. Martin is a tenured faculty employee at Wellesley College and a scholar on Marcus Garvey, the nineteenth-century black leader. Martin's courses were cross-listed with other departments (e.g., history) making it possible for students to satisfy multiple distribution requirements for degree purposes. Early in the spring semester several Jewish students complained about *SR* being sold in the Wellesley College bookstore, and several more students were complaining about Martin's teaching style. Those complaints claimed he was adamantly resistant to any class discussion, particularly any disagreement or criticism of the course material or his lectures. Students, faculty, and the administration were uncomfortable with Martin's style, which was often mercurial. An earlier incident in 1991 had left the college scrambling to protect itself against a lawsuit filed by a former student because of Martin's behavior.

During October 1991, Martin accosted a white female student monitor in one of the dormitories where a lecture was being given. He had been denied access to the private areas of the dorm by this young lady; an appropriate action considering her status as a security monitor. Her actions so infuriated Martin that he verbally assaulted her with a withering stream of invectives. It was later reported by Alyson Todd in a *Heterodoxy* article entitled "Blacks and Jews and the News," May 6, 1993, that he had called her "a white fucking bitch," "a racist," and "a bigot," among other things. "The young woman fell down as a result of his onslaught and Martin bent over [her] to continue to rage at her. Professor Martin became so violent, in fact, . . . that the Head of the House for the dormitory called the campus police." Martin returned to the meeting and said the young woman had stopped him only because he was black.

But the incident didn't end there; in fact it didn't end for several more months. In the aftermath of this verbal assault, Martin complained to a group of his black-student supporters about the young woman. They, in turn, began following her around campus, taunting her with highly personal and pejorative attacks, accusing her of racism. She became increasingly distraught, and finally withdrew from the college. In the months that followed, her family sued Wellesley College and ultimately settled out of court. Although Martin was accused of inciting students to harass the young woman, neither he nor Wellesley's administration ever commented on his role in this incident.

The incident is indicative, in an extreme form, of the turmoil and conflict on Wellesley's campus between some Jewish and black students, as well as of Martin's association with it through his direct verbal assault, his course on African American history, his student supporters, and his public statements. There were students (black, white, Jewish, and Christian) at Wellesley who believed that Martin's teaching fomented antisemitism in some of his students.

The role of Jewish faculty members on the Wellesley campus is one more important ingredient in an already expanding recipe for upheaval. They attempted to meet with Martin and discuss his use of *SR,* as well as some of the students' criticisms of his teaching style, but Martin rebuffed all such requests. The text was his choice, and that was that. The other faculty members (Jewish or not) didn't have to like his choice of books, but he had no obligation to remove it. This is a sensitive issue in academe. Selection of course material and texts is a universally accepted prerogative of the instructor. It goes to the heart of academic freedom and First Amendment constitutional protection.

During the 1992–1993 academic year the controversy swirling around Tony Martin drew in increasingly larger numbers of people. In October 1992, Martin angered a great many people on the Wellesley campus by self-publishing a four-page broadsheet entitled "Blacks and Jews at Wellesley News." He brought large quantities of his broadsheet on campus and handed it out to faculty and students alike. The broadsheet featured articles and comments on black separatism, the supposed Jewish conspiracy against blacks in the media, the Jewish control of the African slave trade, the international prostitution of women (primarily Jewish women), and the participation by Jews in the "extermination of the Native Americans." Mary Lefkowitz, a renowned scholar of Greek and Roman classics and a professor of classics at Wellesley College, came under withering ridicule in the broadsheet with Martin attacking Lefkowitz for criticizing the scholarship of a well-known author of the Afrocentric movement, Martin Bernal, *Black Athena: The Afroasiatic Roots of Classical Civilization* (1987). Lefkowitz characterized Bernal's claims for the African sources of Greek culture as fanciful notions based on myth. Martin's characterization and attack on Lefkowitz, a fellow faculty member, were so grievous that in March 1993 Wellesley College's president issued a formal statement defending Professor Lefkowitz and deploring Martin's attack on her.

February and March 1993 proved to be busy months in the conflict developing at Wellesley College. In February 1993, Selwyn Cudjoe, chair of the department of Africana Studies (and Martin's academic boss), repudiated Martin's use of *SR* in his African American history course. A month later, on March 4, 1993, the Wellesley College Academic Committee, in an all-college faculty meeting, formally censured Martin. Not to be outdone by the establishment, Martin proceeded to personally attack and insult several of the faculty members at that meeting.

In increasing numbers, students in Martin's course and in the general Wellesley population began lining up on either side of this controversy. Martin was not without his admirers or supporters. A number of black students were quick to heap praise on Martin's teaching, and his unofficial role as spokesman for black rights and black history. A flurry of e-mail messages were exchanged concerning Martin. A professor Cain explained his criticisms of Martin, and Martin responded with explosive force. A Wellesley Hillel senator wrote a letter of support for Martin, and in response a former Hillel senator criticized the previous student's comments and Martin's lack of judgement in selecting *SR* as a text to begin with. By April, the Boston JAOs were deeply involved in the furor at Wellesley College.

Collaborative decision making by the JAOs is exceptional because of the infrequency with which it happens. Each of these organizations has different charters and sees itself as serving different populations within the American Jewish community (see chapters three, four, five, and six). Consequently, issues of common interests/concerns to Jews will be approached by each of the JAOs in decidedly different ways. It is rare that any issue will be of such magnitude that all four of the JAOs will make a conscious decision to join hands and speak with a single voice. The issues that surfaced at Wellesley College formed the basis for one of those rare exceptions to past practice. The text that follows is a continuous narrative of the issues and provocations that unfolded at Wellesley College in spring 1993. It was constructed from the multiple observations of the principal players in the JAOs and at the college and was elicited over the course of several interviews.

Each of the JAOs' recommendations about what should be done to combat Martin's distorted rhetoric, and his accompanying antisemitism, moved from pronouncements based on their separate ideologies to agreement that a unitary course of action was called for. After a great deal of work, they finally agreed on a jointly authored press release as the vehicle that would reach the largest audience possible and would best express their outrage and concern over the events unfolding at the college. But, each of the organizations' "take" on how this press release evolved and what role each of them played in the final wording is varied and nuanced.

Understanding how this process evolved calls to mind the image of *Rashomon*, the well-known Japanese film that depicted the retelling of a single event in a small town from the perspective of several different persons. The observations and conclusions of each party about the incident was filtered through deeply held beliefs that formed the basis of their view of the world. In the same way, the narratives provided by the JAOs and people at, or close to, Wellesley College were a "Rashomonic" exercise in the best sense of that term. The different participant's retellings of the events that took place at Wellesley were deeply influenced by four factors: their worldviews; their organizational charters; the demands made on them by their lay leaders; and their personal experience with other antisemitic incidents.

The ADL's eastern states civil rights director, Sally Greenberg, was the first of the JAOs contacted by people at Wellesley College complaining about Professor Martin and his use of the *SR* in his course. A student had called Greenberg and related the story of Martin's verbal attack on the white female student dorm monitor. Greenberg's attempts to talk to college officials were rebuffed, and she was told ADL's help was not needed. The ADL, however, continued to get calls from other students and parents about Martin's behavior, both in class and out of class, and his course on African American history and his choice of the *SR* as the course text. Parents were calling to complain about Martin's antisemitic attack on Jews (in both the historical and modern context). Alumnae were complaining, as well, expressing fear for the school's reputation. Faculty members had also begun to complain to all of the JAOs about what was happening that spring on the Wellesley campus.

There was a certain logic in contacting the ADL first. Discrimination, hate crimes, and antisemitism are the ADL's stock in trade. The ADL had a relationship with the college that went back several years. At one point during the 1950s Wellesley (like other prominent colleges and universities in the United States) maintained restrictive quotas on the number of Jewish students and faculty it would permit on campus. The ADL was a significant player in getting these quotas dropped and, in general, in improving the atmosphere on campus toward Jews. Today, the college has a department of

Judaic studies. In recent years the town of Wellesley has called upon the
ADL to help it with a rash of antisemitic graffiti. The ADL was perhaps better known to the college for these reasons (Auerbach, 1984).

The first official on-site contact with a Wellesley college official was made
by Leonard Zakim, eastern regional director of the ADL, and Sally Greenberg.
The event that triggered the ADL's decision to get involved with Wellesley
College was Tony Martin's publication of a four-page broadsheet entitled
"Blacks and Jews at Wellesley News," Spring, 1993 (Auerbach, 1993). It was
not an approved college publication, but Martin brought quantities of it on
campus and handed it out to faculty and students alike. At this point, the ADL
reasoned, the college could benefit from their advocacy. A meeting was
arranged with Nanerl O. Keohane, Wellesley's president at the time. The ADL
director recalled, "Our general sense was that academic freedom protected
whatever he [Martin] was teaching, and while it might be offensive to us or
other people, we weren't about to dictate what teachers taught in their classrooms, but the broadsheet, 'Blacks and Jews at Wellesley News' was just a
polemic against the Jewish community. When 'Blacks and Jews at Wellesley
News' came out we all began to discuss it. The other advocacy organizations,
and us, felt that the faculty and students who had called us, and some alumnae, and parents, were very upset by it. We felt it was no longer just an issue
of classroom teaching. We decided then that we wanted to do something a little more aggressive, and we sat down with the other organizations and worked
out some language" (Zakim, ADL, interview by author, July 5, 1994).

The JCRC saw the incident at Wellesley a little differently. It was an isolated incident, and the college needed to deal with it themselves. The JCRC's
executive director, Nancy Kaufman, had received calls from Wellesley's
alumnae voicing their serious concern about Tony Martin and all of the uproar the situation was creating on campus. The JCRC's director reasoned
that it was Wellesley's problem and unless (and until) they requested specific
help, it was "not for us as outside groups to decide that is was our problem"
(Kaufman, JCRC, interview by author, July 7, 1994).

Kaufman was reluctant to intrude on an internal matter. She said, "we've
got to be very careful as community relations organizations to understand our
role" (Kaufman, JCRC, interview). The image that was beginning to develop
was one of "Jewish organizations tripping over each other to see who was going to defend Wellesley from the antisemites" (JCRC, interview). By the end of
March 1993, the JCRC had decided that its place was beside those of the
other JAOs in creating and cosigning a joint statement of some sort that would
be seen as a collective statement on the part of all the JAOs, regardless of their
individual ideologies. The fourth JAO to join this unitary action was the AJCg.

The American Jewish Congress in Boston was the last of the JAOs to involve
themselves in the incident at Wellesley College. In the AJCg's opinion, if one or
two of the advocacy organizations were involved in an antisemitic incident,
then it wasn't automatically necessary for the AJCg to be there just to show

that it cared. At some point too many advocacy groups could create more confusion than clarity. The principal reason that prompted the AJCg to participate in this exercise was, according to their Boston director, Sheila Decter, the AJCg's long history of defending academic freedom. The decision by the AJCg to participate in a joint press release came only after lengthy discussion and debate among the four JAOs and officials in their national offices. The AJCg's director wanted to be sure that the statement neither said nor implied that Tony Martin should be fired. Decter explained, "The statement asked the college to use American Association of University Professors [AAUP] standards in determining whether or not Wellesley was appropriately responding to this incident, and whether or not Tony Martin was fulfilling his obligations as a teacher, and whether the college was using the right standards to judge him in using those standards" (Decter, AJCg, interview, June 30, 1994).

As Decter saw it, if the university applied its own standards (AAUP) and still found Professor Martin wanting, then his continued employment became a separate issue. The AJCg vigorously supports academic freedom but at the same time does not believe that faculty members are free to teach anything they want under any circumstances in the classroom. Participation by the AJCg in drafting the joint press release came after several weeks of discussion and the continuing worsening of the issues at Wellesley College. Until this time only two of the JAOs had been directly involved in the turmoil at Wellesley College, the AJC and the ADL.

With an escalating number of phone calls to the AJCg complaining about Martin, his antisemitic rhetoric, and his use of *SR*, it became increasingly apparent that all of the JAOs, including the AJCg, would have to come together and agree on a course of action concerning the events at Wellesley College. In Decter's opinion, this was not a situation any of the JAOs could sit out. They all had members who were concerned about what was happening at Wellesley (Decter, AJCg, interview). This concern coupled with Martin Goldman's (AJC) insistence on pursuing a common path of complaint culminated in the joint press release.

On later reflection, Decter believed that the JAOs' collective involvement helped Wellesley's new president, Diana Chapman Walsh, to cope with a quickly developing "next round" of accusations by Martin on the campus. The JAOs, by their actions, had helped Wellesley's Jewish faculty members feel a little less isolated. Their actions had helped the college's Hillel group to see there were people outside of Wellesley who wanted to help, and finally, in Decter's opinion, they had helped Wellesley students who believed they had done the right thing by participating in discussions and asking questions about some very troubling issues (Decter, AJCg, interview).

Adverse publicity of the sort that developed about Wellesley College could have eventually cost the college money. Donor money can dry up, or be withheld, if the college is embroiled in too much conflict or too much negative publicity. Did that happen at Wellesley College? It has certainly happened at other colleges around the country, and over much less incendiary issues. It would be naive to think Wellesley College was immune to a similar reaction. It would be surprising if some, at least, of the Jewish donors to Wellesley did not pull back in their contributions to the college in the aftermath of the Wellesley incident. Still, there is no independent way to verify such action, unless prominent donors make their displeasure public knowledge. In the aftermath of the events at Wellesley, Dr. Nancy Kolodny, acting dean, received a number of threats by alumnae to withhold contributions to the college. But, beyond the money issue, Decter discussed another, equally serious implication of the bad publicity at Wellesley—new enrollments.

There is every likelihood parents would decide *not* to send their children to Wellesley College because of this very public conflict. Given today's cost of an education at a private college, it is unlikely many parents would want their money, or their child's education, dissipated in a conflict-laden environment. One of these parents expressed his anger by saying, "I spent $25,000 for my daughter to listen to this baloney; now I suppose I will have to spend another $25,000 so she can get the education she came here to get in the first place" (quoted by Sheila Decter, interview by the author, June 30, 1994). The final and perhaps most fateful ingredient in this multiple decision to collaborate on a joint press release was the American Jewish Committee and its associate director, Martin Goldman.

The AJC's participation and involvement in this incident was somewhat different from that of the other three organizations, and in the final analysis theirs was perhaps the most traumatic. The AJC's associate director, Martin Goldman, had a central role in the Wellesley incident, and the AJC's director, Dr. Lawrence Lowenthal, stayed more in the background. Goldman's participation, visibility, and presence on the Wellesley campus ultimately cost him his job with the American Jewish Committee. Consequently, his comments provide some valuable insights into the decision-making process in the Wellesley incident. Goldman's insights also provide a point in this narrative from which to introduce a question that has not yet been raised. Namely, who stood to benefit most from a public and highly visible Jewish response to Tony Martin and the events that transpired at Wellesley College?

Goldman had been associate director of the Boston AJC for three years when the incident at Wellesley College began emerging in public. Prior to the AJC, he had been director of education for the Boston ADL for eight years. He continued a close and harmonious relationship with his former boss (Leonard Zakim) at the ADL.

Before his association with either of the JAOs, Goldman had pursued a Ph.D. in black history, but did not complete his dissertation because of a substantial disagreement with the college where he was pursuing his doctorate. He had taught courses in black history at several Boston area colleges while pursuing the doctorate and had earned a notable reputation as an emerging scholar of black history. He had written several articles on black and American history and had published three historical biographies. When Clark University (the college where Goldman had begun his Ph.D.) refused to consider him for a teaching position in black history because he was not black, Goldman left in response to what he perceived as discrimination.[1]

Goldman had investigated Martin's verbal assault in 1991 on the young woman in the Wellesley dormitory building. The young woman (or her parents) had written to the AJC in New York City complaining about Martin and his verbal harassment. The complaint was, in turn, routed to the Boston chapter of the AJC. This is a typical practice among the major Jewish organizations. Every attempt is made to investigate complaints as close to the source as possible. Goldman did not believe Wellesley College had done enough in terms of sanctioning Martin's behavior over that incident. While he did not think Martin should have been fired for it, he did point out that a white professor who had engaged in such behavior would very likely have been terminated. In the course of investigating the young woman's complaint, Goldman developed a strong personal antipathy toward Martin and a less-than-enthusiastic attitude toward the administrative processes at the college. But Goldman was clear in his condemnation of what he considered Martin's unethical behavior in rallying a group of black students to follow the young woman around campus accusing her of being a racist. He was just as clear in his condemnation of the college for not firing Martin for what he considered Martin's inexcusable behavior as a human being (Goldman, interview by author, August 29, 1995).

It seems everybody on campus knew what was going on, but nobody, according to Goldman, did anything to help the young lady or to stop the harassment. The Wellesley College newspaper was told not to write about it. But, eventually it was written about in a student publication called *Heterodoxy*, barely a month after the JAOs had published their joint press release condemning Martin in the spring of 1993. Wellesley is too small a college and the incident was too highly visible to be kept under wraps for very long (Goldman, interview).

At this point Goldman went on campus at the invitation of several students to talk to them and to try to understand what was happening in the aftermath of the harassment charges that had been leveled at Martin. The students wanted the involvement of the Jewish organizations, even if the college, and as it turned out the campus Hillel organization, did not. Goldman did not feel he was ever welcome in the eyes of the Hillel director. She was new to her job, and as Goldman recalls, "The rabbi was very protective of her turf, and very unfriendly. I knew she was upset, didn't want me around, didn't want any of the Jewish organizations around" (Goldman, interview).

There was never any direct confrontation between the two, but Goldman is convinced that the Hillel rabbi called Goldman's boss (Dr. Lawrence Lowenthal, the AJC director) to complain about his presence on campus. Goldman suspects she may have called other people in the Boston Jewish

Community as well, because in Goldman's words, "[it] got out that I was putting my nose where it wasn't wanted. I hadn't done anything, yet; all I had done was talk to people. I hadn't written a memo, hadn't decided on a main course of action" (Goldman, interview). Wellesley College, its alumnae, its Hillel Branch, and certainly Tony Martin did not want Goldman or any of the other JAOs on their campus. But there they were, and they were now on the verge of writing a joint press release. From this point on, Goldman recalled, "No one got into it as deeply as I did; I think for a couple of weeks [in the spring of 1993] I didn't do anything else. I just spent all my time on this thing" (Goldman, interview).

Goldman's persistence in believing that the JAOs had to act collaboratively was credited with being the driving force that actually made that happen. In interviews with all of the JAOs, they were, to a person, very supportive and flattering of Goldman's energy and dedication to the task of confronting Martin and his antisemitism on the Wellesley campus, and doing so in some unified action. On March 26, 1993 (approximately ten days before the release of the joint press release), Goldman sent a confidential, "for your information only" memo to the other JAOs outlining four possible courses of action they could collectively pursue: (1) a joint press release; (2) a press conference; (3) a series of articles condemning Martin that would be "planted" in different media; (4) a joint press conference with several black supporters and friends of the JAOs. He exhorted his colleagues to "meet, strategize, and act as a united community. With the strength of all of our organizations, the force of our statement will be much more powerful than if we, in more typical fashion, tried [*sic*] to get into the press on our own." He closed his request by saying, "We should meet as soon as possible and strategize, and then we should act in concert" (Goldman memo to JAOs, March 26, 1993 on file). They did meet, several times, and ultimately decided that a joint press release would be the most appropriate vehicle for expressing their collective outrage at the events taking place at Wellesley College.

Goldman's prominence in the issues, coupled with his presence on the Wellesley campus, would place him in a position of professional peril. He had become overidentified with the Wellesley incident. He recalled his error as one of overinvolvement, something the New York office of the AJC did not want. "[W]e got ahead of ourselves," Goldman recalled. "I quarterbacked it with the ADL, and [in the process] I blindsided Larry [Lowenthal] on it. Usually those things get cleared [by AJC, New York], and you have to go through a long process, but we had some time problems. Martin was making some kind of an appearance somewhere, and all the agencies had the same time problem [the impending Jewish holidays]. I don't think we cleared that [press] release with New York; I'm sure that was a problem. New York was not happy with that press release, because we actually did call for Wellesley to look at his tenure. We didn't say fire him; we asked them to review the AAUP regulations" (Goldman, interview).

Goldman didn't believe that anything he or the other agencies did would have resulted in Martin's termination. They did believe that referencing a recognized set of academic guidelines on tenure was a good strategy for putting the "ball back in Wellesley's court." The issue Goldman wanted to shine a strong light on was the fact that Wellesley had done nothing about Martin's outrageous behavior.

While the language of a full-fledged press release was being considered, the ADL began pursuing another line of inquiry. They had contacted the American Association of University Professors (AAUP) to obtain a copy of their disciplinary guidelines for colleges. This step was taken to provide guidance to Wellesley College that came from an authoritative academic source on disciplinary mechanisms that might be available to the college, if they felt they needed, or wanted it.

The ADL director was confident at this point that if he had called for Martin's tenure revocation, he would have been supported in that decision by his national headquarters; the other JAOs felt differently. The AJCg, in particular, has always been a prominent supporter of academic freedom and the inherent protection of dissent found within the AAUP tenure guidelines. They didn't feel it was the JAOs' position to venture into matters that were clearly the college's domain. The ADL's director added, "The AJC seemed more hamstrung [than us] because they had a number of prominent lay leaders who were also Wellesley alumnae or [who] were married to alumnae of Wellesley. The AJCg was the litigator [in] the community, and they were very focused on making sure that we weren't stepping on anybody's First Amendment rights. We worked closely with AJCg to make sure that the toughness we wanted to put forward in the joint letter was also clearly respectful of Martin's academic freedom" (Zakim, ADL, interview).

The Boston director of the AJCg had discussed the issues at Wellesley with her national office, internal advisors, and external resources. One of these advisors was retired Judge Lawrence Shubow (an early director of the Boston AJCg). The JCRC had pursued a similar tack and had talked to several of its advisors about a proposed joint communication condemning Tony Martin. Insofar as possible, the JAOs did not want to be seen as forcing themselves on Wellesley College, and possibly making matters worse, nor did they want to make a martyr out of Tony Martin.

In the midst of all this energetic planning, consulting, and cross-checking, Goldman publicly debated Tony Martin on two separate occasions. The first time was on a local radio program, and the second on a locally sponsored PBS television station. Martin did not belong to the Nation of Islam (NOI), but was, instead, a very prominent and vocal supporter of the NOI. Based on the things he was saying, and what he was teaching, the NOI was quick to extol Martin's virtues wherever he and they went. Martin's nonmembership in the NOI is what permitted Goldman to appear in public with Martin. The AJC's policy of nonappearance with the NOI would have otherwise clearly forbidden his participation in any public debate with a member of the NOI.

At this point, the media in other parts of the country had begun following the events unfolding at Wellesley (e.g., the *Chicago Tribune* ran "Debate over Farrakhan Book Engulfs College" by Mike Dorning, on April 28, 1993; and the *Washington Post* printed "Farrakhan 101 at Wellesley" by Richard Cohen on Febuary 11, 1994). One of the reasons fueling the increased media interest in Wellesley College and Tony Martin was the very public battle going on at City College New York (CCNY), and its attempts to fire a tenured black professor, Leonard Jeffries, for much the same behavior as Tony Martin.

Leonard Jeffries had sued CCNY, claiming violation of his First Amendment rights, and sought $300,000 in damages in addition to reinstating him in his former position as chair of the Black Studies Department; initially he won. On appeal, however, the higher court reversed the decision and dismissed the financial settlement, while ordering the school to reinstate Jeffries to his position of chair. The Jeffries case raised considerable adverse publicity for CCNY, and in the opinion of many in the academic and legal communities, CCNY could have handled its differences with Jeffries more judiciously, thereby avoiding the $300,000 penalty, but still censuring Jeffries for his conduct. As it later turned out, the penalty was voided, and CCNY closed down the Black Studies Department. Jeffries stayed on as a tenured faculty member of the school, as reported in an article by David Stout entitled "City College Closing Black Studies Department" in the *New York Times*, March 19, 1996.

Early in 1993, in a Baltimore speech, Leonard Jeffries talked about the Tony Martin case at Wellesley and praised Martin for his use of *SR* in his class. At this point, the JAOs were not actively seeking any media exposure of the issues at Wellesley, but someone else was. While the JAOs were meeting among themselves, an enterprising reporter at the *Boston Jewish Times* had written a feature piece on Wellesley College and Tony Martin and was about to release it. Susan Bloch's story was about Tony Martin, but from the perspective of Wellesley College and how it was coping with the multiple conflicts that were identified with Martin's presence on campus. Bloch's article pointedly and intentionally omitted the possibility of any Jewish communal response to the incident. In fact, according to the ADL, the *Boston Jewish Times* wasn't interested in talking to the JAOs. Bloch knew there had been campus visits by various members of the advocacy organizations (Greenberg from the ADL and Goldman from the AJC), but her story was about Wellesley College and how they were responding, not about how the Jewish communal world saw it. It would be a mistake, however, to read anything antagonistic in this decision. Bloch's article was simply written from another perspective, that of the college rather than the Jewish community.

The Bloch article, entitled "Furor at Wellesley College over Anti-Semitic Text," appeared on April 1, 1993, and it triggered two outcomes: First, it told the Boston Jewish community what Wellesley College was doing to cope with overt antisemitism on its campus; second, it provided the final *raison d'être* for the JAOs to prepare their own response. Within hours of the *Boston Jewish Times* story, other local (and national) newspapers were asking the AJC and the ADL what their roles in the Wellesley incident were or would be. The ADL was also hearing from Jews in Boston and from members of its own board of directors. The question was always the same: "What are you doing about Wellesley?"

From what has been said thus far it would appear that Wellesley College was sitting quietly with its hands folded waiting for something to happen. Far from it! This was an incident that had galvanized the entire campus. Students, faculty, administrators, alumnae, and parents were all involved, and more than a few heated exchanges had already taken place. For example:

- A formal complaint had been filed against Martin for harassing and threatening a female student.

- Mary Lefkowitz, a renowned classics scholar and professor of classics at Wellesley, was attacked and ridiculed as a "Jew" by Martin in his four-page broadside, "Blacks and Jews at Wellesley News." This for having rejected as fanciful or as myth several claims made by Afrocentric scholars on the source of Greek culture.

- Selwyn Cudjoe, the department chair of Africana Studies at Wellesley (and Martin's boss), flatly rejected Martin's demagoguery and use of the *SR* in Martin's African American history course.

- At an all-college faculty meeting, Martin was censured by 121 members of the academic committee. He proceeded to verbally abuse and curse several of the attendees.

- For weeks e-mail messages were produced by the pound commenting on the pros and cons of the college's reaction to Martin and Martin's reaction to the college, its faculty, administration, and students.

On March 7, 1993, Wellesley's president, Nanerl O. Keohane, issued a formal statement defending Professor Lefkowitz and deploring Professor Martin's attack on her. Keohane would leave Wellesley shortly after that statement for a new job at Duke University (see Cudjoe, 1994; Auerbach, 1993). All of this occurred before the *Boston Jewish Times* article appeared and before the JAOs had made any decision to intervene. In the JAOs' estimation the college was doing its work. The ADL reflected, "In late February 1993, it was clear to us that it was healthier to let the Wellesley process work its way, since they obviously had internal stuff they had to do. With the release of the 'Blacks and Jews at Wellesley News' things began to change and with the speech by Leonard Jeffries (in Baltimore), it was no longer a local issue, but that wasn't what motivated us. We got our first call in February of '93, and we were then developing a response to the book *SR*. Now we're moving towards the end of March and we were meeting as a group about the book" (Leonard Zakim, interview by author, July 5, 1994).

Several people from the JAOs had been on campus, but only on an invited capacity to visit with students, faculty, alumnae, and parents. These visitors included the director of AJCg, the associate director of the AJC, and the civil rights director from the ADL.

While the ADL's director and his colleagues at the other JAOs had some reservations about the strength of Keohane's response to Martin, they felt it was adequate. Wellesley was not the enemy. Wellesley was not a situation like CCNY, or Kean College in New Jersey, or Howard University in Washington, DC, all sites where prominent members of the NOI had delivered very noisy and public antisemitic diatribes. The JAOs trusted the players at Wellesley and felt their internal processes would work things out. But when the "Blacks and Jews at Wellesley News" began circulating and the *Boston Jewish Times* article was published, the JAOs were compelled to respond directly, and quickly, to the events at Wellesley.

With pressure growing on the advocacy organizations from their own members and advisors to do something, the discussions within each advocacy organization escalated quickly to joint meetings and strategizing sessions on what form a response should take to events at Wellesley. The JAOs began writing the multiauthored press release they had earlier agreed would be their best course of action. From the very beginning it was a process attended by conflicting pressures. The ADL wanted stronger language than did the AJC. The AJCg wanted to be sure that communication did not infringe on Martin's freedom of speech or academic prerogatives, and the JCRC wanted the memo to employ language that would not derail existing community relations' discussions in Boston, particularly with the black community.

The tugging and hauling over the language and intent of the press release was not confined to just the four directors of the JAOs. Three of the four JAOs had national offices to contend with. The fourth, the JCRC, was local but closely affiliated with the CJP and had to keep them informed as the process unfolded. A steady stream of faxes and phone calls went back and forth between Boston and New York. The wording of the press release that one JAO wanted, another did not. When the Boston office of the AJCg thought the wording was satisfactory, its national office said, "No, it has to be changed." The implicit message in all of this was that without *home office* approval, a joint press release would not be written or, if written, would not be released.

An additional factor that added considerable pressure to an already tight time schedule (approximately three days from start to finish) was the Jewish observance of Passover. It would start at sundown, April 6, 1993. Even though the JAOs are secular organizations, many of the JAOs' employees are religiously observant Jews. Historically, Passover was a time for religious observance combined with several days of annual vacation. If a response to the issues, long fulminating, at Wellesley (and now written about in a leading Jewish newspaper) was not issued until after the Passover holiday, a great deal would be lost; the press release's value rendered moot. The efficacy of advocating for the Jewish community inside and outside of Wellesley would be lost. The opportunity to demonstrate organizational presence in the face of blatant antisemitism would be lost. The political necessity of saving face because the JAOs were not mentioned in the *Boston Jewish Times* article would be lost. The joint press release had to go out before Passover, not after!

The joint press release was finally written, approved by everyone involved in the process, and released to the Boston press with only minutes to spare to meet the media and religious deadlines. It carried the logo of each of the four advocacy organizations that were signatories to the letter. Only later was it noticed that the director of the AJC had not appeared on the masthead of the joint press release; his associate director's name had, and it was an hierarchical error that would haunt both men in the near future. The press release wasn't perfect; it didn't say everything everyone wanted, but it was a solidly written response deploring Martin's actions and his use of an antisemitic book, plus his anti-Jewish rhetoric. The ADL's director observed, "It was a collaborative effort, and the first joint statement [on the part of all four organizations]. . . . [I]t really did reflect the various angles and different approaches of each organization's structure. . . . [I]t seemed to be a communal strategy that worked. I think a lot of people in the community thought we were going too slow, but we were willing to give Wellesley College the chance to do the right thing" (Zakim, interview).

From an advocacy standpoint, once that joint statement had gone to press, the matter was closed. The matter had been dealt with, and the JAOs had done their job: they had advocated. But as soon as the joint press release was published it began to backfire. On April 17, 1993, the *Boston Globe*, in the article "Jewish Group Raps Wellesley Professor" by Chris Black reporting on the JAOs' joint press release, strongly suggested that the JAOs were ". . . demanding a review of his [Martin's] contract and tenure status." The joint communiqué made no such request. It said, "Reports of intellectual intimidation of students who challenge the anti-Semitic propaganda throughout the book and the Professor's unwillingness to allow free and uninhibited questions of the book in class or on campus without fear of sanctions, further evidences violation of the statement of 'Principles of Academic Freedom and Tenure' promulgated by the American Association of University Professors and the Association of American Colleges." The memo had encouraged Wellesley College to utilize already available mechanisms in dealing with Martin.

The ADL acknowledged that the college may have concluded that the JAOs had only aggravated an internal problem, but like a great many institutions, "they circled their wagons when threatened" (Zakim, interview). The ADL's director added, "We understand your problems and limitations, but you have to understand we have a constituency that we have to respond to."

In the aftermath of the press release, the Wellesley Hillel and some of the Wellesley faculty invited the ADL on campus to conduct seminars and workshops on discrimination, prejudice, and antisemitism. Two or three meetings were held with the support of the college's administration, but they were only sparsely attended. The ADL's director recalled, "You could see there was a division between the faculty, administration, and the dean of the college, who is herself involved in the Jewish community. She felt she was caught between the two groups because she was acting dean [at the time] and a lot of bureaucratic cracks had developed" (Zakim, interview). Colleges and universities are often insulated from the community that surrounds them. So, it is not surprising that a lot of attention from advocacy groups (of whatever stripe) could be unsettling. In addition, Wellesley College was experiencing a backlash from its own alumnae who expressed the belief that the JAOs had gone too far and had ignored Wellesley's reputation in the process.

The backlash also came from several quarters outside the Wellesley College campus community, largely in response to one portion of the press release that involved the issue of Martin's employment and tenure at Wellesley. This paragraph particularly troubled leading educators who complained that these were not sanctions for which the Jewish community could ask. The press release hadn't, but that was the interpretation the Boston press had given it; with this coloration a very large bag of feathers was emptying out all over the country, and there would be no retrieving them. For example:

- The black press in Boston, the *Bay State Banner*, admitted to the ADL, "This is too complicated." The reporter had spoken to Martin and one other person and concluded that this was "a black guy who stood up and was getting trampled" (Zakim, interview).

- Louis Farrakhan had referred to Tony Martin as a "black cultural icon for the truth he spoke."

- In an interview with the author (as part of a video production on black/Jewish relations), Selwyn Cudjoe, the chair of the Africana Studies Department at Wellesley (and Tony Martin's boss), expressed the opinion that Wellesley College had already solved its problems with Tony Martin. The publication of the JAOs' joint press release on April 6, 1993, came too late and only stirred up sour feelings that had already been put to rest (Blakeslee, 1993).

- Another participant on the same video panel (Prejudice: An Equal Opportunity Destroyer), the director of the AJCg defended the JAOs' collective advocacy in the Wellesley incident by pointing out that various groups of people at Wellesley (students, faculty, and the campus Hillel) had sought their guidance and support. When the media began reporting on the Tony Martin situation, a lot of people inside and outside of the Jewish community wanted to know what the JAOs would do. "We had no choice at that point; we had to respond to the press's requests for a formal statement. Because of the anti-Semitic nature of the situation, we decided to speak with a single voice" (Blakeslee, 1993).

The ADL was disappointed to learn of Cudjoe's opinion, but firmly believed that Wellesley had "pulled in its head, admitted the situation was wrong, but still took the position that life [at Wellesley] hadn't [basically] changed" (Zakim, interview). The ADL considered that thinking to be a strategic mistake. While Martin may have been censured, the ADL didn't feel the college had dealt adequately with several other deep-seated problems. Several of the alumnae, faculty, and students felt the JAOs had been capable of bringing a stronger light to bear on several issues that were still unresolved. For one thing, there had been an increase in antisemitism on campus that many believed the incident had triggered, quite apart from Tony Martin, the book he used, or Martin's polemics.

There was also the issue of multicultural education and its curriculum; an issue that, up to that point, the college had simply sidestepped. The JAOs were getting calls from prominent faculty members, like Mary Lefkowitz, seeking their intervention. The college had opened itself up to substantial criticism by allowing the distribution on campus of a noncollege publication, "Blacks and Jews at Wellesley News." When Leonard Jeffries (CCNY) praised Martin in a speech that spring, it transformed the incident into a national issue, not just Wellesley's little secret (Zakim, interview). In spite of the claims made by the college, plus those of Selwyn Cudjoe, that the incident had been resolved, it was clear to the JAOs that these other issues had not been resolved.

The college was in a difficult position at this time, because it was caught between the departure of the college's current president, Nanerl Keohane, and the national search for a new president. The acting dean was doing her best to balance a lot of different agendas (Zakim, interview). Had the Jewish advocacy organizations pushed the college a little too hard for some people's comfort? There were some who thought the whole response to Tony Martin had been engineered by the ADL. This would not be an accurate assessment. The AJC, AJCg, and the JCRC all played an active role in this advocacy effort. The role of advocacy is often perceived as "stepping on someone's toes"; it is part of the process (Zakim, interview).

The fallout from the incident didn't end with the college censuring Martin, or with the joint press release by the JAOs. A second decision began taking shape almost immediately in the aftermath of the original confrontation with Martin; one that would again involve the JAOs.

THE JAOs' CONTINUING INVOLVEMENT
AT WELLESLEY COLLEGE

In the days following the joint press release, the JAOs were busy cementing relations with their advisors, board members and significant intercommunity alliances. Back at Wellesley College, two developments occurred in close proximity to one another: (1) Tony Martin did not remain quiet for very long in the aftermath of all this negative publicity. He wrote, published, and released (in the span of eight months) a slim volume entitled *The Jewish Onslaught: Dispatches from the Wellesley Battlefront* (1993). The content of the first seventy-nine pages repeats many of his earlier accusations of Jewish responsibility for collective black misery. The other fifty-six pages of his book is a collection of unsigned letters supporting Martin and decrying Wellesley College's treatment of him, as well as that of the entire Boston Jewish community and the activities of the JAOs. (2) The new president of Wellesley College, Diana Chapman Walsh, denounced Martin's book and his attacks on other faculty members in a letter that was mailed to 40,000 Wellesley alumnae, parents, and friends of the college (Walsh letter, December 15, 1993).

In addition to writing the book, Martin had gone on the lecture circuit and was getting paid for his angry rhetoric. The *New York Amsterdam News* article by Herb Boyd entitled "Boston Prof. Hails Jeffries Victory," May 5, 1993, teamed him with Leonard Jeffries, the already controversial figure from CCNY, in a speech in Harlem, New York, where Martin said of his Wellesley experience, "There must be no easy victory for the Jews. . . . In fact, there should be no more victories for Jews, period."

A number of other people were writing about Martin and the issues at Wellesley College. In the July/August 1993 issue of the *Congress Monthly* (a publication of the American Jewish Congress), Jerold S. Auerbach, a professor of history and longtime faculty member at Wellesley, in an article entitled "Anti-Semitism at Wellesley College," recounted the Tony Martin incident from the perspective of the faculty. He was as hard on Wellesley's administration as he was on Martin's demagoguery. He credited the JAOs with applying firm pressure on the college, but admitted that all of the coverage undoubtedly gave Martin and his "racist regurgitation more attention than they deserve" in a second article, entitled "Homegrown Anti-Semitism at Wellesley College," *Wellesley News*, Decmber 12, 1993.

A week later Martin released broadsheet number two of "Blacks and Jews at Wellesley News" and attacked Wellesley College's new president for being under the spell of "Shadowy Figures." He followed up his written comments a short time later on National Public Radio in an interview with Tony Phillips in Atlanta, Georgia, where he held the new president of Wellesley College (Walsh) up for withering criticism and ridiculed her for her naiveté.

On January 29, 1994, the *Boston Globe* picked up Walsh's letter to the Wellesley alumnae and extended the discussion to include Martin's "pernicious polemic" and his attacks on other faculty members. On February 2, 1994, the *Boston Globe* ran an editorial attacking Martin's book, *The Jewish Onslaught*, as "wrong, embarrassing, and an exercise in demeaning scholarship." The next day, February 3, 1994, Selwyn Cudjoe, chair of Wellesley's Africana Studies Department, again publicly criticized Martin in a *Boston Globe* op-ed piece that labeled Martin's polemic in *The Jewish Onslaught* as "one-sided, distorted and mean-spirited." As justifiable as these criticisms were of Martin, a larger question (from the perspective of this study) was where were the JAOs during this public flogging of Martin? The JAOs' public silence was significant.

The ADL expressed the belief that this latest outburst by Martin was a "continuation of the same story" (Zakim, interview). Wellesley had withstood a great deal of criticism at this point and little more would have been gained by another intervention by the JAOs. Wellesley was Hillary Clinton's alma mater, and she was now receiving mail concerning the events transpiring at Wellesley College. Cokie Roberts, another prominent graduate of Wellesley, was discussing the Tony Martin affair on David Brinkley's national TV show. This was not the kind of publicity that Wellesley College had hoped for from two such prominent alumnae (Zakim, interview).

Within days of the public release of Martin's latest screed, the JAOs met to discuss what their response would be to his latest attack on the Jewish community. The director of the JCRC, Nancy Kaufman, called a group meeting of all of the JAOs who had been involved in the earlier joint press release decision. She reasoned that the arrival of Wellesley's new president and her speedy rejection of Martin's demagoguery called for a different response from the one adopted for the joint press release the previous April.

This time she did not wait to be called by someone at Wellesley College, but took a more aggressive posture and called Wellesley's new president to arrange a joint telephone conference call between the college and the JAOs. Kaufman had discussed this strategy earlier with the acting dean, Nancy Kolodny, and they had jointly agreed to give Walsh the benefit of any doubt (Nancy Kaufman, interview by author, July 7, 1994). Wellesley faxed Walsh's letter of December 15, 1993 to Kaufman, and she distributed copies of it to the other JAOs.

What was the rationale for beginning with a conference call? Kaufman said, "I decided on the conference call because I knew that otherwise everything would unravel very quickly. The same thing would have happened [again]. Someone would decide they were going to go to the press, and I had made a personal commitment to Nancy Kolodny that I would do my best to coordinate the agencies; that's our role at the JCRC. Otherwise, everyone would have been on the phone with Diana [Walsh] advising her. Since we had done that joint thing the first time we had created a precedent. Let's do it again, but this time instead of anointing one of us to be the spokesperson, we'll all be in the room, and everyone will have a chance to react; that's what we did" (Kaufman, interview).

It was Kaufman's opinion that the JAOs shared her view that Walsh's letter had been a decent statement; she had done the right thing by the college and by its alumnae. Perhaps most important, Walsh had taken action quickly in the aftermath of Martin's new book, within two months of arriving on campus. In Kaufman's opinion, Wellesley College had handled this latest outburst of Martin's just fine, and there was no reason for the JAOs to send out another press release or to do anything else of an overt nature (Kaufman, interview).

Unfortunately, when the day arrived for the telephone conference call, not all of the concerned parties within the JAOs agreed that a conference call was appropriate. The New York office of the AJC was particularly upset that the Boston JAOs were continuing their involvement in "Wellesley College's affairs." The JAOs' decision to initiate a telephone conference call went well beyond simple strategizing about how to counter Martin's latest outburst. They were sharply focused on how they were interpreting Diana Chapman Walsh's letter to the Wellesley alumnae, dated December 15, 1993. The reaction of some of the JAOs to her letter could best be described as "tepid" (Goldman, interview). That sentiment was communicated to her by the JAOs during their early morning conference call.

Everybody from the JAOs (four directors and one associate director) was on one end of the call and the president of Wellesley College was on the other end. The director of the ADL told Walsh that her remarks were unacceptable; she had not used the word *antisemitism* in her letter. He was not rude, simply firm in making his complaint. Goldman (the associate director of the AJC) recalled that Walsh's reaction to this criticism was swift and unequivocal: she was outraged! She was furious that she had gone out on a very public limb in attacking one of her professors, and the reaction of the organized Jewish community was to tell her her comments were tepid (Goldman, interview). The conference call ended on a sour note. The ADL's director thanked her again for her letter, but repeated his earlier observation, "We must disagree with you on its tone" (Goldman, interview). The ADL's criticism contradicted earlier impressions the JAOs had shared among themselves of the Walsh letter. Not surprisingly, the ADL's comments also embarrassed the other JAOs who had participated in the conference call. The telephone conference call and the criticism of President Walsh also upset the college's alumnae and administration.

There are Wellesley alumnae who are major contributors to, as well as members of, the AJC; when the substance of the Boston conference call reached them, they were just as outraged as their new president at the criticisms that had been leveled by the JAOs. They wasted no time in going directly to the AJC's New York office and protesting, loudly, about the treatment Wellesley's new president had been subjected to; they were listened to. Their message was simple and direct, "Get your Boston office off of Wellesley's case; just pull the plug" (Goldman, interview). While the New York office of the AJC was attempting to find out what had happened to inspire such wrath, Goldman found himself the focus of blame for most of what the alumnae believed had gone wrong at their alma mater. Goldman, in turn, was convinced that the AJC's New York headquarters believed he was somehow pulling the strings in the entire Wellesley affair. He was terminated a few weeks later.

In the aftermath of his departure from the AJC, Goldman admitted that "Larry [Lowenthal] let me run with the ball on Tony Martin; Larry was very supportive" (Goldman, interview). Lowenthal subsequently endured a great deal of criticism because of his associate director's involvement with the issues at Wellesley College. Goldman's intensity over the necessity to publicly confront Martin, *SR*, and the antisemitism on Wellesley's campus created another embarrassment for the AJC. At the time the joint press release became public, a great many people were quick to notice that three of the four JAOs were represented by their director's name; the fourth, the AJC, carried Goldman's name as the signatory, but there was no indication that he was an associate director. Lowenthal admitted this had been an unfortunate oversight on his part, and it also made it impossible for him to protect Goldman against New York's criticism that he had, in fact, been overly identified with the issues at Wellesley College. It is ironic that the person who was the target of all of this effort by the JAOs (Tony Martin) still has his job, and the person who quarterbacked the JAOs efforts was terminated because of his singular intensity in pursuing a distressing and inflammatory situation. Twenty years earlier, Wellesley had hired Tony Martin over Martin Goldman to teach black history. It was a hiring decision that Goldman never forgot, and in the final analysis one has to wonder how strongly this earlier rejection at this college ultimately influenced his decision making and the decision making of all of the JAOs.

The reaction among significant persons on the Wellesley campus to the JAOs' handling of the issues surrounding Tony Martin depends on whom you talk to. Professor Mary Lefkowitz was very appreciative of the JAOs presence on campus, particularly the AJC and the ADL. She had been invited to speak at a couple of AJC-sponsored functions about her criticism of Afrocentrism. She knew that Goldman had played a significant role in the preparation of the joint press release, and she believed the JAOs' criticism of Wellesley was effective as well as warranted. However, she acknowledged that Wellesley had been embarrassed by the publicity and certainly would have preferred that their image had not come under such public assault (Mary Lefkowitz, interview by author, February 27, 1996).

On the other hand, Lefkowitz did not feel that Wellesley College had adequately supported her when Tony Martin sued her for slander. This is where the ADL proved to be both sympathetic and helpful. They helped her find competent legal advice to protect herself from Martin's accusations. Martin's lawsuit against Lefkowitz has had a long life. The initial suit was dismissed in February 1996, but Martin appealed and the suit was reinstated. It was dismissed a second time in early 1998 as being without substance; Martin has again filed for an appeal. His appeal for reinstatement of the lawsuit is now being weighed by a panel of judges, and Professor Lefkowitz remains confident that it will finally be dismissed once and for all. She continues a highly successful academic career at Wellesley College while this nagging historical remnant from an incident that started over six years ago grinds to a slow and inexorable halt (Lefkowitz, interview).[2]

There is another view of this entire affair from a key person at Wellesley College, and it is neither as flattering nor as supportive of the JAOs as was that of Professor Lefkowitz. In contrast to Lefkowitz's supportive statements about the role of the JAOs, Dr. Nancy Kolodny, acting dean of the college, was dismayed by the JAOs involvement. She was caught in the middle of all of the events that transpired that spring. She was helping the college negotiate the exit of one president and the search for a replacement. When the issues surrounding Tony Martin became known, Kolodny had already been in touch with the JCRC and the ADL. She knew the ADL from years past, and she had a favorable opinion of its work on behalf of Wellesley College, as well as the town itself. Based on her conversations with the JCRC and the ADL, Kolodny felt the JAOs had betrayed her and Wellesley College. She believed the whole affair with Tony Martin was going to be resolved internally with advice and counsel from the JAOs (Nancy Kolodny, interview by author, Febuary 27, 1996). She never clearly understood why the issue had become such a media event. She surmised that quite likely the national offices of the JAOs had forced the debate to become public because of Martin's notoriety and the support he was receiving from the NOI. Kolodny knew who the directors of the AJCg, JCRC, and ADL were, but as far as the AJC was concerned, "I had no direct interaction with them" (Kolodny, interview).

Part of her dismay can be traced to the fact that she knew virtually nothing about the extent of Goldman's all-consuming pursuit of a unified Jewish response to the issues unfolding at Wellesley College. His name was marginal in her recollection of the events leading up to the publication of the press release. She didn't remember ever speaking to him directly and only knew through hearsay from other people at Wellesley that he had been an occasional presence on campus. It came as a complete surprise to her that Goldman had as much influence over the eventual decision as his own comments claim. She thought she had been working directly with only the top people at the JAOs (Kolodny, interview). The year following the press release was trying for Kolodny. A part of her job required her to travel throughout the United States to meet with alumnae groups, parents, and financial supporters of the college. For all of that year, Kolodny could travel nowhere in the country without spending a considerable amount of her time responding to questions: "What was the story with Tony Martin?" "What influence was he having on how courses were taught at the college; and what efforts was Wellesley taking to protect itself from such an incident in the future?" In a few isolated cases, a financial contributor threatened to withhold her/his annual donation to the college. The parents of some prospective students expressed their dismay at what had transpired at

Wellesley the year before, and wondered out loud if this was still a school where their children could get a top-notch education, as advertised (Kolodny, interview).

The future will undoubtedly unfold along different lines for both Wellesley College and the Boston JAOs. A few things, however, are evident at this writing: Wellesley clearly does not want to go through another public laundering of its private linens. Tony Martin is a tenured faculty member of Wellesley College. He still has that job, and he is still using *The Secret Relationship between Blacks and Jews* and *The Jewish Onslaught: Dispatches from the Wellesley Battlefront* as required reading for his courses in African American history. He is largely isolated from the rest of the campus because of the earlier faculty censure vote, and his courses are not accepted as meeting course requirements in other departments (most notably history). He staunchly dismisses any criticism of his course material as a Jewish conspiracy to discredit him.

How do the JAOs feel about Martin using this material in a future classroom situation, particularly with undergraduates? The ADL says, "People use *Mein Kampf* [in classrooms]. We don't want *The Secret Relationship* used, but we never said he couldn't use it. We felt it needed to be used in the proper context. If you look through his statements, he refuses to let the facts confuse him. He continues to distort what our statement said, and there are still people at Wellesley who thought that we actually called for his tenure to be revoked" (Zakim, interview).

The antisemitism at Wellesley College was a local problem that quickly drew national attention with the release of the joint press release, and the furor that attended President Walsh's letter in December 1993. It became national in scope because of the extensive media coverage after the JAOs became involved. It is unlikely the issue would have received the attention it did based on a single article in the *Boston Jewish Times*. It became increasingly national as Tony Martin was linked to the activities of Leonard Jeffries at CCNY. The Jeffries case was proof positive in the eyes of many (including the ADL) of how not to handle such a situation, either organizationally or academically. As a result of CCNY's lesson in administrative and legal bungling, the ADL is convinced that the strategizing (albeit, limited) undertaken by the Boston JAOs resulted in better decisions being made at Wellesley College and produced an end result that more people could live with. The ADL's director didn't feel the Wellesley incident had particularly helped the Jewish community, but unlike the Black/Jewish Historical Exhibit incident and the AJC, neither had it damaged it.

Is there likely to be another Wellesley incident? If there is, it is unlikely it will be over the same issues as before, including Tony Martin. The present Wellesley president has demonstrated a much less forgiving attitude toward derogatory and pernicious polemics than her predecessor. As reported in the *Chronicle of Higher Education* in an article entitled "Wellesley Rethinks Its

Multicultural Requirement," April 28, 1995, the entire Martin incident prompted Wellesley to create special committees to examine its multicultural curricula requirements, as well as an ongoing review of the college's entire curriculum requirements. The *Chronicle* article pointed to the Tony Martin incident as the starting point for this extensive reexamination of requirements and objectives. The Martin issue was one that few on Wellesley's campus want to see repeated at any time in the future. As for the JAOs, they are painfully aware that they do not always agree on tactics, even when they are in the same room with one another. There are sometimes drastic end results when the interests of contributors clash with the best intentions of confronting antisemitism in public forums.

The Nation of Islam has figured prominently in the first two incidents reported in this book, and it does so again in the third and final incident. All three of these antisemitic incidents took place within months of one another, and in the cases of the Black/Jewish Historical Exhibit, and the antisemitism at Wellesley College, they were literally happening at the same time. The third incident, an antisemitic speech by Minister Louis Farrakhan (leader of the NOI) at the University of Massachusetts, followed the first two incidents by a matter of months.

NOTES

1. Goldman is now the director of the Christian/Jewish Study Center at Merrimack College, Andover, Massachusetts.

2. In mid-June 1999 the Board of Appeals for the Massachusetts Superior Court upheld Lefkowitz's summary judgment against Martin. Case closed.

Incident Number Three: Minister Louis Farrakhan's Anti-Jewish Rant on Campus

On Wednesday evening, March 9, 1994, Louis Farrakhan, the fiery leader of the Nation of Islam (NOI), delivered a two-part four-hour speech to an audience estimated at 2,000 to 4,000 at the University of Massachusetts at Amherst, Massachusetts (hereafter, UMass-Amherst). While the television, radio, and press people were in attendance, Farrakhan focused his comments on black pride, individual sobriety, personal responsibility, and the elimination of black against black crime. The media was compelled to leave around 11:00 P.M. to meet their respective deadlines, and at this point Farrakhan's speech shifted to a highly polemical format.

He upbraided Jews for their alleged control of the African slave trade, and he suggested that powerful sources including Jews were attempting to tie Farrakhan to the murder of Malcolm X on February 21, 1965. In his comments Farrakhan also asserted that not one Jewish rabbi had protested the wanton killing of over one hundred Arab men and boys who gathered for morning prayers at a mosque in Hebron, Israel, and were subsequently massacred by a deranged Jewish extremist. Leaders of three of the four Boston Jewish advocacy organizations were in attendance at Farrakhan's speech.

The next day, March 10, 1994, three of the four advocacy organizations (AJC, AJCg, and ADL) quickly convened a conference of the major media participants from the evening before, and issued a lengthy correction to the media's truncated report of Farrakhan's speech the night before.

Martin Goldman, the soon to be former associate director of the Boston AJC, recalled that people from three of the four JAOs journeyed to UMass-Amherst as a group to hear the Farrakhan speech. The director of the JCRC did not make the trip. Goldman took copious notes over the course of the entire evening, and he described Farrakhan as crafty and skilled at working the media. Farrakhan spoke for approximately four hours. During the first two hours he focused on issues of concern and interest to the black community. Goldman couldn't find much to criticize in Farrakhan's comments that condemned black crime against blacks, blacks assuming greater responsibility for their families, and eschewing drugs and violence. But when the media packed up and left to file their stories and film, Farrakhan's rhetoric took a dramatic shift. For the next two hours Farrakhan (according to Goldman) "started his antisemitic bullshit! His antisemitic craziness" (Martin Goldman, interview by author, August 29, 1995).

At this point in the evening, Farrakhan knew that no record of his anti-Jewish raging would reach the airwaves or the front page of the local paper. "[T]hat's when he got real crazy," according to Goldman. Farrakhan's followers were in the audience to root for everything he had to say. It was a packed house that night, and estimates range from a low of 2,000 to over 4,000 people in attendance. The crowd reacted enthusiastically to every one of Farrakhan's Jew-baiting remarks with "cheering, wild cheering" (Goldman, interview).

Farrakhan claimed "the Jews were behind the assassination of Abraham Lincoln and [were] the instigators of the Civil War. That one I had never heard before" (Goldman, interview). At one point Farrakhan linked the Jews to the Nat Turner episode. Jews were supposedly responsible for suppressing the Nat Turner rebellion. This allegation also appears in the Nation of Islam's publication, *The Secret Relationship Between Blacks and Jews, Volume 1* (1991, hereafter *SR*). Goldman had written a book about the Nat Turner revolt (*Nat Turner and the Southampton Revolt of 1831*, 1992), and he understood better than most people in the audience that night how Farrakhan had made his "Jewish connection" with the Nat Turner revolt. Goldman explains, "They [the NOI] simply went to the muster lists of the regiments that were called up in the Virginia militia, and there were thousands of people [on those lists], and they picked out a couple of Jewish names. I'm not even convinced that Farrakhan has ever read his own book (i.e., *SR*). That's how they do their 'research.' If they can find a Jew anywhere in the wood pile, they pick him out" (Goldman, interview).

In spite of all the wild cheering and enthusiasm from the highly partisan audience, there were dissenting black voices in that crowd. Professor Michael Thalwell of the Black Studies Program at UMass-Amherst called out to Farrakhan, "You were involved in the assassination of Malcolm X; what about that?" Goldman recalls that Thalwell's confrontation of Farrakhan was a brave act. The audience was clearly incensed by Thalwell's question, and said so, loudly, but according to Goldman, "Farrakhan got real rattled at this. He had to deal with it, and he did. In fact his answer was not a bad one. . . . [H]e did say he didn't like Malcolm X, and he was opposed to Malcolm X, but then he tried to worm out of any responsibility for the killing of the former NOI leader" (Goldman, interview).

During the long ride back to Boston in the early morning hours of March 10, there was not a lot of discussion about what to do next, in light of what had just transpired over the past several hours. The JAOs' level of exhaustion far exceeded anyone's ability to think straight at that point. Within hours after his early morning return to Boston, Leonard Zakim (director of the ADL) pulled together the directors of the other three JAOs for a strategy meeting. It was decided during this morning meeting that as many of the media as could be located from the night before would be invited to joint conference later that day at the JAOs' headquarters building in Boston, and the entire content of Farrakhan's speech would be discussed with them. Goldman was an invited guest, but had little to contribute. It was not for any lack of opinions on his part, but rather because the directors of the three organizations were the decision makers on this occasion and nothing was called for from him except his quiet attention.

Sheila Decter, director of the AJCg, discussed several aspects of the decision-making process that took place during this incident. Any decision to challenge Farrakhan's speech at UMass-Amherst was not made in a vacuum, at least not on the part of the AJCg. Its primary interest in any issue it got involved in has always been the legal and constitutional implications of the incident and how it might apply any findings to a population that goes beyond only Jews.

Farrakhan's speech at UMass-Amherst the night before was the kind of incident that generated a good deal of strategizing by the JAOs, if not with one another, then with other organizations intimately connected to the upcoming speech by Farrakhan. They had been in contact with a variety of people at UMass-Amherst, and well before Farrakhan arrived on campus. Decter recounts, "We contacted the UMass Hillel Foundation and tried to find out what was happening on their campus and what kind of help they needed. We did this based on what we knew about prior visits [to college campuses] by the NOI" (Sheila Decter, interview by author, June 15, 1994).

One of the first issues that surfaced was the question of security on the night of the speech; security for people attending the speech as well as for the speaker and the university. During one of those early contacts with UMass-Amherst, Decter learned that the NOI security branch, called the Fruit of Islam, was going to be paid by UMass-Amherst to act as a security service on campus on the day of Farrakhan's speech. Decter did not want that to happen, if at all possible.

In the past, at several other locations, the Fruit of Islam was allowed to search (frisk) students and other attendees for weapons. Their appearance in semimilitary garb is imposing; their presence is frequently described as intimidating. The legal issue here is that the Fruit of Islam is a subdivision of a group (the NOI) that claims to be a religion, a self-proclaimed black separatist group, and an offshoot of main line Islam. Decter felt the overriding issue was the students' civil rights at UMass-Amherst on the night of the speech. "[W]e did not believe that a price for going to this speech was that you gave up your rights to be free from invasion of your body by an outside force like that [of the Fruit of Islam security frisk]" (Decter, interview).

She had discussed this civil rights issue with UMass-Amherst officials and had also taken her concerns to the Massachusetts attorney general's office. She wanted to be sure that both of those organizations would take the appropriate measures to ensure "that the rights of all students were not going to be denied in terms of the Farrakhan visit to UMass. We laid out for the attorney general and for the university what we thought [were] the appropriate ways of dealing with the situation. We said if the university believes that the kind of security needed involves checking to be sure people do not have weapons, we do not believe it should be done by a frisk. That takes away the rights of all students" (Decter, interview). This was, after all, a university, a place of learning, not an entertainment spectacle.

"If you think this is a controversial speech which students have a right to hear, then you can't say, as a price of coming to hear it, you need to be frisked. If you think this security is an issue, then the university has an obligation to provide security themselves, and to provide it in such a way that students' rights are not taken away; students have the right not to be frisked by the Nation of Islam" (Decter, interview).

Whether it was the AJCg's direct efforts, or the combined efforts of several groups working in harmony on a common issue, the university announced that the NOI would not be allowed to frisk students. A New York security firm was hired and provided metal detectors, and they noninvasively screened persons who attended the speech. The Fruit of Islam would be allowed to observe, but not participate in any security screening. This was a significant outcome, because it had not happened in this way at other campuses throughout the country. In those other locations, a not too subtle form of blackmail had been used by the NOI. They said, in effect, "We will cancel Farrakhan's [or whoever] appearance if you won't allow us to do it [security] our way!" The university was convinced that AJCg had been instrumental in effecting a significant change in this practice by the NOI. It is also a reflection of how the AJCg attempts to resolve any issue in which it involves itself. "We did not have an outright confrontation with the NOI. We did look to see if there were excesses on the part of the NOI, but not necessarily to curtail Farrakhan's visit to the university. We also did not write the university saying, 'You can't have him,' or directly object to him being on their campus" (Decter, interview).

In addition to protecting students' civil rights, there was the long-standing issue for the AJCg of the separation of church and state. In this case, there was a question whether state money could be used to pay the Fruit of Islam (because it is part of a religious body) and for Farrakhan's speech which would be presented on public property. The AJCg did what it does best, it quickly moved to protect the civil and constitutional rights of large numbers of people under a compelling circumstance, whether or not they were Jewish; in this case, the student body at UMass-Amherst.

The Fruit of Islam is a security force established by Farrakhan, and it travels everywhere with key NOI personages. In addition to bodyguard duties, members of the Fruit of Islam have been contracted to provide security services to public housing projects in various cities in the United States. Their success rate in these undertakings has been mixed. In a few cases they have been lauded for the ability to curtail crime, drugs, and violence. In other cases, they have been fired from the projects and accused of causing more trouble than they prevented. The AJCg filed a court case against the Fruit of Islam under the separation of church and state provisions, demanding that the Fruit of Islam as a division of a tax-exempt religious organization be barred from bidding on security contracts that involve government funding. Other events that took place in the aftermath of his speech at UMass-Amherst would involve Farrakhan and the NOI again in serious questions about the separation of church and state.

While the AJCg was conferring with the university and state officials, Decter was also meeting with her colleagues from the AJC and the ADL. Not extensively or for long periods, but, "two maybe three times, for an hour or so, and we discussed what each other was doing, and [we met] to get a feeling for what other organizations we were each working with" (Decter, interview). There was no specific attempt among the JAOs to find a unifying theme or voice for this incident, or to work collaboratively (as they had with the Wellesley College incident) on Farrakhan's upcoming appearance; after his speech there was. For one thing, the AJCg had already announced what it was doing (at UMass-Amherst and with the state attorney general's office). They were steps that were consistent with the kind of issues that the JAOs dealt with every day. Decter's comments about communicating with the other two JAOs provides some insights into why the JCRC did not go to the university to hear Farrakhan's speech along with the other three JAOs and why the JCRC did not attend the press conference the next day.

The JCRC excused itself from attending the Farrakhan speech because of an earlier commitment. On the other hand, it was appropriate for the three national JAOs to coordinate their decision-making strategy about Farrakhan's appearance at UMass-Amherst, because they all have statewide responsibility. The JCRC is a local umbrella organization, and would not ordinarily involve itself in an out-of-town incident. This incident also involved other organizations besides the JAOs. From the very beginning it involved UMass-Amherst personnel and people at the UMass Hillel Foundation. Farrakhan's speech would be given on their campus, and, to a significant degree, it was their situation to manage. The JAOs were there to provide help, advice, and guidance where and when requested. The discussions among the other three organizations were based on finding out what one another was doing and to be sure they were not tripping over one another in their efforts to help the students and the university.

The night of Farrakhan's speech, the ADL rented a van, and the AJC, AJCg, plus other invited guests of the ADL went to UMass-Amherst to listen and observe. A protest rally organized by the campus Hillel group had already taken place earlier in the day. The field house where the speech was given was large; it held over 2,000 people that night, but only half of those in attendance were students. Decter recalled, "The audience's reactions, in addition to Farrakhan's comments, were very disturbing to us. Whenever Farrakhan made comments that were anti-Jewish, the audience applauded with great enthusiasm. The largest amount of applause came at a statement [Farrakhan made] which was factually wrong. He said that after the Hebron [Israel] tragedy, not a single Jewish organization rose up to discredit Baruch Goldstein [the assassin] or to say that it was wrong, and the audience stood up and cheered when he said this! In fact, every single Jewish organization that I know of made a statement by the next day, and this included many orthodox rabbis who said this [killing] was not acceptable. The fact that it was factually inaccurate made no difference to the audience. Farrakhan's inaccurate statement made it sound as if Jews were really out for the blood of their enemies. The implication was clear—no one [Jews] spoke up for the Palestinians. Thus, if Jews were willing to do nothing for Palestinians, then clearly they [Jews] were out for African American blood as well. The audience was probably a quarter white, and they were incapable or unwilling to exercise critical judgment in listening to this demagogue. They accepted what he said, and they were enthusiastic in their response. This was overt antisemitism. It was not deceptive; it was not hidden" (Decter, interview).

There were several other disturbing characterizations in Farrakhan's speech: The amount of antisemitic rhetoric in Farrakhan's speech picked up noticeably as the evening wore on; The largest numbers of press and media people had left after the first hour of the speech; several more left after the second hour, and only a few remained until the speech ended sometime after midnight. At one point in his speech Farrakhan said, "You know, if anything ever happens to me or you find me dead, look to the Jewish community because they want me dead and that's where the source will be!" Farrakhan accused Hollywood Jews (Warner Brothers) of bribing Spike Lee with "thirty *shekels* of silver" ($300 million) to produce a sanitized film version of Malcolm X's life (Decter, interview).

As lopsided and distressing as Farrakhan's demagoguery was, the JAOs that departed Amherst for Boston in the early morning hours were too emotionally drained to make any complex decisions about what they would do next. The morning papers provided their first answers. All of Boston's newspapers and the morning newscasts characterized Farrakhan's speech of the night before as "conciliatory." In the AJCg's opinion it was anything but conciliatory. The last half of Farrakhan's speech was an all-out attack on Jews. With these first press reports as an impetus, an early morning strategy session was assembled by the ADL comprising the three organizations to decide how to correct the inadequate media version of Farrakhan's speech the night before.

They convened a press conference for later that same day and confronted the omissions and the distortions within the press's coverage of the speech. The press responded well and immediately prepared a series of clarifying articles. The Sunday following (March 13, 1994) this meeting, the *Boston Globe Sunday Edition* ran a three-quarter page article detailing virtually all of Farrakhan's Wednesday night speech, including his antisemitic rhetoric. But would the press have initiated this follow-up without the coordinated pressure from the three Jewish advocacy organizations; probably not.

Within a week of the speech at UMass-Amherst, Farrakhan was back in Boston to speak to an audience that advertised it would allow entry only to black men. It was to be held at the Strand Theater in Roxbury. The Strand Theater building is owned by the city of Boston and is legally required to observe the open seating laws. The AJCg was not yet through with Minister Louis Farrakhan. This second speech by Farrakhan aimed at "black men only" was a violation of other people's civil rights as far as the AJCg was concerned. The issue turned on the city ownership of the building that housed the Strand Theater. Publicly owned facilities cannot deny entry to anyone based on race, religion, or gender. The Nation of Islam and Farrakhan's second speech proposed to violate the city's civil rights provision, that is, women and white males would be barred from entering the building during Farrakhan's speech.

In a brief conversation that had occurred several days before, the AJCg had discovered that one of the coordinators for Farrakhan's upcoming speech at the Strand Theater did not realize that the building was owned by the city of Boston and therefore carried certain legal requirements about open admission. The leasing agent for the Strand notified the local mosque of the NOI and informed them of these requirements. The leasing agent felt confident that the NOI had reconsidered its original position and would admit women (Decter, interview).

On the night of the speech, all women were barred from entering the building. One of these women was a reporter from a local television station. This exclusion of women from attending his speech generated a great deal of criticism and, in the end, generated more discussion than anything Farrakhan said during his speech. One of the women who was excluded from that speech sued the NOI, and a Boston court ruled that Farrakhan had to appear in court.

In contrast to the speech at UMass-Amherst, the AJCg did not directly involve itself in this civil rights case. The Boston chapter may have wanted to, but its wishes were overruled by the AJCg's New York office. The national office for the AJCg did not believe it was up to the director of the Boston office of the AJCg to enforce these laws. "We were not the only body out there that had to enforce the law. The American Civil Liberties Union [ACLU] was available. I think a decision not to be involved with a [law] suit dealing with the issue of gender was made because of our concern about black/Jewish relations, and our feeling that we did not have to be the point-person on this particular incident. We made no public statement about the issue of the gender and, in part it came from [our] feeling about fairness. We often try to put ourselves in someone else's shoes. For example, there are times when feminists might want to meet and will say, 'We really want to have a meeting that is primarily women, and we don't want an antifeminist presence.' In the same way we did not think the notion of talking to just black men is so completely outrageous that we need to deal with that. We thought that the women, who had come and wanted to hear the speech, had the right to hear it, but we did not elect at this particular point in time to spend every ounce of our available time fighting this man" (Decter, interview).

The director of the Boston ADL saw the advocacy response to Farrakhan's speech at UMass-Amherst as a coordinated, professionally driven response; that is, professionals within the JAOs working closely with the UMass-Amherst administration and campus Hillel personnel to accomplish two things: (1) to share important information about Farrakhan's upcoming visit to the UMass-Amherst campus; (2) to discuss the kind of action each would take in anticipation of Farrakhan's arrival, as well as on the evening of his speech, and any issues that might develop in the speech's aftermath. The ADL became the communications link with the other JAOs, and the campus Hillel organization became the communications link with the other UMass-Amherst campus groups who had an interest in the Farrakhan speech. It should be pointed out that UMass-Amherst had had over the years at least five incidents on the campus involving racial, ethnic, or religious differences among the student body. One of those involved a speech by Louis Farrakhan in 1989.

The UMass-Amherst Hillel director, Saul Perlmutter, had called the ADL requesting its support and strategic involvement in the upcoming Farrakhan speech. The ADL had worked with the UMass-Amherst Hillel organization for over twelve years and had established a trusted on-campus reputation with them. It was not possible for the ADL to have developed such a relationship, for instance, with the new Hillel director at Wellesley College. She was virtually brand new in her job and was still finding her own level on that campus when the Tony Martin issues began to take shape.

The AJC and the AJCg were not initially involved and only became involved after the planned appearance by Farrakhan became public knowledge. In this incident there were no lay leaders or prominent members of the JAOs involved as there were in the first two incidents. This does not mean the national offices of the three organizations were not constantly aware of what was going on; they were, but in this incident, the decision making was almost entirely driven by local personnel.

The ADL had worked with the UMass-Amherst Hillel group for over twelve years. The Hillel group's call to the ADL requesting assistance is one more example of the public's inclination to call the ADL first in the event of an antisemitic attack or a hate crime. The other JAOs may become involved at some point, particularly if the incident has national implications; they are not likely to be called first. The director of the ADL pointed out, "We have been in this business a long time. We're number one—we've been through it before" (Leonard Zakim, interview by author, July, 28, 1994).

On each occasion that Farrakhan (or one of his followers) made an appearance at UMass-Amherst the ADL had been in the audience. The ADL reasons that its presence creates a visible assurance to the black community that what the ADL knew about Farrakhan; it had learned it from firsthand observation, not simply what the papers reported. On this occasion, the ADL's director felt it was important for members of his board of directors to attend this speech. "[W]e invited members of our board to [hear Farrakhan] rather than just [read] newspaper clippings. [T]he tenor in the room, the audience climate, the way in which he is introduced and the warmup speeches, etc., are all part of a general picture that gives us reason to believe that he is a significant problem in terms of the Jews. [I]t is part of a serious program, and we thought it was important for our people to observe it firsthand" (Zakim, interview).

In early March 1994 the ADL's director had decided to attend Farrakhan's speech, along with the ADL's civil rights director and a handful of board members. A number of decisions were then undertaken: (1) Discussions were held with UMass-Amherst administration about personal safety issues; (2) The AJCg checked out the legal implications of the NOI's private security force (the Fruit of Islam) on the campus of a state university; (3) Several contacts were made with the chancellor's and president's offices (at UMass-Amherst), as well as contacts with the governor's office; (4) There was almost daily contact with the UMass-Amherst Hillel office and its personnel.

Just prior to the day of Farrakhan's speech, the AJC and the AJCg were invited to attend with the ADL. The JCRC turned down the invitation to attend the speech with the others because of a schedule conflict and because the JCRC's director "did not want to drive two and a half hours to hear Louis Farrakhan" (Nancy Kaufman, interview by author, March 13, 1996). There was some speculation at the time that the JCRC's reluctance to attend the speech may have been predicated on a rumor that the ADL was going to the speech to stage a demonstration or protest against Farrakhan. The ADL's director dismissed the speculation as nothing more than rumor with no substance in fact (Zakim, interview). This entire aggregation of JAO personnel and some members of the ADL's board of directors attended Farrakhan's speech in Amherst, Massachusetts. They were back in Boston by approximately 3:00 A.M. the next morning. By 7:00 A.M. the early editions of the local newspapers reflected everybody's fears—the press had completely missed the second half of Farrakhan's speech. "I read that Farrakhan had given a two and a half hour conciliatory speech. I picked up the phone and called the editor of the *Globe*, Max Storin. I made a few other calls around town, and I decided at that point that a response had to go out very quickly, [because] an issue won't go away if it is ignored. At this point I spoke to the other [JAO] people here in the building, and then I called my New York office. . . . [W]ould they have a problem with clarifying Farrakhan's reported remarks? They . . . thought it was a good idea. They were prepared to let us go it alone, but my feeling was because we had invited the AJCg and the AJC, they should be involved [too]" (Zakim, interview).

The directors of the three JAOs, plus their support personnel, met to discuss organizing a press conference that would ask the media to include in the next editions those portions of Farrakhan's speech that the press had not covered. The JCRC's director was not a part of this early morning meeting and, in fact, did not learn of the proposed press conference until "twenty minutes before it was happening. And I tried to stop it" (Kaufman, interview).

Kaufman saw two distinct issues here working at cross-purposes. The first was the issue of the JAOs, as well-known Jewish groups, holding a press conference that day; and the second issue, a black minister's group called the Ten Point Coalition who wanted to hold their own press conference. The Ten Point Coalition had authored a very strong statement (two pages, single-spaced) entitled "A Question of Morality: An Open Letter to Minister Louis Farrakhan." Their letter assailed Farrakhan for his silence over the Malcolm X assassination, as well as several other instances of violence against blacks instigated by members of the NOI. The Ten Point Coalition had planned to read their letter at a press conference at approximately the same time (4:00 P.M.) as the JAOs' press conference. It seemed to the JCRC that publicly rebuking Farrakhan would be seen as far more effective if it came from a prominent group of black ministers than if it came from the Jewish groups.

The JCRC had worked closely in Boston with the Ten Point Coalition, and the JCRC's director was concerned with the possible negative impact a Jewish response would have on the efforts of the Ten Point Coalition to directly confront Farrakhan. She recalled, "They [the Ten Point Coalition] did *not* want this to be a Jewish issue, because the more it was a Jewish issue the harder it [was] for them, because then they would be looked [upon] as pawns of the Jews. They were trying desperately to assert themselves as blacks concerned with Farrakhan's message to blacks. I greatly respected what they were trying to do, and thought it was in our interest to encourage it. They were saying Farrakhan contributed to an environment of violence. They were trying to prevent violence in the black communities, and the NOI is inciting violence. I felt there was either a total disregard, or an unwillingness to acknowledge, what had been an effective strategy on the minister's part" (Kaufman, interview).

The JCRC's director made her plea to her colleagues telling them "[T]hey [the Ten Point Coalition] are going to release their statement at four o'clock. Why not give them the benefit of a full press [conference]? Why make this a

Jewish issue now, what do we gain; . . . what's our goal? Our goal is to discredit Farrakhan . . . everyone knows that Jews don't like Farrakhan, but what no one knows is that there are black ministers in this town who are willing to speak out [against him]; so wouldn't it make sense for us to be a little lower key than usual?" (Kaufman, interview). Her argument did not prevail. The ADL did not see the press conference as an issue of competing values.

The ADL's director recalled, "We weren't talking about Farrakhan's threat to the black community or his alleged connection to the assassination of Malcolm X. We were talking about the media coverage of the event [Farrakhan's speech] the night before, how distorted it was, and what we felt needed to be done to correct those distortions. They got their publicity. It was important what they did, and it was important what we did. Our decision was driven by the strategic necessity to reach people who would pick up the newspaper, and say, 'What is this Farrakhan thing all about?' " (Zakim, interview).

By late afternoon the directors of the three JAOs met with a hastily gathered collection of media people who had been at the Farrakhan speech the night before. The advocacy organizations won two concessions from the media: (1) Publish an article that talked about *everything* Farrakhan had said the night before; and (2) Do a lengthier treatment of all of his comments in the upcoming Sunday edition of the *Boston Globe*.

Their advocacy was successful. The *Boston Globe* ran an article on Friday (March 11, 1994) reporting the displeasure of the JAOs with Farrakhan's comments about Jews ("Jewish Leaders Criticize UMass-Amherst Speech"). On the Sunday following (March 13, 1994) two major, full-page treatments of Louis Farrakhan appeared in the *Boston Sunday Globe*. One of the articles entitled "What I Am Telling You Will Save Your Life" was a collection of excerpts of several attacks on Jews in Farrakhan's four hour speech at UMass-Amherst. The second was an article written by Jonathan Kaufman, the prominent author of *Broken Alliances* (1991), on the black/Jewish relations. His article ("The Fire This Time") was a lengthy opinion piece focused on the demagoguery and distortion of Louis Farrakhan and the Nation of Islam toward Jews.

On the other hand, the JCRC's comments demonstrate the reality and function of interorganizational competition. It suggests it is part ego, part personality, and part competition between individual and organizational goals. Not, perhaps, on a conscious level, but from the above example, it appears that Jewish interests were placed ahead of the interests of the black community: their opposition to Louis Farrakhan and their concern over the proviolence nature of the NOI.

Collaborative decision making by these organizations, even when it is focused on the classic complaint of antisemitism, is episodic at best. There is no overall strategic plan in the Jewish community for dealing with antisemitic attacks, and each individual JAO is on its own to decide what it will do from one incident to the next.

In summary, the three antisemitic incidents and the JAOs' responses to each reveals a number of consistencies in the advocacy used in each situation. On the other hand, the larger question that must be addressed is whether or not the JAOs were actually effective in their advocacy given the multiple needs that were being addressed. It is also important to analyze these incidents in light of the impact they have on how effectively the JAOs are serving the needs of the larger Jewish community. The last chapter of this book addresses these questions of effectiveness, antisemitism as a property serving multiple needs, and the efficacy of the JAOs' activities in the face of serious questions about the future direction of Jewish identity and continuity.

Part Four

New Definitions, New Directions

Chapter 11

Antisemitism, America's Jews, and the Future

INTRODUCTION

Chapter one briefly recounted the history of the Jewish experience in America and the antisemitism that often assailed Jews over much of their journey up to their current status as full citizens. This final chapter addresses the same two topics, that is, America's Jews and antisemitism, but in reverse order. The chapter attempts to provide answers to several questions about these intertwined issues. First, the JAOs publicly take note of every manifestation of antisemitism and rightfully criticize it, but five persistent questions remain: why have the statistics that focus on anti-Jewish beliefs dropped so dramatically over the past fifty years? Or, said another way, what accounts for the substantial improvement in the public's attitudes toward America's Jews since World War II? Second, it is important to revisit the actions of the JAOs in the three antisemitic incidents reported in chapters eight, nine, and ten and attempt to determine whether or not the JAOs are "effective" organizations in their advocacy efforts against antisemitism. It is in this analysis of effectiveness that we begin to appreciate the political significance of antisemitism for the JAOs.

Third, given the dramatic slide in negative opinions about Jews in America over the past fifty years (as well as the steady drop in incidents of direct hostility), how are we to understand what antisemitism actually means, and just as importantly, how are we to measure it? This is a particularly important question in light of earlier comments about the dwindling strength of antisemitic manifestations, but also because of the persistence with which antisemitism maintains its political significance for the JAOs and the emotional strength it continues to possess for substantial numbers of American Jews. Fourth, given the secular nature of the JAOs and their exemplification of a "civil Judaism" (as contrasted with a traditional or religious Judaism), how do these advocacy organizations propose they will represent America's Jews in the coming century? This is a sensitive question, because it focuses on the ways in which three key organizational issues—antisemitism, the State of Israel, and the Holocaust—were transformed into utilitarian goals for the JAOs, but that no longer possess the same significance they held in years past. Finally, how are we to understand the dilemma of Jewish identity/continuity given the impact 100 years of economic, social, and cultural success have had on American Jewish identity? Has the inevitable process of assimilation so far eroded Jewish identity as to render any discussions about "rediscovery," or "reawakening," of a once vibrant community all but moot?

Beginning with how antisemitism should be understood today, it is important to address a question about the statistics presented in chapter two. Those statistics clearly document the slide in antisemitism's attitudinal strength over the past fifty years, a slide that has led to the title of this study, *The Death of American Antisemitism*. What is just as important as tracing this downward spiral in anti-Jewish animus is an answer to the question, "What were the factors that led to this demise, and how large a role was played by the advocacy efforts of the JAOs in this diminishment?"

WHY ANTISEMITISM HAS GRADUALLY DISAPPEARED OVER THE PAST FIFTY YEARS

The discussion of antisemitism in chapter two graphically attests to the drop in antisemitic attitudes among the American public over the past fifty years and the drop in antisemitic incidents in more recent years. The important question that goes unanswered (or, for that matter, is never raised) by the JAOs is "Why have these negative opinions about Jews dropped the way they have over this fifty-year period?" There are seven factors that explain this steady decline in anti-Jewish animus in the United States. No one of these reasons can stand by itself as a totally satisfactory explanation for the decline in negative public opinion about Jews. But, when taken in combination, they collectively form a historically traceable and understandable path along which this long-standing prejudice has inevitably dwindled to its present state of minimal importance in the eyes of the general public. All of these factors have appeared at one point or another throughout this text.

Just as antisemitism was bound up with this nation's history from its earliest days, so too has been its decline. It is useful to highlight these seven factors:

1. Over the past fifty years the drop in negative beliefs about Jews has been facilitated by the educational efforts, advocacy efforts, and advertising of the JAOs.

These efforts cannot be isolated from a score of other pressures, but even without knowing the exact 1:1 relationship those other factors may possess, it is safe to say that the JAOs' collective efforts have had an impact on bringing down negative attitudes toward Jews.

2. Over the past fifty years the drop in antisemitic beliefs has been facilitated by the revelations of virtually every detail of the attempted destruction of European Jewry. The Allied powers and the Jewish organizations knew virtually all of the grisly facts about this genocide beginning late in 1941. But the American public, including America's Jews, did not fully learn of the extent, ferocity, or political certainty of Hitler's annihilation program for several years after the end of World War II. By 1961, and the public trial of Adolf Eichmann in Israel, the entire country (not to mention the rest of the world) came to realize the enormity of the Nazi crime. With these revelations came the realization that even if a certain percentage of Americans persisted in their loathing for Jews, killing them was unacceptable. Then there is the quantity and sophistication of Holocaust scholarship that poured forth in the 1970s and 1980s. It further contributed to reducing negative attitudes toward Jews in this country. Earlier Israeli scholarship was written in Hebrew and focused primarily on the religious and theological significance of the destruction. The scholarship of Lucy Dawidowicz (1975), Raul Hilberg (1985), Yehuda Bauer (1982), Richard Marrus (1987), Martin Gilbert (1985), Leni Yahl (1990), Helen Fein (1984), and John Weiss (1996) were written in English, and their insights were accessible to large audiences possessing a reasonable level of education. For the first time millions of readers, Jewish and non-Jewish, became fully aware of the horrors of the *Shoah* and in extensive detail.

3. Over the past fifty years the complex of events described earlier as "When Jews became white folks" has facilitated the drop in negative beliefs about Jews. The combination of government-supported educational funding, government-supported funding for new housing, and the suburbanization of America forced millions of Americans to live, work, and play with real Jews, not the mythical or fantastical representations of the Jew dredged up from centuries of propaganda. A lot of people found they liked Jews and even started marrying them in substantial numbers.

4. Over the past fifty years the drop in negative beliefs about Jews has been facilitated by decisions on the part of local law enforcement offices and the FBI to cooperate with the Jewish community in identifying and pursuing perpetrators of hate crimes. The apprehension of these perpetrators is in the high 90-percentile range.

5. Over the past fifty years the advances made by the civil rights movement of the 1950s and 1960s have facilitated the drop in negative beliefs about Jews. It placed the issue of intolerance, bigotry, and discrimination on America's nightly television screens and in the newspapers with a never before seen ferocity. Jews participated extensively in this domestic revolution, and even though the principal beneficiaries were blacks, everyone in the country—white, women, and Jews—benefited from the legal abandonment of centuries of inequity and racial segregation. It was a period of unparalleled change, opening up the halls of education and providing employment and housing to millions of citizens who had been denied these basic civil liberties.

6. Over the past fifty years the drop in negative beliefs about Jews has been facilitated by the upward mobility of Jews into top leadership positions in private,
public, and nonprofit organizations. One consequence of this improved social status on the part of America's Jews was that their philanthropy increasingly went to
supporting a wider range of issues and institutions, issues and institutions that
were not solely Jewish in their focus or intent. Jews were identifying with the majority culture.

7. Over the past fifty years the drop in negative beliefs about Jews has been facilitated by the rising intermarriage rate between Jews and non-Jews. Intermarriage
has climbed from approximately 7 to 9 percent in the mid-1950s to somewhere
in the vicinity of 50 percent today. As Jews moved away from the old neighborhoods and spread out across the suburban landscape they came in contact with
increasing numbers of non-Jews. The opportunities these contacts fostered for
friendships, dating, and marriage has changed forever the definition of what it
means to be Jewish in America.

These seven factors have created an inescapable background within which
the antisemitic incidents described in the previous three chapters must be understood. Given this background, it is now necessary to address the second
question asked above, "Are the JAOs effective organizations in their battles
with antisemitism?"

ARE JAOs EFFECTIVE ORGANIZATIONS?

One of the more elusive properties in studying complex organizations is
arriving at a satisfying answer to questions concerning effectiveness. Is the
organization doing what it advertises? Is it meeting its goals? Is this an effective organization, and what does "effective" mean? The investigator in
the private sector possesses concrete markers such as production data, sales
revenues, time and motion studies, stock market performance, and myriad
other measures to analyze organizational effectiveness, but what comparable measures are available to the investigator asking the same effectiveness
questions of the nonprofit organization? How are we to now understand the
word "effective"? How do we know when a JAO is effective? Can a JAO do
what it "advertises," that is, bring all of its talent and resources to bear
against antisemitism, and still not be effective as an organization?

These qualifications about JAOs and their primary mission—to fight antisemitism—immediately suggests that there are multiple explanations for what
signifies effectiveness. Even in the same group of organizations, these different
understandings can produce significant disagreement among observers. Those
disagreements generate considerable conflict, and that becomes a distraction
in understanding whether or not effectiveness has been lost in the ensuing debate. To return to the three antisemitic incidents and the four JAOs, were they
effective or not in the way they handled these incidents? Framed this way the
question elicits the classic sociological answer, yes and no!

To further complicate our answer, we would have to add, It depends on whom you ask, and what bases are used to determine effectiveness. To begin with, advocacy succeeds even if the cause is lost. It is there to represent one side of an argument, and the advocacy does not have to win to succeed. It is only sufficient that a good argument or defense was raised. A closer examination of the three antisemitic incidents clearly indicates that in all three cases the advocacy did not achieve a clear "win," but it did succeed on several levels. It could also be said to have failed on as many levels as well.

In the Black/Jewish Historical Exhibit, a series of bungled communications compromised the AJC's national policy of not appearing in any public forum with the NOI. As a result of this national policy, the AJC's director of public affairs had no other choice but to remove the AJC from the exhibit. This strict adherence to a national policy in a local situation resulted in three negative outcomes:

1. The exhibit continued for another eight months without the AJC's critically acclaimed panels on 350 years of black/Jewish history, but instead, with the NOI's tainted messages about Jews. Two and a half years of planning were lost in a matter of minutes because of the inflexibility of the AJC's policy of nonappearance. Thousands of Boston area residents and school children were permanently deprived of a valuable history lesson on the relationship between blacks and Jews. Perhaps most disturbing, the NOI touted itself as victorious over the AJC for having gotten its way, and in the process, gained thousands of dollars in free advertising because of the publicity the incident generated.

2. A prominent member of the AJC's board of directors resigned in disgust over the way the whole matter was handled. Not just any member of the board, but one who was widely respected for her support of the local black community and a person who had a strongly favorable opinion of the NOI and the work they had done in drug-infested neighborhoods. Her resignation was a clear signal to the black community that the Jewish community did not speak with one voice.

3. The AJC was held up for considerable scorn in both the black and Jewish communities, and challenging the antisemitic rhetoric in the NOI's display panels was not effective either. It made no difference to the point at which it counted most to be discredited in the historical exhibit itself. Some Jews as well as blacks concluded that the antisemitism of the NOI must not be as bad as the AJC contended; the Jewish advocacy organization couldn't even prevail against the NOI in an exhibit the organization itself had sponsored.

In the second antisemitic incident, involving Wellesley College, nobody would deny that the JAOs had mounted a spirited and direct assault on Professor Martin's antisemitism and the highly inflammatory book he chose to use in his course on African American history. But it was also an incident that revealed serious underlying problems in the process of advocacy. First, the writing of the joint press release was a back and forth exercise that frayed everybody's nerves in the JAOs' local offices. Each of the JAOs was in constant contact with its headquarters office, and each of those offices was rigid in its demand that its "spin" would be represented in the forth-coming press release. It is this sort of internecine conflict that has beset the JAOs virtually from their inception and continues to plague them to this day. One of the directors was reduced to tears before the final version of the press release was signed, not because of any brittleness between the local agencies, but only because of the incessant political wrangling about "spin" at the home office level.

Second, in his zeal to see the antisemitism and Professor Martin at Wellesley College successfully confronted and dealt with, the associate director of the AJC lost his job for too vigorously pursuing the incident, and in the process, holding the college up to public ridicule. There were key AJC board members who were also prominent Wellesley College alumnae, and they made heated demands of the AJC's national office that would not be denied—terminate the offending employee! On the other hand, given the long and twisted history of the two men over who was best qualified to teach black history, it is not surprising that the associate director's personal agenda overrode his organizational charter and ended in embarrassment.

Finally, nothing really changed at Wellesley College as a result of the JAOs' advocacy. Professor Martin still teaches there (he's tenured), and he still relies on his academic privilege to assign *The Secret Relationship between Blacks and Jews, Volume 1* as a text for his courses. Added to this is the fact that Martin authored and self-published a thin volume, *The Jewish Onslaught*, that excoriates the Jewish community and the Wellesley academic community for mounting a singular effort to get him fired. The publicity this book raised only gained Martin nationwide recognition. He now uses that book in another of his courses, and his struggle with Wellesley has been favorably treated in a recent attack on political correctness in America's colleges by the prominent legal gadfly Harvey Silverglate and his coauthor Charles Alan Kors in their book *The Shadow University* (1998). In spite of the fact that the college felt it had success-fully dealt with Martin internally, the JAOs charged ahead and turned an academic argument into a public cause. There is no arguing that they con-fronted antisemitism where they found it, but the larger question that lingers over this incident is "Were the best interests of the Jewish commu-nity being served?" What protection did this all-out attack on Martin or the college yield in added protection for the average Jew? It would be hard to find any at all! On the other hand, it produced substantial publicity for all of the JAOs and their spokespersons.

The third incident, Minister Louis Farrakhan's speech at a major college campus, presents similar dichotomies. Three of the four JAOs were in atten-dance at Farrakhan's speech. It has been argued that the JCRC (which was not present) as a Boston-based organization had no reason, or justification, for being at a speech in the central part of the state. But this absence from the speech automatically excluded the JCRC's director from participating in the hastily gathered press conference the next day as well. There is nothing amiss in this omission until recognition is given to the fact that the JCRC was an early and staunch supporter of the local black organization that was attempting to challenge Farrakhan's demagogic rhetoric! In Nancy Kaufman's words, "it became a 'Jewish thing,' and the black group was totally overshadowed" (JCRC, interview by author, March 13, 1996). However carefully worded opposing opinions may be about the JCRC's absence from a speech by Louis Farrakhan, the fact remains that the internecine differences between the agencies and other community groups once again cloud the picture of Jewish organizational effectiveness. Is this political maneuvering really in the best interests of the at-large Jewish community? Again, it is difficult to see how it would be.

In each of these incidents the antisemitism was vigorously pursued, even where it was detrimental to the JAOs' image and, in one case, to the continued employment of one of its own personnel. In this regard the JAOs were effective as organizations in doing what they advertise. All four of these organizations would argue that their actions in these three incidents served three other outcomes that would render them effective:

1. Whatever the JAOs do in one case, the end result is automatically beneficial to all Jews, whether or not they knew the specifics of a particular case or even see any connection to their lives. The protection of one Jew is a protection of all Jews.

2. The actions taken by the JAOs in these three incidents served as a warning to others that they shouldn't pursue antisemitic rhetoric or actions, or the JAOs would come down on them as well. That is an impossible premise to ever prove, but in this case one supporting argument that could be advanced by the JAOs would be that there has not been an antisemitic incident of the scope or dimension of these three in the years since they were confronted by the JAOs. For most people that might prove very compelling evidence that the JAOs had warded off other offenders. On the other hand, those individuals in society that are driven to mount pernicious attacks against Jews are not likely to care much what the JAOs do or think. Said another way, good (even excellent) advocacy on the JAOs' part cannot anticipate the future. Advocacy can't act until someone else attacks the Jewish community.

3. The JAOs' actions are a reflection of what their lay leaders expect of them. This is what they are getting paid to do—fight antisemitism whenever and wherever it occurs. In each of these three incidents that is what the JAOs did. In this regard they were fulfilling the mandates of their leaders, but that raises as many questions as it answers. Abraham Maslow is credited with the story of a man hunting for his car keys under a bright street lamp. When asked by a passerby where he had lost his keys, the man pointed to a dark corner of the street where his car was parked. When asked why he wasn't looking in the vicinity of his car, he answers, "because the light is better over here!" In much the same way, these JAOs are "looking where the light is brighter," but not necessarily where the problem is.

In other words, they are doing what they know best, whether or not it has any
meaningful impact on the Jewish community.

The JAOs know how to combat antisemitism and that is what they will
do, until they find something else they can do as well. The director of the
AJC admitted in interviews that the most serious problem facing the Jewish
community was not antisemitism, but the increasingly severe problem of
Jewish continuity. But knotty issues like Jewish identity and continuity are
not problems the AJC knows how to do anything about; for that matter, neither do any of the other Jewish organizations. Unfortunately Maslow's
metaphor also raises the specter of moral entrepreneurship, that is, fighting
demons that may or may not exist because that meets the expectation of a
particular organizational power structure; in this case, the reigning oligarchy
in each organization. To examine this relationship between what the JAOs
did and what it was their lay leadership wanted of them (i.e., combat antisemitism), each organization was asked if antisemitism is still a threat to
Jewish security. Their answers are revealing, and they go directly to the heart
of the political importance of antisemitism for the JAOs.

THE CONTINUING SIGNIFICANCE OF ANTISEMITISM
FOR THE JAOs

Antisemitism is a deeply rooted ideological issue for the JAOs, and even
though it is not their only issue, the JAOs' leadership will never allow anyone to move antisemitism from its long-standing position of organizational
importance. Consider the following response to a question asked of each of
them concerning antisemitism and its relationship to present-day Jewish
safety.

The director of the AJC felt certain that: "[T]he biggest threat to Jewish
security is certainly not antisemitism. It is the reverse of antisemitism . . . the
fear of disruption of Jewish continuity is what is foremost on people's mind.
. . . [P]eople acknowledge it but they don't know what to do about it"
(Lawrence Lowenthal, AJC, interview by author, July 12, 1994). He admits
that the (organizational) Jewish community does not know what to do
about the intermarriage rate or its implication for Jewish continuity in
America (Lowenthal, AJC, interview).

On the other hand, he acknowledged that antisemitism is still something
the JAOs know how to deal with: "[Antisemitism] is dramatic . . . it races
the adrenaline. . . . *We've always got to be in that combat arena, against the
antisemites*" (Lowenthal, AJC, interview; emphasis added). Every pro-
nouncement made about Jewish progress in America has to be qualified with
the obligatory reminder that as good as things are the seeds of destruction
and animosity are always there. An executive in one of the JAOs, such as
this director, places himself at great risk if he downplays antisemitism in any

way: "You can get into terrible trouble. You're perceived as having your head in the clouds. They will say [to you], 'Aren't you aware of the undercurrent of antagonism toward the Jews in this country?' You are seen as dismissing a real threat that still exists. You can't be perceived that way, not in the Jewish organizational world. You will have your head handed to you!" (Lowenthal, AJC, interview).

The director of the AJCg sees threats to the Jewish community from a historical perspective: "[M]uch of what we do deals with issues of antisemitism. We believe that a great deal of antisemitism existed historically in relations between certain religious groups, various Christian religious groups and the Jewish community" (Sheila Decter, AJCg, interview by author, June 15, 1994). The AJCg also deals with antisemitism in political groups (both right and left), feminist groups, and labor unions. Such antisemitism takes many forms, ranging from the use of code words to describe Jews, such as "progressive," "New York types," and "radical," up to desecrations, vandalism, discrimination, anti-Israel commentary, and hate speech.

Since the AJCg views antisemitism as a manifestation of several interlocking social pressures (e.g., poverty, racism, and economic inequality), it does not want to focus too tightly on such things as the fiery rhetoric of a Louis Farrakhan. "[I]t diverts us from the real areas where blacks and Jews are working together. The demagogue has to be confronted, and the canards dealt with, *but too much time is distracting, and not enough time is seen as avoiding a clearly stated obligation*" (Decter, AJCg, interview; emphasis added).

The ADL differentiates between threats to the safety of an individual Jew and threats to the safety of the entire Jewish community. A Jew standing in line at a store and hearing someone refer to the cash register as pressing the "Jew button" may feel insulted, but not every denigrating comment about Jews is politically significant. The ADL believes the uneasiness of large numbers of America's Jews is not based on any one incident or any one demagogue, but an accumulation of these stimuli over an undefined period of time.

The director of the ADL considers antisemitism "a threat too easily underestimated" today. "There is . . . a very strong sense in the American Jewish community that we are living perhaps in the best of times, but we are in jeopardy, and the biggest threat to us is to ignore threat . . . *what undermines Jewish security is the failure to respond to antisemitism*" (Leonard Zakim, ADL, interview by author, June 28, 1994; emphasis added).

Finally, is antisemitism a serious enough impediment to the process of Jewish community relations to be considered a primary objective? The JCRC's director does not think so. "I don't see a whole lot of antisemitism in Boston or in [its] black community. Nationally, I see a small part of the black community, the Nation of Islam, deciding that it's in their political and public relations interest to use this issue [antisemitism] to get headlines. They're using the Jewish community" (Kaufman, JCRC, interviews by author, July 7, 1994; May 24, 1995). "I think the biggest threat to Jewish security is the potential disappearance of the Jewish community. I think it's intermarriage; it's assimilation and the lack of a solid Jewish education. It's the total acceptance of Jews that most threatens us, and that is the opposite of antisemitism" (Kaufman, JCRC, interviews, July 7, 1994; May 24, 1995). Yet, as two of the three incidents reported earlier reveal, the JCRC was deeply involved in both incidents, and particularly the incident at Wellesley College.

These comments by leaders in each of the JAOs are consistent with each organization's worldview. However, one thing is abundantly clear, there is substantial political risk in ever letting the real state of anti-Jewish beliefs blur the continuing necessity to keep its historical image foremost in each of the organization's identity profile. This collection of comments on the seven factors that led to the steady decline of antisemitism and the continuing political necessity on the part of the JAOs to retain antisemitism as a central organizational issue brings us to an answer to one of the three questions raised at the beginning of this study, namely, "How many Jewish organizations does it take to fight antisemitism in America today?"

The simple answer is not four! The more complex answer involves determining which organization(s) should take the lead in assuming responsibility. The clear front runner is the ADL. Its long and public history of successful defense and advocacy of Jews have made it the organization to reckon with in the field of hate crimes. It has expanded its efforts beyond antisemitism to combat prejudice and discrimination against other groups as well, for example, blacks, Asians, and gays. The AJCg is not financially strong enough to go on splitting its energies and limited budget into too many areas. Its major legislative battles are won, and today it is best known for the work of the CLSA. The sensible course of action for the AJCg would be to preserve its resources and talent and seek an organization with which it can merge. The ADL is a logical candidate because of the similarity in the two organizations' parallel legal actions. They have filed joint *amicus curiae*, they have supported one another on the issue of church and state, and have both pursued active attacks on violations of the separation of church and state. These similarities may overcome the reluctance of the still largely German Jewish constituency of the ADL to combine with the largely East European leadership of the AJCg. These ideological differences remain a central reason why the AJC and the AJCg have been unsuccessful on at least two separate occasions to arrive at terms that would have allowed them to effect a merger years ago. Given the persistence of these ideological differences between the power structures of the two organizations there is a zero probability that another attempt at merger could be brokered. One allegation as to why the last merger attempt in 1994 did not come off is because the leaders of the AJC did not want any of those "Bolsheviks" walking around the hallways of the AJC![1]

If such a thing as a "sacrilege" could be said to exist in Jewish organizational life (at least the advocacy side of it), it would be to suggest resurrecting the 1951 MacIver study, and in doing so, give serious consideration to its recommendations concerning the reorganization of the JAOs. Even if the JAOs were willing to consider such an idea, it is one that would undoubtedly have to rest on an entirely new study of the JAOs as they are currently organized and led. On the other hand, the JAOs are little different in their worldview from forty-seven years ago, and given the overlap in their pursuit of antisemitism, it is not unreasonable to suggest that the results of any new study would closely parallel MacIver's recommendations of nearly fifty years ago. Two of MacIver's original recommendations to the JAOs are still appropriate today, and a third recommendation naturally suggests itself. First, recognize the special expertise of each organization, and then shift responsibility for that expertise to that organization best qualified to execute it. Second, conserve financial and human resources by consolidating or merging some of the activities of these organizations. The third recommendation grows out of the first two, and that is, carefully reexamine the "organizational effectiveness" question discussed above in light of the dwindling importance of antisemitism as an organizational issue, and reexamine the Jewish continuity debate as the paramount issue. This recommendation, and its thoughtful consideration by the JAOs' leadership, must force the JAOs to ask themselves the compelling question, "What business are we in—and—why?"

Given the past histories of these organizations and the divisiveness that accompanied several of their previous attempts to work together, it is unlikely that anything so bold as the resurrection (or creation) of a MacIver analysis is anything but wishful thinking. However, even if such a recommendation is wishful thinking, the fact remains that the way in which these organizations deal with antisemitism in the future clearly must change. They have a collective and individual responsibility to define with much greater precision what the anti-Jewish beliefs are that they are combating, and in so doing, devise entirely new and more realistic measurement questions to determine anti-Jewish animus in American society. It would also represent a very large step forward in allaying much of the suspicion and uneasiness seen in surveys of Jews who continue to believe antisemitism is a substantial and continuing threat to their personal safety.

One of America's most respected observers of the Jewish community, Earl Rabb, points to a continuing "sense of foreboding" in the attitudes of significant numbers of America's Jews about antisemitism and its continuing latency in the United States. To the extent to which Jews fear antisemitism, they will continue to see themselves as a people under attack and susceptible to future attack (Earl Rabb, interview by author, October 1, 1996). Although antisemitism is dropping in every opinion poll, many Jews believe that given the right circumstances, antisemitism would reappear (Lipset and Rabb, 1995).

The comments of the JAOs' leaders are revealing for two reasons: First, the intensity of the comments by the JAOs clearly demonstrates the stature antisemitism still possesses in their eyes, a stature well beyond its documented reality. Second, there is persistent attachment to a past that morally compromises the JAOs in the fulfillment of other priorities in the Jewish community. The political implications are clear—antisemitism, regardless of its intensity or frequency—is a fixed and sensitive membrane in the JAOs' mentality and mission.

These reactions also help to explain why this sense of foreboding among some Jews is also likely to continue in the future. The advertising, press releases, and media conferences heighten the apparent existence and depth of antisemitism in ways that are dramatic and confrontational. In the aftermath of the third incident, the speech by Louis Farrakhan, one of the leaders of the black ministers' Ten Point Coalition group bemoaned that being upstaged by the Jewish press conference was "just the ADL doing its thing. Farrakhan is the best thing that ever happened to the ADL and its need for constant publicity" (Eugene Rivers, interview by author, Febuary 26, 1996). While these press conferences and press releases may be good advocacy technique, they are questionable in the effect they have on parallel advocacy organizations and their efforts, as well as the reinforcing effect they are having on the negative beliefs of some Jews. It is not hard to understand why an already nervous community thrust into constantly speculating if antisemitism isn't staging a comeback in the aftermath of some dramatic (albeit, remote) outburst continues to tell opinion polls that it is apprehensive about its safety.

To stay with the emotional influence antisemitism has on some American Jews for a moment longer, there is a disturbing undercurrent that this antisemitism possesses for some of these same Jews, both in terms of its diminished reality and in terms of its historical image. It is important to frame this undercurrent in the reality of how Jews identify themselves as Jews. It is not an identity based on any strong religious attachment (accept for a small percentage of the very observant), nor is it coming from any deeply rooted ethnic pride. That ethnic closeness ended when America moved to the suburbs and when intermarriage between Jews and non-Jews began to climb. It is an undercurrent that prompts a classically sociological explanation for the continuing emotional appeal of antisemitism, even if there is little, if any, possibility of it involving a particular Jew. It is the power antisemitism possesses to foster a continuing Jewish identity.

Several decades ago, the sociologist Leon Festinger ([1957] 1965) proposed a theory of "cognitive dissonance." It is the state of negative emotional tension a person experiences when his cognitive orientation toward a behavior or predisposition is seriously challenged by new facts. Faced with this uncomfortable dilemma most people attempt to reduce this dissonance and maintain their sense of equanimity with their situation. There are few situations sociologists could analyze that would better exemplify this theory than the persistent belief by some American Jews that antisemitism is a continuing serious problem. They have been raised and educated since infancy to accept that there are evil people in this world who don't like Jews, and they have the incidents and statistics to prove their point, up to and including the epochal expression of antisemitic destruction—the Holocaust. Now, after generations of believing Jews are beleaguered on all sides (and throughout history), they are told that the statistics really tell another story. They are not under personal threat, and the likelihood of their being involved in any of the pernicious canards or life threatening incidents portrayed in their life long education is negligible. How do they deal with that news, and further, what does this absence of threat say about how America's Jews understand their Jewish identity? Enter the power of cognitive dissonance. Antisemitism (according to one interviewee) "fires the blood, it gives identity to the victim; it becomes the way in which members of this group stand out from the general population." It is the time-honored prejudice imposed on the "outsider," the "stranger group"; it provides some Jews with a tangible referent for their identity. If Jews are apprehensive about their increasing absorption into the dominant society, then these occasional outbursts of antisemitism serve to provide them with an anchor (a negative one, to be sure) to which they can attach their continuing quasi-ethnic, if not religious, presence in a polyglot society. "Take away the antisemitism, and there goes what's left of my identity!" said this person![2]

In a controversial essay, "How the Jews Use Antisemitism" (in Chanes, 1995:337–47), Arthur Hertzberg presents a larger discussion of the quoted comments above. According to Hertzberg, antisemitism has supplanted the necessity to define what being Jewish in America means; it means "those people" are against me, and that is sufficient to make me a Jew without any effort on my part. Further, Hertzberg points to the inevitable dilemma of actually conquering antisemitism in the Diaspora, "What will the American Jewish organizations do with themselves?" (in Chanes, 1995:334). These organizations must compete with one another for dollars and recognition; this is part and parcel of "moral entrepreneurship." If the evil associated with antisemitism isn't explicit any longer (i.e., in the statistics or incidents), then it has been repackaged as a more subtle threat, or something more deviously dangerous, and the JAOs have rejustified their continued need as an organization.

But, as palpable as antisemitism is to those who continue to see it as a problem (or necessity), it is a problem/necessity that eludes a clear definition. The reluctance by the JAOs to redefine what anti-Jewish hostility means today goes hand in hand with the acquiescence of substantial numbers of American Jews to the role antisemitism plays in supporting their fractured sense of identity. The JAOs have actively preserved the confusion and impression of "antisemitism" because so much can be done with it to preserve their own legitimacy and fund raising requirements; "Why tamper with a good thing?" Hertzberg captures this sentiment in a poignant witticism left to him by his father "that when fundraising is in decline, the organizations pray for a small, and hopefully, not too murderous pogrom" (in Chanes, 1995:346).

REDEFINING ANTISEMITISM

Antisemitism is the model prejudice. It is the basic model from which spring all other studies of minority group prejudice. It is a prejudice that has existed in one form or another for centuries, yet this long history has only complicated the task of analyzing it. In spite of that sordid history, it is a property of Jewish group identity that must be reevaluated from time to time in the same way we reevaluate scores of other social indicators in a pluralistic society. The progress or position of any group in a social system that has previously been labeled as "outsiders" or "others" must be reevaluated with fresh insights from time to time to determine the group's social progress. In the case of the present study, it is not responsible scholarship to continue using descriptors of anti-Jewish sentiment from decades ago when they no longer have meaning in the context of modern-day American life. The second half of this observation is the absolute necessity for a new definition of negative attitudes toward Jews that until now we have conveniently mislabeled as antisemitism. But if antisemitism is not the label of choice, what is?

When asked what this antisemitism is that they are so concerned about, the usual Jewish response is one that parallels Justice Potter Stewart's lament when asked to define obscenity, "I can't define it, but I know it when I see it." A great many Jews will say the same thing—they "know" antisemitism when they see it—but they are still unable to define what it is they know with any precision. In fact they will argue it is so much a part of society that it doesn't need any definition; everybody knows what antisemitism is, don't they? This Jewish definition is sometimes referred to as the *kishke* factor, a Yiddish word that roughly translates as "gut feeling." This internalized belief on the part of Jews that antisemitism is a societal given is captured in the classic observation: What is a Jewish telegram? "Start worrying. Letter follows." But, as we shall very shortly see, there is more than one way to describe this long-standing prejudice. Unfortunately, this inability or unwillingness on the part of many Jews to more carefully define the expression "antisemitism" (beyond a gut feeling) makes every hostile incident and every percentage point in a public opinion poll susceptible to overwrought interpretation, particularly on the part of the JAOs.

There are few expressions in any language that conjure up such an immediate reaction on the part of the listener that on hearing it he is convinced he knows exactly what it means as does the expression "antisemitism." Yet, when put to the test, the definition of antisemitism is as slippery and misleading as the property it is supposedly describing. Jerome Chanes suggests antisemitism is "all forms of hostility manifested toward the Jews throughout history" (1995:5). While this definition is all encompassing, it also implies that every expression of hostility toward Jews was intentionally antagonistic simply because the object of hostility was Jewish. This is too simple a definition and too far reaching to be helpful in the present study. A second and more complex definition is found in Paul Grosser and Edward Halperin's book, *The Cause and Effect of Anti-Semitism*: "Attitudes and actions against Jews based on the belief that Jews are uniquely inferior, evil, or deserving of condemnation by their very nature or by historical or supernatural dictates" (1978:5). This is somewhat more satisfying, because it asks questions about the formation of the respondent's basic beliefs, but according to Grosser and Halperin, those beliefs were formed through experience with Jews based on certain specific political, social, or religious experiences. The determination of the respondent's beliefs toward Jews becomes so complicated in its determination that the average individual would have an impossible time trying to keep straight in his/her head the multiple levels of involvement that the authors' model suggest.

One of the best attempts to define antisemitism came from the pen of the renowned philosopher Jean-Paul Sartre in the aftermath of the Holocaust. Sartre said, "If a man attributes all or part of his own misfortunes and those of his country to the presence of Jewish elements in the community; if he proposed to remedy this state of affairs by depriving Jews of certain of their rights, by keeping them out of certain economic and social activities by expelling them from the country, by exterminating all of them we say that he has anti-Semitic opinions" (1965:7). This definition, while accurate for the "culture of racism" (Weiss, 1996:viii) that pervaded Nazi Germany during its reign of terror, is (in contrast to Chanes) too narrow for our purposes here. It must be a definition of a collection of beliefs about Jews that is not connotative of the brief historical period represented by World War II and its murderous rampage on European Jewry. It must be possible to define anti-Jewish hostility or negativity without the sentence ending in the mass extermination of all Jews. It must be possible, as the American experience demonstrates, to find Jews culturally distasteful in some or several ways without killing them as an end product of that antipathy. We have already succeeded at that definitional task with scores of other groups, and there remains no good reason why Jews should be the last holdout in the struggle for clarity. To complete this examination of useful properties for defining anti-Jewish beliefs, it is essential to examine the extensive treatment of anti-Jewish hostility provided by Gavin Langmuir (1990). Langmuir, a medieval classicist, has exhaustively examined the social, political, and religious roots of anti-Semitism that emerged from the middle ages. He brings forward all of that scholarship to the present time, and then synthesizes a handful of understandable and useable tenets that are extremely useful in fashioning a new, more contemporary set of definitions of anti-Jewish opinion.

Langmuir proposes three assertions be adopted in attempting to describe the behavior or character of Jews. The first assertion is the "realistic" one that condemns a specific Jew because he/she has engaged in the same kinds of objectionable behavior for which we would condemn any other citizen and for which Jews should expect no more leniency than is extended to anyone else, certainly none based on the Jewish identity of the wrongdoer. Second, the "xenophobic" assertion is one that attempts to condemn all Jews based on the behavior of a few. The classic accusation here is that of Jews as "Christ killers." In chapter one, I cited the Birmingham report on crime in New York City in the early years of the twentieth century. A principal assertion of the report's language is that it indicts all Jews for the criminal misbehavior of a few; anyone who has ever been a part of an "out group" always recognizes what is coming when they hear someone talking (or writing) about the actions of "those people." Several of the canards that make up the antisemitic index, that is, "Jews care only for their own kind," "Jews are unscrupulous in business," and "Jews are only interested in money," are of this xenophobic variety of assertions about the nature of Jews as a group. Yet, even here, we must remain mindful of the fact that all groups are subject to xenophobic assertions, not just the Jews. But by combining a xenophobic assertion with Langmuir's third assertion, the chimerical, or fantasy, the resultant accusation may indeed represent something that is properly reserved only for Jews.

Langmuir's third assertion is the "chimerical." These are assertions about Jews that are based in pure fantasy, for example, blood libel, host piercing, and well poisoning, as three examples. Nobody has ever actually seen these behaviors, and absolutely no empirical evidence exists (going back to medieval times) to support the reality of any of these chimerical assertions. But in the hands of even semiliterate propagandists, the use of such contrived assertions creates and reinforces the mythical and fantastical image of "the Jew."[3] Langmuir's principal argument is that we must be sure that whatever it is we find objectionable about Jews is a genuine property of being Jewish, and not something that could be said of anyone, or could not just as easily describe persons in any one of several other groups. To accomplish this, we must devise a definition that more appropriately describes what it is in Jewish behavior that is both objectionable and Jewish. The expression "antisemitism" cannot, and in fact has never, been able to do that.

Langmuir's three-part discussion of anti-Jewish antipathy has the greatest potential for reframing negative beliefs about Jews. A discourse of this sort would yield a clearer understanding of the nature and extent of anti-Jewish sentiment in America, and it would do it without resorting to the language of the enemy. But it goes further than wresting a definition from the discussion. It means reconstructing the questions asked of ordinary citizens about Jews. Even here, it isn't simply a matter of which canard or statement people believe describes Jews, but the extent to which those assertions possess any reality in the daily lives of the respondents. What I am describing is not an easy assignment for the American Jewish community, but it is certainly one that is both long overdue and well worth undertaking.

It is a constant source of puzzlement why Jews have so readily and completely acquiesced to a definition of loathing created by their enemies! Jews are not a race, and yet they throw around this term "antisemitism" without realizing that the origins of the expression in 1889 (by Wilhelm Marr) were specifically created to give a racial legitimacy to the Jew-hatred then current in Germany. It became the racial justification that fit neatly into the pseudoscience of the eugenicists and fully realized itself in the murderous policies of the Nazi regime. If, in this day of politically correct descriptions, a blind person becomes "visually impaired," then I see nothing irregular in abandoning the completely false connotations associated with the expression "antisemitism" and replacing it with a more accurate expression, such as "antipathy toward Jews," "aversion to Jews," or "anti-Jewish beliefs." Whatever definition is finally agreed upon, it must be accompanied by an expression that has grown out of a thoughtful examination of real characteristics of Jews that possess a descriptive ability to reflect negatively on Jewish character or behavior. In this way scholars will no longer be forced to twist themselves into intellectual knots attempting to justify the use of an inappropriate expression (i.e., antisemitism), while at the same time arguing for its exact opposite. We then can concentrate on describing the circumstances, social, political, religious, and cultural, that give rise to and support the extent of such aversions, antipathies, or beliefs about Jews.

A NEW SURVEY FOR PROBING ANTI-JEWISH BELIEFS

Questions that can only be answered by yes or no are of limited value in analyzing social behavior. These dichotomized, or forced-choice, questions leave more unsaid than said in their answers. For example, "Is the lamp on: yes or no?" If the lamp is *not* on, we still do not know if there is any need for a lamp to begin with. If the answer is yes, we still do not know if the lamp is providing sufficient light, or if it is so dim as to render its usefulness problematic.

So it is with the questions that make up the "antisemitism index"; their answers shed little light on what a yes/no answer signifies. To extend this example a little further, take the statement, "Jews have a lot of irritating faults." Regardless of how many people answer "yes." The larger "so what" question persists, that is, "So what . . . does this tells us about Jews?" Answer: nothing; but it tells us a little bit about the respondents. For example, they believe, for whatever reason, that Jews are irritating. Why would this come as a particular surprise? Every group you can name has irritating faults according to someone's perception. But does that make this perception antisemitic? No, no more than the same question when asked of blacks makes the respondent racist, or if asked about gays makes the respondent homophobic, or if asked about Catholics renders the respondent anti-Catholic.

"Wait a minute," the supporters of this type of question will argue, "if a person says 'yes' to several of these negative statements then they are anti-semitic." Once again I do not buy this simplistic logic. If one yes/no question tells me nothing about Jews, how will three or more answers tell me any-more; they won't, and they never have. These are supposed Jewish attributes created by enemies of the Jews. On the other hand, almost any xenophobic allegation can be made about any group and one or two members of that group can be found to support the underlying distortion. What is more im-portant about this collection of yes/no answers is what it reveals about the respondent. It tells me that given a choice of only two answers, the respon-dent is forced to make a series of compromised choices; very little in life is "yes or no." The respondent is never given the opportunity to say, "I don't know," "I don't care," or "I never think of Jews, blacks, gays, or Catholics, and so on, in these terms." Those additional possible answers have always been distinctly absent from thirty-five years of asking the same eleven ques-tions to successive populations.

A second major methodological problem is embedded in the antisemitic index, and it further diminishes the index's usefulness. It is the recommen-dation by index supporters that a certain number of "yes" answers catego-rizes the respondent as mildly, moderately, or very antisemitic, but why? This is a question that is never satisfactorily addressed by the index's sup-porters. The fundamental reason why this assignment of guilt is so unsatis-factory is that no attempt has been made to determine which of these eleven items is more egregious when compared to the other items. The list should be rank-ordered from most serious negative belief about Jews to least seri-ous negative belief about Jews. For example, I would put irritating faults at the bottom of such a ranking. On the other hand, what should go at the top of such a ranking? Is it "Jews have too much power in the business world," "Jews stick together too much," or perhaps, "Jews care only about their own kind"? Until and unless we assemble a group of randomly selected test subjects and make this ranking, we must concede that clumping their an-swers into some tripartite determination of antisemtism is wholly arbitrary, and misleading.

In years past, five "yes" answers rendered the respondent very antisemitic. In recent years, with the steady decline in antisemitic attitudes, the ADL in-creased that number to six. But which six out of the eleven items are most important in making that determination? Again, the reader does not find out. This undifferentiated lumping of items into a fixed categorization is se-riously misleading. Two other points: first, why these eleven items? After thirty-five years it is time to examine the items themselves for their continu-ing validity as measurement items. These items do not mean the same thing today that they did three decades ago. Second, the questions as they now stand mean different things to different groups of people. For example, blacks find two of these items characteristics to be emulated—Jews stick together too much and Jews only care about their own kind; those are values that helped Jews succeed, and blacks believe that there is a lesson in this for improving their success as well. But those two answers (alone) negatively skew the supposed level of antisemtism in the black community. So, answering "yes" to a question that one population sees as a positive attribute actually results in their being labeled as "more antisemitic than whites."

Finally, the antisemitic index possesses the same problem as all attempts at measuring negative beliefs, opinions, or prejudices about individuals or groups based on self-reporting, and that is, how do these results translate to action? At what point does the person with five or six negative opinions about Jews become the person who now throws a rock through a synagogue window or leads a riot in a Jewish community that leads to the murder of a young Hasidic scholar? Social scientists have not yet deciphered this dilemma, nor have the Jewish advocacy organizations; our entire collection of analyses of discriminatory behavior is based on hindsight. All of the opinion surveys in the world have never been successful in deciphering who among a population of respondents is ever likely to take action on his beliefs, or at what point in time, or under what provocation.

By way of a summary we can safely conclude three things about the antisemitic index. First, the eleven items in the antisemitic index are outdated and in serious need of revision or outright elimination. Second, the response to each item is restricted by a forced choice of yes or no; the bandwidth for possible responses has to be increased. Third, taken in the aggregate, the index possesses no ability to differentiate between people who don't like Jews and people who don't like anyone else who is different from themselves, regardless of what their attributes, behavior, or racial/ethnic/religious composition may be. The time is long overdue to scrap this entire index and construct one that will accurately reflect the general public's opinion about Jews (positive as well as negative) at this point in time. The deeper and more troublesome intellectual challenges associated with making connections between attitudes and behavior (i.e., prejudice and discrimination) is not the purpose of an opinion survey instrument; that is a separate, but nonetheless important study for another forum.

Rather then continuing a lengthy methodological discussion about what a new survey instrument for probing anti-Jewish beliefs would look like, I decided to approach the present discussion of a new survey from an end results perspective. Social scientists can struggle with the very legitimate questions of survey construction, item wording, and factorial integrity, pre-testing for validity and reliability, in another forum. What, I asked myself, would I want to know about non-Jewish opinion about me as a Jew? With that question in mind, I constructed a laundry list of possible results. To begin with there would be few questions that could be answered "yes" or "no." They must all be answerable with a range of responses from strongly agree (SA) to strongly disagree (SD), or very frequently (VF) to very infrequently (VI). A response must be available that allows the respondents to express their uncertainty (?) about a particular item, and a response that lets them admit to having had no experience (NE) with Jews on the opinion being sought. It is also necessary, with such a response schema, to carefully define the meaning of an SA, A, ?, D, SD, or NE response. Given these qualifications as a thin structure on which to hang some questions, I would want to know what characteristics or beliefs about Jews the respondent does *not* like, and which characteristics about Jews they *do* like. I would then ask the respondent to rank order these two lists of characteristics (like and dislike) about Jews from most to least.[4]

I would want the same questions asked about blacks, Hispanics, Asians, and others to provide a larger canvas of differences on which to base comparisons and conclusions about Jews. This would be particularly important for beliefs that focus on power, control, or ambition. I would want to know in what ways Jews were similar as well as different from these several other groups. I would want to know what group(s) the respondent believes Jews are most like, least like, and why. There are two other questions I would want answers to: (1) "In the normal course of your life, how often do you think about Jews—daily, weekly, monthly, yearly, or never?" and (2) "Based on your personal experiences with Jews over the past year, what is it about them you find most objectionable/most appealing, and why?" Then repeat the same questions for all of the other groups mentioned above. It is important to determine how the respondent feels about Jews as a group, but it is essential to understand those beliefs in the context of the several groups that make up the pluralistic fabric of American society. Finally, I would want to reexamine the original eleven items in the antisemitic index, but scaled with the new descriptors. For example:

"Jews have too much power."   SA   A   ?   D   SD   NE

Finally, it would be necessary to make the same comparisons here with other groups as it was with the other beliefs that questionnaire would probe.

Historians regularly point out that even the best-written book about a particular war is not the war itself, and in the same way social scientists must clarify reality from reports. Opinions about anti-Jewish beliefs are not the same as the social reality of the respondents who provided them. We need more than their answers to survey questions; we need to know why they answered those questions in the ways that they did. Just as it is important to construct worthwhile questions to determine the extent of anti-Jewish beliefs, it is equally important to find out what drives those opinions. So, a second and equally necessary part of this exercise is to assemble groups of those respondents and find out why they answered their questions the ways they did. In so doing we will obtain a broad sense of what non-Jews believe about Jews, and we will also obtain a broad sense of what predisposes those opinions.

A NEW SURVEY OF JEWISH FOREBODING

If it is important for social scientists and pollsters (who are attempting to determine non-Jewish opinions about Jews) to create new and more appropriate questions, then it is equally important for those same social scientists and pollsters to change the questions they ask Jews concerning their apprehension about the extent of anti-Jewish beliefs in the United States. It is just not adequate to the task or intellectually responsible to ask Jewish respondents, "Do you believe antisemitism/anti-Jewish sentiment is a problem?" Of course it is a problem; so is racism, poverty, unemployment, and hundreds of other social afflictions, prejudices, and discriminations. What is essential to determine in this examination of opinions is what gives rise to the apprehension on the part of ordinary Jews that leads them to conclude that their safety and peace of mind in this country are in jeopardy from legions of Jew-haters. It is important to ask these questions of Jews who are not affiliated through membership or employment with the major Jewish organizations. This should not be too difficult to arrange since 80 percent of all Jews in America are not dues paying members of the Jewish organizational world. Does this mean we should not ask organizationally affiliated Jews the same questions? Certainly not, but with both sets of data we are better able to assess the reality of perceived threat to Jewish security from anti-Jewish beliefs and that which reflects a persistently constructed social reality based on the educational and advertising efforts of the JAOs.

The *1998 Annual Survey of American Jewish Opinion* conducted by the AJC is a case in point. The sixty-seven-item questionnaire (some items with several subparts) was designed and administered to 1001 "self-identified" Jews by Market Facts, Inc. (a survey research firm). What is not made clear is that the "self-identified" Jews are members of the AJC. This makes for a lopsided report because of the respondent's vested interest in the worldview of the AJC. If any ordinary, non–AJC affiliated Jews answered this questionnaire there is no way to determine that distinction in this survey. The results generated (June 1998) were based on questions probing everything from Israel/Arab relations to U.S. political and social issues, antisemitism, Jewish identity, and opinions on various AJC programs and publications. Four of the survey's results are particularly important to the present discussion:

1. The extent to which antisemitism was currently thought to be a problem in the United States. (#40)
2. Which is a greater threat to Jewish life in the United States, intermarriage or antisemitism? (#39)

3. The importance of various activities to the respondent's Jewish identity. (#34)

4. Agreement or disagreement about how badly the Jewish community is divided. (#38)

The answers to these four questions are revealing. To the first question, 95 percent of all respondents believe that antisemitism is a very serious to somewhat serious problem in the United States (37). Secondly, "A majority of American Jews believe that anti-Semitism [*sic*] is a greater threat to Jewish life in the United States today than is intermarriage" (25). To the third question, the most important issue checked was "remembrance of the Holocaust." This response was more popular than synagogue attendance, Jewish study, the Jewish holidays, and others (23). Finally, 68 percent of the AJC's respondents agreed that the American Jewish community is "badly divided" (25). These are results that literally cry out for further clarification, but the AJC's study, unfortunately, does not provide it.

Just as we are asking the social scientists and pollsters to broaden their data to include comparisons and beliefs about groups other than Jews, so too must we ask the same of polls revealing the opinions of Jews about their belief in the strength of anti-Jewish hostility in this country. For example, I would want to know if these respondents think racism and ageism (to take but two examples) are serious problems, and what other prejudices that arise from living in a pluralistic society they would include in their list of serious problems. I would want to know what personal experience the respondents have had with anti-Jewish hostility. Have they been deprived of a job, a college admission, service at a restaurant, an opportunity to run for public office because they are Jewish? How have they been deprived of complete civil participation because they are Jewish? Have they received a threatening phone call or have threatening letters, leaflets, or pamphlets been slipped under their door or in their mailbox because they are Jewish? Have their places of worship been vandalized, set aflame; their cemeteries desecrated? Have groups of people assembled in their streets or at political rallies demanding that they leave the country? As you can see, the potential for personal risk is long. At one time or another these things have all happened to Jews in this country (and occasionally they still do), but in the main they don't anymore, and they haven't in decades. There is nothing on the horizon, including the fringe groups, that suggests to law enforcement officers or civil rights groups that a great resurgence in Jew-hatred is brewing in the United States. Personal safety, however it is construed, is far more tenuous in the black community, among the openly gay, or for those advocating for abortion, than it is for the Jews of this country.

The fact of the matter is that the average Jew's potential susceptibility to any of the offenses cataloged above is so low as to make computation nearly impossible. Jews have never been safer in America than they are today! It is time to stop regurgitating tales of discrimination from a long ago past in some contrived effort to keep Jews frightened about their security and peace of mind. It is the wrong way to keep Jews Jewish. But there are still other things I would want to know of those Jews who fear for their safety.

What vehicles or mechanisms are telling them that anti-Jewish hostility is a serious problem in this country? In other words, "Who says so?" This is a question that has been answered for decades by the JAOs: they said so, and that was enough. But as we have already seen, the importance or significance of the message has changed dramatically over those many decades. On the other hand, the reporting of a threat, even a diminished threat—one that now approaches the insignificant—can be so inflated in its reporting that it is bound to keep Jews apprehensive about their safety and security. Consider the newspaper ads and reports cited in the opening pages of chapter one. "1 out of 8 Americans has hard-core anti-Semitic feelings;" and "more than 35 million Americans have anti-Semitic attitudes." These blazing declarations of supposed hostility toward America's Jews were not written to inform the general public. They are the ones whose negative opinions have dropped like a shot for decades. The reports were written for America's Jews. Headlines were (and are) written to constantly remind them of a threat to their security that in fact has virtually no reality. The ADL admits that 53 percent of Americans are not antisemitic—whatever that means. A careful reading of ads, articles, and news clips reveals some serious inconsistencies.

For example, according to the December 30, 1998, "National Briefs" in the *Boston Globe*, one out of eight Americans is approximately 12.5 percent of the U.S. population, which currently stands at 271,645,214. That comes to approximately 34 million people, but who are these people? Does the ADL mean to include children under the age of six? What qualified these 34 million citizens as "hard-core" antisemites? We never find out from the ads or the news articles. Perhaps more problematic is the ADL's own publication *Frontline* ("What Americans Think of Jews," December 1998:1) that reassures the reader that antisemitism has dropped from 20 percent to 12 percent since 1992. But, why has it dropped so significantly in a scant six years? Once again, we never find out. The same article later points out that, "more than 20 million Americans [are out there] with hard-core anti-Semitic feelings" (1). Now, which is it: 34 million, 35 million, or 20 million? At what point does the ADL tell us the real numbers, or isn't that what matters? It matters if you are attempting to accurately report a genuine social reality, but it does not matter if the intent is to simply keep a lot of Jews frightened about their safety. Permit me to take this criticism a little further. If I am already paranoid about the level of supposed animosity toward Jews in the general population, nothing I read in those ads or reports is likely to go very far in allaying my underlying fear or my belief that there hasn't been any diminution of antisemitism in America. If the purpose of these results is to subtly imply that I am being defined as Jewish by my enemies, then it is an ad campaign that is succeeding. This casualness about numbers and the imprecision in reporting them is not helping anyone, particularly the JAOs. It casts a continuing cloud of suspicion over the reliability (let alone the validity) of their data, and I am hard pressed to understand from this distortion of reality how the JAOs can say they are serving the best interests of America's Jews. They are not; it is their own best interests that are being served.

Finally, in what ways and at what times will this supposedly high level of hostility toward America's Jews actually affect their daily lives: this year, next year, when? What form of attack is it that people who don't like Jews will take? I am fully aware that one of the surest responses to this question is to point to the infuriating rhetoric of Louis Farrakhan and his spokespeople in the Nation of Islam. But the fact remains that all of that inflamed rhetoric has only served one purpose—the political ambitions of a small religious movement within the black community. Minister Farrakhan has found the number one way to get a lot of free publicity—attack the Jews—even if most of those attacks are blatant distortions. It has worked. Jewish organizations have sprung into action and decried Farrakhan from every media source imaginable, but to what avail? The black separatists are not the ones desecrating Jewish cemeteries or painting swastikas on synagogues, however infrequently this may be happening.

I do not want to be understood as minimizing or dismissing the vicious rhetoric Louis Farrakhan and his ardent spokesmen are spewing about Jews, whites, Catholics, or gays. That noise must be countered every time it occurs, but it shouldn't take the entire force of the organized Jewish community to do it! That much attention to one ideologue is akin to killing a fly with a charge of dynamite. The AJCg already knows this and pays little attention to Farrakhan and his followers, because too much attention engenders the opposite effect. It doesn't stop him, or cool his messages of hate. It actually has the reverse outcome of portraying him as the victim, and consequently, making him and his message more appealing. The AJCg does not want to do anything that wastes its time and talent on providing free publicity for demagogues.

It is not blacks, particularly ordinary blacks, who are after the Jews. In fact, we know very little about the extent or source of hostility toward Jews from the general black community, no more so than what the existing and badly flawed surveys already tell us. The black community in America needs to be surveyed on their attitudes toward Jews in a different format from the one that has been used for decades to plumb the attitudes of the white community. However, nobody in the Jewish community is rushing forward to undertake this difficult task. It is easier to simply paint the black community with the same statistics that have been used in the white community for decades. Incidentally, why is it we never see such pointed references to survey results from the Hispanic, or the Asian, or the gay community, or Roman Catholics? Is it that they are not as antisemitic as blacks, and if not, how are we to understand the absence of animosity from these groups? As usual, we never get any explanation from the JAOs.

If the near-disappearance of anti-Jewish hostility in America has removed a fundamental corner of the organizational table supporting the JAOs' rationale for being, then that table is being further destabilized by a deepening weakness in two other prominent issues—the Holocaust and the State of Israel. A fourth issue that has aroused a great deal of public commentary by the JAOs in the name of the American Jewish community—Jewish identity/continuity—is actually a nonissue for the JAOs. I will say more about identity/continuity and its relationship to the JAOs a little later.

THE HOLOCAUST AS AN ORGANIZATIONAL ISSUE

For millions of Jews the Holocaust represents the nadir in the Jews' history of struggle for survival and rebirth after terrible destruction. As Woocher (1986:131) observes, "The Holocaust's power lies in its capacity to provoke an absolutely predictable response on the part of American Jews." The generations of American Jews born after the Holocaust have been educated on every conceivable facet of the *Shoah*. But what those Jews and, for that matter, everybody else in America were learning about was the Jew as victim. It was the attempted destruction of Europe's Jews that quickly became the ultimate manifestation of centuries of antisemitism. Rabbi Michael Goldberg (1995:53) describes the fascination of America's Jews with the *Shoah* as a "Holocaust cult." Recalling the horrors of the Holocaust every year has become the annual Jewish observance that reminds Jews that they are Jews. Its best known shrine (what Hertzberg [1990:342] refers to as the "national Jewish Cathedral") is the United States Holocaust Museum in Washington, DC. It sits on public ground and is funded largely through taxpayers' dollars; it is a monumental sign of the success Jews have had in defending themselves from prejudice and discrimination. Yet, it is paradoxical that the God of the Jews and the religion of the Jews are never mentioned anywhere in the museum's sprawling edifice to destruction and death. It can't—to do so would be a violation of the separation of church and state provisos involving publicly supported buildings. The most recent reflections on the centrality of the Holocaust can be found in Michael Novick's new book *The Holocaust in American Life* (1999).

Jews are no longer struggling for their survival in the United States, and this will, in time, affect the power the Holocaust has on people's imaginations as well as the evocativeness of its symbolism. Over the next twenty years (as the remaining survivors of the Holocaust die), the horrors of the Holocaust will become less of a living presence and more a tragic symbol of an age and of conditions long since passed. While it is unlikely that the Holocaust will lose that symbolic power anytime soon, as a major organizational issue for the JAOs it suffers from severe limitations.[5]

Disasters ultimately fade into history, and this has been true, as well, of Jewish disasters. It isn't even a question of the legitimacy of the Holocaust as a Jewish issue, it is certainly that, but rather, how viable will it remain as an organizational issue for the JAOs; and this is where the currents of history have always worked against the most successful organizations. It is possible to reinvent an organization based on its past glories for a little while, but ultimately the organization's supporters realize that the battle has been won or that the issue is not as sensitive as it once was. In other words, the world has moved on to other concerns and other disasters, and the organizations must follow suit or cease to function.

More than fifty years have passed since the Nazis were defeated, and from that day forward, the Nazi campaign to make Europe *Judenrein* (free of Jews) has gripped most people's imaginations and in turn come to symbolize the darkest translation of Jew-hatred. It was also an event that served to unite Jews as one people under the banner "Never Again." For a great many American Jews this expression became the single most significant reminder of what it means to be Jewish, and over the years it steadily came to replace the more difficult Hebrew prayer that had, for millennia, represented the universal Jewish prayer, the *Sh'ma*: "*Sh'ma Yisrael: Adonai Elohenu, Adonai Echad!*" (Hear O Israel, the Lord Our God, the Lord is One!). If God's covenantal promise to the Jewish people had died in the furnaces of Poland, then Jews everywhere had to realize that survival was now their business; and if they understood the profound message in this death, they had better create political mechanisms to protect themselves and their heirs forever. Enter the State of Israel.

The historical proximity of the Holocaust and the founding of the State of Israel was an inescapable eventuality. To a large degree the foundation of the State of Israel was only successful because of the Holocaust. But the connection between the two ends there.[6] In the case of the Holocaust, Jews have an indelible memory of the destructive power of racial nationalism. It is a memory of a historical tragedy that had an end-point—the end of World War II. Israel, on the other hand, represented the birth of a Jewish nation, but also, the rebirth of a near-decimated people.

ISRAEL AS AN ORGANIZATIONAL ISSUE

The only recognized heresy in civil Judaism is in an unwillingness to support Israel. But, what happens to this loyalty if the Israeli government and most of its citizens are not interested in the opinions or the concerns of the American Jewish community even after it has donated large sums of money for fifty years?

Israel needs U.S. foreign aid ($3 billion annually), but it does not welcome American Jewish involvement in its internal affairs. For example, Goldberg (1996) reports that in 1988 Yitzhak Shamir proposed an amendment to Israel's "Law of Return" (first enacted in 1950) that would have disenfranchised people who had attempted to convert to Judaism in Israel through any other branch of Judaism than the Orthodox. Persons who had converted to Judaism through the Reform or Conservative branches of Judaism are still entitled to full-citizenship privileges if they move to Israel (337–40). In response to the Shamir amendment, the Boston and Atlanta federations voted to withhold $16 million earmarked for Israel from their United Jewish Appeal (UJA) contributions; Los Angeles reduced their contribution to the UJA from 47 percent to 34 percent, and Milwaukee, Indianapolis, and Detroit reported similar reductions (Abrams, 1997:145 n16).

A more compelling example of this Israeli distaste for American Jewish involvement in their internal affairs, came in the aftermath of a series of highly contentious meetings in 1992 that took place between the leaders of key Jewish communal organizations. Yitzhak Rabin, on his first U.S. visit, told American Jews their input was no longer needed, because "their view did not matter anyway" (Goldberg, 1996:347).

During a visit to the United States in 1992 Deputy Foreign Minister Yossi Beilin asked American Jews to challenge Israel about the merit of some of its decisions. The American Jewish organizations said they were there to support Israel not to criticize it. Their worldview was so pro-Israel that they literally could not imagine criticizing anything that Israel did or didn't do. As Goldberg (1996:348) relates it, "Beilin complained in a series of speeches and interviews [that UJA fundraisers] were portraying Israel as a pauper. In fact, it was now a high-tech regional superpower, and [it] had no need of charity. He suggested that American Jews keep their money at home and look for ways to save themselves from assimilation." The JAOs have largely ignored this sea change in Israel's attitude toward the United States and continue to believe that their wisdom and their money are still welcome. However, cracks have begun to appear in this unquestioning defense of Israel.

The growing distance between the two most prominent Jewish communities in the world is due, in large part, to their religious differences. A total of 80 percent Israeli Jews are secular (or nonreligious); Israelis who are religious are overwhelmingly Orthodox. By contrast, over 78 percent of America's Jews are Reform or Conservative and approximately 15 percent are nonreligious (NJPS, 1990). Reform and Conservative Jews are publicly and stridently outspoken in their belief that, as Jews, they are as entitled as the Orthodox to equal representation in Israeli life. At present in Israel the ultra-Orthodox Knesset officials hold a significant (and growing) influence on establishing the criteria that determine who is Jewish. In these identity debates, the Orthodox have gone so far as to suggest that at some point in the future non-Israeli Jews might not be recognized as Jews if they are adherents of the Reform or Conservative branches of Judaism. These same Orthodox legislators have already attempted to label Reform and Conservative expressions of Judaism as another religion, much like Christianity, and certainly not Judaism.

The increasing instances of conflict between the Orthodox Jews in Israel and the more liberal Jews in the United States have intensified in recent months and become increasingly spiteful, even dangerous. In a recent report, Rabbi Eric Yoffie (the current head of the Reform movement in the United States) said that the Orthodox leaders in Israel have condemned Jewish liberals as "Satans of the Jewish World." As reported in a January 8, 1999 article by Michael Arnold for *Forward*, Yoffie went on to predict that American giving to Israel would drop off by as much as $100 million in the year ahead (1). Other incidents involving personal vilification and physical attack have occurred repeatedly at one of world Jewry's most sacred places, the Western Wall (the *Kotel*).

During the summer of 1998 a group of Conservative Jews and their families from the United States were tormented by a group of Orthodox Jews who threw bags of garbage at the visiting Jews. The Jews from America had come to pray at the Western Wall. They were forced to stop their prayers and were hurriedly escorted away from their tormentors by Israeli soldiers. Several of the visiting Jews were concerned for their and their family's personal safety.

In her article "Orthodox Confront U.S. Reform Rabbis at Western Wall" (*New York Times*, international, February, 2, 1999), Deborah Sontag reported a more recent incident: a group of Orthodox hard-liners attempted to evict a group of visiting U.S. Reform rabbis from the Western Wall with taunts that included, "Go back to Germany—to be exterminated." This behavior does not represent all Israelis. The majority of Israelis find these incidents as deplorable as we do, but the unfortunate fact remains: it is the troublemakers who get the press attention. These repeated incidents, rebuffs, and outright physical attacks on the part of Orthodox Jews are not engendering any support for the Israelis among growing numbers of American Jews, and the JAOs are not able to create reasons why such behavior is in any way acceptable. For many American Jews, the behavior of the Israeli Orthodox Jews is a distorted and shocking display of Jewish antisemitism! Israel is another corner of the JAOs' issue table that is quickly weakening.

For American Jews Israel is a spiritual and emotional icon, while for Israeli Jews the American Jewish community has no spiritual or emotional significance (Goldberg, 1996:342).[7] For American Jews it is important that Israel survive, if only as a sign that for the first time in history Jews have a land of their own, its citizens are safe from harm, and, as a consequence, all Jews everywhere are safer. For American Jews Israel is that romanticized image of a safe haven for all Jews, the land that will take in any Jew and protect all Jews from attack. But it is an impossible dream to harbor the belief (let alone to encourage it) that the Israeli government would take in 5.5 million American Jews if they were in mortal danger. Forget for the moment just how that many people could be quickly transported to Israel. What happens to them after they get there? Where would they live, work, simply exist? There is not enough habitable space in the entire country of Israel to put another five million people on short notice, or long notice for that matter. Not enough similarity exists between American Jewish communities and Israeli communities to ensure that the trust and confidence that has characterized American/Israeli relations in the past would survive in such intimate circumstances.

Like the dwindling force of antisemitism in the United States, the symbolic meaning of Israel as a safe haven has a problematic quality, and the JAOs in turn have another softening organizational issue that they are trying to support. The hostility the Orthodox Jews in Israel are displaying toward non-Orthodox Jews from other parts of the world will one day result in two Jewish communities. The one in Israel, and the Jews in the rest of the world. It remains to be seen how the Jews in the rest of the world, particularly those in the United States, will choose to identify themselves as Jews (if at all), and given those definitions, what they portend for the continued presence of Jews in a pluralistic American society.

JEWISH IDENTITY AS AN ORGANIZATIONAL NONISSUE

If the ability of the JAOs to speak to or for America's Jews already rests on three shaky foundations, that is, antisemitism, the State of Israel, and the Holocaust, then their ability to make any contributions to the current debate about Jewish identity is nil. It is for this reason that I have termed Jewish continuity/identity a nonissue for the JAOs. Their inability to make any impact on this vital issue arises from a combination of two interwoven realities: the rapid assimilation of Jews into American society and the secular ideology of the JAOs.

American Jews, Intermarriage, and Assimilation

Jews have always been a small percentage of the population in every land in which they have settled, Israel being the obvious modern exception. (Ancient exceptions can be found in the period of Hellenization when Jews represented approximately 30 percent of Athens's population.) In America, demographers and census trackers could not register a partial percentage for a Jewish presence until 1776 when it was estimated at .04 to .10 percent of the entire population (Sarna, 1986:296). This background suggests that no matter how successful Jews in America may be in defining their identity and expanding their physical presence, they are not likely to assume large numbers. But, even if the American Jewish community remains small in absolute numbers and as a percentage of the general population, do individual Jews possess any interest in their identity as Jews as well as the energy to create a visible and vibrant community for themselves? Further, with the classic trend toward lower birthrates in highly developed nations, will American Jews (however defined) reproduce themselves beyond a basic replacement level? Jewish fertility today parallels that of the rest of the United States, approximately 1.8 children per household. Based on the current trends in intermarriage and fertility, the outlook for increased Jewish identity or increased Jewish numbers is, at best, grim.

However, to speak of America as the first Jewish settlement that faced the dual questions of Jewish identity and continuity is to ignore a great deal of Jewish history. Throughout the centuries Jews have everywhere and always intermarried and become a part of the community in which they resided. During the murderous days of the Middle Ages when Jews were forcibly converted to Christianity (*Conversos* and *Marranos*), many secretly continued to cling to their Judaism, but the majority did not.

The Enlightenment of the eighteenth century was accompanied, in most major European countries, by the emancipation of the Jews. Jews all across Europe were granted citizenship and access to a secular education (and the universal values that went with it), which represented an education that went well beyond the established ingredients of a Torah-focused Jewish education. The Jews of Germany, France, Holland, and England quickly came to regard themselves as national citizens first and second as Jews by religious predisposition. This was a status not unlike their Catholic and Protestant neighbors, and Jews flourished in this new environment of freedom.

While the German states granted Jews citizenship, they never fully embraced the principles of the Enlightenment or the emancipation. As this collection of princely states formed itself into a country, it continued to argue its "Jewish question" right up to the days of the Nazi regime and the Holocaust. The emancipation, however, was something that never reached the bleak Jewish communities of East Europe or Russia. For many of the poverty stricken *Ostjuden* their first encounter with an open and democratic society was upon their arrival in America. These new arrivals quickly discovered that the goal of already settled Jews was to "Americanize" them from their bumbling status as newcomers (greenhorns) to that of Americans and to do so as quickly as possible. The powerful leaders of the newly forming JAOs had always aspired to be Americans first and Jewish second as a matter of religious choice, and they wanted the same things for all other Jews coming to America, regardless of their far-flung origins. The Jews coming to America from East Europe only thought of themselves as Jews, never as citizens of their home countries.

The flood of East European Jews who began arriving in this country at the turn of the century had practiced a traditional Judaism in the old country, but it would be a mistake to think of them as Orthodox in the present sense of that word. They simply had no other alternatives available to them in the *shtetls* of Russia. On arrival in America they frequently (and quickly) gave up the trappings of that traditional Judaism in their pursuit of economic success. When they reached a point of even modest success they readopted many, if not all, of those earlier accoutrements of traditional Judaism. This readoption was often accomplished in less than one generation. But denominationalism as it is understood in the Protestant sense of the word did not exist in the American Jewish community. Those Jews who were already in the United States considered themselves Reform, with the exception of a small handful of earlier Sephardic Jews who had continued to observe a traditional form of Judaism in their own temples.

The Reform branch of Judaism was the dominant form of Jewish religious expression in America. It arrived with its German adherents and persisted for decades before any other form of worship exhibited itself. Although small in actual numbers of congregants (it was the Judaism of the German elite), it remained the dominant expression of Judaism until approximately 1913 and the emergence of the Conservative movement. This new branch of Judaism satisfied millions of East European Jews who could not see themselves as "modernized" Reform Jews, but who could not return to the rigidity of scriptural interpretation and ritual observance that traditional Judaism had stood for in the old world (Lawrence Grossman in Linzer et al., 1998:85). A third branch of Judaism established itself in America at almost the same time as the Conservative movement, and it was the Orthodox movement. It too had its origins in early-nineteenth-century Germany.

Neo-Orthodoxy was a small movement in Germany in the nineteenth century. These were Jews who were educated and emancipated, but who could not accept the freer, less traditional tenets of Reform Judaism. Orthodoxy sought, instead, to adhere to many of the traditional translations and ancient rituals by virtue of free choice, not compulsion. They were always a small percentage of all Jews, but as Lawrence Grossman (in Linzer et al., 1998:88) points out, in America the Orthodox were often lumped in with the traditional East European Jewish immigrants. Modern Orthodoxy in America began at about the same time as the emergence of the Conservative movement in 1913. Today, Orthodoxy is split between the fervently Orthodox (40 percent), what Samuel Heilman and Menachem Friedman (1991) refer to as "Haredi," and the other 60 percent who are modern or centrist Orthodox. But the absolute numbers of all Orthodox Jews, Haredi or modern, are quite small in terms of all religiously identified Jews. These numbers are significant for what they reveal about being Jewish in America over the past 100 years and the impact assimilation has had on the Jewish community.

In 1935 there were approximately 4.5 million Jews in the United States (Sarna, 1986b:296). Of those Jews who said they were religiously affiliated and attended synagogue, approximately 1 million were Orthodox, 300,000 were Conservative, and 200,000 were Reform (Hertzberg, 1990:279). By the time of the 1990 National Jewish Population Survey (NJPS) those figures had changed dramatically, and in the opposite direction. Orthodox was now the expressed preference of only 5 to 7 percent of American Jews, or approximately 375,000; Conservative Judaism was the expressed preference for approximately 40 percent (slightly more than 1 million); and 38 percent of the Jews surveyed said Reform Judaism was their expressed preference for a total of slightly less than 1 million (Lazerwitz, 1998:10–11).[8] Not all of these Jews attend synagogue or temple regardless of their expressed preferences: 2 percent of the Orthodox, 17 percent of the Conservative, and 22 percent of the Reform do not attend temple. Lastly, another 850,000 identified themselves as nonreligious or "just Jewish" in the 1990 survey. It must be further noted that only about 10 percent or less of those Jews who state a preference for Conservative or Reform attend religious services regularly. Among the Orthodox regular synagogue attendance is in the ninetieth percentile range.

There is a disconcerting suspicion surrounding the number of Jews who identify a preference for Reform Judaism, and it is that Reform is a default choice. These are Jews who pay fees each year for attendance at High Holy Day (Rosh HaShanna and Yom Kippur) services, and this is their only synagogue attendance all year. This sort of loose association permits them the privilege of participating in a host of life-cycle events (marriages, baby namings, funerals, etc.) by simply paying for them. They hold no interest in the congregational calendar of the temple and seldom observe any of the other rituals that are associated with Judaism. In effect, for a few dollars once in awhile, they can call themselves "affiliated Jews," but without the inconvenience of doing anything particularly religious.

An initial conclusion from these statistics on denominational preference would seem to suggest that Judaism in America thrived between 1935 and 1990. That is true insofar as the growth among those claiming a preference for the Reform and Conservative branches of Judaism. However, much of this growth in the Reform and Conservative branches occurred in the years immediately following World War II and the rapid suburbanization of America. Hundreds of temples and synagogues of the Reform and Conservative variety were built (see Jick, [1976] 1992; Wertheimer, n.d.). But the decline in numbers among the Orthodox is symptomatic of a far more important phenomenon than a loss of interest in Orthodoxy. It is a smaller version of the denominational choices available to Jews that parallels the denominational switching that occurs in Christian faith communities. Secondly, it is an important barometer concerning the staying power of Orthodoxy from generation to generation, and this in turn is a reflection of the power of assimilation in pluralistic societies such as the United States. In the case of Orthodoxy, second-generation offspring of Orthodox parents typically move away to a Conservative affiliation, and the third generation of the same family moves again to a Reform affiliation. The Lazerwitz et al. (1998) study on this denominational switching is important to our understanding of Jewish identity and continuity for three reasons. It is the first attempt to examine in careful detail (1) How those denominational switches took place from generation to generation; (2) How the function of intermarriage between Jews and non-Jews impacts denominational choice; and (3) The role denominational preference has on "in-marriage" conversions to Judaism.

In all cases this denominational naming and switching are visible indications of the inroads 100 years of assimilation have made on the American Jewish community and their steady absorption into the general society. Beyond a core of approximately 2.5 million Jews who base their identity on a religious affiliation, there is that number who see themselves as nonreligious, ethnic, secular, or "just Jews" who hold no particular affection for the religion or the ethnic markers. Secondly, those Jews who switch out of Reform Judaism, as a last step toward abandoning any religious identity whatsoever, frequently do so through marriage to a non-Jewish partner. The inroads that intermarriage have made on the Jewish community parallel those found in other immigrant communities and first became a subject of genuine concern to Jewish leaders with the release of the 1971 NJPS results, the first of its kind for the entire U.S. Jewish community. This was in contrast to the local and regional studies of Jewish demographics that had been done up to that time.

In 1971 the NJPS found that the intermarriage rate between Jews and non-Jews had risen sharply. Prior to 1965 the Jewish intermarriage rate was thought to be in the vicinity of 9 to 11 percent, but between 1966 and 1970 that rate climbed to approximately 31.7 percent (Masserik and Chenkin, 1973:292–93). The Jewish communal organizations, including the JAOs, expressed shock and concern at the advancing rate of intermarriage between Jews and non-Jews as evidenced in the NJPS results, but as an organization they did nothing. Nor did they feel it was their province to do anything: Jewish identity had always been someone else's responsibility. They were secular organizations and did not involve themselves in matters religious.

In 1990 the second NJPS survey found that the intermarriage rate had risen to approximately 52 percent, depending on how the statistics were interpreted for various parts of the country. This 52 percent figure represented the period 1986–1990. A hard reality made itself apparent in these latest statistics—Jewish intermarriage was not a temporary aberration. Secondly, with the exception of the Orthodox, Jews were not reproducing themselves in sufficient numbers to maintain themselves proportionately to other groups in the United States. From 1965 to 1990 their percentage representation had dropped from 3.7 to approximately 2 percent (Abrams, 1997:1). In 1971 the Jewish population of the United States was approximately 5.5 million; today it is approximately the same or slightly less (NJPS, 1971, 1990). Assimilation theory suggests that intermarriage across ethnic lines, but particularly across religious lines, is the strongest indicator a group has that they are moving from ethnic or religious "otherness" to a status of acceptance and absorption into the general society of which they are a part (Gordon, 1964. See also Wirth, 1945; Alba, 1985, 1995).

Over the past 100 years generation upon generation of immigrant groups who came to the United States have gradually given up their sense of a distinct and separate identity. This has happened through the inexorable process of acculturation (adopting the appearances, mannerisms and speech of the larger society), and assimilation (marriage into the general society). The accelerating rate of Jewish intermarriage is slightly behind the experience of the Irish, Italian, Polish, and other European immigrant groups who already considered themselves fully assimilated Americans. The fifth generation is the key generation in this absorption process. It is at this point that the immigrant group sees itself as fully assimilated, and its ethnic or religious markers are historic reminders of families' pasts, but not a central ingredient in their identities. For example, by 1963 the intermarriage rate among Italian Americans was 41 percent; by 1979 it was 80.5 percent (Abrams, 1997:100). In 1990 the intermarriage rate among Irish Americans had reached 65 percent, and for Polish Americans it had reached 84 percent (Abrams, 1997:101).

This accelerating intermarriage pattern is just as apparent among Asian immigrant groups as their European counterparts. The Japanese American intermarriage rate today is approximately 50 percent (Abrams, 1997:100). The intermarriage rate of Chinese Americans in New York City is approximately 24 percent; in Los Angeles it is over 40 percent; and in the older Chinese communities in Hawaii, it is approximately 75 percent (Abrams, 1997:100). By the fifth generation, group differences are virtually trivial and additional assimilation is inevitable (Abrams, 1997:101). The assimilation "wave" that Abrams laments is not bearing down upon the Jewish community; it has already rolled over it; it is a wave that cannot be turned back.

This is where the American Jewish community finds itself at the dawn of the third millennium and the twenty-first century. It is absolutely inevitable that the NJPS plan for the year 2000 will reveal still more erosion of the Jewish presence in America, largely because of intermarriage with non-Jews. Given these gloomy predictions of further assimilation and intermarriage, how are we then to understand Jewish identity/continuity? It would be all too easy to conclude that there is no problem with Jewish identity or continuity: a combination of assimilation and intermarriage has taken care of it; say goodbye to American Jewry as we have known it. Perhaps, but that strikes me as too simple an answer to the complex issue of identity in a pluralistic society.

The oft-repeated lament of Simon Rawidowicz, "Israel, the ever-dying people" (1986:54), is too often interpreted as describing a community that is constantly wringing its hands in the face of destruction and disappearance in every generation. The message is that every generation of Jews is convinced that it is the last generation who knows what it means to be Jewish, and the future is indeed bleak. This is an incorrect reading of Rawidowicz and always has been. A closer reading of his text clearly reveals that he meant exactly the opposite! The Jewish community has never perished from the face of the earth regardless of the forces ranged against it. It has always survived to live another day, and frequently prospered in the process. It is precisely at these confrontations in history that Jews have made a conscious decision to survive, again. Today we are witnessing another of those historical junctures, a "Rawidowiczian Juncture," if you please, when Jews must once again make up their minds if they are going to survive and maintain a presence in the vast pluralistic labyrinth that represents modern American culture. Today, and in the future, all Jews will be Jews by choice, or not, by choice.

This is a historical juncture at which every American Jew will have to determine for him- or herself what it means to possess a Jewish identity and whether it is worth continuing. Perhaps even more important than whether or not to identify oneself as Jewish is the intriguing question, Why be Jewish, at all? That is the provocative title (*Why Be Jewish*) of Barry W. Holz and Steven Bayme's small but significant monograph on Jewish identity. Both authors provide satisfying suggestions to answer their own question (Holz with eight, and Bayme with another eight), but all of their suggestions are embedded in a rediscovery of the religious side of Judaism. For millions of American Jews that course isn't even a consideration. But if Jewish identity is to have a self-sustaining property about it (as it has had for millennia), then at some point it must connect with its ancient past in modern-day religious formulations. Then Jews of whatever stripe can liberally dip into this font of wisdom, direction, and civilization in their quest for an identity and as a basis for a physical continuity. But even in making the suggestion that the ancient religion of the Jews holds some direction for the future, another dilemma is imposed on this discussion—whose wisdom, whose direction, whose interpretation of Judaism? Which of the many Judaisms will be our guide—Reform, Conservative, Orthodox, or some other translation? The divisiveness within the American Jewish religious community is one of staggering proportions.

Wertheimer (1993b) presents an incisive exploration of the problems for Jewish continuity based on religious observance. Each branch of Judaism has interpreted its faith and its observance very differently, leaving no room in its liturgies for accommodation. These differences are exacerbated by the right-wing Orthodox members of the Israeli Knesset who want to rule out any conversions in Israel other than Orthodox, and who have the sympathy, if not outright agreement, of substantial numbers of American Orthodox Jews. This identity/citizenship issue in Israel has only deepened the gulf between the Orthodox, on the one hand, and Reform and Conservative Jews, on the other, in the United States.[9] This divisiveness is further exacerbated by the relentless inroads that civil Judaism has made on the average Jew's sense of identity. Affiliation with the formal branches of Judaism is overridden to a large extent by the sense of the Jew's commitment to civil justice, and that has become the meaning of Jewish identity for millions of Jews. It is an iden-

tity that is content to let the vast armies of Jewish social and legislative advocates carry out the work of Judaism in the secular world by simply writing
out a check! Here the JAOs reenter the picture again. The question that must
be addressed to them is, given all of this background on religious dissent
among Jews, and a clear preference on the part of the average Jew for some
civil interpretation of Judaism, what is the role of the JAOs in fostering
Jewish identity? They have none, and that is why I framed this part of the discussion as a "nonissue."

The JAOs have always been secular organizations, and for their leaders
this secularism has always been their expression of their Jewish identity. As
a consequence, the JAOs have no power over Jewish identity or continuity
from the perspective of religious observance. Given their historically secular
background, the leaders of these JAOs are unlikely to believe that adopting
a religious perspective would be in their best interests. But, precisely what is
this civil Judaism that inhibits any genuine action on the part of the JAOs toward helping to resolve the question about why American Jews should continue being Jewish?

This secularism has been the Jewish religion of the JAOs' leaders. They
have never attempted to understand Jews from the joint perspectives of religious origins or religious affiliations. Now the very secularism that has
served these organizations so well in the past in carrying out scores of hu-
manitarian efforts may be the very impediment that will finally bring them
down in the ongoing assimilation of America's Jews. It is important to understand what constitutes this "secular Judaism" and the substantial difficulties it poses for the continued effectiveness of the JAOs.

CIVIL JUDAISM, JEWISH IDENTITY, AND THE JAOs

Civil Judaism is tightly tied to the four long-standing issues previously discussed: antisemitism, the Holocaust, the State of Israel, and Jewish iden-
tity/continuity. These four issues form the core of the JAOs' secular ideology,
an ideology that is based on the civil translation of Judaism rather than on
a traditional or religious understanding of Judaism. Jonathan Woocher
(1986:20) describes this civil Judaism in the following way: "The American
Jewish civil religion prescribes a model of Jewishness which synthesizes eth-
nicity and religiosity and places both firmly within the embrace of American
pluralism. It links American Jews to the totality of the Jewish people at a
level beyond ideological diversity. Perhaps most important, it gives
American Jews transcendent purposiveness by holding out to them a vision
of Jewish destiny and mission in which they have a central role to fulfill."

The ideological diversity Woocher refers to is the substantial differences
that exist among the three major denominational branches of Judaism, that
is, Reform, Conservative, and Orthodox. Civil Judaism represents the public life of Jews, not the spiritual or existential. The political/social order be-

comes the focus of religious sentiments (Woocher, 1986:14). Woocher clearly demonstrated that civil religion is the principal form of Jewish identity for most American Jews. By examining hundreds of documents, speeches, and articles, he identified a set of basic tenets and what he calls a "pervasive rhetoric" (89) that identifies the major issues civil Judaism addresses. I have condensed and paraphrased Woocher's longer treatment of each of these tenets that appear in his pages 68 through 89:

1. The Unity of the Jewish People. "We are one" was adapted as a powerful fundraising slogan by the United Jewish Appeal several years ago. The phrase captured the emotional content resident in the reality of the Holocaust and the emerging significance of the State of Israel. It was a phrase that gave instant legitimacy to the Jewish communal organizations. This oneness is both contemporary and historic: it is a property that binds Jews of today to Jews of earlier millennia. The pressure is to preserve this "oneness," even if no one can quite explain what that "oneness" is. The slogan "We are one" is the core of civil Judaism.

2. Mutual Responsibility. Not only are Jews one (as in one people), but they are also responsible for one another. This translates into the genuine action on the part of a handful of Jewish agencies (71) and is found everywhere in the promotional literature and annual reports of all of the Jewish communal organizations. Jews everywhere are entitled to support from America's Jews. "Are we our brother's keeper?" Yes, and that includes everywhere our brother is around the world.

3. Jewish Survival in a Threatening World. Jewish survival is what the community is all about. It is today's consuming passion. Jews exist in a basically hostile environment. Jews are persistently endangered. The Jewish philosopher Simon Rawidowicz called it "Israel, the ever-dying people." Jewish life constantly stands on the edge of extinction. Jewish survival means, first and foremost, physical survival. The Holocaust, Israel's precarious existence, and a constant vigilance against any manifestation of antisemitism are at the very center of this concept of a threatening world. Survival also means enhancing Jewish life. It has become a broad, legitimating canopy for almost anything Jewish. But why is it important? The answers do not come forth quickly or easily. A Jew's life takes on significance when he or she fights to protect the life of other Jews: you survive by helping others survive.

4. The Centrality of Israel. A great many things Jewish come together in the State of Israel—Jewish survival, mutual responsibility, Jewish identity, ancient Jewish history, and the hope for a united Jewish people. These factors all intersect in the State of Israel. Israel is at one and the same time the manifestation of everything possible for Jews everywhere and the result of continuous efforts for over 2,000 years by implacable foes to destroy it and everything sacred to Jews. Jews in America are one of the few groups of Jews in the world who are financially capable of supporting Israel without the necessity of living there.

5. The Enduring Value of Jewish Tradition. There exists respect for attitudes toward a select number of issues of Jewish tradition ranging from a "benevolent neutrality" to the reification of the Holocaust following World War II. These are the traditions of "*mitzvah*" translated as a financial sacrifice that pinches, more so than this

tradition as it is found in the spirit of Abraham. It is the Jewish polity as advocates
for Jewish study and tradition. If being Jewish is not attached to these larger and
older traditions, Jews will simply drift off into another collection of liberal organizations seeking to do good. But this borrowing, on the one hand, and promulga-
tion, on the other is not directed toward a greater understanding of a Jewish
religious tradition (italics added) that has come forward from the Enlightenment period to the present. Instead, it touts the ethical dimension of Jewish civil life. Civil
Judaism has done a good job in *not* taking denominational sides. All expressions
of Judaism are considered appropriate, and one doesn't outweigh another. It cannot, because favoring one denomination (Reform, Conservative, or Orthodox)
threatens the financial support that comes from the other branches.

6. *Tzedakah*: Philanthropy and Social Justice. This is the philanthropic thread that
   runs throughout Jewish life in all times and under all circumstances. It isn't just
   charity, but the pursuit of justice. It becomes more than charity or securing justice
   for the downtrodden; it is the very heart of being Jewish and, because of this,
   tzedakah becomes the standard or model for all of society, not just Jewish society.
   So it includes support for civil rights, government support programs, the war on
   poverty, and relieving the urban crisis.

7. Americanness as a Virtue. Jews have prospered in the United States and Jews are
   expected to participate fully and enthusiastically in all phases of American life. "A
   good Jew is a good citizen *and* a good American." This underlying pluralism requires Jews to see themselves as Americans, not as Americans who happen to be
   Jewish. It means contributing to America, not just living in it. It is the active encouragement of a diverse, pluralistic society. It is the insistence on being citizens
   of two worlds: one Jewish, the other American. American social and cultural
   norms are in no way a contradiction to the expression of one's Jewishness; a Jew's
   mission is fulfilled by helping America fulfill its mission.

These seven tenets have been formed and refined by a long and complex
Jewish history, a history that is both religious and civil. The JAOs, as secular
organizations, are firmly committed to these historical traditions and religious antecedents. They provide immediately visible legitimacy and confir-
mation for their civil values and their work (purportedly) in the name of
America's Jews.[10]

The central theme of religious Judaism is a Jewish identity grounded in a
common, and unbroken, covenant with God, and in the pursuit of a public
and private life through study and observance of the Torah (the five books
of Moses). Civil Judaism, by contrast, has no such central theology and is instead intended to unite Jews through a set of common civil/social values,
even though their religious beliefs may differ. It is a secular mentality that
borrows heavily from the language and traditions of Judaism to facilitate its
civil activities, but it is a language that does not include the divine or the rituals of formal, religiously grounded Jewish observance. Since 1967 (the wa-
tershed year for the Jewish organizational return to specifically Jewish
interests), the majority of American Jews have readily anchored their Jewish
identity in this civil Judaism.

In spite of the constant divisiveness among the major branches of Judaism over everything from observance of rituals to the interpretation of holy writ, traditional Judaism is firmly anchored in a history and theology that have reproduced themselves over the span of 100 generations. Civil Judaism, by contrast, has no self-sustaining theology and is dependent for its existence on a continuous supply of civil issues to sustain itself. In the final analysis, civil Judaism cannot reproduce itself over several generations.

Civil Judaism as a way of life is constantly reinforced through the decisions made by the key decision makers in the JAOs. As discussed earlier, these decision makers are largely male, over fifty years of age, and men who have been deeply influenced by the Jewish immigrant experience (they are typically second-, third-, and some fourth-generation Jews). Just as often, they have been influenced by firsthand experiences with antisemitism, their discovery of the Holocaust, and their participation in the establishment of the State of Israel. The lay leaders in these organizational oligarchies can take steps (if only through wise investment decisions) to guarantee the future of their organizations, but they cannot reproduce their experience of being Jewish in America over the past 100 years. Succeeding generations of Jews (fifth and sixth) will define differently what it means to be Jewish in America and what constitutes challenges to that presence. This is a reality in the Jewish community that Hertzberg (1990:377) refers to as "the end of the immigrant experience, and what will replace it?"

In summary, the four central issues that occupy much of the JAOs' time and budgets have a legitimacy that is at best problematic and at worst are nonissues. Antisemitism, the first issue, is at the cornerstone of the JAOs' mission statements. The general attitude polls they conduct of their constituency, while badly outdated, virtually assure that antisemitism will remain a central issue in the JAOs' future, despite its nearly nonexistent role in American life. The second issue is that the impact of the Holocaust may not evoke the same emotional response for succeeding generations of Jews as it has for past generations. Third, the relations between Israel and the American Jewish community are strained and may continue to deteriorate. As a consequence, it is likely that the Jewish community in the United States will not be socially allied with Israel as it is now. Finally, Jewish continuity is a grave question for the JAOs, but they are not equipped to develop any programs that will influence how Jews in the United States will choose to identify themselves as Jews in the decades ahead.

CONCLUSION

William Julius Wilson presented the black community with a startling thesis twenty years ago in his study, *The Declining Significance of Race* (1978). Unfortunately, for all of Wilson's brilliance and accuracy, his thesis did not convince large numbers of prominent blacks that racism was declining in America. In a similar fashion, I am not overly confident that my arguments about the death of American antisemitism will convince the JAOs and their lay leaders that antisemitism is no longer a threat of such magnitude that it continues to require the talents of several organizations and millions of dollars annually to combat it. Neither am I convinced that my arguments will sway a significant group of American Jews to give up their self-absorption concerning the seriousness of antisemitism and realize how misplaced it is in a country where Jewish security has never been higher. To return to Maslow's metaphor of searching for identity under the bright lights of antisemitism, it is well-nigh time to move on to seeking identity and continuity where the real problem resides—with Jews themselves.

Any threat of antisemitism in America pales in comparison with the galloping inclination of Jews to marry non-Jews at increasingly greater rates and the obvious biological impact this is going to have on how many Jews will populate America in the next two generations. I am convinced that the grandchildren of this generation and the next must not be educated about being Jewish by scaring the daylights out of them with well-worn tales of ancient prejudices and discriminations or the incalculable horror of the Holocaust. These historic properties of being Jewish did happen to millions of Jews, and they must be understood and honored for their historical importance, but neither antisemitism nor the Holocaust are sufficient reasons to remain Jewish, nor are they the principal reasons for pursuing an actively Jewish lifestyle. The history, religion, and civilization of the Jews comprise one of the most exciting stories in the history of the human race, and it is an excitement that has much to teach future generations about the unceasingly complex task of living a good life. It remains to be seen if we, as Jews, will put aside our self-interest and religious divisiveness long enough to pay attention to the possibility of an American future that does not include us and to determine how to best forestall that event.

NOTES

1. Comment provided on assurances of anonymity for the author.

2. Anonymous comments by one executive in one of the JAOs, September 9, 1995.

3. In the early 1990s a poster began appearing on telephone poles around St. Cloud, Minnesota that said, "Where are our missing children—Jewish Ritual Murder." The poster contained several of the supposed reasons why Jews needed the blood of Christian children. As mysteriously as the posters went up, they came down. Nobody in town admitted to knowing who put them up (see Kleg, 1993:6).

4. These items cannot be taken from folklore or conjecture. A separate exercise is called for that would determine precisely what characteristics would be incorporated in a new survey and would be consistent with a revised definition of anti-Jewish beliefs.

5. Rabbi David Wolpe, speaking at Temple Mishkan Tefila, Chestnut Hill, Massachusetts, in November 1994, suggested that 300 years from now the only people interested in the Holocaust will be Jewish theologians.

6. One of the best analyses of the linkage between the Holocaust and the founding of the State of Israel can be found in Tom Segev, *The Seventh Million* (1993), New York: Hill and Wang.

7. In the fall of 1993 I spent a semester on the campus of Brandeis University (Waltham, Massachusetts). I had the opportunity to visit with several Israeli exchange students during that time. To a person they agreed they could not imagine what being Jewish could possibly mean in a country like the United States. They were Jews and they lived in Israel; that's where Jews lived as Jews. None of these delightful young people was the least bit antagonistic, but neither was any of them the least bit curious about how it might be possible to be very Jewish and very American at the same time.

8. Lazerwitz's percentages reveal an unexplained difference with the results from the original 1990 NJPS. In those results 7 percent of respondents identify Orthodox, 38 percent Conservative, and 42 percent Reform. A possible explanation may lie in the distinction between "what branch of Judaism were you raised in: Orthodox, Conservative, or Reform" (the CJF report), and the refashioning of the question to reflect "expressed preference" (Lazerwitz). See *Highlights of the CJF National Jewish Population Survey.*

9. The June 13, 1997 issue of *Forward* discusses the financial impact of the pluralism issue on giving by U.S. donors. The July 4, 1996 *Jewish Advocate* examines Netanyahu siding with the "unity over pluralism" issue.

10. Jonathan Woocher (1986) points out that the communal agency with the most influence on civil Judaism is the United Jewish Appeal.

References

Abrams, Elliott. 1997. *Faith or Fear: How Jews Can Survive in a Christian America.* New York: Free Press.

Adorno, Theodor E. Frankel-Brunswick, D. J. Levinson, and R. N. Sanford. 1950. *The Authoritarian Personality.* New York: Harper & Row.

Alba, Richard. D. 1985. *Italian Americans.* Englewood Cliffs, NJ: Prentice-Hall.

———. 1995. "Assimilation's Quiet Tide." *Public Interest,* no. 119 (spring): 14.

Allport, Gordon W. [1954] 1979. *The Nature of Prejudice.* Reading, MA: Addison-Wesley Publishing Co.

American Jewish Committee. 1925, 1995, 1996. *The American Jewish Year Book.* New York: Jewish Publication Society of America.

———. 1984. *National Survey of American Jews: Political and Social Outcomes.* New York: American Jewish Committee.

———. 1994. *Antisemitism in America.* New York: American Jewish Committee and National Opinion Research Center.

———. 1997. *1997 Annual Survey of American Jewish Opinion.* Conducted by Market Facts, Inc. New York: American Jewish Committee.

———. 1998. *1998 Annual Survey of American Jewish Opinion.* Conducted by Market Facts, Inc. New York: American Jewish Committee.

American Jewish Historical Society. 1992. *The Jewish People in America.* 5 vols. Edited by Henry L. Feingold. Balitimore, MD: Johns Hopkins University Press.

Andrews, Holly. 1992. "Dillaway-Thomas House to Open in Eliot Square." *Roxbury Heritage News* (fall).

Anti-Defamation League. 1992. *Highlights from an Anti-Defamation League Survey on Anti-Semitism and Prejudice in America.* New York: Anti-Defamation League.

———. 1993. *A Survey of Antisemitic Attitudes.* Boston, MA: Anti-Defamation League and Martilla and Kiley.

———. 1995. *Annual Audit of Anti-Semitic Incidents.* New York: Anti-Defamation League.

———. 1998. *Litigation Docket*. New York: Anti-Defamation League.

Antin, Mary. 1912. *The Promised Land*. Boston, MA: Houghton Mifflin.

Arenson, Karen W. 1995. "Donations to Jewish Philanthropy Ebb." *New York Times*, 27 December.

Arnold, Michael. 1999. "Conversion Crises Will Cause $100 Million Drop-off in American Giving to Israel, Reform Leader Warns." *Forward*, 8 January.

Auerbach, Jerold S. 1984. "Anti-Semitism at Wellesley College." *Sh'Ma*, 16 November.

———. 1993a. "Anti-Semitism at Wellesley." *American Jewish Congress Monthly*, July.

———. 1993b. "Homegrown Anti-Semitism at Wellesley College." *Wellesley News*, September.

Baron, Salo W. 1952–76. *A Social and Religious History of the Jews*. 2d ed. 16 vols. New York: Columbia University Press.

Bayme, Steven. 1996. "Whither American Jewry?" *Contemporary Jewry* 17: 148–54.

Belth, Nathan C. 1979. *A Promise to Keep: A Narrative of the American Encounter with Anti-Semitism*. New York: New York Times Publishing Co.

Ben-Sasson, H. H., ed. 1976. *A History of the Jewish People*. Cambridge, MA: Harvard University Press.

Berman, Paul, ed. 1994. *Blacks and Jews: Alliances and Arguments*. New York: Delacorte Press.

Bernal, Martin. 1987. *Black Athena: The Afroasiatic Roots of Classical Civilization*. New Brunswick, NJ: Rutgers University Press.

Berry, Jeffrey. 1989. *The Interest Group Society*. 2d ed. New York: HarperCollins.

Black, Chris. 1993. "Jewish Group Raps Wellesley Professor." *Boston Gobe*, 17 April.

Blakeslee, Spencer. 1993. *Prejudice: The Equal Opportunity Destroyer*. Boston, MA: Northeastern University Press. Video.

Bloch, Susan. 1993. "Furor at Wellesley College over Anti-Semitic Text." *Boston Jewish Times*, 1 April.

Bogin, Frederick D., ed. 1993. *The American Jewish Committee*. Vol. 17 of *Archives of the Holocaust: An International Collection of Selected Documents*, edited by Henry Friedlander and Sybil Milton. New York: Garland Publishing.

Boyd, Herb. 1993. "Boston Prof. Hails Jeffries Victory." *New York Amsterdam News*, 22 May.

Brackman, Harold. [1993?]. *The Historical Record: Responding with Fact to Charges in The Secret Relationship between Blacks and Jews*. New York: American Jewish Committee (2 pages).

———. 1994. *Ministry of the Lies: The Truth Behind the Nation of Islam's "The Secret Relationship between the Blacks and Jews."* New York: Four Walls Eight Windows Press.

Brodkin, Karen. 1998. *How Jews Became White Folks and What That Says About Race in America*. New Brunswick, NJ: Rutgers University Press.

Cahan, Abraham. 1993. *The Rise of David Levinsky*. New York: Penguin Books.

Cantor, Aviva. 1995. *Jewish Women/Jewish Men: The Legacy of Patriarchy in Jewish Life*. San Francisco, CA: HarperSanFrancisco.

Chanes, Jerome A. 1994. "The Voices of the American Jewish Community." Originally published in *Excerpts from a Survey of Jewish Affairs*. 1989. New York: National/Jewish Community Relations Advisory Council.

————. 1995. *Antisemitism in America Today: Outspoken Experts Explode the Myths.* New York: Carol Communications.

Cohen, Jeremy. 1982. *The Friars and the Jews: The Evolution of Medieval Anti-Judaism.* Ithaca, NY: Cornell University Press.

Cohen, Naomi N. 1972. *Not Free to Desist: The American Jewish Committee 1906–1966.* Philadelphia: Jewish Publication Society (of America).

Cohen, Oscar, and Stanley Wexler, eds. 1989. "Not the Work of a Day." *Anti-Defamation League of B'nai B'rith Oral Memories.* Vol. 3. New York: Anti-Defamation League.

Cohen, Rich. 1998. *Tough Jews: Fathers, Sons, and Gangster Dreams.* New York: Simon & Schuster.

Cohen, Richard. 1993. "Farrakhan 101 at Wellesley." *Washington Post*, 11 February.

Cohen, Steven M. 1985. *1984 National Survey of American Jews: Political and Social Outlooks.* New York: American Jewish Committee.

Cohn, Norman. [1968] 1996. *Warrant for Genocide: The Myth of the Jewish World Conspiracy and the Protocols of the Elders of Zion.* London, England: Serif.

————. 1970. *The Pursuit of the Millennium.* New York: Oxford University Press.

Cole, Donald B. *Immigrant City: Lawrence, Massachusetts 1845–1921.* Chapel Hill, NC: University of North Carolina Press.

Council of Jewish Federations. 1971, 1990. *National Jewish Population Study.* New York: Council of Jewish Federations.

Cudjoe, Selwyn. 1994. "When Academic Freedom Is Used to Spread Hatred." *Boston Globe*, 3 February.

Davis, David Brion. 1992. "Jews in the Slave Trade." *Culturefront* (fall): 42–45.

Diner, Hasia R. 1977. *In the Almost Promised Land: American Jews and Blacks, 1915–1935.* Westport, CT: Greenwood Press.

————. 1994. "Jewish Self-Governance, American Style." *American Jewish History* 81 (spring–summer): 287.

Dinnerstein, Leonard. [1968] 1987. *The Leo Frank Case.* New York: Columbia University Press.

————. 1982. *America and the Survivors of the Holocaust.* New York: Columbia University Press.

————. 1994. *Antisemitism in America.* New York: Oxford University Press.

Dinnerstein, Leonard, ed. 1971. *Anti-Semitism in the United States.* New York: Holt, Rinehart and Winston.

Dorning, Mike. 1993. "Debate over Book Engulfs College." *Chicago Tribune*, 28 July.

Dowdy, Zachary R. 1993. "In Shift, Jewish Group to Allow Exhibit to Remain in Roxbury." *Boston Globe*, 2 July.

Dwork, Deborah. 1986. Immigrant Jews on the Lower East Side of New York: 1880–1914." In *The American Jewish Experience*, edited by Jonathan Sarna. New York: Holmes and Meier.

Elazar, Daniel J. [1976] 1995. *Community and Polity: The Organizational Dynamics of American Jewry.* Philadelphia: Jewish Publication Society of America.

————. 1982. "The Jewish Community as a Polity." In *Understanding American Jewry*, edited by Marshall Sklare. New Brunswick, NJ: Transaction Books.

―――. 1991. *Authority, Power and Leadership in the Jewish Polity: Cases and Issues*. Lanham, MD: University Press of America.

Feiden, Douglas. 1994. "Restructure World Jewry WJC Insists." *Forward*, 25 February: 1, 5.

Feingold, Henry L. 1981. *A Jewish Survival Enigma: The Strange Case of the American Jewish Committee*. New York: American Jewish Committee.

―――. 1987. *The American Jewish Committee: Past as Prologue*. New York: American Jewish Committee.

Festinger, Leon. [1957] 1965. "A Theory of Cognitive Dissonance." Reprinted in *Social Psychology: The Study of Human Interaction*, edited by Theodore Newcomb, Ralph Turner, and Phillip Converse. New York: Holt, Rinehart and Winston.

Fillipow, David. 1998. "Public Discontent Fuels Hate in Russia." *Boston Globe*, 16 December.

Finger, Seymour Maxwell, ed. 1984. *American Jewry during the Holocaust: A Report by the Research Director and His Staff and Independent Research Scholars Retained by the Director for the American Jewish Commission on the Holocaust, March, 1984*. New York: City University of New York; released for sale by Holmes and Meier, New York.

Fishman, Sylvia B. 1993. *A Breath of Life: Feminism in the American Jewish Community*. New York: Free Press.

Friedman, Murray. 1994. "Going Our Own Way." *Moment Magazine*, June: 36–39, 72.

―――. 1995. *What Went Wrong: The Creation and Collapse of the Black/Jewish Alliance*. New York: Macmillan Publishing Co.

Frommer, Morris. 1978. "The American Jewish Congress: A History, 1914–1950," 2 vols. Ph.D. diss., Ohio State University.

Gates, Henry Louis. 1992. "Black Demagogues, and Pseudo-Scholars." *New York Times*, 22 July.

George, Henry. 1942. *Progress and Poverty*. Classics Club. New York: W. J. Black.

Glasscock, Jean, ed. 1975. *Wellesley College 1875–1975: A Century of Women*. Wellesley, MA: Wellesley College.

Glazer, Nathan. [1957] 1989. *American Judaism*. 2d ed. Chicago: University of Chicago Press.

Glock, Charles Y., Gertrude Selznick, and Joe L. Spaeth. 1966. *The Apathetic Majority: A Study Based on Public Responses to the Eichmann Trial*. New York: Harper & Row.

Glock, Charles Y., and Rodney Stark. 1966. *Christian Beliefs and Anti-Semitism*. New York: Harper & Row.

Glock, Charles Y., Robert Wuthnow, James Piliavin, and Michael Spencer. 1975. *Adolescent Prejudice*. New York: Harper & Row.

Gold, Michael. [1930] 1996. *Jews without Money*. New York: Carroll and Graf Publishers.

Goldberg, J. J. 1996. *Jewish Power: Inside the American Jewish Establishment*. Reading, MA: Addison-Wesley Publishing Co.

Goldberg, Michael. 1995. *Why Should Jews Survive: Looking Past the Holocaust Toward a Jewish Future*. New York: Oxford University Press.

Goldman, Julia. 1998. "Anti-Semitism in U.S. Drops, but Stays High Among Blacks." *Jewish Advocate*, 27 November.

Goldman, Martin S. 1992. *Nat Turner and the Southampton Revolt of 1831.* New York: B.F. Watts Publishers.

Goldstein, Judith. 1972. "The Politics of Ethnic Pressure: The American Jewish Committee as Lobbyist, 1906–1917." Ph.D. diss., Columbia University.

Gordon, Milton M. 1964. *Assimilation into American Life.* New York: Oxford University Press.

Goren, Arthur A. 1986. "The Kehillah Vision and the Limits of Community." In *The American Jewish Experience*, edited by Jonathan Sarna. New York: Holmes and Meier.

Grosser, Paul E., and Edward G. Halperin. 1978. *The Cause and Effects of Anti-Semitism.* New York: Philosophical Library.

Hacket, Alice P. 1949. *Wellesley: Part of the American Story.* New York: E.P. Dutton & Co.

Hall, Peter Dobkin. 1987. "A Historical Overview of the Private Nonprofit Sector." In *The Nonprofit Sector: A Research Handbook*, edited by Walter W. Powell. New Haven, CT: Yale University Press.

Hall, Richard H. 1987. *Organizations: Structures, Processes and Outcomes.* 4th ed. Englewood Cliffs, NJ: Prentice-Hall.

Hall, William, David Ruderman, and Michael Stanislawski, eds. 1984. *Heritage: Civilization and the Jews, Source Reader.* Westport, CT: Praeger Publishers.

Haraven, Tamara K. 1978. *Amoskeag: Life and Work in an American Factory City.* New York: Pantheon Books.

Harding, John, Bernard Kutner, Harold Proshansky, and Isidore Cohen. 1954. "Prejudice and Ethnic Relations." In *Handbook of Social Psychology*, vol. 1, edited by Gardner Lindzey. Cambridge, MA: Addison-Wesley Publishing Co.

Hasenfeld, Yeheskel. 1983. *Human Service Organizations.* Englewood Cliffs, NJ: Prentice-Hall.

Heilman, Samuel, and Menachem Friedman. 1991. "Religious Fundamentalism and Religious Jews: The Case of Haredim." In *Fundamentalisms Observed*, edited by Martin E. Marty and R. Scott Appelby. Chicago, IL: University of Chicago Press.

Herberg, Will. 1955. *Protestant, Catholic, Jew: An Essay in American Religious Sociology.* New York: Doubleday & Co.

Hertzberg, Arthur. [1990] 1998. *The Jews in America, Four Centuries of an Uneasy Encounter: A History.* New York: Touchstone Press.

Himmelstein, Jerome L. 1993. "The Place and Meaning of the Nonprofit Sector." *Qualitative Sociology* 16 (fall): 319–29.

Historical Research Department. 1991. *The Secret Relationship between Blacks and Jews.* Vol. 1. Boston, MA: Nation of Islam.

Holz, Barry W, and Steven Bayme. 1993. *Why Be Jewish?* New York: American Jewish Committee.

Hourwich, Isaac. [1912] 1969. *Immigration and Labor.* New York: Arno Press.

Howe, Irving. 1990. *World of Our Fathers.* New York: Schocken Press.

Igmatier, Noel. 1995. *How the Irish Became White.* New York: Routledge.

Israel, Sherry. 1985, 1995. *Boston's Jewish Community: The 1985 Combined Jewish Philanthropies Demographic Study.* Boston, MA: Combined Jewish Philanthropies.

Jaher, Frederic Cople. 1994. *A Scapegoat in the New Wilderness: The Origins and Rise of Anti-Semitism in America.* Cambridge, MA: Harvard University Press.

Jewish Community Relations Council. 1994. *Fifty Years of the JCRC—Boston: Highlights 1930–1994*. Boston, MA: Jewish Community Relations Council.

Jewish Publication Society. Biblical passages in chapter one come from *Tanakh: The Holy Scriptures*. The New Jewish Publication Society Translation According to Traditional Hebrew Text. Philadelphia: The Jewish Publication Society.

Jick, Leon A. [1976] 1992. *The Americanization of the Synagogue, 1820–1870*. Hanover, NH: Brandeis University Press.

Joly, Maurice. 1864. *Dialogue aux enfers entre Montesquieu et Machivelli*. Brussels, Belgium with a Geneva Imprint.

Karp, Abraham J. 1985. *Haven and Home: A History of the Jews in America*. New York: Schocken Books.

Kaufman, Debra R. 1991. *Rachel's Daughters: Newly Orthodox Jewish Women*. New Brunswick, NJ: Rutgers University Press.

Kaufman, Jonathan. 1988. *Broken Alliance: The Turbulent Times between Blacks and Jews in America*. New York: Scribner.

———. 1994. "What's a Jewish Liberal to Do?" *Moment Magazine*, June: 40–42, 73.

Kleg, Milton. 1993. *Hate Prejudice and Racism*. Albany, NY: State University of New York Press.

Konvitz, M. R., ed. 1950. *Alexander Pekelis: Law and Social Action: Selected Essays*. New York: Ithaca Press.

Kors, Charles Alan, and Harvey Silverglate. 1999. *The Shadow University: The Betrayal of Liberty on America's Campuses*. New York: Free Press.

Kosmin, Barry A., Sidney Goldstein, Joseph Waksberg, Nava Lerer, Ariella Keysar, and Jeffrey Scheckner. 1991. *Highlights of the CJF 1990 Jewish Population Survey*. New York: Council of Jewish Federations.

Langmuir, Gavin I. 1990. *Toward a Definition of Anti-Semitism*. Berkeley, CA: University of California Berkeley Press.

Lazerwitz, Bernard, J. Alan Winter, Arnold Dashefsky, and Ephraim Tabory. 1998. *Jewish Choices: American Jewish Denominationalism*. Albany, NY: State University of New York Press.

Lederman, Douglas, and Stephen Burd. 1996. "High Court Refuses to Hear Appeal of Ruling That Barred Considering Race in Admissions." *Chronicle of Higher Education*, 12 July.

Leo Baeck Institute Yearbook. 1967. Volume 10. New York: Leo Baeck Institute.

Levine, Hillel, and Lawrence Harmon. 1992. *The Death of an American Jewish Community: A Tragedy of Good Intentions*. New York: Free Press.

Levy, Richard S. 1991. *Antisemitism in the Modern World: An Anthology of Texts*. Lexington, MA: D.C. Heath.

Lewin, Kurt, R. Lippitt, and R. K. White. 1939. "Patterns of Aggressive Behavior in Experimentally Created 'Social Climates.' " In D. S. Pugh, ed. 1971. *Organization Theory*. Baltimore, MD: Penguin Books.

Linzer, Norman, David J. Schnall, and Jerome Chanes. 1998. *A Portrait of the American Jewish Community*. Westport, CT: Praeger Publishers.

Lipset, Seymour M., ed. 1990. *American Pluralism and the Jewish Community*. New Brunswick, NJ: Transaction Books.

Lipset, Seymour M., and Earl Rabb. 1970. *The Politics of Unreason: Right Wing Extremism in America, 1790–1970*. New York: Harper & Row.

———. 1995. *Jews and the New American Scene*. Cambridge, MA: Harvard University Press.

Loury, Glenn. 1994. "The Alliance Is Over." *Moment Magazine*, June: 32–35, 68.

MacIver, Robert M. 1951. *Report on the Jewish Community Relations Agencies*. New York: National Community Relations Advisory Council.

Magner, Denise. 1995. "Wellesley Rethinks Its Multi-Cultural Requirement." *Chronicle of Higher Education*, 28 April: A45.

Mansbridge, Jane J. 1980. *Beyond an Adversary Democracy*. New York: Basic Books.

Marcus, Jacob Rader. 1990. *To Count a People: American Jewish Population Data 1585–1990*. Lanham, MD: University Press of America.

———. 1995. *The American Jew, 1585–1990: A History*. New York: Carlson Publishing.

Martin, Tony. 1993. *The Jewish Onslaught: Dispatches from the Wellesley Battlefront*. Dover, MA: Majority Press.

Marx, Gary T. 1967. *Protest and Prejudice: A Study of Belief in the Black Community*. New York: Harper & Row.

Massarik, Fred, and Alvin Chenkin. 1973. "United States National Jewish Population Study: A First Report." In *American Jewish Year Book*. New York: American Jewish Committee.

Matire, Gregory, and Ruth Clark. 1982. *Anti-Semitism in the United States: A Study of Prejudice in the 1980s*. New York: Praeger Publishers

Merton, Robert K. 1967. *On Theoretical Sociology*. New York: Free Press.

Meyer, Marshall W., and Lynne G. Zucker. 1989. *Permanently Failing Organizations*. Newbury Park, CA: Sage Publications.

Michalczyk, John J. 1995. *Stars and Shamrocks: The Jews and Irish of Boston*. New York: First Run Features. Video.

Michels, Robert, 1958. *Political Parties: A Sociological Study of the Oligarchic Tendencies of Modern Democracy*. Glencoe, IL: Free Press.

Minkoff, Debra C. 1993. "Shaping Contemporary Organizational Action: Women's and Minority Social Change Strategies, 1955–85." Paper presented at American Sociological Association Meeting: 13–17 August, Miami Beach, FL.

———. 1995. *Organizing for Equality: The Evolution of Women's and Racial-Ethnic Organizations in America, 1935–1985*. New Brunswick, NJ: Rutgers University Press.

Moore, Deborah Dash. 1981. *B'nai B'rith and the Challenge of Ethnic Leadership*. Albany, NY: State University of New York Press.

———. 1990. "The Relationship between the Jewish Political Tradition and Jewish Civil Religion in the United States." *Jewish Political Studies Review* 2 (spring): 105–19.

Morse, Athur D. [1967] 1998. *While Six Million Died: A Chronicle of American Apathy*. New York: The Overlook Press.

Newsome, Yvonne D. 1991. "A House Divided: Conflict and Cooperation in African American–Jewish Relations." Ph.D. diss., Northwestern University.

Nilus, Serge. 1920. *The Protocols and World Revolution, Including a Translation and Analysis of the "Protocols of the Meetings of the Zionist Men of Wisdom."* Boston, MA: Small, Maynard, & Co. Publishers.

Novick, Michael. 1999. *The Holocaust in American Life.* Boston, MA: Houghton Mifflin.

Palmer, Phyllis. 1989. *Domesticity and Dirt: Housewives and Domestic Servants in the United States, 1920–1945.* Philadelphia: Temple University Press.

Parrillo, Vincent N. 1997. *Strangers to These Shores: Race and Ethnic Relations in the United States.* 5th ed. Boston, MA: Allyn and Bacon Publishing.

Peck, Abraham J., ed. 1987. *Blacks and Jews, "The American Experience."* Cincinnati, OH: American Jewish Archives.

Peters, Madison C. 1908. *Justice to the Jew: The Story of What He Has Done for the World.* New York: Free Press.

Poliakov, Leon. 1965. *The History of Anti-Semitism.* Vol. 1. New York: Vanguard Press.

Quinley, Harold E., and Charles Y. Glock. 1979. *Anti-Semitism in America.* New York: Free Press.

Rabb, Earl. 1991. *The Modern Practice of Jewish Advocacy and Community Relations.* Waltham, MA: Perlmutter Institute Publication.

———. 1995. *A Survey of Jewish Attitudes about Anti-Semitism.* San Francisco, CA: Bay Area Jewish Community Relations Council.

Random House Dictionary of the English Language. 1987. 2d ed. New York: Random House.

Rawidowicz, Simon. 1986. *Israel: The Ever Dying People and Other Essays,* edited by Benjamin C. I. Ravid. Cranbury, NJ: Associated University Presses.

Ribbufo, Leo P. 1986. "Henry Ford and *The International Jew.*" In *The American Jewish Experience,* edited by Jonathan Sarna. New York: Holmes and Meier.

Richen, Moses. [1962] 1997. *The Promised City: New York's Jews 1870–1914.* Cambridge, MA: Harvard Press.

Rosenbaum, Gerald. 1992. "The Educational Efforts of the American Jewish Congress to Combat Anti-Semitism in the United States, 1946–1980." Ph.D. diss., University of Chicago.

Roth, Henry. 1934. *Call It Sleep.* New York: Noonday Press.

Rubinstein, William D. 1997. *The Myth of Rescue: Why the Democracies Could Not Have Saved More Jews from the Nazis.* London: Routledge Press.

Rufner, Frederick G., and Margaret Fisk, eds. 1996. *Encyclopedia of Associations.* 39th ed. Detroit, MI: Gale Research Co.

Sacher, Howard M. 1992. *A History of the Jews in America.* New York: Alfred A. Knopf.

Sanders, Ronald. 1969. *The Downtown Jews: Portraits of an Immigrant Generation.* New York: Harper & Row.

Sarna, Jonathan. 1986a. "American Anti-Semitism." In *History and Hate: The Dimensions of Anti-Semitism,* edited by David Berger. Philadelphia: Jewish Publication Society.

———. 1986b. *The American Jewish Experience.* New York: Holmes and Meier.

Sarna, Jonathan, and Ellen Smith, eds. 1995. *The Jews of Boston.* Boston, MA: Combined Jewish Philanthropies of Boston.

Sartre, Jean-Paul. 1965. *Anti-Semite and Jew.* New York: Schocken Books.

Segal, Robert E. 1985. *The Early Years of the Jewish Community Council of Metropolitan Boston.* Boston, MA: Jewish Community Relations Council.

Segev, Tom. 1993. *The Seventh Million: The Israelis and the Holocaust.* New York: Hill and Wang.

Seltzer, Robert M. 1980. *Jewish People, Jewish Thought: The Jewish Experience in History.* New York: Macmillan Publishing Co.

Selznick, Gertrude J., and Stephen Steinberg. 1969. *The Tenacity of Prejudice: Anti-Semitism in Contemporary America.* New York: Harper & Row.

Shevitz, Susan L. 1991. "Communal Planning in a Nonrational World: A Shift in Paradigm and Practice." In *Changing Jewish Life: Service Delivery and Planning in the 1990s,* edited by Lawrence I. Sternberg, Gary Tobin, and Sylvia Barack Fishman. Westport, CT: Greenwood Press.

Silberman, Charles E. 1985. *A Certain People: American Jews and Their Lives Today.* New York: Summit Books.

Sills, David. 1957. *The Volunteers, Means and Ends in a National Organization: A Report.* Glencoe, IL: Free Press.

Sontag, Deborah. 1999. "Orthodox Confront U.S. Reform Rabbis at Western Wall." *New York Times,* International, 2 February.

Sorauf, Frank J. 1963. "The Released-Time Cases." In *The Third Branch of Government,* edited by C. Pritchet, Herman Westin, and Alan Westin. New York: Harcourt Brace Jovanovich.

Stark, Rodney, Bruce Foster, and Charles Y. Glock. 1971. *Wayward Shepherds: Prejudice and the Protestant Clergy.* New York: Harper & Row.

Stember, Charles H. 1966. *Jews in the American Mind.* New York: Free Press.

Stern, Kenneth S. 1996. *A Force upon the Plain: The American Militia Movement and the Politics of Hate.* New York: Simon & Schuster.

Stout, David. 1996. "City College Closing Black Studies Department." *New York Times,* 19 March.

Sung, Betty Lee. 1990. "Chinese American Intermarriage." *Journal of Comparative Family Studies* 21, no. 2 (summer): 351.

Supple, Barry E. 1986. "A Business Elite: German-Jewish Financiers in Nineteenth-Century New York." In *The American Jewish Experience,* edited by Jonathan Sarna. New York: Holmes and Meier.

Svonkin, Stuart G. 1995. "Jews Against Prejudice: American Jews and the Intergroup Relations Movement from World War to Cold War." Ph.D. diss., University of Wisconsin–Madison.

Telushkin, Rabbi Joseph. 1991. *Jewish Literacy: The Most Important Things to Know about the Jewish Religion, Its People, and Its History.* New York: Wm. Morrow and Co.

Tenofsky, Elliot. 1979. "Interest Groups and Litigation: The Commission on Law and Social Action of the American Jewish Congress." Ph.D. diss., Brandeis University.

Theodorson, George A., and Achilles G. Theodorson. 1969. *Modern Dictionary of Sociology.* New York: Thomas Y. Crowell Publishers.

Tobin, Gary, and Sharon Sassler. 1988. *Jewish Perceptions of Anti-Semitism.* New York: Plenum.

Todd, Alyson. 1993. "Blacks and Jews and the News." *Heterodoxy,* 6 May: 1.

Truman, David B. 1971. *The Government Process: Political Interests and Public Opinion.* 2d ed. New York: Alfred A. Knopf.

Weiss, John. 1996. *Ideology of Death: Why the Holocaust Happened in Germany.* Chicago, IL: Ivan R. Dee.

Wertheimer, Jack. 1972. "The Founding of the ADL." Unpublished paper, Jewish Theological Seminary, NY.

———. 1993b. *A People Divided: Judaism in Contemporary America.* New York: Basic Books.

———. 1995. "Jewish Organizational Life in the United States since 1945." In *American Jewish Year Book, 1995.* New York: American Jewish Committee.

Wertheimer, Jack, ed. 1993a. *The Modern Jewish Experience: A Reader's Guide.* New York: New York University Press.

Whitt, J. Allan, Gwen Moore, Cynthia Negrey, Karen King, and Deborah White. 1993. *The Inner Circle of Local Nonprofit Trustees: A Comparison of Attitudes and Backgrounds of Women and Men Board Members.* New Haven, CT: Program on Non-Profit Organizations Institution for Social and Policy Studies, Yale University.

Wilson, William J. 1978. *The Declining Significance of Race: Blacks and Changing American Institutions.* Chicago, IL: University of Chicago Press.

Wirth, Louis. 1945. "The Problem of Minority Groups." In *The Science of Man in the World Crisis*, edited by Ralph Linton. New York: Columbia University Press.

Wise, Stephen S. 1916. "American Israel and Democracy." Address delivered at the Preliminary Conference for the Organization of the American Jewish Congress held at the Hotel Walton, Philadelphia, March 26, 27, 1916. Issued by the Executive Organization Committee for the American Jewish Congress, New York.

Wistrich, Robert S. 1991. *Antisemitism: The Longest Hatred.* New York: Schocken Books.

Woocher, Jonathan S. 1986. *Sacred Survival: The Civil Religion of American Jews.* Bloomington, IN: Indiana University Press.

———. 1991. "The Democratization of the American Jewish Polity." In *Authority, Power and Leadership in the Jewish Polity: Cases and Issues*, edited by Daniel J. Elazar. Lanham, MD: University Press of America.

Wyman, David S. 1985. *The Abandonment of the Jews: America and the Holocaust, 1941–1945.* New York: Pantheon Press.

———. 1990. *America and the Holocaust.* 13 vols. New York: Garland Publishing. This documents Wyman's *The Abandonment of the Jews.* Volumes 2, 3, 5, 7, and 13 contain references to actions and correspondence by the American Jewish Committee.

Yezierska, Anzia. [1925] 1975. *Bread Givers: A Struggle between a Father of the Old World and a Daughter of the New.* New York: G. Braziller Publishing.

Zakim, Leonard. 1993. *Coalition Building: Insights in Jewish Advocacy.* Waltham, MA: Brandeis University Press.

Zald, Mayer N., and John D. McCarthy. 1990. *Social Movements in an Organizational Society.* New Brunswick, NJ: Transaction Books.

Zelin, Richard D. 1992. "Ethnic and Religious Group Politics in the United States: The Case of the American Jewish Committee, 1982–1987." Ph.D. diss., University of Wisconsin–Madison.

ARCHIVAL RECORDS

American Jewish Committee, Blaustein Library, New York. The Official Meeting Records of the American Jewish Committee. Vol. 1. February 3, 1906 to March 19, 1911 (330 pages).

American Jewish Congress, at the American Jewish Historical Society, Waltham, MA. The History of the American Jewish Congress. Box 1, 1916–1965, letters and memos.

Anti-Defamation League of B'nai B'rith, Boston, MA. Not in a Lifetime: An Oral History of the Anti-Defamation League. Vol. 4 of 7.

ORGANIZATIONS AND PERSONS INTERVIEWED

Academic Community

Professor Selywn Cudjoe, Wellesley College

Professor Mary Lefkowitz, Wellesley College

Professor Jack Wertheimer, Jewish Theological Seminary

American Jewish Committee

Mr. Martin Goldman, (former) Associate Director

Dr. Lawrence Lowenthal, Director

Dr. Howard Weintraub, Regional President

American Jewish Congress

Mr. Phillip Baum, Director AJC-National

Ms. Sheila Decter, Director

Anti-Defamation League

Ms. Sally Greenberg, Director of Civil Rights

Mr. Leonard Zakim, Director

Jewish Communal Leaders

Rabbi Douglas Kahn, Director of the Bay Area JCRC

Dr. Earl Rabb, (retired) Director of the Bay Area JCRC

Dr. Gary Tobin, Director, Brandeis Institute for Religion in Community

Jewish Community Relations Council

Ms. Barbara Geffen, Associate Director

Ms. Nancy Kaufman, Director

National Jewish Community Relations Advisory Council

Mr. Jerome Chanes

Private Citizens

Reverend Eugene Rivers, Director, Ten Point Coalition
Mr. George Russell, Director of Public Affairs for the State Street Bank
Lawrence Shubow, (retired) District Court Judge, Brookline, MA

Subject Index

Name Index

Adler, Cyrus, 67, 96
Adorno, Theodor E., 42, 70
Alan X, 157–159
Allport, Gordon, 41
Antin, Mary, 28, 66
Arenson, Karen W., 145
Arnold, Michael, 234
Auerbach, Jerold S., 186
Augustine of Hippo (354–430), 11
Aviva, Diana, 146

Bache, Semon, 23
Bakke, Allan, 105–106
Bauer, Yehuda, 209
Baum, Phillip, 110, 146–147
Bayme, Steven, 241
Beilin, Yossi, 233
Belth, Nathan, 82, 85, 92
Bergman, Alexander, 31–32
Bernal, Martin, 172
Bingham, Theodore, 30
Birmingham, Stephen, 22
Black, Chris, 183, 250
Blakeslee, Spencer, 40 nn.1, 2, 184, 247
    n.7
Bloch, Susan, 180
Boas, Franz, 31
Boyd, Herb, 186
Brackman, Harold, 6, 157

Brandeis, Louis D., 96
Brinkley, David, 187
Brodkin, Karen, 38
Bronfman, Charles, 147
Bronfman, Edgar, 146
Brudnoy, David, 157
Buchalter, Louis "Lepke," 30

Cahan, Abraham, 28, 66
Cantor, Aviva, 134–135, 138
Cantor, Eddie, 67
Chanes, Jerome, 16, 97, 123, 219–221
Clark, Ruth, 51
Clay, Henry, 20
Clinton, Hillary, 187
Coakley, Steve, 5
Cohen, A. K. (Judge), 87, 92
Cohen, Alfred M., 83
Cohen, Isidore, 43
Cohen, Jacob I., 19
Cohen, Jeremy, 10, 11
Cohen, Naomi, 65, 69
Cohen, Oscar, 82, 83, 86, 87, 93, 94
Cohen, Richard, 180
Cohn, Norman, 11–12, 15, 63, 64, 65,
    69, 83
Columbus, Christopher, 17
Conley, Jim, 81
Cooper, James Fenimore, 20

About the Author

SPENCER BLAKESLEE teaches sociology at Framingham State College. Professor Blakeslee has published essays on the Holocaust, Jewish traditions, and Black-Jewish relations. He was coordinator of The Boston Holocaust Study Group from 1993 to 1998.